THE CAMBRIDGE COMPANION TO
THE AFRICAN AMERICAN SLAVE NARRATIVE

The slave narrative has emerged as a fundamental genre within literary studies. This Companion examines the slave narrative's relation to transatlantic abolitionism, British and American literary traditions including captivity narratives, autobiography, and sentimental literature, and the larger African American literary tradition. The volume also explores the history of the genre, including its rediscovery and authentication, its subsequent critical reception, and its continued importance to modern authors such as Toni Morrison and Edward P. Jones. Attention is paid both to well-known slave narratives, such as those by Olaudah Equiano, Frederick Douglass and Harriet Jacobs, and to a wide range of lesser-known narratives. With its chronology and guide to further reading, the Companion provides both an easy entry point for students new to the subject and comprehensive coverage and original insights for scholars in the field.

AUDREY FISCH is Professor in the Departments of English and Elementary and Secondary Education at New Jersey City University.

THE CAMBRIDGE
COMPANION TO

THE AFRICAN
AMERICAN SLAVE
NARRATIVE

EDITED BY
AUDREY A. FISCH
New Jersey City University

CAMBRIDGE
UNIVERSITY PRESS

CAMBRIDGE UNIVERSITY PRESS
Cambridge, New York, Melbourne, Madrid, Cape Town, Singapore,
São Paulo, Delhi, Dubai, Tokyo, Mexico City

Cambridge University Press
The Edinburgh Building, Cambridge CB2 8RU, UK

Published in the United States of America by Cambridge University Press, New York

www.cambridge.org
Information on this title: www.cambridge.org/9780521615266

© Cambridge University Press 2007

First published 2007

A catalogue record for this publication is available from the British Library

ISBN 978-0-521-85019-3 Hardback
ISBN 978-0-521-61526-6 Paperback

For Mark Flynn and Max Flysch

CONTENTS

CONTRIBUTORS

DICKSON D. BRUCE, JR., is Professor of History at the University of California, Irvine. His books include *Black American Writing from the Nadir: The Evolution of a Literary Tradition, 1877–1915* (1989) and *The Origins of African American Literature, 1680–1865* (2001). His most recent book, *The Kentucky Tragedy: A Story of Conflict and Change in Antebellum America*, was published in 2006.

VINCENT CARRETTA is Professor of English at the University of Maryland. His publications include the following editions: Olaudah Equiano, *The Interesting Narrative and Other Writings* (1995; rev. edn. 2003); *Letters of the Late Ignatius Sancho, An African* (1998); Quobna Ottobah Cugoano, *Thoughts and Sentiments on the Evil of Slavery and Other Writings* (1999); Phillis Wheatley, *Complete Writings* (2001); and *Unchained Voices: An Anthology of Black Authors in the English-Speaking World of the Eighteenth Century* (1996; rev. edn. 2004). With Philip Gould, Carretta has co-edited and contributed to *Genius in Bondage: Literature of the Early Black Atlantic* (2001). His most recent book is *Olaudah Equiano, the African: Biography of a Self-Made Man* (2005).

JOHN ERNEST is the Eberly Family Distinguished Professor of American Literature at West Virginia University. He is the author of *Resistance and Reformation in Nineteenth-Century African-American Literature: Brown, Wilson, Jacobs, Delany, Douglass, and Harper* (1995) and *Liberation Historiography: African American Writers and the Challenge of History, 1794–1861* (2004). His editions of texts by nineteenth-century African American writers include William Wells Brown's *The Escape; or, A Leap for Freedom* (2001) and William Craft's *Running a Thousand Miles for Freedom; Or, The Escape of William and Ellen Craft from Slavery* (2000).

AUDREY A. FISCH is Professor in the Departments of English and Elementary and Secondary Education at New Jersey City University. She is the co-editor of *The Other Mary Shelley: Beyond Frankenstein* (1993) and the author of *American Slaves in Victorian England: Abolitionist Politics in Popular Literature and Culture* (Cambridge, 2000).

PHILIP GOULD is Professor of English at Brown University and Director of the American Seminar at Brown. He is the author of *Barbaric Traffic: Commerce and Antislavery in the Eighteenth-Century Atlantic World* (2003).

ROBERT S. LEVINE is Professor of English at the University of Maryland. He is the author of *Conspiracy and Romance* (Cambridge, 1989) and *Martin Delany, Frederick Douglass, and the Politics of Representative Identity* (1997), and the editor of *The Cambridge Companion to Herman Melville* (Cambridge, 1998), *Martin R. Delany: A Documentary Reader* (2003), and several other volumes.

DEBORAH E. MCDOWELL is Professor of English and African American Studies at the University of Virginia. McDowell is the author of various scholarly texts, including *"The Changing Same": Studies in Fiction by Black American Women* (1995), co-editor with Arnold Rampersand of *Slavery and the Literary Imagination* (1988), and an editor of the *Norton Anthology of African-American Literature* (1996).

YOLANDA PIERCE, an Associate Professor of English and African American Studies at the University of Kentucky, teaches and publishes in the fields of American Religious History, African American Literature, and Black Atlantic Studies. Her most recent book is *Hell without Fires: Slavery, Christianity, and the Antebellum Spiritual Narrative* (2005). She is currently at work on a monograph about religious ecstasy.

ROBERT F. REID-PHARR is Professor of English and American Studies at the Graduate Center of the City University of New York. He is the author of *Conjugal Union: The Body, the House and the Black American* (1999); *Black Gay Man: Essays* (2001) and *Once You Go Black: Choice, Desire and the Black American Intellectual* (spring 2007).

XIOMARA SANTAMARINA teaches English and Afro-American and African Studies at the University of Michigan, Ann Arbor. She is the author of *Belabored Professions: Narratives of African American Working Womanhood* (2005).

KERRY SINANAN is lecturer in the long eighteenth century at the University of the West of England. She teaches courses on eighteenth-century literature and Romanticism. Her research focuses on the black Atlantic, slavery, and travel, and she is currently completing a monograph, *Slave Masters and the Language of Self*. She has written on slave masters' accounts of their own enslavement in *Colonial and Post-Colonial Incarceration* (2001).

STEPHANIE A. SMITH is associate professor of English and American Studies at the University of Florida. She is the author of three novels, *Snow-Eyes* (1985), *The*

Boy Who Was Thrown Away (1987), and *Other Nature* (1995), and the author of two critical studies, *Conceived By Liberty* (1995) and *Household Words* (2005).

VALERIE SMITH is the Woodrow Wilson Professor of Literature and Director of the Center for African American Studies at Princeton University. The author of *Self-Discovery and Authority in Afro-American Narrative* (1987) and *Not Just Race, Not Just Gender: Black Feminist Readings* (1998), she is also the editor of *African American Writers* (2000); *Representing Blackness: Issues in Film and Video* (1997); and *New Essays on Song of Solomon* (Cambridge, 1994). At present, she is writing a book on the Civil Rights Movement in cultural memory.

JOHN STAUFFER is Professor of English, African and African American Studies, and the History of American Civilization at Harvard University. He is the author of *The Black Hearts of Men: Radical Abolitionists and the Transformation of Race* (2002), winner of the Frederick Douglass Book Prize and the Avery Craven Book Prize, and the Lincoln Prize runner-up. Other publications include the Modern Library edition of Frederick Douglass's *My Bondage and My Freedom* (2003), an anthology on John Brown, *Meteor of War: The John Brown Story* (2004), and a collection on abolitionism, *Prophets of Protest: New Essays on American Abolitionism* (2006). He is completing two new books, *Imagining Equality: American Interracial Friendships in History and Myth* (forthcoming 2008), and *Douglass and Lincoln: The Lives of Self-Made Men* (forthcoming 2009).

CINDY WEINSTEIN is Professor of English at California Institute of Technology. Her most recent publications include *Family, Kinship, and Sympathy in Nineteenth-Century American Literature* (Cambridge, 2004) and the edited volume, *The Cambridge Companion to Harriet Beecher Stowe* (Cambridge, 2004).

ACKNOWLEDGMENTS

Ray Ryan, editor at Cambridge University Press, asked me to edit this volume. I am immensely grateful for his confidence in me and his unwavering support throughout this project.

Of course, there wouldn't be a Cambridge Companion to the African American Slave Narrative if it weren't for the difficult work of so many scholars over the years, for which many of us are thankful. I am personally grateful to Donald Gibson for introducing me to and helping develop my knowledge of the genre.

I am thankful to the contributors to this volume and to Chris Jackson and Jayne Aldhouse at Cambridge for joining in my vision of the project with good humor and collegiality.

I wouldn't have been able to conceive of this volume without my students at New Jersey City University, whose questions, ideas, and interests have been in my mind throughout this project. I hope this volume will help students like mine think carefully and critically about slave narratives with their own students some day.

Support from my university came in the form of colleagues' precious time and energy. Thanks to Hilary Englert and Ellen Garvey for helpful feedback on the project, and especially to the reference and interlibrary loan departments, including James Brown, Fred Smith, Toby Heyman, and Michele Hoban, who cheerfully dealt with my numerous requests. I would never have been able to complete this project without their help. Thanks also to the Office of Academic Affairs for releasing me from the teaching of one course so that I might devote some of my time to this volume.

To Cindy Weinstein I am grateful for regular encouragement throughout this project, and to Bob Levine I am thankful for some quick help at the right moment. To Lisa Botshon and Elise Lemire, who are always with me in writing, I am always in debt.

Finally, this book is dedicated, with love, to Mark and Max.

CHRONOLOGY

<table>
<tr><td>1510</td><td>The Spanish begin importation of African slaves into the Caribbean</td></tr>
<tr><td>1619</td><td>A Dutch ship sells twenty slaves kidnapped from Africa to the English settlers at Jamestown, Virginia, establishing slavery in the New World</td></tr>
<tr><td>1662</td><td>Virginia passes a law making slaves any children born to enslaved women</td></tr>
<tr><td>1701</td><td>Samuel Sewell writes The Selling of Joseph, the first antislavery document published in America</td></tr>
<tr><td>1702</td><td>Adam Negro's Tryall is recorded by the Colonial Society of Massachusetts</td></tr>
<tr><td>1712</td><td>Slave uprising in New York City</td></tr>
<tr><td>1713</td><td>The Treaty of Utrecht, concluding the War of the Spanish Succession, grants England the exclusive right to supply slaves to Spain's American colonies</td></tr>
<tr><td>1739</td><td>Slave rebellion in South Carolina</td></tr>
<tr><td>1750</td><td>Approximate population of the thirteen American colonies is 236,000 black slaves and 934,000 whites.</td></tr>
<tr><td>1754</td><td>John Woolman publishes Some Considerations on the Keeping of Negroes</td></tr>
<tr><td>1758</td><td>The Society of Friends in London and Philadelphia condemns slavery and the slave trade at their annual meetings</td></tr>
<tr><td>1760</td><td>Tacky's Revolt in Jamaica leads to the death of more than sixty whites and four hundred blacks; the first American slave</td></tr>
</table>

narrative, Briton Hammon's *Narrative of the Uncommon Sufferings, and Surprising Deliverance of Briton Hammon, a Negro Man* is published in Boston

1767   Anthony Benezet publishes *A Caution and Warning to Great Britain and the Colonies*

1769   Granville Sharp publishes *A Representation of the Justice and Dangerous Tendency of Tolerating Slavery in England*

1772   Lord Mansfield decides in favor of the slave James Somerset, and the *Somerset* decision declares that slavery cannot exist within England and that a slave brought to England is free and cannot be returned to slavery in the colonies (much slavery continued in England nonetheless)

1774   John Wesley publishes *Thoughts upon Slavery*; the US Continental Conference adopts a resolution banning the importation of slaves and American participation in the slave trade after December 1

1775   The royal governor of Virginia, Lord Dunmore, promises freedom to slaves who desert their American masters and fight in the King's service

1775–83   American Revolution

1776   Virginia slave owner Thomas Jefferson writes the Declaration of Independence; in it, he asserts that "all men are created equal; that they are endowed by their Creator with certain unalienable rights; that among these are life, liberty and the pursuit of happiness"; Jefferson also writes in a draft statement that "the present King of England . . . has waged cruel war against human nature itself, violating its most sacred rights of life and liberty in the persons of a distant people who never offended him, captivating and carrying them into slavery in another hemisphere, or to incur miserable death in their transportation hither," but these words are omitted in the final document

1777   Vermont prohibits slavery in its constitution; in subsequent years, Pennsylvania, Connecticut, and Rhode Island adopt gradual emancipation laws

1781   The *Zong* massacre occurs, in which the captain of a slave ship orders 133 slaves thrown overboard and drowned so ship owners can collect insurance money

1783   Anthony Benezet publishes *The Case of Our Fellow Creatures, the Oppressed Africans*

1784   James Ramsay publishes *Essay on the Treatment and Conversion of African Slaves in the Sugar Colonies*

1786   Thomas Clarkson publishes *Essay on the Slavery and Commerce of the Human Species*; the Committee for the Relief of the Black Poor is established in London and begins planning a freed slave colony in Sierra Leone

1787   Quobna Ottobah Cugoano publishes *Thoughts and Sentiments on the Evil and Wicked Traffic of the Slavery and Commerce of the Human Species*; the US Constitutional Convention forbids Congress from ending the slave trade until 1808, provides for the return of fugitive slaves, apportions representation for slaves as the equivalent of three-fifths of a free person, and enacts the Northwest Ordinance, prohibiting slavery in the territories north of the Ohio and east of the Mississippi Rivers; the Society for Effecting the Abolition of the Slave Trade is established in London; Olaudah Equiano, Cugoano, and others campaign as "Sons of Africa" against slavery by sending letters to prominent people and periodicals

1788   John Newton publishes *Thoughts upon the African Slave Trade*

1789   Olaudah Equiano publishes in England *The Interesting Narrative of the Life of Olaudah Equiano*; William Wilberforce introduces in the British Parliament twelve resolutions against the slave trade, but Parliament decides to regulate, not end, the English slave trade

1790   Slave revolts and civil war in Saint Domingue

1791   William Wilberforce's bill for the abolition of the slave trade is defeated in the House of Commons

1792   Freetown in founded in Sierra Leone with 1,190 blacks from Nova Scotia and 119 Europeans from England

1793   Eli Whitney invents the cotton gin, a machine that separates the seed from the cotton fiber, and thus paves the way for large-scale cotton cultivation and the need for slave labor throughout the South; William Wilberforce's second bill for abolition passes the House of Commons but is defeated in the House of Lords

1800   US census lists 108,395 free colored people, 893,041 slaves, and 4,304,489 whites

1804   Haiti becomes an independent nation

1807   A bill abolishing the slave trade within the British colonies is passed in the House of Lords, and Britain abolishes the slave trade; the United States also bans the importation of slaves

1808   Thomas Clarkson publishes *History of the Rise, Progress and Accomplishment of the Abolition of the African Slave-Trade by the British Parliament*; Henri Grégoire publishes *De la littérature des nègres*, subsequently translated and published as *An Enquiry Concerning the Intellectual and Moral Faculties and Literature of Negroes*

1810   Portugal adopts gradual abolition of the slave trade

1812   War between the USA and Britain

1815   Spain adopts gradual abolition of the slave trade

1816   The American Colonization Society is formed to promote the colonization of Africa by freed slaves; George Bourne publishes *The Book and Slavery Irreconcilable*; slaves revolt in Barbados

1820   As part of the Missouri Compromise, the USA admits Missouri as a slave state and forbids slavery north of the 36° 30′ latitude

1822   Founding of a colony for freed slaves (later named Liberia) on the West African coast

1823   The Society for the Mitigation and Gradual Abolition of Slavery is formed under Thomas Folwell Buxton and establishes *The Anti-Slavery Reporter*; William Wilberforce publishes *An Appeal to the Religion, Justice, and Humanity of the Inhabitants of the British Empire*; Thomas Clarkson publishes

Thoughts on the Necessity of Improving the Condition of the Slaves in the British Colonies; slaves revolt in Demerara and Guyana

1824   Robert Wedderburn publishes *The Horrors of Slavery*

1826   James Stephen publishes *England Enslaves by Her Own Colonies*

1828   Lord Stowell rules, in the case of an Antiguan slave named Grace, that residence in England does not guarantee freedom for a slave who voluntarily returns to the colonies

1829   Mexico abolishes slavery; David Walker publishes *Walker's Appeal in Four Articles*

1831   William Lloyd Garrison begins publishing *The Liberator*; Mary Prince dictates her story to Susanna Strickland and the first slave narrative authored by a woman is published to public controversy in London as *The History of Mary Prince*; the largest slave rebellion in the British West Indies, known as the "Christmas Rebellion" or the "Baptist War" and led by Samuel Sharpe, takes place in western Jamaica; Nat Turner leads a slave rebellion in Virginia which ends with the deaths of 57 whites, 100 blacks, and the death by hanging of Turner and 19 of his followers

1833   Parliament passes the Emancipation Act, emancipating 780,000 slaves in the West Indian colonies but requiring them to serve their masters for six years as apprentices; William Lloyd Garrison forms the American Anti-Slavery Society

1834   The British Emancipation Act begins to take effect

1838   The British abandon apprenticeship and give full freedom to former slaves

1839   Theodore Weld publishes *Slavery as It Is*

1840   The World Antislavery Convention takes place in London, with Thomas Clarkson presiding

1845   Frederick Douglass publishes *The Narrative of the Life of Frederick Douglass, an American Slave*

1848	Slavery is abolished in the French Caribbean
1850	The US Congress passes the Compromise of 1850, which includes the Fugitive Slave Law
1851	Harriet Beecher Stowe begins publishing *Uncle Tom's Cabin* in *National Era*, an abolitionist weekly newspaper; the novel is published in full in 1852 and becomes a world-wide bestseller
1857	The US Supreme Court in the *Dred Scott* case rejects the claim of freedom of Scott, a slave, after being taken to a free territory; instead, the Court rules that the federal government cannot outlaw slavery in the US territories and that African Americans have "no rights which the white man was bound to respect"
1859	Abolitionist John Brown executes a raid on a federal arsenal at Harpers Ferry, Virginia, in order to arm nearby slaves and begin a slave revolt; Brown is captured by Marines, tried for treason and murder, and executed
1860	Abraham Lincoln is elected president of the USA on a platform that opposes the extension of slavery; Southern states begin seceding from the Union
1861	Harriet Jacobs publishes *Incidents in the Life of a Slave Girl*, the first slave narrative written by a woman
1861–65	American Civil War
1862	Congress abolishes slavery in Washington DC and passes a law freeing slaves who escape from the Confederacy
1863	President Lincoln issues the Emancipation Proclamation, freeing all slaves
1865	The 13th Amendment to the US Constitution declares "Neither slavery nor involuntary servitude, except as punishment for crime whereof the party shall have been duly convicted, shall exist within the United States, or any place subject to their jurisdiction"
1901	Booker T. Washington publishes *Up from Slavery*
1936	The Federal Writers' Project begins a two-year project of interviewing and recording the stories of more than 2,000 former slaves

1967   William Styron receives the Pulitzer Prize for *The Confessions of Nat Turner*

1976   Alex Haley publishes *Roots* and wins the Pulitzer Prize and the National Book Award

1987   Toni Morrison wins the Pulitzer Prize for *Beloved*

2004   Edward P. Jones wins the Pulitzer Prize for *The Known World*

Cambridge Companions to . . .

AUTHORS

Edward Albee edited by Stephen J. Bottoms

Margaret Atwood edited by Coral Ann Howells

W. H. Auden edited by Stan Smith

Jane Austen edited by Edward Copeland and Juliet McMaster

Beckett edited by John Pilling

Aphra Behn edited by Derek Hughes and Janet Todd

Walter Benjamin edited by David S. Ferris

William Blake edited by Morris Eaves

Brecht edited by Peter Thomson and Glendyr Sacks

The Brontës edited by Heather Glen

Byron edited by Drummond Bone

Albert Camus edited by Edward J. Hughes

Willa Cather edited by Marilee Lindemann

Cervantes edited by Anthony J. Cascardi

Chaucer, second edition edited by Piero Boitani and Jill Mann

Chekhov edited by Vera Gottlieb and Paul Allain

Coleridge edited by Lucy Newlyn

Wilkie Collins edited by Jenny Bourne Taylor

Joseph Conrad edited by J. H. Stape

Dante edited by Rachel Jacoff (second edition)

Charles Dickens edited by John O. Jordan

Emily Dickinson edited by Wendy Martin

John Donne edited by Achsah Guibbory

Dostoevskii edited by W. J. Leatherbarrow

Theodore Dreiser edited by Leonard Cassuto and Claire Virginia Eby

John Dryden edited by Steven N. Zwicker

George Eliot edited by George Levine

T. S. Eliot edited by A. David Moody

Ralph Ellison edited by Ross Posnock

Ralph Waldo Emerson edited by Joel Porte and Saundra Morris

William Faulkner edited by Philip M. Weinstein

F. Scott Fitzgerald edited by Ruth Prigozy

Flaubert edited by Timothy Unwin

Brian Friel edited by Anthony Roche

Robert Frost edited by Robert Faggen

Elizabeth Gaskell edited by Jill L. Matus

Goethe edited by Lesley Sharpe

Thomas Hardy edited by Dale Kramer

Nathaniel Hawthorne edited by Richard Millington

Ernest Hemingway edited by Scott Donaldson

Homer edited by Robert Fowler

Ibsen edited by James McFarlane

Henry James edited by Jonathan Freedman

Samuel Johnson edited by Greg Clingham

Ben Jonson edited by Richard Harp and Stanley Stewart

James Joyce edited by Derek Attridge (second edition)

Kafka edited by Julian Preece

Keats edited by Susan J. Wolfson

Lacan edited by Jean-Michel Rabaté

D. H. Lawrence edited by Anne Fernihough

David Mamet edited by Christopher Bigsby

Thomas Mann edited by Ritchie Robertson

Christopher Marlowe edited by Patrick Cheney

Herman Melville edited by Robert S. Levine

Arthur Miller edited by Christopher Bigsby

Milton edited by Dennis Danielson (second edition)

Molière edited by David Bradby and Andrew Calder

Nabokov edited by Julian W. Connolly

Eugene O'Neill edited by Michael Manheim

Ovid edited by Philip Hardie

Harold Pinter edited by Peter Raby

Sylvia Plath edited by Jo Gill

Edgar Allan Poe edited by Kevin J. Hayes

Ezra Pound edited by Ira B. Nadel

Proust edited by Richard Bales

Pushkin edited by Andrew Kahn

Philip Roth edited by Timothy Parrish

Shakespeare edited by Margareta de Grazia and Stanley Wells

Shakespeare on Film edited by Russell Jackson

Shakespeare on Stage edited by Stanley Wells and Sarah Stanton

Shakespearean Comedy edited by Alexander Leggatt

Shakespearean Tragedy edited by Claire McEachern

Shakespeare's History Plays edited by
Michael Hattaway

Shakespeare's Poetry edited by Patrick Cheney

George Bernard Shaw edited by
Christopher Innes

Shelley edited by Timothy Morton

Mary Shelley edited by Esther Schor

Sam Shepard edited by Matthew C. Roudané

Spenser edited by Andrew Hadfield

Wallace Stevens edited by John N. Serio

Tom Stoppard edited by Katherine E. Kelly

Harriet Beecher Stowe edited by
Cindy Weinstein

Jonathan Swift edited by Christopher Fox

Henry David Thoreau edited by Joel Myerson

Tolstoy edited by Donna Tussing Orwin

Mark Twain edited by Forrest G. Robinson

Virgil edited by Charles Martindale

Edith Wharton edited by Millicent Bell

Walt Whitman edited by Ezra Greenspan

Oscar Wilde edited by Peter Raby

Tennessee Williams edited by
Matthew C. Roudané

Mary Wollstonecraft edited by
Claudia L. Johnson

Virginia Woolf edited by Sue Roe and
Susan Sellers

Wordsworth edited by Stephen Gill

W. B. Yeats edited by Marjorie Howes and
John Kelly

TOPICS

The Actress edited by Maggie B. Gale and
John Stokes

The African American Novel edited by
Maryemma Graham

The African American Slave Narrative edited by
Audrey A. Fisch

American Modernism edited by
Walter Kalaidjian

American Realism and Naturalism edited by
Donald Pizer

American Women Playwrights edited by
Brenda Murphy

Australian Literature edited by
Elizabeth Webby

British Romanticism edited by Stuart Curran

Canadian Literature edited by
Eva-Marie Kröller

The Classic Russian Novel edited by
Malcolm V. Jones and Robin Feuer Miller

Contemporary Irish Poetry edited by
Matthew Campbell

Crime Fiction edited by Martin Priestman

The Eighteenth-Century Novel edited by
John Richetti

Eighteenth-Century Poetry edited by John Sitter

English Literature, 1500–1600 edited by
Arthur F. Kinney

English Literature, 1650–1740 edited by
Steven N. Zwicker

English Literature, 1740–1830 edited by
Thomas Keymer and Jon Mee

English Poetry, Donne to Marvell edited by
Thomas N. Corns

English Renaissance Drama edited by A. R.
Braunmuller and
Michael Hattaway (second edition)

English Restoration Theatre edited by
Deborah C. Payne Fisk

Feminist Literary Theory edited by
Ellen Rooney

The French Novel: from 1800 to the Present
edited by Timothy Unwin

Gothic Fiction edited by Jerrold E. Hogle

Greek and Roman Theatre edited by
Marianne McDonald and J. Michael Walton

Greek Tragedy edited by P. E. Easterling

The Irish Novel edited by John Wilson Foster

The Italian Novel edited by Peter Bondanella
and Andrea Ciccarelli

Jewish American Literature edited by Hana
Wirth-Nesher and Michael P. Kramer

The Latin American Novel edited by
Efraín Kristal

Literature of the First World War edited by
Vincent Sherry

Medieval English Theatre edited by
Richard Beadle

Medieval Romance edited by Roberta L. Krueger

Medieval Women's Writing edited by Carolyn
Dinshaw and David Wallace

Modern American Culture edited by
Christopher Bigsby

Modern British Women Playwrights edited by
Elaine Aston and Janelle Reinelt

Modern French Culture edited by
Nicholas Hewitt

INTRODUCTION

AUDREY A. FISCH

It wasn't until the very end of my education that I first read a slave narrative. Growing up in Rochester, New York, once an abolitionist stronghold, I knew about slavery and encountered evidence of it both in the classroom and the community. I vividly remember being taken as a small child to see a hidden room in a local restaurant which was a "stop" on the Underground Railroad. But I never read or was asked to read a slave narrative until the end of my coursework in graduate school.

My experience was not unique. In the not-so-distant past, few students read slave narratives in secondary school, in universities, or even in graduate school. For a variety of reasons, including political change caused by the Civil Rights movement, the steadfast work of many devoted scholars, and a radical shift in notions of what literature is and why we read it, the value of the slave narrative has multiplied exponentially. Today, students at every level are likely to encounter these narratives of slavery, escape, and freedom written by fugitives of British colonial and American slavery in a wide range of courses.

Indeed, the existence of this volume is a testament to that sea change. Volumes in the Cambridge Companion series offer what Cambridge University Press describes as "lively, accessible introductions to major writers, artists, philosophers, topics and periods." The publication of this Companion confirms that the African American slave narrative is now recognized as a "major" genre, firmly established in the academic canon of what should be read and studied.

This Cambridge Companion, then, covers a rare phenomenon: a "major" genre that, because of its unusual history, may still be relatively unknown to some readers. For this reason, my goal in editing this volume has been to answer even the most basic questions about the genre: What is a slave narrative? When, why, and by whom were these narratives written? Who read them? At the same time, I have chosen essays which introduce readers to the now broad range of scholarship in several of the different contexts in which the slave narrative is now studied.

The first part, "The slave narrative and transnational abolitionism," examines what may be the most obvious context for the slave narrative: abolition. First and foremost, the slave narrative is a text with a purpose: the end of slavery. The slave narrative is a key artifact in the global campaign to end first the slave trade (the practice of transporting slaves across international waters), then colonial slavery (in British Caribbean colonies like Jamaica), and finally US slavery. In the first essay of the volume, "The rise, development, and circulation of the slave narrative," Philip Gould sketches for us the ideologies of the religious and political groups that shaped the language and themes of the narratives. At the same time, he cautions that "slave narratives cannot be reduced to these different ideological influences" and unpacks for the reader the ways in which the narratives "creatively engage the expectations of these groups in order to create cultural spaces in which the project of self-representation takes place." Gould also explores how the material and economic realities surrounding the slave narratives' publication shaped their content and format. This opening essay sets the parameters for the volume as a whole with its careful discussion of a wide range of slave narratives and its focus on the narrative's presence and importance both in England and the USA from the early 1770s until the American Civil War and, in other essays in the volume, beyond.

In chapter two, "Politics and political philosophy in the slave narrative," Dickson D. Bruce, Jr. focuses on one of the subjects identified by Gould – the political philosophy of the slave narrative – while maintaining a similar broad focus and referencing a range of narratives. Bruce explores how, in order to counter proslavery ideas, slave narratives engage with the conventional ideas, images, and rhetorical conventions about slavery and freedom that were familiar to the reading public. By embracing distinctly American ideals and values – of Christian faith, of the centrality of the family, and of a notion of freedom that encompasses individualism and independence – that were rooted in and central to the newly emerging Republic, the narratives, according to Bruce, are able to argue effectively for the abolition of slavery.

One early text, and indeed one figure, Olaudah Equiano, is pivotal to the interplay between the slave narrative and abolition, and thus deserves his own essay. Vincent Carretta's "Olaudah Equiano: African British abolitionist and founder of the African American slave narrative" explores Equiano's "rise from the legal status of being an object to be sold by others to become an international celebrity, the story of whose life became his own most valuable possession." While describing the success of this "founder" of the slave narrative in redefining the image of the slave, Carretta explores the latest research, including his own, on how Equiano invented and constructed his story, based only partially on the facts of his life. For Carretta, Equiano's achievement lies not merely in this artful construction of his narrative, however, but also in his mastery of the publication process which ensured his own financial success and allowed him to resist many of the constraints other former slaves faced telling their stories in the white-controlled literary marketplace.

If Equiano was able to master the fraught dynamics of the abolitionist marketplace, others struggled to negotiate this genre that was often defined by the needs and values of white abolitionists. Kerry Sinanan, in the fourth and final chapter of this first part of the volume, examines several case studies that exhibit the "signs of exchange, argument, and debate" between slaves and white abolitionists as these two groups worked together in the fight against slavery. "The slave narrative and the literature of abolition" moves from Equiano's skillful incorporation of a range of texts and sources as an exploitation of "the rhetorical and mythical power of the west's own literature" to several different attempts by Frederick Douglass to resist the dominant abolitionist discourse and assert an independent identity for himself. In her discussion, Sinanan reminds readers that the slave narrative is not simply a hybrid form drawing on preexisting literature to create a form of autonomous self-expression for the ex-slave. Abolitionist literature also modeled itself on and even copied slave narratives, and Sinanan explores this complex interdependence in the work of several black and white writers, including Harriet Beecher Stowe, the author of *Uncle Tom's Cabin*, and the slave narrator Josiah Henson.

The second part of the volume, "The slave narrative and Anglo-American literary traditions," examines the ways that these narratives, which were written to change the world, also function as literary texts and engage the generic expectations of readers of other important literary forms of the same time. This part points to the vast area of current research aimed at exploring the interchange between the slave narrative and other literary traditions.

In chapter five, the first essay in this part, "Redeeming bondage: the captivity narrative and the spiritual autobiography in the African American slave narrative tradition," Yolanda Pierce examines the narratives of Venture Smith and George White, and focuses on how each employed the conventional genres of the captivity narrative and the spiritual autobiography to tell their "unconventional" stories of slavery and freedom. The captivity narrative, a distinctly American popular literary genre, tells the story of abduction, trial, and escape faced by "innocent" colonists who resist the savagery of their Native American captors and generally glorify the Christian way of life. The spiritual autobiography was a more widespread and longstanding literary tradition, "loosely modeled after the biblical account of Paul's conversion," in which a convert to Christianity documents the personal trials of his life and his spiritual conversion to "the true light of Christian doctrine." Both of these genres, with their emphasis on spiritual enlightenment, provided a recognizable and culturally acceptable template for the slave narrator, and Pierce explores how Smith and White, like other narrators, not only employ but also transform these genres to "restore honor and worth to the status of 'African' in early American culture."

In chapter six, "The slave narrative and the revolutionary tradition of American autobiography," Robert S. Levine turns to a more secular tradition, that of the autobiography. Some critics have concluded that the slave narrative does not attain the stature of autobiography because of the many constraints slave narrators faced in crafting and producing their stories. But the "'classic' white-authored autobiography" is as structured and delimited by generic conventions, argues Levine, as is the slave narrative. In this chapter, Levine demonstrates that many slave narrators found Benjamin Franklin's *Autobiography* an enabling, if also challenging, model, which they did not "blindly or un-self-consciously follow." As Levine explores a wide range of narratives, he finds that the American revolutionary tradition affords the slave narrators a powerful connection between "the individual uplift of the black persona" and "the revolutionary cause of freedom."

While Pierce and Levine consider the slave narrative in relation to earlier and contemporaneous literary traditions, focusing on how slave narrators exploited and transformed these forms for their own purposes, Cindy Weinstein asks us to think about the contribution slave narratives made to an Anglo-American antebellum literary tradition, the sentimental novel. In chapter seven, "The slave narrative and sentimental literature," Weinstein argues that sentimental literature and the slave narrative intersect with, challenge, and should be read in dialectical relation to each other. In her discussion, Weinstein reads several white-authored sentimental novels, including *Ida May* and *Marcus Warland*, and suggests that how a "sentimental heroine becomes free, how she experiences her bondage, and how her experience is told" was frequently informed by generic conventions of the slave narrative, which functioned for readers as "a lens through which to view the sentimental experience."

The third part of the volume, "The slave narrative and the African American literary tradition," examines a longstanding context for the slave narrative: African American literature. While the academic world has only "discovered" the slave narrative in recent years as an important and interesting genre, the slave narrative has always served as an essential, if sometimes vexing, model for African American writers.

Robert F. Reid-Pharr opens this part with chapter eight, "The slave narrative and early Black American literature," where he asks us to rethink "linear and singular conceptions of the development of Black American culture." In particular, Reid-Pharr wants to challenge the notion that the slave narrative articulated "simple truths" and that the literature that followed these narratives was "more muddled and less sophisticated." Reid-Pharr reads *Clotel*, *The Garies and Their Friends*, and *Our Nig* as works that do not transcend but rather are influenced by the same complex political and material forces that shaped the slave narrative. For Reid-Pharr, it is this "messy, parodic, over-determined, promiscuous, multiform and naive tradition" that is "the best part of the fantastic legacy" of the slave narrative.

In chapter nine, Deborah E. McDowell takes as her subject an historical span ranging from post-Reconstruction to the Harlem Renaissance, and, like Reid-Pharr, she asks how African American writers "grappled with the generic conventions of the slave narrative." She finds that, amid racial uplift and a "zeitgeist of progressivism" – the optimistic spirit of the age – African American writers could not "exorcise" the legacies of slavery and the slave narrative. Indeed, in a chapter that considers the work of Frances Harper, Booker T. Washington, Charles W. Chesnutt, W. E. B. Du Bois, James Weldon Johnson, and Zora Neale Hurston, McDowell notices "the frequency with which shame appears" as these writers struggle to "will away" slavery.

In contrast to the literary era that McDowell considers, the late twentieth century has witnessed a need to grapple with slavery and the slave narrative that has proved both enduring and energizing for African American writers. So much writing has emerged about slavery that a term, the "neo-slave narrative," was coined in 1987 by Bernard W. Bell in his *The Afro-American Novel and Its Traditions*. In chapter ten, "Neo-slave narratives," Valerie Smith sets out to capture the "range and complexity of this genre of writing." She discusses Toni Morrison's *Beloved* at length, along with Edward P. Jones's recent and acclaimed *The Known World*, as well as a wide variety of other texts that will intrigue students of the slave narrative.

The final part of the volume, "The slave narrative and the politics of knowledge," examines the critical history of the slave narrative and reflects on the overall direction of the field. Why were these texts once ignored? And what are we ignoring in our current study of the genre? Which texts aren't being read? What questions aren't being asked?

Stephanie A. Smith begins the discussion in chapter eleven, "Harriet Jacobs: a case history of authentication." In a review of the critical history of Jacobs's *Incidents in the Life of a Slave Girl*, Smith reflects on its new position in the literary canon, made possible by the work of Jean Fagan Yellin within the context of larger changes in the field, including the emergence of feminist criticism. As Smith shows, the treatment of *Incidents* constitutes both a unique story related to the particularities of Jacobs's text and a representative instance of the general devaluation of the work of African American and women writers in the first half of the twentieth century. Racism, sexism, and a modern literary aesthetic that eschewed sentimentalism combined to ensure that this narrative would not be visible, and Smith asks us to read this case history "as a cautionary tale about aesthetic value and literary politics."

Frederick Douglass, a writer and intellectual who was much lauded as a "representative American man," forms a sharp contrast to Harriet Jacobs, whose narrative was for so long denied both validity and representational value. John Stauffer, however, in chapter twelve, allows us to reflect on the ways Douglass was engaged, like Jacobs, in a difficult enterprise of self-creation. In "Frederick Douglass's self-fashioning and the making of a representative American man," Stauffer explores Douglass's speeches, his 1845 *Narrative*, and his 1855 *My Bondage and My Freedom* in order to consider the ways in which Douglass, over time, fashioned and re-fashioned himself as a representative American man, and not a slave or a thing.

Chapter thirteen, "Beyond Douglass and Jacobs," considers the fact that Douglass, long a "representative man," and Jacobs, the newly representative woman, stand at the center of what has become this "major" genre: the African American slave narrative. John Ernest asks readers to think not just about why certain narratives are now deemed representative and therefore taught with regularity, often to the exclusion of others, but also about what it means to try to understand slavery through a handful of narratives written by former slaves. Ernest worries about whether the slave narrative's acceptance as part of the "settled knowledge represented by the [literary] canon" will produce a "dangerously simplified view of the past," particularly when students of the genre begin to read only the same few texts and ask of them the same few questions. Ernest's chapter raises a fundamental challenge for the study of the slave narrative to which this volume has tried to respond.

The final chapter in the volume reminds us that issues of representativeness and the concomitant problems of exclusion were always present for women trying to utilize the vehicle of the slave narrative and enter into public debate. Moreover, Xiomara Santamarina's discussion of a range of women's texts in chapter eleven, "Black womanhood in North American women's slave narratives," reminds us that Harriet Jacobs's recuperated text is not the only female-authored slave narrative that has proved problematic in literary history. Her discussion of Mary Prince, Sojourner Truth, Ellen Craft, Louisa Picquet, and Elizabeth Keckley offers us "a rich archive about race and gender" and the "multidimensionality of black women's lives" and might be read as a fruitful response to John Ernest's challenge to think "beyond Douglass and Jacobs." I hope the same may be said for this volume as a whole.

In 1987, when Henry Louis Gates, Jr. edited *The Classic Slave Narratives*, a volume containing the narratives of Olaudah Equiano, Mary Prince, Frederick Douglass, and Harriet Jacobs, he brought these narratives together in a convenient and inexpensive format that could be used both in classrooms and outside of them. Today, the narratives of Equiano, Douglass, and Jacobs are widely available in myriad editions, but so too are many others. Indeed, as part of "Documenting the American South," a major digital publishing initiative, sponsored by the University of North Carolina, Chapel Hill, William L. Andrews has compiled a comprehensive bibliography of slave narratives with links to full-text electronic versions for most citations.[1] With the wealth of electronic and critical editions of the narratives available today, students of the slave narrative have little excuse for reading only, as John Ernest writes, "one complete narrative and about one-seventh of another."

If the availability of primary material has exploded, so too has the critical literature around the slave narrative. My hope is that this volume will follow in the estimable tradition of John Sekora and Darwin T. Turner's *The Art of Slave Narratives* (1982) and Deborah E. McDowell and Arnold Rampersad's *Slavery and the Literary Imagination* (1989) in capturing something of the rich variety of this dynamic and evolving field while still allowing those for whom the genre is new to keep up with the conversation.

NOTE

1. See http://docsouth.unc.edu/neh/index.html

PART I

The Slave Narrative and Transnational Abolitionism

I

PHILIP GOULD

The rise, development, and circulation of the slave narrative

In the late eighteenth century, important cultural and philosophical changes facilitated the rise of antislavery movements. These developments are rich, complex, and usually fall under the rubric of "Enlightenment" ideology. The historian David Brion Davis has identified three of them. One was the rise of secular social philosophy, based on humanitarian principles and contractual terms for human association and government, found in such thinkers as Baron Montesquieu and John Locke, which drastically narrowed the traditional Christian rationale for slavery as the natural extension of the "slavery" of human sin.[1] Another important development was the rise of sentimentalism in the eighteenth century, which, related to evangelical religion, popular fiction, and urban cultures of refinement, raised the importance of the virtues of sympathy and benevolence as well as the cultural refinement accompanying them. A third development, especially important in the 1790s, was the proliferation of more radical and revolutionary ideas about natural rights vis-à-vis state and social forms of authority.

The slave narrative first emerged during the 1770s and 1780s in the context of these transatlantic political and religious movements which shaped the genre's publication history, as well as its major themes and narrative designs. These late eighteenth-century works reveal what Paul Gilroy calls the "transcultural international formation" of the "Black Atlantic" – that fluid geographical area encompassing the West African littoral, Britain, British America, eastern Canada, and the Caribbean – through which black subjects traveled as free persons and as slaves.[2] The conditions and contexts for publishing these early narratives were in many ways unique. Evangelical Christian groups often sponsored and oversaw their publication. By the 1780s, new political organizations, like the English Society for Effecting the Abolition of the Slave Trade (1787) and the Pennsylvania Abolition Society (1775/1784), dedicated to the abolition of the slave trade, also played a role in encouraging and publishing these narratives.

These religious and political groups helped to shape the language and themes of the eighteenth-century slave narrative: they helped to influence the genre's treatment of the black protagonist's physical and spiritual journey. Not until the organization of more radical antislavery societies in America during the 1830s and 1840s, which now called for the immediate emancipation of slaves, did the genre turn its energies upon Southern plantation slavery. Such an important change did not entirely nationalize or secularize the slave narrative, but it did produce new literary conventions, rework traditional ones, and effectively standardize all of them to the point where the slave narrative was an easily imitated – and sometimes forged – literary form. While earlier narratives were published, read, reviewed, and reprinted as much for their religious as racial experiences, the antebellum slave narrative sharpened its focus and became an increasingly popular and effective political means of fighting slavery.

Slave narratives cannot be reduced to these different ideological influences, but they do creatively engage the expectations of these groups in order to create cultural spaces in which the project of self-representation takes place. Whether actually writing or only orally relating their lives, slave narrators drew on multiple discourses as a way of cultivating such complex identities that lay ambiguously within and without contemporary norms.

Context, genre, theme

The first black autobiographers largely wrote within the norms of "civilized" or "Christian" identity – one that was more often than not associated directly with "Englishness." The *Narrative of the Uncommon Sufferings and Surprising Deliverance of Briton Hammon, a Negro Man* (1760) appropriates such a civilized persona. The narrative, which recounts Hammon's thirteen-year odyssey of shipwreck and captivity in the Caribbean, contrasts his self-image as a "free" English subject with his presumably barbaric captors, Native Americans or the Spanish in Havana. The *Narrative* concludes with Hammon's fortuitous rediscovery of his "good Master" Winslow on board a ship bound from England to New England, and his symbolic reunification with him. Hammon leaves the terms of his "service" to Winslow deliberately ambiguous as a way of being able to access the language of English liberty, which was especially resonant for British and British American readers during the Seven Years War (1754–63), and to thereby legitimize himself by exploiting the period's anti-Catholic fervor and assuaging anxieties about slave unrest in Massachusetts.[3] By manipulating this ideal of the rights of Englishmen, moreover, Hammon suggests the kind of thinking that, a decade later, would underlie the famous decision by Lord Mansfield in the case of James Somerset (1772). This case ruled on the complaint of a black slave who had traveled to England with his master and did not wish to return to the West Indies. The Court ruled, albeit reluctantly, that slavery was incompatible with English liberty and that slaves who set foot in England were, in effect, free.

The genres upon which Hammon draws also suggest important historical realities about the publication, popularity, and expectations of the early slave narrative. One should recognize that, unlike the antebellum slave narrative, eighteenth-century narratives were more generically fluid. They were published and read as many things at once. The generic field includes spiritual autobiography, the conversion narrative, the providential tale, criminal confession, Indian captivity narrative, sea adventure story, and the picaresque novel. In Hammon's case, the publication history suggests that it was read as an Indian captivity narrative and an adventure story, and one that also "proved" the piety and loyalty of African Americans. The Boston publishing firm of Green and Russell (who were associated with Fowle and Draper, the leading publishers of captivity stories) took a chance on Hammon not out of antislavery convictions but out of a belief in the market potential of a picaresque tale of captivity. Edited by an English Methodist minister, John Marrant's *Narrative* similarly exemplified the edifying faith of its black subject, but its tale of captivity – already an established popular genre by the 1780s – significantly contributed to its popularity and continual republication between the 1780s and 1810s. (Until recently, it was republished in anthologies of Indian captivity narratives.) *The Life and Confession of Johnson Green* (1786) describes another autobiographical genre related to the slave narrative: the criminal conversion narrative, often published in broadside form. Many of these texts displayed an uneasy tension between evangelical didacticism and titillating commercial value.

The early slave narrative drew as well on less marketable genres. If we take a larger view of the development of the slave narrative, between the 1770s and 1830s, we see a genre arising not only from religious and popular contexts but also along with important kinds of political writing that directly took up the issues of race and slavery. Ever since the 1770s, for example, the political petition was an important antislavery genre that, like the slave narrative, critiqued slavery in terms of natural rights and humanitarian principles. The famous petition by a slave named Belinda to the Massachusetts legislature in 1782, for example, asked for compensation from the seized estate of her former Loyalist master. The petition was re-published in 1787 in Mathew Carey's *The American Museum, or Repository of Ancient and Modern Fugitive Pieces, Prose and Poetical*. Her petition employs two strategies that will become staples to the antebellum slave narrative: the sentimental drama of the slave trade's disruption of the African home, and the moral bankruptcy of social law compared with natural law. As with the works of Marrant and Hammon, generic classification here becomes messy. Political writing overlaps with and is animated by sentimental autobiography – the slave's story of the loss of family and home.

Slave narratives that drew on the context of political writing found similar expression in essays and epistles that were published as pamphlets or in newspapers: Caesar Sarter's "Essay on Slavery," which appeared in 1774 in *The Essex Journal and Merrimack Packet*, Benjamin Banneker's famous letter to Thomas Jefferson, Daniel Coker's *A Dialogue Between a Virginian and an African Minister* (1810), and James Forten's *Letters from a Man of Color* (1813), which was written in response to a proposed Pennsylvania state law prohibiting further immigration of free blacks. "We hold these truths to be self evident," Forten declared, "that God created all men equal . . . is one of the most prominent features in the Declaration of Independence and in that glorious fabric of collective wisdom, our noble constitution." These early works, written by ex-slaves as well as freeborn blacks, blend personal experience with political polemic, lending political arguments the emotional weight of autobiography, and providing a source of political arguments for the developing slave narrative.

The early slave narrative, however, might be read as a religious genre. With some exceptions of course – *A Narrative of the Life and Adventures of Venture, a Native of Africa* (1798), for example, which has an almost exclusively economic focus on the slave's capacity to buy his own freedom – virtually all of these early narratives were as much stories of spiritual as bodily captivity and liberation. Why was this so? Rhetorically, of course, the languages of spiritual and physical liberation overlapped considerably. The ability of black autobiographers to signify on religious and political registers simultaneously lay largely in the elasticity of the language they used. The Bible itself provided a crucial source of the language of liberation – of salvation – that could be construed by black writers in highly creative ways. One could easily place, for example, the passage from 2 Corinthians 3:17 ("Now the Lord is that spirit, and where the Spirit of the Lord *is*, there *is* liberty") as the epigraph to most of the major slave narratives from the late eighteenth century.

But the material and economic realities of publication provide the most important context for understanding the religious qualities of early slave narratives. Evangelical groups like the Methodists and Baptists, who emphasized the central importance of the individual's "new birth" (and which, as Africanists have noted, resembles the West African tradition of ecstatic soul possession), took an interest in black autobiographies because of their spiritual value in disseminating religious ideas and thereby converting souls. These groups often assumed the role of publisher – the agent financing and taking risk on publication.

This was true of *An Account of the Life of Mr. David George, from Sierra Leone in Africa*, which was published in *The Baptist Annual Register* (London, 1793). The title page informs readers that the narrative was "given by himself in a Conversation with Brother Rippon of London, and Brother Pearce of Birmingham." It begins by stating that he was "without knowledge" of God and that his African parents "had not the fear of God before their eyes." Similarly, *Memoirs of the Life of Boston King, a Black Preacher. Written by Himself, during his Residence at Kingswood School* was published in the Wesleyan *Methodist Magazine* (London, 1798). Other autobiographies, such as *A Brief Account of the Life, Experience, Travels, and Gospel Labors of George White, an African* (1810), *The Life, History, and Unparalleled Sufferings of John Jea, the African Preacher*, and *The Life Experience and Gospel Labors of the Rt. Reverend Richard Allen* (1833), recounted the dual stories of physical and spiritual liberation as well as their subjects' newfound identities as itinerant preachers and their ensuing struggles with established religious authorities. These works were, in one sense, the heirs to earlier religious writing by Briton Hammon, Phillis Wheatley, and Ukasaw Gronniosaw.

With strong ties to evangelical interests, *A Narrative of the Most Remarkable Particulars in the Life of James Albert Ukasaw Gronniosaw an African Prince* (1772) is arguably the first narrative that directly addresses the evils of slavery. Like Phillis Wheatley's *Poems*, the first edition of the *Narrative* was dedicated to the Countess of Huntingdon, the leader of a prominent Methodist religious group in England. It was first published in Bath in 1772, and over the next two decades republished in Bath as well as Dublin, Ireland, and Newport, Rhode Island.[4] The fact that it was published in serial form in the *American Moral and Sentimental Magazine* in 1797 suggests that the *Narrative*'s autobiographical tale of enslavement and liberation was, at least for some readers, meaningful in terms of its thematic structure of religious conversion – its preface, after all, emphasizes the passage from African heathenism to Protestant Christianity. Gronniosaw's *Narrative* also emphasizes the virtue of benevolence that was so important to the evangelical style of piety. It ends bitterly with his lament about his poverty, which in effect takes readers full-circle to the *Narrative*'s preface: "Reader, recommending this Narrative to your perusal, and him who is the Subject of it to your charitable Regard."

By the end of the eighteenth century, then, the demonstration of one's religious conversion and Christian feeling was an important convention of the slave narrative. This development registers the institutional and cultural forces shaping the very meaning in these writings of "liberty" and "slavery." Evangelical Protestantism provided many of the categories and tropes through which black autobiographers – whether they were speaking or writing – fashioned "civilized" identities for public consumption. Even a thoroughly worldly slave narrator like Olaudah Equiano makes sure to demonstrate his spiritual path to religious salvation; like much of the period's Methodist writing, he emphasizes the importance of dreams and visions to his spiritual life. The portrait of Equiano on the frontispiece of the *Interesting Narrative* shows him holding a bible opened at Acts 4:12 ("Neither is there salvation in any other, for there is none other name under heaven given among men whereby we must be saved"). And, as in many black writings during this period, the famous itinerant minister George Whitefield makes an important appearance in the *Interesting Narrative*, which further strengthens Equiano's religious credentials and thereby his authority as a writer.

The politics of abolition

Another crucial context shaping the slave narrative during this early period was the rise of organized antislavery movements. From the early 1770s until 1807, when the slave trade was abolished in Britain and the USA, new political organizations assailing the African slave trade were quite active on both sides of the Atlantic.[5] Organizations like the English Abolition Society lobbied Parliament as well as American colonial (and later state) assemblies to abolish the slave trade. They were truly transatlantic movements, insofar as their members corresponded vigorously with one another across national boundaries. They also supported and patronized the work of black writer-activists like Equiano and Quobna Ottobah Cugoano. These organizations significantly generated a great deal of antislavery literature: books, pamphlets, epistles, institutional reports and proceedings, published sermons and orations, as well as a lot of visual and iconic materials meant to sentimentalize the plight of African slaves. Composed largely, though not exclusively, of Quakers and humanitarians, these groups helped to form a kind of transatlantic print culture, which overlapped with those of evangelicalism, political radicalism, and popular culture.

Antislavery print culture provided the slave narrative with flexible rhetorical strategies and helped to sharpen its political focus. Its growing influence on the slave narrative is apparent, for example, in the dedication of *The Interesting Narrative of the Life of Olaudah Equiano, or Gustavus Vassa, the African* (1789) to the English Parliament. Here Equiano openly connects the writing of autobiography to the politics of abolishing the African slave trade. Similarly, Cugoano's two major works, *Thoughts and Sentiments on the Evil and Wicked Traffic of the Slavery and Commerce of the Human Species* (1787) and *Thoughts and Sentiments on the Evil of Slavery* (1791), are explicitly shaped by antislavery politics and provided perhaps the most radical assault on the African slave trade and West Indian slavery by any writer, white or black, during this era. Cugoano is careful to frame his arguments within the context of the larger antislavery culture. The title of Cugoano's first work culls from English abolitionist Thomas Clarkson's *An Essay on the Slavery and Commerce of the Human Species* (1785); the latter work expressly acknowledges the English abolitionists Granville Sharp and William Wilberforce. Cugoano's prose style, moreover, reveals the radical turn in contemporary antislavery politics. Cast in the language of the jeremiad, his outraged tone is far more apparent than, for example, either Gronniosaw's or Marrant's. (This radical approach likely contributed to the fact that his works were not advertised or reviewed in Britain.)

The changing political culture of abolitionism also opened up more ideological room in the slave narrative for secular arguments. The early writers Hammon and Gronniosaw, for example, did not make extended economic arguments against the slave trade or slave-keeping – these would have been out of step with the personae they wished to create for themselves and the constituencies to which they were appealing. By contrast, Equiano, writing later in the 1780s, drew upon Enlightenment authorities to argue against the economic rationale for slavery. The *Interesting Narrative* echoes Adam Smith's *Wealth of Nations* (1776) as it analyzes the potential advantages for the British economy of converting slave labor into free labor. Equiano's use of personal experience and empirical observation lent further force to this argument.

Slave narratives also pursued the antislavery strategy during this period by reinterpreting Locke's philosophy about natural rights. Whereas proslavery writers traditionally justified slavery according to "natural" rights to property, antislavery writings re-possessed Locke's ideas to argue for the absurdity of equating human beings – who inherently possessed the right to life – with material possessions. This was certainly true of a wide array of British and British American writers, including, for example, Thomas Paine, Anthony Benezet, Clarkson, and Granville Sharp. Black writers like Venture Smith, John Marrant, and James Forten took such an argument and pushed it even further, both logically and emotionally, calling upon the rhetorical power of personal experience. Indeed, part of the interest in Smith's life lay in his prodigious capacity for work, his ability to mix his labor with the land, and thereby purchase his liberty.

In keeping with this major shift in antislavery polemic was the slave narrative's central proposition about the full humanity of the African. The genre made extensive use of a wide array of Christian and Enlightenment philosophy that posited the singular nature (or what is known as the "monogenist" view) of humanity as well as the moral responsibility to uphold humanitarian ideals. Phillis Wheatley's famous autobiographical poem, "On Being Brought from Africa to America," employs the language of salvation (albeit with complex layers of irony) to achieve this racial theme. Other antislavery writers, white and black, were aware of and employed the biblical evidence found in Acts 17:26 ("And hath made of one blood all nations of men"). In contrast to Wheatley, Equiano draws upon secular racial theorists of the Enlightenment such as John Mitchill to make a case for the singular view of humanity.

During the 1830s and 1840s, changes in abolitionism drastically affected the thematic and formal features of the slave narrative. Partly in reaction to colonization movements in Britain and America, abolitionism became more radical and more organized in the antebellum era. The rise of the Massachusetts Anti-Slavery Society in 1831, and its heir, the American Anti-Slavery Society (AASS) in 1833, under the leadership of William Lloyd Garrison, changed the political direction of antislavery politics. Even though the AASS was often condemned for its radical beliefs – the immediate emancipation of all slaves, non-violent resistance, moral suasion as opposed to political negotiation, and the proslavery character of the US Constitution – the Garrisonians helped to shift the center of political gravity in American antislavery. Its newspaper *The Liberator* became an important public forum for disseminating ideas. By the late 1830s, however, the abolitionist movement in America had fragmented into different organizations, like the American and Foreign Antislavery Society, due largely to social and gender issues dividing conservative religious members from others. Many other antislavery constituencies, moreover, like the Free Soil Movement and the Liberty Party, simply lacked the moral and religious commitment to helping African Americans. Notwithstanding these political divisions, the movement as a whole created an expansive antislavery print culture. There were now many more – and more widely circulating – abolitionist periodicals, newspapers, and yearbooks: the *National Anti-Slavery Standard*, the *American and Foreign Antislavery Reporter*, the *Anti-Slavery Record*, the *Anti-Slavery Bugle*, and the *Herald of Freedom*, to name only a few. Renowned slave authors like Frederick Douglass, William Wells Brown, and Henry Bibb, for example, also became active in the abolitionist press and published or edited periodicals of their own.

The impact of these changes was immense on the slave narrative. The central abolitionist project of exposing the evils of the Southern plantation (and the false paternalistic myths supporting it) became the absolute priority of the antebellum slave narrative. The genre now focused, often with painstaking vigilance, on the actual, daily conditions of slave life, because abolitionist readers and publishers desired – indeed required – that kind of detailed evidence. A good example of this is the *Narrative of James Williams* (1838), which was edited and transcribed by the poet and abolitionist John Greenleaf Whittier. Its preface and appendices, written and compiled by Whittier, are nearly half as long as Williams's story, and they densely document the horrors of plantation life. Sandwiched between this editorial apparatus, the Williams narrative (which was later withdrawn because of controversy over its authenticity) unsurprisingly duplicates this emphasis.

So the antebellum slave narrative came of age in the context of the abolitionist obsession with "evidence" and the new documentary compendia meant to fill that role. In this sense, the slave narrative has a reciprocal relation with influential antislavery documentaries like Theodore Dwight Weld's *American Slavery As It Is* (1839) and Harriet Beecher Stowe's *A Key to Uncle Tom's Cabin* (1853). It borrows from them and provides factual material for them, so that these genres inter-animate one another, and the major rhetorical tropes of antislavery circulate freely in both of them. Many of the narrative and thematic conventions, which were apparent yet not fully developed in eighteenth-century works, take shape in this period – the depravity of Southern planters and the irrepressible fact of sexual miscegenation, the hypocrisy of Southern Christianity, scenes of brutal whipping and torture, rebellious slaves who are murdered, and the strategic mechanisms by which the plantation maintains what Douglass called the "mental and moral darkness" of enslavement – and all become standard fare.

These conventions were usually rehearsed orally before they appeared in print. The abolitionist lecture circuit was an important development shaping the style and content of the antebellum slave narrative. Most slave narrators made their names as speakers before they became writers per se. Some – Douglass, William Wells Brown, J. W. C. Pennington, Samuel Ringgold Ward, to list a few – were known just as much as orators as writers. Indeed, many entered into the world of print because of their powers in oratory (which was a largely masculine mode of expression in this era). Some – Douglass, Brown, William and Ellen Craft, Henry "Box" Bown – even gained international renown by traveling to Britain and Europe and giving public lectures about the evils of slavery. We should remember, however, that Garrisonian abolitionists themselves were never considered a "mainstream" political group, principally because they believed the Constitution was a proslavery document and a "covenant with death." Even though radical abolitionists were out of step with most Americans, their forceful message about the evils of Southern plantation slavery was effective over time. Most importantly, the abolitionist forum became a vitally important arena of expression for ex-slaves. Abolitionist newspapers and periodicals published and reviewed as many, if not more, oral testimonies against slavery and ex-slave speeches as "written" narratives.[6]

However, the abolitionist meeting also put limits on black expression in public and literally staged their bodies for public consumption. Ex-slaves were asked only to state the basic "facts" of their lives; they sometimes bared their backs as texts that "proved" their stories. These dramatic conventions only further heightened the stakes for African Americans of establishing their own voices as speakers and as writers. As Douglass puts it in *My Bondage and My Freedom*, during the abolitionist meeting William Lloyd Garrison "took me as his text." The abolitionist forum provides a crucial rhetorical context – the limitations of voice, the bounds of propriety, the humility of self-presentation – for evaluating the slave narratives during this period. Important slave narratives from this period self-consciously stage scenes of speaking and wield tropes of utterance to counter the constant prospect of being silenced.

If the politics of slavery were, as we might expect, central to the slave narrative in the antebellum period, the narrative continued to express religious ideas and employ Christian tropes about the nature of enslavement and liberation. One central reason for this is that antebellum culture was still highly religious; evangelical institutions exerted significant influence on the world of antebellum publishing. Religious reading continued to play a major role in most Americans' lives: bibles, religious primers, devotional handbooks, psalters, hymnals, and John Bunyan's *The Pilgrim's Progress* still were standard fare. The framing devices editors used to portray ex-slaves continued to emphasize moral virtue and Christian feeling. For example, the preface to *A Narrative of the Adventures and Escape of Moses Roper* (1837), written by the British evangelical and antislavery activist Thomas Price, notes how Roper continues his religious education so that "he will be eminently qualified to instruct the children of Africa in the truths of the gospel of Christ." The *Narrative*'s publication in effect fulfills this financial goal. Roper's patron, John Morison, was an English evangelical, who obviously influenced Roper's presentation of himself as the biblical Joseph, the victim of slavery who eventually forgave his oppressors. The traditional intertwining of physical and spiritual journeys, moreover, continued to characterize the genre. In *Running a Thousand Miles for Freedom; or, The Escape of William and Ellen Craft from Slavery* (1860), William Craft likens his journey north to the allegorical protagonist of *The Pilgrim's Progress*: "I thought I might indulge in a few minutes' sleep in the car; but I, like Bunyan's Christian in the arbour, went to sleep at the wrong time, and took too long a nap."

Publication and reception

From the outset, the slave narrative appears to have been a popular genre on both sides of the Atlantic, though exact sales figures for eighteenth-century narratives are more difficult to calculate. We do know, however, that between the 1770s and 1810s the narratives of Gronniosaw, Marrant, and Equiano went through multiple editions and apparently sold quite well. These works were published in London and, with the advent of provincial printing in the eighteenth century, later re-published in places like Dublin and Edinburgh (and sometimes in America). The source of their appeal lay in a number of factors: an evangelical reading market, the motifs of captivity and enslavement, the allure of sea narrative and high adventure, and, often, the allure of the exotic. Most importantly, these narratives were able to combine multiple genres – spiritual autobiography, travel narrative, ethnography, political commentary – as well as religious, sentimental, and gothic discourses. They were flexible enough to appeal to various readerships simultaneously.

Perhaps this is the reason for the financial success of Equiano's *Interesting Narrative*. As Vincent Carretta has shown, Equiano was commercially savvy enough to keep the copyright to the *Interesting Narrative*, rather than allowing a publisher (usually a bookseller) to assume the risk of printing costs.[7] Later African American ex-slave narrators like Henry Bibb pursued the same strategy. Equiano also marketed the *Interesting Narrative* through subscription, which was not an uncommon strategy at this time (Ignatius Sancho's and Cugoano's works were published in this way), since it significantly decreased financial risks. The *Interesting Narrative* subsequently went through thirteen editions in the first five years after its London publication in 1789. It was re-published in 1791 in New York and was translated into Dutch, German, and Russian. By 1850 it had gone through thirty-six editions.[8] By comparison, Marrant's *Narrative* went through (perhaps) ten printings in 1785, the year of its initial publication, and almost forty by the middle of the nineteenth century.[9] The economic potential of this genre was such that even smaller publishing houses sometimes participated in re-publishing those works that had proven their market value. When Gronniosaw's work was re-published in Salem, New York in 1809, it was re-titled simply *The Black Prince* (adapting the phrase "an African Prince" from its original, lengthy title), a move that suggests a different kind of marketing strategy.

The literary world of eighteenth-century London reviewed works by black writers in general seriously though not always positively. Wheatley's *Poems on Various Subjects, Religious and Moral* (1773) and *The Letters of Ignatius Sancho, an African* (1782), for example, generally upheld standards of morality and cultural refinement and were less politically volatile. In contrast, the writings of Equiano and especially Cugoano were more radical, and the mainstream English press often cast doubt on the plausibility of these and other narratives in terms that were particularly condescending about the possibilities of black authorship. For example, *The Monthly Review* disparagingly noted of the *Interesting Narrative* that "it is not improbable that some English writer has assisted him in the compliment, or, at least, the correction of the book: for it is sufficiently well-written." The *Gentleman's Magazine* claimed the *Interesting Narrative* was "written in a very unequal style," but offered this praise together with the negative assertion that "there is no general rule without an exception." These magazines also critiqued the authenticity (and even the interest) of Equiano's and Marrant's accounts of their religious conversions. The critiques in general are more than tinged with racial hostility, but they may also reflect the cultural friction between secular and evangelical reading publics at this time.

We might even broadly re-conceive the term "review" as it affects early black writing in general and the slave narrative in particular. Traditional reviews of writers like Equiano and Marrant were only one kind of discourse evaluating early black writing. Indeed, the prefatory material framing – and legitimating – these works functioned as promotional reviews. There is probably no better example of this than the preface that the minister William Aldridge wrote for John Marrant's *Narrative*, which highlights the interest of Marrant's Indian captivity and simultaneously asks readers to read that captivity as a spiritual allegory of the soul. Even as editors lowered the bar for the writing skills of "uncultivated" or "untutored" minds, they nevertheless made the case for the value of these works. This was especially resonant at a time when the "literary" was associated with "letters" generally and was never separated from writing's moral edification.

Expanding the category of the review, however, cuts both ways. David Hume and Thomas Jefferson disparaged black writing in important philosophical and historical works like Hume's "Of National Character" (1764) and Jefferson's *Notes on the State of Virginia* (1785). Hume likened the Jamaican poet Francis Williams to a "parrot," and Jefferson infamously debunked the quality of Wheatley's poems and even used her as an example testifying to the inferiority of Africans in general. Their comments did not go unanswered, however. Writers as diverse as Gilbert Imlay and the French prelate Abbé Gregoire publicly came to the defense of Wheatley,

Equiano, and many others. The important idea here is that the "review" of the slave narrative, whether a traditional review or in the form of prefatory material, was a highly politicized form. Literary evaluation and the politics of race and slavery were deeply enmeshed in one another: judgments of the aesthetic value of the slave narrative were inseparable from transatlantic debates over the morality of the African slave trade and the nature of the African.

Between the 1770s and 1840s, however, the slave narrative became part of an emerging, capitalist literary market, and the genre was promoted and reviewed accordingly. This is to say that the rising popularity of the slave narrative was due as much to the changing conditions of print capitalism as to the rising tide of abolitionist sentiment. The publishing industry in America underwent expansive changes at the same time that abolitionist groups were promoting the publication of slave narratives to advance their political cause. A number of factors contributed to the development of a modern book industry in America: larger publishing firms, with greater resources to finance and market their products; changes in the technology of printing, which decreased costs, controlled prices, and enabled far greater levels of production; improvements in transportation routes and distribution techniques; and marketing strategies that targeted expanding readerships on an increasingly national scale. All of these changes have complex histories and did not occur quickly. But they did change the economic conditions under which slave narrators, publishers, printers, and abolitionist patrons all operated.

The genre was also affected by the emergence of modern publishers in America. These firms assumed the risk of financing print and distribution costs, and they were often more concerned with the genre's market potential than its political efficacy. Abolitionist societies, however, sometimes assumed the role of publisher – the AASS financed the publication, for example, of Douglass's first autobiography and the *Narrative of William Wells Brown, a Fugitive Slave* (1847). But the publishing history of other narratives suggests their status as commercial ventures. For example, after the enormous success of Harriet Beecher Stowe's novel *Uncle Tom's Cabin* (1852), and her subsequent suggestion that her characterization of Uncle Tom was taken in large part from *The Life of Josiah Henson* (1849), John and Henry Jewett re-published Henson's narrative in 1858 as *Truth Stranger Than Fiction: Father Henson's Story of his Own Life* – and included a new preface by Stowe herself to enhance its marketability. This was also true of *Slavery in the United States: A Narrative of the Life and Adventures of Charles Ball* (1836), which went through nine US editions, two British editions, and one German edition. As with Henson's autobiography, however, its popularity took off when it was (misleadingly) re-titled *Fifty Years in Chains; or the Life of an American Slave* (1859) and packaged in a more attractive binding. By the eve of the Civil War, then, the slave narrative had become simultaneously a more mature literary form and a more sensationalist print commodity.

In light of these changes, antebellum narratives enjoyed much greater sales than had earlier slave narratives and reached audiences beyond the pale of radical abolitionism. *The Narrative of the Life of Frederick Douglass, an American Slave* (1845), for example, sold 5,000 copies in four months and 11,000 copies in two years, and Solomon Northrup's *Twelve Years a Slave* (1853) sold 27,000 copies in two years. The popularity of these narratives extended beyond America. Most popular slave narratives were soon reprinted in Britain, and many were translated into other languages and published in Europe. Douglass's *Narrative* underwent nine British editions in the 1840s and was also re-published in Ireland as well. William Wells Brown's *Narrative* had a London edition and was later translated into Dutch. *A Narrative of the Adventures and Escape of Moses Roper, from American Slavery* (1838) was first published in London and then in Philadelphia, and represents perhaps the most Anglicized slave narrative of this period; it went through ten editions in twenty years, selling more than 20,000 copies.[10]

Editorial decisions continued to shape the rhetorical and thematic designs of the slave narrative. Black writers negotiated political and economic forces in order to tell "free" stories. Perhaps the most extreme case of this is *The Confessions of Nat Turner* (1831), edited by Thomas Gray, which was published immediately after Nat Turner's Rebellion in order to discredit Turner as a fanatic and to suppress future slave insurrections. But, to a lesser extent, the same issues of editorial manipulation were present in narratives sponsored by antislavery constituencies. Witness the difficult relationship between Garrison and Douglass, whose second autobiography, *My Bondage and My Freedom*, published in 1855, was in many ways an open break from Garrison's mentorship. Its preface, written by an African American physician, openly addressed the problems Douglass experienced in asserting his independence among white abolitionists. Published in Boston in 1849, the first edition of Henry "Box" Brown's narrative was edited and transcribed by the abolitionist Charles Stearns, who subjected the text to stylistic excesses, overblown rhetoric, and melodramatic commentary. Its title suggests as much: *Narrative of Henry Box Brown who Escaped from Slavery Enclosed in a Box Three Feet Long and Two Wide Written from a Statement Made by Himself. With Remarks upon a Remedy for Slavery. By Charles Stearns.* In 1850, however, the newly empowered Fugitive Slave Law forced Brown to flee to England, where he set up (much to the dismay of British abolitionists) his own traveling exhibition of his famous escape, complete with the eponymous box in which he had escaped. The second edition of his auto-biography, published in Manchester in 1851, presents a more compact and stylistically controlled work, due to Brown's editorial control. It was entitled simply the *Narrative of the Life of Henry Box Brown, Written by Himself*.

During the antebellum period, when the political stakes of the slave narra-tive's authenticity became intensified, antislavery reviewers usually defended the veracity of the slave narrative as well as the moral character of the slave narrator. Such praise often relied on available cultural tropes and set the terms through which slave narrators reconstructed their own identities. Lydia Maria Child, for example, included a letter from Amy Post in the first edition of Harriet Jacobs's *Incidents in the Life of a Slave Girl* (1861) that praised the protagonist as a "naturally virtuous and refined" slave woman with "a natural craving for human sympathy." Reviewers, moreover, generally took a pragmatic attitude toward the genre, evaluating its ability to combat slav-ery in the USA. One of the most famous reviews of slave narratives in this period was Ephraim Peabody's, which appeared in 1849 in the Unitarian *Christian Examiner*. While heaping praise on Douglass, Josiah Henson, and others, Peabody still cautioned that Douglass's "mode of address" (read: his anger, wit, and irony) was "likely to diminish, not only his usefulness, but his real influence."[11] An anonymous review of Charles Ball's autobiography, appearing in *The Quarterly Anti-Slavery Magazine*, was happy about this "simple" and "plain" narrative composed by a writer "who is no more than the recorder of facts detailed to him by another."

Reviewers were highly self-conscious about the subject of race in light of the rise of pseudo-scientific theories about racial difference, which were related to the fields of natural history, ethnology, and phrenology (the study of human traits according to the configuration of the human skull). Even the best-intentioned reviewers, however, reveal racial condescension that often takes the form of romantic primitivism – the idea that "native peoples" were more virtuous since they were removed from the corrupting influ-ences of modern society. When slave narrators like Harriet Jacobs confessed moments of their own moral weakness, we should remember they did so in the midst of an abolitionist culture that readily figured African Ameri-cans as culturally deficient. Even in antislavery circles, representations of the "poor slave" often had primitivist tendencies that reflected some form of the "noble savage" trope noted above. The editor of Venture Smith's *Narra-tive* likened him to a Benjamin Franklin in a "state of nature"; antebellum admirers of Douglass similarly attributed his oratorical and literary gifts to the same sources. Reviewing Douglass's *Narrative* in the *New York Tribune*, for example, Margaret Fuller praised it as "simple, true, coherent, and warm with genuine feeling." Arguing against racial prejudice, Fuller nevertheless noted the African race's "peculiar element" – its "talent for melody, a ready skill in adaptation and imitation, [and] an almost indestructible elasticity of nature." This was supposed to be a compliment.

By the 1850s reviews of major slave narratives also registered the importance of the genre to American literary culture. The period between the American Revolution and Civil War was characterized by chronic laments about America's literary reputation, and was punctuated by famous declarations of national cultural independence by Emerson, Whitman, and others. As a form of increasingly popular, distinctly American autobiography, the slave narrative further enabled this national cultural project. Not all reviewers embraced the genre as a high form of literature, and sectional and racial politics continued to shape all literary evaluations. Yet even pragmatic and condescending reviewers like Peabody recognized the capacity of the slave narrative to stand as an "American" literary genre in the eyes of the literary world. What further enhanced this literary reconfiguration was the romantic cachet the slave narrative possessed – its scenes of isolation, suffering, and solitary flight from the barbarities of society – that suited well romantic culture's thematic motifs and master tropes. Even the ways in which these narratives were prefaced and packaged suggest their modern literary appeal. As the preface to the *Narrative of Henry Bibb* (1849) demonstrates, the book was presented as much for picaresque adventure as for antislavery themes. The "Opinions of the Press" that Bibb included for promotional purposes contained praise from magazines like the *New York Evangelist* ("a work adapted to produce . . . proper Christian sympathy") and *The Liberator* (a work of "thrilling interest"). The slave narrative's entrance into this literary and commercial culture produced tensions in its literary development. While adhering to higher principles, the slave narrative had to compete in an increasingly capitalized and modern print culture; while abdicating the role of professional "writer" who merely sought money, the slave narrator nevertheless was conscripted into the modern "American" literary scene.

NOTES

1. David Brion Davis, *The Problem of Slavery in the Age of Revolution, 1770–1823* (Ithaca: Cornell University Press, 1975).
2. Paul Gilroy, *The Black Atlantic: Modernity and Double Consciousness* (Cambridge: Harvard University Press, 1993).
3. See Robert S. Desrochers, Jr., "'Surprizing Deliverance'?: Slavery and Freedom, Language, and Identity in the Narrative of Briton Hammon, 'A Negro Man'" in *Genius in Bondage*. Vincent Carretta and Philip Gould, eds. (Lexington: University of Kentucky Press, 2001), pp. 153–74. See also John Sekora, "Red, White, and Black: Indian Captivities, Colonial Printers, and the Early African American

Narrative" in *A Mixed Race: Ethnicity in Early America*. Frank Shuffelton, ed. (New York: Oxford University Press, 1993), pp. 92–104.

4. See Vincent Carretta, ed., *Unchained Voices: An Anthology of Black Authors in the English-Speaking World of the Eighteenth Century* (Lexington: University of Kentucky Press, 1996).

5. See Philip Gould, *Barbaric Traffic: Commerce and Antislavery in the Eighteenth-Century Atlantic World* (Cambridge: Harvard University Press, 2003).

6. See John W. Blassingame, *Slave Testimony: Two Centuries of Letters, Speeches, Interviews, and Autobiographies* (Baton Rouge: Louisiana State University Press, 1977).

7. Vincent Carretta, "'Property of Author': Olaudah Equiano's Place in the History of the Book" in Carretta and Gould, *Genius in Bondage*, pp. 130–52.

8. See Charles T. Davis and Henry Louis Gates, Jr., eds., *The Slave's Narrative* (New York: Oxford University Press, 1985).

9. See Adam Potkay and Sandra Burr, eds., *Black Atlantic Writers of the Eighteenth Century* (New York: St. Martin's Press, 1995).

10. See Yuval Taylor, ed., *I Was Born a Slave: An Anthology of Classic Slave Narratives* (Chicago: Lawrence Hill, 1999). 2 vols.

11. Davis and Gates, *The Slave's Narrative*, p. 24.

2

DICKSON D. BRUCE, JR.

Politics and political philosophy in the slave narrative

The slave narratives were intensely political documents. Although one may find many motivations behind their writing, all were published to play a role in the fight against slavery. Encouraged by the rise of the abolitionist movement in the 1830s, the narratives quickly became that movement's most essential texts, providing eyewitness accounts of slavery's brutal reality. Most of the authors were themselves active abolitionists who had told their stories on the platform prior to setting them down in print. Both they and their colleagues believed the narratives could strike a telling blow against slavery.

The narratives' political purposes also contributed to their shape and content. Written to serve the abolitionist cause, the narratives quickly developed a set of rhetorically effective conventions with great political resonance in antebellum America, based on significant, systematic political ideas.

The political character of abolitionism was itself a complex matter. The movement's roots, and those of the slave narrative, lay in efforts to oppose slavery that had appeared both in Britain and its American colonies by the 1680s. During the eighteenth century, and into the era of the American Revolution, such former slaves as Ayuba Suleiman Diallo (Job ben Solomon) and Olaudah Equiano, their works well known on both sides of the Atlantic, recounted their experiences in order to further that opposition. Still, both in Britain and the United States, the development of the slave narrative as a form was closely connected to the rise of American abolitionism as an organized force, formally marked, beginning in 1833, by the formation of the American Anti-Slavery Society (AASS), led by William Lloyd Garrison, Robert Purvis, and others. The slave narrative not only flowered with the growth of abolitionism, but also simultaneously shaped and was shaped by the movement's goals and the political environment within which it operated, an environment marked by conflict and change.

Politically, slave narratives tended to look in three distinct, though related, directions. First, as contributions to the abolitionist movement, they played a critical role in antebellum debates over slavery. With the growth of abolitionism, there developed a large body of proslavery writing defending the institution and creating an array of arguments on its behalf. Slave narratives countered proslavery arguments by undermining the ideas and images on which those arguments were based, and did so explicitly through the special role that African Americans – and former slaves – claimed in the debate.

Secondly, the slave narratives participated in larger processes of democratization taking place in the antebellum United States. Built on ideas and values going back to the American Revolution, democratic rhetoric and practices became dominant modes in the nation's politics, especially after the mid-1820s. Imperfectly realized, these modes were nevertheless widely embraced as standards against which political processes were judged. Slave narratives both drew on and helped to shape this process.

Finally, this was an era in which the idea of freedom itself was increasingly both valued and contested. Given the focus of abolitionism, and of the narratives, it is not surprising that they should have played a role in this discussion. The narratives brought together abolitionist ideology with ideas of freedom that had evolved out of the distinctive experiences of African Americans, especially people who had lived in bondage, in a way that had particular political resonance for antebellum American readers.

The narratives in the abolitionist movement

The primary political impulse behind the slave narratives grew out of the nineteenth-century debates over slavery. Proslavery arguments took the form they did in large part because slavery's defenders had to respond to abolitionist attacks; abolitionism had to answer proslavery as well. The ex-slaves who recounted their experiences entered self-consciously into this debate. The specific episodes they recounted were often offered as explicit replies to proslavery assertions. Several writers openly addressed prominent proslavery figures, challenging them with facts that undermined proslavery claims.[1]

Antebellum debates over slavery focused on several key issues. Some of these had to do with race. Since at least the early nineteenth century, race had served as a cornerstone for slavery's defenders, who argued that people of African descent were intellectually and morally inferior to Europeans and Euro-Americans and were, therefore, fit only for slavery. Abolitionists rejected such arguments, asserting the common humanity of all people. Race, they said, could provide no defense for slavery or any other form of discrimination.

The slave narratives had an obvious role to play in the abolitionist case, as ex-slaves – articulate, intelligent men and women – challenged proslavery racism by example. In an introductory note to his second autobiography, *My Bondage and My Freedom* (1855), Frederick Douglass wrote that not only was slavery on trial but "the enslaved people are also on trial" as "*so low* in the scale of humanity" as to be unable to speak for themselves. Writing his "own biography" enabled Douglass to demonstrate his own abilities and, by extension, to prove those of others.[2]

The importance of such a demonstration was widely acknowledged. Most of the narratives included introductions and other testimony from established abolitionist leaders – often white, but sometimes African American – stressing their authors' accomplishments and ability.

Racist ideas were widely shared during the antebellum period, even among some white abolitionists. Such ideas probably represented the strongest assumptions upon which slavery's defenders could build. The narratives' power to counter such assumptions was real, but the necessity to do so was greater still. The assertion of racial equality was central to the narratives' political role in the debate over slavery.

But the debate over slavery revolved around more than race. With the rise of abolitionism, as slavery's defenders felt increasingly threatened by antislavery efforts, they advanced an argument presenting the institution as a "positive good" for the nation and for the slaves as well. The slave narratives challenged that argument by providing first-hand testimony contradicting some of its most crucial contentions.

The most widely advanced of such contentions was the assertion, consistent with notions of African American inferiority, that slavery had provided slaves with a "school for civilization." According to this argument, slavery had enabled Africans and their descendants to come in contact with European and Euro-American customs and achievements, exposing them to virtues they would otherwise not have been able to learn.

The oldest version of this argument, with roots actually predating the rise of abolitionism, had to do with religion, as slavery's defenders claimed that slavery created an arena in which the slaves could be taught the Christian religion. Slave narratives contradicted this claim. Most of the narrators were dedicated Christians who documented religion's importance to themselves and to other slaves. But they also showed that, far from encouraging faith and piety, slaveholders tended to persecute true believers, denying them opportunities to worship and pray, even punishing those who sought to live Christian lives.

The narrators also portrayed religion in the slave South as a perversion of true Christianity. Slaveholders, they said, were willfully blind to Christian principles. "We have man-stealers for ministers, women-whippers for missionaries, and cradle-plunderers for church members," Frederick Douglass wrote.[3] Moses Roper told the story of a young man whipped to death by his "devout" master for "breaking the Sabbath" to complete a task the slaveholder had given him the day before.[4]

Ex-slaves demonstrated that Southern churches sought to inculcate a religion that served slavery more than God. Henry "Box" Brown, whose escape from slavery was legendary, wrote that he had even been raised to believe that "old master was Almighty God, and that his son, my young master, was Jesus Christ," hardly a teaching designed to give slaves "true knowledge of the eternal God."[5] Harriet Jacobs, recounting a sermon in which the slaves were told, "If you disobey your earthly master, you offend your heavenly master," noted that her companions were "highly amused" by such a "gospel teaching" (*Incidents*, p. 71). Writing for a largely Christian audience, and demonstrating, by their words, an impressive grasp of Christian ideals, these narrators powerfully condemned the hypocrisy of Christian slaveholders even as they pointedly refuted proslavery assertions of the missionary value of slavery to the slaves.

Narrators also documented slaveholder hostility to education, often reinforcing religious concerns by portraying Southern persecution of those slaves who had learned to read and understand the Bible. Slaveholder opposition to slave literacy was well known; several Southern states even made it a crime for slaves to learn to read and write. Such opposition clearly contradicted any defense of slavery based on its purported benefits to the slaves.

In addition, at least some of what was portrayed in the narratives not only contradicted positive good arguments but also helped to emphasize, by contrast, how slavery corrupted slaves and slaveholders alike. At the center of such portrayals were issues of family and sexuality. Family ideals were extremely important in antebellum America. The family was seen as the center of social life; bonds of family affection served as a model for an array of social ties.

The narratives made the case that Southern slavery, however, destroyed the family. Among slaves, husbands and wives, children and parents, could all be separated, sold away according to the financial needs – or at the whim – of their owners. The narrators vividly evoked the sufferings of family members who lost their loved ones, the anguish of mothers or children, wives or husbands suddenly sent away, knowing they would never see each other again. As the prominent fugitive Henry Bibb wrote, remembering his separation from his wife and child, "I can never describe to the reader the awful reality of that separation," and, as he made clear, it was a reality he could never forget.[6] Slavery's proponents defended their actions on the ground that such values among their slaves were weak, lacking the depth that white Americans could feel. Slave narratives countered such a claim.

When someone like Bibb described his wife's uncontrollable weeping as he was taken away, he demonstrated that slaves' family ties were no weaker than were those of anyone else.

Bibb, like others, also portrayed the open hostility of slaveholders to the slaves' family ties. He did so, most vividly, by describing a violent scenario of separation. About to be torn apart, Bibb and his family knelt to pray. Their owner – a Methodist deacon – responded, not with sympathy, but by severely beating Bibb's wife even as she wept inconsolably over the loss of her husband. Slavery's hypocritical defenders were aware of the strength of slave families; the narratives made the case that slaveholders just did not care.

If anything, slave masters actually manipulated family ties to augment the brutality that their slaves had to face. Lewis Clarke was one of many who told of husbands forced to whip their wives, as masters sought to create a display of power over both, while increasing the suffering of both as well. In one such case, according to Clarke, a husband was even forced to whip his wife to death.[7]

The evocation of proslavery hypocrisy was especially striking in regard to sexuality. The portrayal of male slaveholders as sexual predators was common. As the narrators said, slaveholders had the power to compel slave women to submit to sexual advances, and they used it. The classic episode along these lines was Frederick Douglass's account of the horrific beating of his aunt, Hester, especially as he told it in *My Bondage and My Freedom*. Hester's owner had made constant sexual advances toward her; she had consistently refused them. Her love for another slave had only increased her owner's rage and desire. Finally, in a fit of frustration, he tied and stripped her, beating her senseless. In doing so, the cruel man proved, as Douglass wrote, how much "a slave-woman is at the mercy of the power, caprice and passion of her owner" (*My Bondage and My Freedom*, p. 176).

The fullest account of sexual corruption on a Southern plantation, however, is Harriet Jacobs's *Incidents in the Life of a Slave Girl* (1861). Writing that the "slave girl is reared in an atmosphere of licentiousness and fear," Jacobs said that, from her teenage years, "The lash and the foul talk of her master and his sons are her teachers" (*Incidents*, p. 51). Thus, Jacobs recounted a story of continual sexual threats and intimidation. She told her story in a uniquely blunt way that explicitly belied the proslavery case. Slave women, Jacobs and others stressed, were like other American women in valuing chastity; slavery itself made chastity a virtue that could be all too easily violated. And slaveholders violated their slave women with impunity.

The focus on sexuality allowed fugitives to make some telling points against both the racial and moral pretensions of proslavery writers. Jacobs put the matter succinctly when, discussing the "doctrine that God created the Africans to be slaves," she asked, "Who can measure the amount of Anglo-Saxon blood coursing in the veins of American slaves?" (*Incidents*, p. 45). Other writers suggested the possibility of being their owners' children; a few also identified slaves who were descended from prominent, slaveholding American statesmen. Such slaves were living refutations of their owner's dedication to family ideals, living proof of slaveholders' willingness to abandon their own wives and families to pursue uninhibited sexual passions.

Narrators also commonly pointed out one of the uglier possibilities created when slaveholders fathered slave children. These were children, in J. W. C. Pennington's words, "held at such a price, even to their own father, that they could be sold to any interested party." This could even entail, as in a case Pennington described, the selling of one's own daughters into prostitution.[8] Such stories stressed slavery's power to corrupt everyone it touched, including slaveholders. Cohering with more general abolitionist portrayals of slavery as a blot on the national character, these accounts of slaveholder perversity put forward an argument against the institution that could carry weight even with those who were less concerned than were many abolitionists with the humanity and equality of the slaves themselves.

Underlying such portrayals, however, was a final dimension of the narratives' role in the debate over slavery. By the 1830s, that debate had become closely connected to sectional divisions in the United States, as, after about 1800, slavery had come to exist only in the Southern states, having been abolished in or excluded from those in the North. Sectional rivalries led political ideologues to construct pervasive images of regional differences. Southern defenders of slavery created pictures of the South focusing on what they portrayed as a patriarchal plantation system, one involving happy slaves and kindly slaveholders working together in harmony and peace.

The narratives exposed a more antagonistic undercurrent to slave society. It was, the narratives showed, a system based on force and exploitation, something slaveholders well knew. John Thompson was one of many who described a master who followed the practice "to whip occasionally, whether there was cause or not,"[9] simply to keep his slaves in line. Emphasizing the centrality of violence to slavery as a social form and a labor system, the slave narratives unmasked the idyllic South of slavery's defenders, demonstrating that patriarchal images were slaveholder fantasy.

The slave narratives thus had an important political role in the debates over slavery. They had significant impact, as well. The narratives did much to focus and to shape antislavery ideas and to bring people into the movement. Much of the literature of abolitionism, including such novels as Harriet Beecher Stowe's *Uncle Tom's Cabin* (1852), derived from the slave narratives.

Memoirs of abolitionists and other texts demonstrate the extent to which individuals – white and black – were moved to greater fervor as a result of what the narratives revealed.

And the narratives definitely put proslavery writers on the defensive. Slavery's defenders knew what was in the narratives; narratives have even been found in some slaveholders' libraries. Proslavery writers responded to the narratives in several ways. For one thing, they sought to discredit the narratives' authenticity. Many individual narratives, including those by Frederick Douglass, were attacked by proslavery critics who claimed that no African American could be so articulate, and that the narratives were ghostwritten by white abolitionists. There were, in fact, instances of fraudulent narratives, as well as narratives dictated to, and strongly shaped by, abolitionist editors, providing significant grist for the proslavery mill. In such cases as Douglass's, and in most others, however, these charges were unfounded, related more to the racist premises of slavery's defenders than to the narratives' origins, reflecting, more than anything, proslavery anxieties about the narratives' effect.

Slavery's defenders also sought to deny specific charges the narratives raised. They denied, for example, charges of sexual promiscuity; they asserted their dedication to a Christian mission. At the same time, a few proslavery leaders, stung by the narratives' claims, proposed "reforms" to correct abuses documented in the narratives. They urged legislation, for example, to prevent family separations and suggested that slaves should be given at least basic literacy. Such proposals made little headway but do further indicate the political impact of the testimony the narratives provided.

The narratives and democratization

Apart from their role in the debate over slavery, the political character of the narratives reflected more general developments during the time in which they were written. The direction of antebellum American politics was toward an increasingly democratic order and an increasingly influential democratic rhetoric. Political participation was broadened during the era, as democratic ideals provided standards against which policy and politics alike were measured. The emergence of Andrew Jackson and "Jacksonian democracy" beginning in the mid-1820s helped to synthesize and consolidate processes of democratization that continued to strengthen up to the time of the Civil War.

The imperfections of this process were notable. It was, for the most part, a process that benefited white adult males. Women were excluded from politics, as were most African Americans, even in the Northern states, where virtually all were free. If anything, processes of democratization had a perverse effect on African American political participation. In several states, as more white men were included in the political system – through expanded suffrage, for example – African Americans faced greater restrictions on their right to vote and to hold office.

Nevertheless, democratization was not only about voting and holding political office. It was also about who could participate in political deliberation, and how. In this, democratization may be understood in terms of the notion of a "public sphere" which includes those whose voices can influence how political decisions are made. And here, democratization was far more expansive, because the antebellum public sphere came to include many people otherwise excluded from the political order. This was particularly the case as the antebellum public sphere came to be shaped by the explosion of print culture during the era, an explosion that brought many formerly excluded voices, including those of women and African Americans, into the political order.

The slave narratives were part of this expanded public sphere, as their role in shaping debates over slavery suggests. The narratives' authors and audiences agreed that individuals who had experienced slavery had something to say about the character of the institution, and that what they had to say could not be ignored – although slavery's defenders might have preferred otherwise. Such views were not confined to people in the abolitionist movement. For example, Abraham Lincoln, uncomfortable with both slavery and abolitionism (and sharing the era's racist ideas), responded to a proslavery argument by remarking that it was important to ask the slaves' "opinion on it."[10]

The narratives should also be seen, however, as part of a demand for a still more fully inclusive public sphere. To some extent, this demand was made within the parameters of the abolition movement, which was itself devoted to the cause of democratization. Abolitionists demanded emancipation, racial equality, and full citizenship for African Americans, and saw the narratives as a powerful means for asserting an African American voice into American public life. Hence, as a major element in the movement's print culture, the narratives highlighted both the radical quality of abolitionism's demands and the more specific goals of the movement.

Within the context of an enlarging public sphere, however, the specifically African American character of the narratives had implications that went beyond simple questions of inclusion. The narratives' authors also asserted a privileged African American voice that could offer a distinctive commentary on American society and politics. Implicit in the significance assigned to the narratives was an appreciation for the authority of experience. "Facts are stubborn things," wrote fugitive Austin Steward, and no one could talk about slavery better than one who "has seen and *felt it himself.*"[11] Such a claim may seem obvious, but it was also part of an expanding public sphere. Prior to the antebellum period, authority, status, and a public voice were closely connected to each other. Grounding authority in experience broke the connection between status and authority in fully democratic ways even as it supported abolitionist goals. It was a shift of which the narratives' authors and other abolitionists were well aware.

There were, however, implications to ideals of democratization that posed more complex problems for the narratives, even within the context of abolitionism. American democratic ideals included values of individualism and independence, values directly opposed to slavery, and in an obvious way. As the authors described their feelings about slavery, they made clear that, whatever the specific abuses, the most galling fact was the inability to control one's destiny, to have one's fate placed in the hands of another person.

This drive for self-control entered into the creation of the narratives, as such, and even helped to create a division within abolition that was related to questions of independence, democratization, and the public sphere. Though sometimes exaggerated by historians and critics, there was a tendency among white abolitionists to control the African American voice, to define and delimit the content and character of the narratives. The famous episode Douglass recounted in *My Bondage and My Freedom* has often been cited in this regard. Having been involved in abolitionism for some time, he had reached a point at which "new views" had begun to concern him. When he sought to present them, however, he had been told by white colleagues to stick with his narrative. "Give us the facts," one had said, "we will take care of the philosophy" (*My Bondage and My Freedom*, p. 367). Such limits were, as Douglass understood, patronizing, even racist. They were also, as he acknowledged, connected to internal divisions within abolitionism, and a marker of the significance that white and black abolitionists alike gave to African American testimony. But Douglass's response was ultimately evidence of the extent to which he and other African American authors appreciated the ideals of self-definition and self-determination connected with democratic ideals. As Douglass said, "I must speak just the word that seemed to *me* the word to be spoken *by* me" (ibid.).

The narratives and the meaning of freedom

The issue of self-definition and self-control was also related to the third key dimension of the politics and political philosophy in the slave narratives: their representations of freedom. Although freedom was an evolving idea during the antebellum period, with numerous and vague definitions, for many thinkers, especially in the Jacksonian period, it was closely connected to ideals of independence and understood as the freedom to do whatever one felt to be right or necessary, without any external constraints. This was often given an economic twist that emphasized the right to pursue, without restraint, one's own well-being.

Such was the view of freedom embodied in the slave narratives. It was a view that had broad appeal within the abolitionist movement. Bringing together abolitionist ideals with notions of freedom deeply rooted in slave culture, the narratives' authors gave voice to political aspirations that had been shaped in slavery itself. For the authors of the slave narratives, freedom meant, above all, freedom from coercion. The narrators accurately represented slavery as a forced labor system maintained by the continual threat of physical violence. In so portraying slavery, however, the authors went beyond the evocation of brutality to describe a world which ran counter to the most deeply held American ideals of freedom, including the economic notions of freedom that many held dear. Slaves, as the narrators repeatedly emphasized, were forced to work not for their own ends but for those of their owners. Slavery violated connections among labor, independence, and freedom in unmistakable ways.

It was in this regard that slave culture and abolitionist ideals were most clearly related. It is not surprising, first, that slaves should have developed a sense of freedom on their own, given the coercive, exploitative nature of the slave system – and its American setting in an environment that valued economic achievement and independence. They could easily contrast their own condition with that of their masters. Solomon Northup, a free man kidnapped in New York and enslaved in Louisiana for twelve years, wrote that it was "a mistaken opinion" to believe that slaves fail to "comprehend the idea of freedom." He said, "They understand the privileges and exemptions that belong to it – that it would bestow upon them the fruits of their own labors, and that it would secure to them the enjoyment of domestic happiness."[12]

Still, slaves' ideas of freedom did not develop in a vacuum. Plantation owners tried to keep their slaves isolated from the larger currents of antebellum American thought, fearing, especially, the influence of abolitionist ideas. But those ideas did penetrate the plantation world, as did other elements of antebellum political ideology and rhetoric. There were significant contacts between slaves and free people of color (many of them former slaves) living in the North. Literate slaves gleaned news, often at great peril, from newspapers and periodicals, and that news traveled rapidly over informal but efficient interplantation networks.

From such sources, popular American ideas of economic autonomy along with tenets of what is usually called "free labor" ideology were as well known inside the plantation world as outside. The notion that one should receive the benefit from one's labor and, moreover, that one should be able to negotiate the terms under which one worked was a notion many slaves knew and valued. As the authors of the slave narratives evoked their experiences and feelings under slavery, they emphasized their own awareness of that notion and conveyed their sense of the injustice of the institution as a coercive, exploitative system.

In their contemplation of freedom, however, the authors were able to capture still deeper themes in antebellum thought. They did so through their portrayals and analyses of the master–slave relationship, a relationship they put at the heart of the institution. As slaves, they and their peers felt themselves entirely at the mercy of those who claimed to own them, and, as the narrators also emphasized, slaveholders tended to exert their power arbitrarily as well as cruelly.

Here, one may see particularly well an integration of slave cultural traditions with more widespread American ideas about freedom. Slave cultural traditions – expressed through religion and folklore – had long given centrality to the master–slave relationship and focused on the arbitrariness of slaveholder coercion. But concern about arbitrary power was deep-seated in American political rhetoric and ideology. Even prior to American independence, Americans had rejected the legitimacy of arbitrary power. In the most heated antebellum debates over the nature of freedom, no one accepted the view that arbitrary power could exist in a free society. Slavery, the narrators demonstrated, was based on arbitrary power, a premise that was central to the narratives' rhetorical thrust as political documents and to the philosophical underpinnings upon which their arguments rested.

Looking back on their experiences, ex-slaves found several ways to characterize slave owners' will to arbitrary power. For one thing, they recounted their experiences with slaveholders who had no respect for contracts or agreements. Josiah Henson, having negotiated a price to buy his own freedom, and having paid it, could not claim that freedom when his mistress simply repudiated the agreement and demanded a much higher price. Henson wrote that he was "alternately beside myself with rage, and paralyzed with despair," knowing he was at her mercy.[13]

As the authors of slave narratives portrayed the arbitrariness of slavery, however, there was another dimension to it that also went straight to the heart of antebellum political thought. Inevitably, they portrayed slaveholding men and women as people driven by passion, whose exercise of brutal authority was not only arbitrary but also unrestrained. Connecting arbitrary power to uncontrolled passions, the authors drew on motifs and themes that go back to the Revolutionary era, but, adapting those themes to portrayals of slavery, enriched them and made them even more powerful.

Slave narratives provided examples of an ungovernable brutality on the part of slaveholders that entered into every area of the master–slave relationship, especially in regard to labor. The narratives' authors invariably presented episodes in which even the most diligent efforts on the part of slaves were met with cruel violence as the slaveholder seized upon the most trivial shortcomings as pretexts for "punishment." William Wells Brown, for example, described the case of Aaron, working in a St. Louis hotel, who was subjected to fifty lashes – a debilitating number – when a knife was not as clean as the owner demanded.

Moreover, as many of the ex-slaves also showed, such slaveholder violence often slipped over into sadism: ingenious, gratuitous, even inflicted for pleasure. Douglass's account of the beating of Hester moved in this direction. So did Solomon Northup's account of the brutal beating of his friend Patsey, irrationally hated by a mistress who continually demanded that the young woman be flogged. Ultimately, after a brief absence from the plantation, Patsey was seized by the master, stripped, staked to the ground, and whipped until she lost consciousness. The mistress looked on with what Northup described as "an air of heartless satisfaction" (*Twelve Years a Slave*, p. 196).

Ex-slaves also described patterns of torture designed to intensify the slaves' suffering. Moses Roper's owner was one of several who liked to put slaves in painful contraptions, each more ingenious than the last. Roper recounted how one slave woman was given an excessive dose of castor oil, then entrapped under a small box overnight, in intense agony. Many authors described how slaves, their backs shredded by whipping, were washed down with solutions of salt and red pepper to prolong and intensify the pain.

Such events did occur on Southern plantations. The stories of physical torment told in the slave narratives have been corroborated by other historical documents and artifacts. Sadism was both possible and prevalent in the slave regime. One should not minimize the political impact of the stories of this violence. There was, for one thing, a more general antebellum American reaction against pain and suffering to which such accounts appealed. Americans were concerned about a gamut of issues, ranging from the use of corporal punishment in childrearing to capital punishment in response to crime. Accounts of plantation brutality resonated with such concerns.

But fugitive authors also connected accounts of brutality with problems of power and restraint as they created portrayals of slaveholding men and women driven by the cruelest impulses. Charles Ball's 1836 narrative described a mistress who severely beat a young female slave nursing an infant because the baby had begun to cry. As Ball's narrative said, here was a woman who "possessed no controul [sic] over her passions" and who, when enraged, "would find some victim to pour her fury upon, without regard to justice or mercy."[14]

The presence of such figures highlights not only the political underpinnings of the narratives but also their rhetorical thrust. Recognizing and sharing in the rejection of arbitrary power, the narratives portrayed a slave regime that was the embodiment of arbitrariness. In doing so, they exposed the presence of an economic, social, and political elite in America – the plantation owners – that violated the most deeply held American standards for authority and order.

It was a portrayal that stung. Fears of a dominating "slavocracy" became rampant in the late antebellum period, reinforcing the abolitionist movement and its appeal. Within the framework of their paternalistic ideology, moreover, slavery's defenders were quick to assert that plantation power was exerted neither brutally nor arbitrarily. Faced with the narrators' portraits of slavery, they claimed that plantation "government" should be, and usually was, systematic and ordered, based on clearly defined rules under which punishment was to be both understandable and restrained. Such claims, incidentally, had little validity. Based on the evidence, the slave narratives' emphasis on arbitrariness was both justified and real, as well as one with great rhetorical effect.

There was yet another dimension to the narratives' approach to freedom that was politically important. None of the fugitive slaves who wrote a narrative was ever simply given his or her freedom, and a key element in every narrative was a story of freedom valued and achieved despite the most intense opposition and despite the most formidable barriers.

The political implications of such a story were numerous. For one, they further established the significance of the narratives in the debate over slavery. At least one corollary to the idyllic images of plantation life presented by slavery's defenders was the idea that slaves were happy with their lot and, despite abolitionist contentions, had no desire for freedom. The narrators accurately portrayed a deep desire for freedom that directly contradicted such proslavery assertions. Douglass famously wrote of the point at which the "silver trump of freedom" (*Narrative*, p. 42) began to sound in his heart, creating an ever-present desire to escape from bondage. But virtually every ex-slave pointed to a similar moment when, as with Henry Bibb, the "voice of liberty" (*Narrative*, p. 368) began to thunder in his soul.

No less significantly, the ex-slaves also emphasized their willingness to take risks for freedom. Every narrative documented a fight for freedom and did so in a manner that fit into a larger context of ideas that had been pervasive in America since the era of the Revolution. These ideas were built on the notion that the people who most deserved freedom were those who were willing to risk their lives for it.

The narratives built on this idea. They did this when fugitives described their resistance to arbitrary force, as many did. Frederick Douglass's oft-noted account of his resistance to the notorious "slave-breaker" Covey, which, he said, "rekindled the few expiring embers of freedom, and revived within me a sense of my own manhood" (*Narrative*, p. 65) was only one example of this. Similar episodes appeared in many of the narratives.

But these authors most graphically dramatized their willingness to risk their lives for freedom when they described the dangers they had faced in trying to escape the system, knowing they faced brutal reprisals or death if captured. Most described desperate hunger and hardship as they made their ways through the wilderness, traveling on foot, usually at night. Then there was the ingenuity and sacrifice displayed by Henry "Box" Brown, who acquired his nickname as a result of having himself surreptitiously shipped out of the South in a box three feet long by two feet wide! William and Ellen Craft, also displaying great ingenuity, escaped slavery when the light-complexioned Ellen successfully posed as a slaveholder traveling to the North, with her husband William playing her servant. But they also recounted how, in the constant presence of hostile whites, their effort was never free of the possibility that they should be discovered and remanded to bondage. The threat plagued fugitives even in the nominally free states, where authorities were liable, and after the Fugitive Slave Law (1850) legally required, to capture the escaping fugitives and return them to the South – not only to slavery but also to what was certain and cruel retribution.

The language in which fugitives and their supporters described these undertakings was strongly based in the American rhetoric of freedom. Samuel Ringgold Ward, describing the risks he took to escape, asserted that he would never "seek or accept peace at the expense of liberty," a sentiment virtually everyone echoed.[15] Harriet Jacobs made the connection with American ideals especially clear when she wrote that, having decided to escape, "'Give me liberty, or give me death,' was my motto" (*Incidents*, p. 101), quoting the famous phrase from the American Revolutionary Patrick Henry. Douglass, too, cited Henry in his two antebellum autobiographies, *The Narrative of the Life of Frederick Douglass* and *My Bondage and My Freedom*. In this he echoed the abolitionist leader William Lloyd Garrison's comparison of Douglass to Henry in a preface to the *Narrative*. The comparison was applied to Henry "Box" Brown as well. In making such a comparison, the narratives emphasized their authors' devotion to freedom as well as their claim to its blessings.

Such portrayals also reinforced that authorial stance apparent in the authors' assertion of a role in the American public sphere. Few in the narrators' audiences had taken as personal a risk for freedom as had the authors of the slave narratives. Recounting his own entry into free territory, William Wells Brown wrote "none but a slave could place such an appreciation upon liberty as I did at that time, because few had earned liberty at such great price."[16] Moreover, as the narrators set up the contrast between themselves and their oppressors, they could even use their experiences and their sacrifices to emphasize a certain political superiority. The lives of the fugitives demonstrated not only a superior devotion to freedom but also a superior understanding of its meaning and significance. Thus, Samuel Ringgold Ward suggested that, "in the matter of liberty and progress," African Americans, as a result of their experiences, would become the teachers and whites the taught "ere the struggle be over" (*Autobiography*, p. 100). The narrators represented the embodiment of an ideal that few Americans could match.

The slave narratives as a body of writing are rich in their literary and historical characteristics and implications. One should be careful never to reduce them to any single dimension. Neither should one ignore their political purposes or their political underpinnings in the context of antebellum history. Intended to present an irrefutable case against slavery, they entered into a debate that divided the nation, while resonating strongly with American political concerns. And they also did so in ways that contributed significantly to bringing slavery to an end.

NOTES

1. See, e.g., Harriet Jacobs, *Incidents in the Life of a Slave Girl*, ed. L. Maria Child (1861. Rpt. San Diego: Harcourt, 1973), pp. 124–25. Subsequent references will be cited parenthetically within the text.
2. Frederick Douglass, *My Bondage and My Freedom* in Douglass, *Autobiographies*. Henry Louis Gates, Jr., ed. (New York: Library of America, 1994), p. 106, italics in original. Subsequent references will be cited parenthetically within the text.
3. Frederick Douglass, *The Narrative of the Life of Frederick Douglass* in Douglass, *Autobiographies*, p. 97. Subsequent references will be cited parenthetically within the text.
4. Moses Roper, *A Narrative of the Adventures and Escape of Moses Roper, from American Slavery* (1840) in *African American Slave Narratives: An Anthology*. Sterling Bland, ed. (Westport, CT: Greenwood Press, 2001), p. 58.
5. Henry "Box" Brown, *Narrative of Henry Box Brown, Who Escaped from Slavery in a Box 3 Feet Long and 2 Wide* (1849) in Bland, *Narratives*, pp. 454, 455.
6. Henry Bibb, *Narrative of the Life and Adventures of Henry Bibb, an American Slave. Written by Himself* (3rd edn., 1850) in Bland, *Narratives*, p. 412. Subsequent references will be cited parenthetically within the text.

7. Lewis Clarke, *Narratives of the Sufferings of Lewis and Milton Clarke* (1846) in Bland, *Narratives*, p. 135.
8. James W. C. Pennington, *The Fugitive Blacksmith; or, Events in the History of James W. C. Pennington* (3rd edn., 1850) in Bland, *Narratives*, p. 548.
9. John Thompson, *The Life of John Thompson, a Fugitive Slave* (1856) in Bland, *Narratives*, p. 640.
10. Abraham Lincoln, *Collected Works of Abraham Lincoln*, ed. Roy Basler (New Brunswick, NJ: Rutgers University Press, 1953). 9 vols. Vol. III, p. 204.
11. Austin Steward, *Twenty-Two Years a Slave and Forty Years a Freeman* (1857) in Bland, *Narratives*, p. 700, italics in original.
12. Solomon Northup, *Twelve Years a Slave* (1853), eds. Sue Eakin and Joseph Logsdon (Baton Rouge: Louisiana State University Press, 1968), p. 200. Subsequent references will be cited parenthetically within the text.
13. Josiah Henson, *Truth Stranger than Fiction: Father Henson's Story of his Own Life* (1858. Rpt. Upper Saddle River, NJ: Gregg Press, 1970), p. 75.
14. Charles Ball, *Slavery in the United States: A Narrative of the Life and Adventures of Charles Ball, a Black Man* (1836. Rpt. Detroit: Negro History Press, 1970), p. 268.
15. Samuel Ringgold Ward, *Autobiography of a Fugitive Negro* (1855. Rpt. New York: Arno Press, 1968), p. 12. Subsequent references will be cited parenthetically within the text.
16. William Wells Brown, *Narrative of William W. Brown, A Fugitive Slave. Written By Himself* (2nd. edn., 1847) in *The Travels of William Wells Brown*. Paul Jefferson, ed. (New York: Markus Wiener, 1991), p. 65.

3

VINCENT CARRETTA

Olaudah Equiano: African British abolitionist and founder of the African American slave narrative

The most important and most widely published author of African descent in the English-speaking world of the eighteenth century, Olaudah Equiano founded the genre of the African American slave narrative. Writing in 1913, W. E. B. Du Bois recognized Equiano's autobiography as "the beginning of that long series of personal appeals of which Booker T. Washington's *Up from Slavery* is the latest."[1] *The Interesting Narrative of the Life of Olaudah Equiano, or Gustavus Vassa, the African. Written by Himself* (London, 1789) established all of the major conventions reproduced in the vast majority of nineteenth- and twentieth-century factual and fictional African American slave narratives: an engraved frontispiece, a claim of authorship, testimonials, an epigraph, the narrative proper, and documentary evidence.[2]

Equiano writes that he was born in 1745 in what is now southeastern Nigeria. There, he says, he was enslaved at the age of eleven and sold to English slave traders who took him on the Middle Passage to the West Indies. Within a few days, he tells us, he was taken to Virginia and sold to a local planter. After about a month in Virginia he was purchased by Michael Henry Pascal, an officer in the British Royal Navy, who ironically renamed him Gustavus Vassa and brought him to London. Slaves were often given ironically inappropriate names of powerful historical figures like Caesar and Pompey to emphasize their subjugation to their masters' wills. Gustavus Vasa (sic) was a sixteenth-century Swede who liberated his people from Danish tyranny.

With Pascal, Equiano saw military action on both sides of the Atlantic Ocean during the Seven Years' War. Known in North America as the French and Indian War, the Seven Years' War actually lasted from 1754 to 1763. Fought on several continents between Britain and France, eventually joined by Spain, the conflict was arguably the first world-wide war. As the fighting was coming to an end in 1762, Pascal shocked Equiano by refusing to free him, selling him instead into West Indian slavery. Escaping the horrors of slavery in the sugar islands in the Caribbean, Equiano managed to save enough money to buy his own freedom in 1766. In Central America he helped purchase and supervised slaves on a plantation. Equiano set off on voyages of commerce and adventure to North America, the Mediterranean, the West Indies, and the North Pole. Equiano was now a man of the Atlantic. A close encounter with death during his Arctic voyage forced him to recognize that he might be doomed to eternal damnation. He resolved his spiritual crisis by embracing Methodism in 1774. In 1779 he unsuccessfully petitioned the Bishop of London to be sent to Africa as a missionary. During the 1780s he became an outspoken opponent of the slave trade, first in his letters to newspapers and then in his autobiography. Equiano's brief involvement with the project to resettle poor blacks from London to Sierra Leone nearly sent him to Africa as the representative of the British government in 1787. He married an Englishwoman in 1792, with whom he had two daughters. Thanks largely to profits from his publications, when Equiano died on March 31, 1797, he was probably the wealthiest, and certainly the most famous, person of African descent in the Atlantic world. Towards the end of the eighteenth century, an English family of four in London could live modestly but comfortably on £40 a year; a gentleman could support a significantly higher standard of living for himself on £300 a year. In 1816 Equiano's surviving daughter inherited nearly £1,000 from his estate, equivalent today to roughly $150,000.

Over the past thirty-five years, historians, literary critics, and the general public have come to recognize the author of the *Interesting Narrative* as one of the most accomplished English-speaking writers of his age, and unquestionably the most accomplished author of African descent. Several modern editions are now available of his autobiography. The literary status of the *Interesting Narrative* has been acknowledged by its inclusion in the Penguin Classics series. It is universally accepted as the fundamental text in the genre of the slave narrative. Excerpts from the book appear in every anthology and on any website covering American, African American, British, and Caribbean history and literature of the eighteenth century. The most frequently excerpted sections are the early chapters on his life in Africa and his experience on the Middle Passage crossing the Atlantic to America. Indeed, it is difficult to think of any historical account of the Middle Passage that does not quote his purportedly eyewitness description of its horrors as primary evidence. Interest in Equiano has not been restricted to academia. He has been the subject of television shows, films, comic books, and books written for children. The story of Equiano's life is part of African, African American, and Anglo-American, African British, and African Caribbean popular culture.

Attempts to pin Equiano down to either an American or a British identity are doomed to failure. Once he was free, Equiano judged parts of North

America reasonably nice places to visit, but he never revealed any interest in voluntarily living there. By Equiano's account, the amount of time he spent in North America during his life could be measured in months, not years. Whether he spent a few months, as he claims, or several years, as other evidence suggests, living in mainland North America, he spent far more time at sea. He spent at least ten years on the Atlantic Ocean and Mediterranean Sea during periods of war and peace between 1754 and 1785. The places he considered as a permanent home were Britain, Turkey, and Africa. Ultimately, he chose Britain, in part because Africa was denied him, despite his attempts to get there. Truly a "citizen of the world" (p. 337),[3] as he once called himself, Equiano was the epitome of what the historian Ira Berlin has called an "Atlantic creole":

> Along the periphery of the Atlantic – first in Africa, then in Europe, and finally in the Americas – [Anglophone-African] society was a product of the momentous meeting of Africans and Europeans and of their equally fateful encounter with the peoples of the Americas. Although the countenances of these new people of the Atlantic – Atlantic creoles – might bear the features of Africa, Europe, or the Americas in whole or in part, their beginnings, strictly speaking, were in none of those places. Instead, by their experiences and sometimes by their persons, they were part of the three worlds that came together along the Atlantic littoral. Familiar with the commerce of the Atlantic, fluent in its new languages, and intimate with its trade and cultures, they were cosmopolitan in the fullest sense.[4]

Recent biographical discoveries have cast doubt on Equiano's story of his birth and early years. The available evidence suggests that the author of the *Interesting Narrative* may have invented rather than reclaimed an African identity. If so, Equiano's literary achievements have been vastly underestimated. Baptismal and naval records say that he was born in South Carolina around 1747. If they are accurate, he invented his African childhood and his much-quoted account of the Middle Passage on a slave ship.[5] Other newly found evidence proves that Equiano first came to England years earlier than he says. He was clearly willing to manipulate at least some of the details of his life.

Every autobiography is an act of re-creation, and autobiographers are not under oath when they are reconstructing their lives. Furthermore, an autobiography is an act of rhetoric. That is, any autobiography is designed to influence the reader's impression of its author, and often, as in the case of the *Interesting Narrative*, to affect the reader's beliefs or actions as well. No autobiographer has faced a greater opportunity for redefinition than has a manumitted (freed) slave.

Manumission necessitated redefinition. The profoundest possible transformation was the one any slave underwent when freed, moving from the legal status of property to that of person, from commodity to human being. Former slaves were also immediately compelled to redefine themselves by choosing a name. Even retention of a slave name was a choice. Choosing not to choose was not an option. With freedom came the obligation to forge a new identity, whether by creating one out of the personal qualities and opportunities at hand, or by counterfeiting one. Equiano may have done both. In one sense, the world lay all before the former slave, who as property had been a person without a country or a legal personal identity.

Why might Equiano have created an African nativity and disguised an American birth? Unlike African American writers in the nineteenth century, most eighteenth-century abolitionists on both sides of the Atlantic concentrated on trying to end the transatlantic slave trade, rather than on attempting to eradicate the institution of slavery itself. Only after both the United States and Britain outlawed the transatlantic slave trade in 1807 were abolitionists positioned to attack slavery. Before 1789 the abundant evidence and many arguments against the trade came from white voices alone. Initially, opponents of the trade did not recognize the rhetorical power an authentic African voice could wield in the struggle. Equiano knew that to continue its increasing momentum the antislave trade movement needed precisely the kind of account of Africa and the Middle Passage he, and perhaps only he, could supply. An African, not an African American, voice was what the abolitionist cause required. He gave a voice to the millions of people forcibly taken from Africa and brought to the Americas as slaves. Equiano recognized a way to do very well financially by doing a great deal of good in supplying that much-needed voice.

As an "Atlantic creole," Equiano was ideally positioned to construct an identity for himself. He defined himself as much by movement as by place. Indeed, he spent as much of his life on the water as in any place on land. Even while he was a slave, the education and skills he acquired with the Royal Navy rendered him too valuable to be used for the dangerous and backbreaking labor most slaves endured. Service at sea on Royal Naval and commercial vessels gave him an extraordinary vantage point from which to observe the world around him. His social and geographical mobility exposed him to all kinds of people and levels of Atlantic society. The convincing account of Africa he offered to his readers probably derived from the experiences of others he tells us he listened to during his many travels in the Caribbean, North America, and Britain. His genius lay in his ability to create and market a voice that for over two centuries has spoken for millions of his fellow diasporan Africans.

Equiano followed with great interest the rapid development of the abolition movement during 1788. He did what he could in person and print to help it succeed. He recognized that the secular conversion narratives of former slave owners, slave-ship surgeons, and slave-ship captains moved the public toward the abolitionist position. He saw that effective witnesses to the cruelty of the slave trade could influence legislators. And he certainly noticed how large the market was for information about the trade. Most importantly of all, he understood that what the abolitionist cause needed now, and what readers desired, was exactly what he had positioned himself to give them – the story told from the victim's point of view. Initially, not even black opponents of the trade recognized the rhetorical power an authentic African voice could wield in the struggle. When Equiano's friend, collaborator, and future subscriber Quobna Ottobah Cugoano published *Thoughts and Sentiments on the Evil and Wicked Traffic of the Slavery and Commerce of the Human Species* in London in 1787, he chose not to describe Africa or the Middle Passage in much detail. A member of the Fante people from the area of present-day Ghana who had been kidnapped into slavery around 1770, Cugoano believed that "it would be needless to give a description of all the horrible scenes which we saw, and the base treatment which we met with in this dreadful captive situation, as the similar cases of thousands, which suffer by this infernal traffic, are well known."[6]

Equiano had spent years developing contacts with abolitionists through his friendship with James Ramsay, his association with Granville Sharp, and his involvement with the project to resettle the 'Black Poor' in Africa. He had spent recent months defending his integrity, establishing himself as a public figure participating in the debate over abolition, and honing an African identity. He had learned the art of self-promotion and the usefulness of making the right enemies. Equiano's success had earned him the attacks in the press by the pseudonymous "Civis," whose comments, despite his intentions, only increased interest in the life of his African opponent. The attention "Civis" gave him acknowledged Equiano's prominence as the leading black abolitionist. Arguments by "Civis" and others over the literary abilities and achievements of people of African descent, and hence their suitability for enslavement, indicated that a black voice needed to be heard. Equiano's status in the black community meant that it should be his.

Equiano's *Interesting Narrative* is a remarkable achievement. It is very difficult, if not impossible, to classify in terms of its genre. Among other things, it is a spiritual autobiography, captivity narrative, travel book, adventure tale, slave narrative, rags-to-riches saga, economic treatise, apologia, testimony, and possibly even a historical fiction. Equiano's own descriptions of his autobiography's contents accurately reflect his book's heterogeneous nature, as well as his desire to appeal to as wide an audience as possible. Some of his book's generic components are less noticed today than they would have been in the eighteenth century. For example, few readers now recognize the degree to which his autobiography is an apologia, or formal defense, of his conduct and motives, particularly in regard to the Sierra Leone resettlement project between 1786 and 1787. Equiano had been fired from his role in the plan to send hundreds of the London poor, many of them people of African descent who had found refuge with the British forces during the American Revolution. A white colleague had falsely accused him of misconduct and troublemaking.

Rather than seeing the *Interesting Narrative* as a relatively late example of a spiritual autobiography, most twenty-first century readers approach the *Interesting Narrative* as the progenitor of later, more secular African American slave narratives. Historically and generically, Equiano's autobiography lies between earlier seventeenth- and eighteenth-century captivity narratives, many by European whites abducted into alien cultures, and the nineteenth-century North American slave narrative epitomized by *The Narrative of the Life of Frederick Douglass, an American Slave. Written by Himself* (Boston, 1845).[7] Like the authors of captivity narratives, and unlike later slave narrators, Equiano experiences slavery, he tells us, between periods of freedom. The story of his life begins and ends in freedom.

The earliest commentators on the *Interesting Narrative* considered the book a "life," a "history," or "memoirs," indicating that eighteenth-century readers most likely received it as an example of history writing, which included autobiography (memoirs), biography, and the treatment of the manners, customs, and activities of people below the rank of statesmen and military heroes. But whether we approach Equiano's *Interesting Narrative* as a spiritual autobiography, a history, or an anticipation of later slave narratives, we cannot fail to recognize that the author had designs upon his audience when he wrote it. A careful consideration of the content, organization, and argument of Equiano's book demonstrates that his designs were personal as well as political, and that the personal and political were intimately connected.

The genre of the spiritual autobiography assumes that the spiritual life of an individual Christian, no matter how minutely detailed and seemingly singular his or her temporal existence, reflects the paradigm of progress any true believer repeats. This implicit invocation of the paradigm the author and his overwhelmingly Christian audience shared serves as the most powerful argument in the *Interesting Narrative* for their common humanity. Equiano couples it with a secular argument based on the philosophical premise that the human heart, uncorrupted by bad nurturing, has naturally benevolent feelings for others because it can empathize with their sufferings. Consequently, people of feeling, or sentiment, will share the sufferings of others, and by so doing demonstrate their shared humanity, a humanity that supporters of slavery and the trade denied to people of African descent.

More subtly, Equiano offers the transformation of his own attitude toward the transatlantic slave trade and the varieties of eighteenth-century slavery as a model for the moral progress of his readers as individuals, and of the society he now shares with them. By claiming personal experience and observation, Equiano becomes an expert on the institution of slavery as well as on the effects of the African slave trade. Rhetorically, Equiano had the advantage over most whites of having experienced both sides of slavery. He tells us that he was born into a slave-owning class before he was enslaved, and he was a slave-driver in Central America after he regained his freedom. Initially, slavery was simply one of the many levels that constitute the apparently healthy social order in which Equiano found himself near the top. But, like an infectious disease, the European slave trade with Africa had gradually spread farther inland until it destroyed even the tranquility of Equiano's homeland. The closer his successive African owners were to the European source of the infection, the more inhumane they became. The corruption of the transatlantic slave trade, he discovered, contaminated everyone. But only long after he reached Old England, the land of liberty, "where [his] heart had always been," did he come to see that the trade must be abolished because it cannot be ameliorated.

In the little worlds of the ships of the British Royal Navy and the merchant marine, Equiano offers us a vision of what seems to be an almost utopian, microcosmic alternative to the slavery-infested greater world. The demands of the seafaring life permitted him to transcend the barriers imposed by race, forcing even whites to acknowledge that he merited the position, if not the rank itself, of a ship's captain. He experienced a world in which artificially imposed racial limitations would have destroyed everyone, white and black. But, perhaps because he does not want to distance himself too far from his audience, by the end of the *Interesting Narrative*, like most of his readers he has not quite reached the position of absolutely rejecting slavery itself, usually calling instead for the amelioration of the harsh conditions imposed on the enslaved. Readers can reasonably extrapolate from the progress Equiano has made in his own evolving attitude toward slavery that the next logical step is such total rejection. If he can carry his audience as far as he has come in his autobiography, he will bring them a great way toward his probable ultimate goal. Unlike Cugoano in his jeremiad-like *Thoughts and Sentiments*, or Equiano himself in some of his letters to the newspapers, Equiano rarely engages in lengthy lamentations and exhortations in his

Interesting Narrative. He tries not to lecture to his readers. He teaches by example, inviting them to emulate him.

Conciliatory as he is in the main, Equiano does not refrain from intimating a more combative side. Throughout the *Interesting Narrative* he is willing and able to resist whites in childhood boxing matches or when mistreated by them as an adult. This willingness to resist is almost always limited, however, to threat, and not carried into action, probably lest he alienate his overwhelmingly white readership. He was certainly not reluctant to affront some of his white audience directly. He knew that the news of his marriage to a white woman, included in the fifth and later editions of his *Interesting Narrative*, would appall racist readers like "Civis."

To antagonists like "Civis," who denied that people of African descent were capable of writing literature, publication of the *Interesting Narrative* was itself an act of resistance and aggression. Equiano knew that the most effective way to respond to the charge from "Civis" that he was incapable of doing more than "fetch a card, letters, &c." was to write a book. Writing his *Interesting Narrative* gave Equiano an opportunity to display his learning by citing, quoting, and appropriating the Bible, as well as works by Homer, Sir John Denham, John Milton, Alexander Pope, Thomas Day, William Cowper, and many other literary and religious writers. Moreover, he included his own original poetry to remind his readers that they had never "heard of poems written by a monkey . . . or by an oran-outang."

Sometimes Equiano's intimations of resistance are quite subtle, as when he quotes John Milton, one of the most esteemed icons of his shared British culture, at the end of chapter five.[8] By quoting lines spoken in *Paradise Lost* by Beelzebub, one of Satan's followers, Equiano appropriates a voice of alienation and resistance from within the very culture he is demonstrating that he has assimilated. He similarly used Shakespeare in later editions. From 1792 on, in his initial address to the reader in all the editions that include the announcement of his marriage to a white woman, Equiano appropriates Othello's words. Surely he had bigots like "Civis" in mind when he invoked the image of Britain's most famous literary instance of intermarriage in the tragic figure of African sexuality and power. Even the most venerated icon of British culture, the King James Version of the Bible, became a means of self-expression. At first glance, the image of the author in the frontispiece to the *Interesting Narrative* seems to be a representation of humble fidelity to the text of the sacred book, but as we discover at the end of his "Miscellaneous Verses," which conclude chapter ten, Equiano appropriates Acts 4:12 by paraphrasing the original in his own words, an interactive relationship with the sacred text that may have been influenced by Cugoano's example.

But to demonstrate his rhetorical powers in the abolitionist cause, Equiano had to get his words published. First-time authors trying to get a book into print during the eighteenth century faced as many obstacles as first-time writers in the twenty-first century do. Equiano published his book by first advertising it publicly and selling it openly through booksellers. During the eighteenth century the term *bookseller* was used to describe publishers as well as wholesale dealers and retail sellers of books, whose functions often overlapped in practice. But to have a book to sell, an author needed to acquire funding to enable him to produce it. No one involved in the book trade was normally keen to invest in an unknown author's first attempt at publication, especially if the author wanted to keep his or her copyright rather than sell it. If the aspiring author had sufficient means, he could of course risk investing in himself. If not, he had to find other sources of venture capital.

A traditional way of getting the required capital was to sell the proposed book by subscription, convincing buyers to commit in advance of publication to purchase copies of the book when it appeared. If an author was able to get subscribers to pay at least part of the book's price in advance, he subsequently paid the production costs, found bookseller-agents to distribute the work, and normally sold his copyright. Booksellers would effectively act as the aspiring author's agents in accepting subscriptions, probably receiving a commission for doing so.[9] Subscribers typically were promised the book for a lower price than the one asked for retail sales. With a list of subscribers as proof of a guaranteed market, the novice sought a bookseller-publisher who would produce the book, paying the costs of publication plus a small sum to the author for its copyright. If his book proved to have a market beyond its subscribers, the self-published author could negotiate a premium price for the copyright. With the sale of his copyright, the author also sold any right to profits, or royalties, from any future sales of the book. Just as importantly, by giving up his copyright, an author lost control of the content as well as production of his text. The author would no longer have the legal power to revise his own text in subsequent editions. Nor would he have the authority to choose what, if any, illustrations or other supplementary materials his published book might include.

First-time authors in England had published by subscription since the early seventeenth century, but by the end of the eighteenth the practice had become very uncommon because it was so susceptible to abuse. Too many would-be buyers had been disappointed by people who never produced the promised books. Publication by subscription was liable to far greater abuse if either the author or bookseller required payment in advance from subscribers. They rarely did so.[10] Speaking in 1775 of subscription by advance payment, the bookseller John Murray noted, "That mode (which formerly was fashionable) is so much disliked now that the bare attempt is sufficient to throw discredit upon the performance."[11] Of the 1,063 works Murray is known to have produced between 1768 and 1795, the *Interesting Narrative* was one of only about twenty-five he published by subscription.[12] Unlike the vast majority of eighteenth-century authors near the end of the century, Equiano required partial payment in advance from his subscribers, no doubt to cover his living and production costs. Yet more unusually, Equiano chose not to sell his copyright, even after it proved as popular as he could have hoped.

Although Equiano had never published a book before, his newspaper writings had made him known to his potential audience. Once his book was published, he chose not to sell his copyright cheaply to a bookseller-publisher. He was confident enough in the sales of his autobiography to gamble on self-publication rather than forgo future profits. At least three of his bookseller-agents, James Lackington, Thomas Burton, and John Parsons, shared his confidence. They each subscribed for six copies, undoubtedly expecting to be able to sell the books they had received as payment for acting as Equiano's agents. Another bookseller, Charles Dilly, subscribed for two copies, although he was not one of Equiano's agents. Equiano's 311 original subscribers included more than a dozen others involved in the book trade.

Equiano was so confident about the investment he had made in the story of his life that he registered his copyright with the Stationers' Company. By the end of the eighteenth century, many authors and publishers chose not to register their books with the Company to avoid the expense of depositing the nine copies of a book required for registration. Equiano, however, decided to take the financial risk to protect his copyright. On March 24, 1789 he registered his 530-page, two-volume, first edition of his *Interesting Narrative* with the Company at Stationers' Hall as the "Property of Author," declaring his figurative as well as real ownership of his self. The printer of Equiano's first edition is not certainly known, though he may have been the Thomas Wilkins identified in the imprint to the second edition of the *Interesting Narrative* (December 1789). The second edition is the only one of the nine that Equiano published that identifies a printer.

Many elements in the book itself, not least its frontispiece, further demonstrate Equiano's genius for marketing and self-representation. Retention of his copyright meant that he exercised control over the selection of the visual images in his autobiography. His proposal promised potential subscribers "an elegant Frontispiece of the Author's Portrait." Indeed this "elegant Frontispiece" is mentioned as the last of the "Conditions," as if to emphasize the value it adds to the book's worth. But it also adds value to Equiano's character and visually demonstrates his claim to *gentle* status because it is "elegant" in subject as well as in execution.[13] We see an African man dressed as an English *gentleman*, a figure who visually combines the written identities of both Olaudah Equiano and Gustavus Vassa revealed in print beneath the frontispiece, as well as on the title page opposite it. The bible in his hand open at Acts 4:12 illustrates his literacy and his piety. The frontispiece is "Published March 1, 1789 by G. Vassa." All the evidence we have, such as Equiano's registering his book in his own name at Stationers' Hall and marketing it himself, suggests that he chose the artists to create and reproduce his likeness. For the first time in a book by a writer of African descent, Equiano asserts the equality of his free social status with that of his viewers and readers. Represented as a *gentleman* in his own right, he looks directly at them. As their moral equal, if not superior, he guides his readers to a passage in Acts 4 telling them that spiritual salvation comes through faith alone.

Equiano's readers confronted his dual identity as soon as they opened his book. The initial frontispiece presents an indisputably African body in European dress, and the title page offers us "Olaudah Equiano, or Gustavus Vassa, the African." To call him consistently by either the one name or the other is to oversimplify his identity. Equiano periodically reminds readers of his *Interesting Narrative* that he exists on the boundary between African and British identities.

Purchasers of Equiano's *Interesting Narrative* familiar with the earlier published works of Wheatley, Sancho, and other Anglophone-African writers probably noticed how distinctively Equiano identified and authorized himself on his title page. With the exception of Cugoano, the author of the *Interesting Narrative* was the first writer of African descent to present his work as self-authored and self-authorized, proudly announcing on the title page that it had been "Written by Himself." The phrase "written by himself" appears in more than one thousand eighteenth-century titles of fiction and non-fiction, almost always of works attributed to authors whose presumed levels of education and social status were likely to make readers suspect their authenticity.[14] A familiar example is Daniel Defoe's *Robinson Crusoe* (1719), a fictional text to which Equiano's was compared early in the nineteenth century. Black authors faced greater suspicion than others. Cugoano and Equiano were unusual in publishing their works without any of the authenticating documentation or mediation by white authorities that preface the works of Wheatley, Sancho, and other eighteenth-century black writers. These white voices typically reassured readers that the claim of authorship was valid and implied that the black authors had been supervised before publication.

A second London edition of the *Interesting Narrative* appeared at the end of 1789, suggesting that the first edition was probably the standard run of

500 copies, including subscriptions. As a good man of business, Equiano probably limited his risk of having many unsold books left from a first printing, but once the popularity of his work was clear he increased the number of copies for the second and subsequent editions.[15] Because publication by subscription, with its attendant lists, was itself traditionally a form of self-promotion, the lists must be approached with some caution and skepticism. Authors, publishers, and booksellers all clearly had motive for inflating the number and status of the names of subscribers.

But the increasing number and repetition of names prefacing the multiple editions of Equiano's *Interesting Narrative* render them more credible, and thus more valuable, to the historian than they would be had they appeared in only one edition of the author's work. Clearly, a growing number of people wanted to be publicly associated with the *Interesting Narrative* and its author. Equiano's subscription lists demonstrate how skilled he was at what we now call networking, developing a constellation of influential and powerful contacts through often overlapping categories of individuals connected to one another in smaller groupings. At the top of Equiano's lists, literally and politically, is the Prince of Wales, an especially significant name during the fall of 1788 and the spring of 1789, when King George III's lapse into madness appeared to make a Regency under the Prince's rule inevitable. Equiano had access to the Prince of Wales's patronage through others on the initial subscription list: Richard Cosway was the Prince's official painter; Cugoano was Cosway's servant.

Moreover, the lists connected Equiano explicitly and implicitly with the African British writers of the preceding fifteen years: Cugoano's name appears; Gronniosaw and Phillis Wheatley by association with their patron, the Countess of Huntingdon; and John Marrant by association with his editor, the Reverend William Aldridge. Equiano certainly knew of Wheatley and had read at least some of her poems in Thomas Clarkson's *Essay on the Slavery and Commerce of the Human Species* (London, 1786). Cugoano mentions Gronniosaw and Marrant in his *Thoughts and Sentiments* (1787). Gronniosaw's *A Narrative of the Most Remarkable Particulars in the Life of James Albert Ukawsaw Gronniosaw, an African Prince* (Bath, 1772) was published at least ten times in Britain and America before Equiano first published his autobiography. Marrant's *A Narrative of the Lord's Wonderful Dealings with John Marrant, a Black, (Now Going to Preach the Gospel in Nova-Scotia) Born in New-York, in North-America* (London, 1785) went through at least fifteen London printings before 1790. Both texts were dictated to and revised by white amanuenses. The late Ignatius Sancho appears via his son William. The inclusion on the original subscription list of "William, the Son of Ignatius Sancho" clearly demonstrates

that Equiano wanted to associate himself with earlier black writers. A recognized tradition of African British authors had been established by the
time Equiano published his autobiography, with new writers aware of the
work of their predecessors. This African British canon was being created
by the commentators, who argued about the most representative authors
and works. The publishing success of his predecessors gave Equiano cause
for believing that a market already existed for the autobiography of a black
entrepreneur.

Equiano's publication of several editions outside of London anticipated the
nineteenth-century growth of the provincial press. Anticipating the modern-
day book tour and talk-show appearances, Equiano also bore witness against
the slave trade in person, selling his books and lecturing throughout England,
Ireland, and Scotland from 1789 to 1794. He was a very active and successful
salesman for his book and the abolitionist cause. As he told a correspondent
in February 1792 in one of his few extant manuscript letters, he "sold 1,900
copies of my narrative" during eight and a half months in Ireland. During the
eighteenth century, selling 500 copies of a book meant relative success, and
1,000 copies indicated a bestseller. Individual buyers purchased up to 100
copies of the *Interesting Narrative*, no doubt for resale, or free distribution.
Readers unable or unwilling to pay the full purchase price for books also
had access to Equiano's autobiography through circulating libraries. For
a relatively small annual cost, subscribers to such libraries could borrow
thousands of books.[16]

By 1794 demand for his *Interesting Narrative* was so great that Equiano
decided to raise the price for his ninth edition to five shillings. The reception the public and reviewers gave the *Interesting Narrative* and its author
proved that Equiano had certainly invested wisely in himself. It also found
an international market during Equiano's lifetime. Unauthorized translations appeared in Holland (1790), Germany (1792), and Russia (1794). An
unauthorized reprint of his second edition (1789) was also published in the
United States (1791).[17] Although he could of course neither do anything
to stop them nor to profit directly from them, Equiano cleverly found a
way to use these unauthorized reprintings to further advertise the appeal
of his book and supplement his own efforts at self-promotion. In a passage
added to his fifth (1792) and subsequent editions of the *Interesting Narrative*, Equiano acknowledged the international piracies that he knew about:
"Soon after[,] I returned to London [in 1791], where I found persons of note
from Holland and Germany, who requested me to go there; and I was glad
to hear that an edition of my Narrative had been printed in both places, also
in New York" (p. 235). The international book trade enhanced Equiano's
transatlantic reputation. In 1790 Charles Crawford informed his readers in

Philadelphia that "Olaudah Equiano, or, Gustavus Vassa, the African, is a man of talents, as appears by the narrative of his life, which was written by himself, and published in London, in 1789. The friends of humanity by encouraging the sale of his work, might make him some recompence for the injuries which he has received from mankind."[18] By acting as his own publisher, Equiano kept much of the profit margin for himself. Consequently, we can roughly estimate how much money he made on the sales of his *Interesting Narrative*: Equiano could easily have garnered more than £1,000 in total gross profits from the nine editions.

Equiano's gamble on investing in the publication of the story of his life, whether that gamble was initially voluntary or forced upon him, obviously paid off. Unlike the vast majority of his fellow eighteenth-century authors, he retained his copyright even after it proved to have a high market value. By doing so and acting as his own publisher and principal distributor, he made himself a relatively wealthy man. But the motivation for his behavior may have been as much psychological as financial. Far more than other authors, the formerly enslaved Equiano was aware of the consequences of losing control over one's own physical self and legal identity. That heightened awareness may help explain why he was so resistant to relinquishing control over the verbal and visual representations of his free self. He had spent too much time and effort in establishing an identity to allow anyone else to claim ownership of it.

Through a combination of natural ability, accident, and determination, Equiano seized every opportunity to rise from the legal status of being an object to be sold by others to become an international celebrity, the story of whose life became his own most valuable possession. Once free from enslavement, his every action reflected his repudiation of the constraints that bondage had imposed on him. As if to flaunt his liberty, he traveled the world virtually at will, recognizing the sea as a bridge rather than a barrier between continents and people. His freedom gave him the chance to move socially, economically, religiously, and politically, as well as geographically. Having known what the loss of liberty entailed, once free he took as much control of his life as he could, even revising the events in it to make a profit in a just cause. He became the exemplary "Atlantic creole."

Print allowed him to resurrect not only himself publicly from the "social death" enslavement had imposed on him, but also the millions of other diasporan Africans he represented. By combining his own experiences with those of others he refashioned himself as *the* African. Rejected in his attempts to be sent by Europeans to Africa as a missionary or diplomat, Equiano, through his *Interesting Narrative*, made himself into an African missionary and diplomat to a European audience. In the re-creation of his own life he forged a compelling story of spiritual and moral conversion to serve as a model to be imitated by readers during his lifetime and by authors who followed him.

During Equiano's own lifetime, the *Interesting Narrative* went through an impressive nine editions. Most books published during the eighteenth century never saw a second edition. A few more editions of his book appeared, in altered and often abridged form, in Britain and America during the twenty years after his death in 1797. Thereafter, he was briefly cited and sometimes quoted by British and American opponents of slavery throughout the first half of the nineteenth century. He was still well enough known publicly that he was identified in 1857 as "Gustavus Vassa the African" on the newly discovered gravestone of his only child who survived to adulthood. But after 1857 Equiano and his *Interesting Narrative* seem to have been largely forgotten on both sides of the Atlantic for more than a century, with the notable exception of Du Bois. The declining interest in the author and his book is probably explained by the shift in emphasis from the abolition of the British-dominated transatlantic slave trade to the abolition of slavery, particularly in the United States, following the outlawing of the transatlantic trade in 1807.

Unfortunately, Equiano did not live to see the abolition of the slave trade he had done so much to accomplish. The political triumph of the abolitionist cause in 1807 came ten years too late for him to celebrate. It might not have come that soon, however, had he not contributed to the cause by so skillfully and creatively fashioning the story of his life "to put a speedy end to a traffic both cruel and unjust" (p. 5). He gave the abolitionist cause the African voice it needed. The very act of writing a story of his life was an act of resistance to those who denied the full humanity of people of African descent. The role he played in the last mission of his life earned him the right to claim an African name that "signifies vicissitude, or fortunate also; one favoured, and having a loud voice and well spoken." That role also entitled him to accept the name of a European liberator of his people ironically given him in slavery. He had made himself a true "citizen of the world."

NOTES

1. W. E. B. Du Bois, "The Negro in Literature and Art" in *Du Bois: Writings*. Nathan Huggins, ed. (New York: The Library of America, 1913), p. 863.
2. See James Olney, "'I Was Born': Slave Narratives, Their Status as Autobiography and as Literature" in *The Slave's Narrative*. Charles T. Davis and Henry Louis Gates, Jr., eds. (New York: Oxford University Press, 1985), pp. 148–75, especially 152–53.

3. All quotations from Equiano's works are taken from Vincent Carretta, ed., *The Interesting Narrative and Other Writings* (New York: Penguin Putnam, 1995; 2nd edn. 2003) and are cited by page number parenthetically within the text.

4. Ira Berlin, "From Creole to African: Atlantic Creoles and the Origins of African American Society in Mainland North America," *William and Mary Quarterly* 33 (1996), 251–88; quotation from 254. I have substituted "Anglophone-African" for Berlin's "African American" because his characterization of the "Atlantic creole" can be applied to many English-speaking people of African descent on both sides of the Atlantic during the seventeenth and eighteenth centuries. Berlin uses the term *creole* to refer to a person of mixed cultures and languages. During the eighteenth century, a creole was someone of African or European descent who had been born in the Americas.

5. See my "Questioning the Identity of Olaudah Equiano, or Gustavus Vassa, the African" in *The Global Eighteenth Century*. Felicity Nussbaum, ed. (Baltimore: Johns Hopkins University Press, 2003), pp. 226–35.

6. *Thoughts and Sentiments on the Evil of Slavery*. Vincent Carretta, ed. (New York: Penguin, 1999), p. 15.

7. Examples of the European captivity narrative include Mary Rowlandson's often re-published *The Soveraignty and Goodness of God, Together with the Faithfulness of His Promises Displayed; Being a Narrative of the Captivity and Restauration of Mrs. Mary Rowlandson* (Cambridge [Massachusetts], 1682); John Kingdon's *Redeemed Slaves* (Bristol, 1780?); and Penelope Aubin's fictional *The Noble Slaves* (Dublin, 1736). Eighteenth-century captivity narratives had also been written or recorded by people of African descent: Briton Hammon's *Narrative* (Boston, 1760), James Albert Ukawsaw Gronniosaw's *Narrative* (Bath, 1772), and John Marrant's *Narrative* (London, 1785).

8. Equiano slightly alters lines from Milton, *Paradise Lost* 2: 332–40:

> . . . No peace is given
> To us enslav'd, but custody severe;
> And stripes and arbitrary punishment
> Inflicted – What peace can we return?
> But to our power, hostility and hate;
> Untam'd reluctance, and revenge, tho' slow,
> Yet ever plotting how the conqueror least
> May reap his conquest, and may least rejoice
> In doing what we most in suff'ring feel.

9. Dr. Mark Jones found the subscription proposal among the Josiah Wedgwood papers in the Keele University Library Special Collections, and very kindly brought it to my attention. Wedgwood was one of Equiano's original subscribers.

10. James Green, "The Publishing History of Olaudah Equiano's *Interesting Narrative*," *Slavery and Abolition* 16 (1995), 363, notes the relative rarity of asking for advance payment from subscribers.

11. Letter to William Boutcher, December 30, 1775, quoted in William Zachs, *The First John Murray and the Late Eighteenth-Century Book Trade* (Oxford: Oxford University Press, 1998), p. 69. Zachs notes that Murray reiterates his opinion of publication by subscription in a letter to John Imison, August 27, 1784.

12. Murray is the first bookseller-agent listed in Equiano's subscription proposal. He was one of Equiano's principal distributors. Equiano may have been drawn to Murray because he published the monthly *Political Magazine and Parliamentary, Naval, Military and Literary Journal* (London, 1780–91), which presented both sides of the slave-trade debate.

13. For a fuller discussion of how and why Equiano represents himself as a *gentleman*, see my "Defining a Gentleman: The Status of Olaudah Equiano or Gustavus Vassa," *Language Sciences* 21 (2000), 385–99.

14. The ongoing *English Short Title Catalogue* identifies 1,110 titles of fiction and non-fiction as "Written by Himself." Another 135 titles claim to be "Written by Herself."

15. Green, "The Publishing History," 364–65, estimates that the size of the first edition was 750 copies. At least 1,900 copies of the fourth (1791) edition were produced.

16. In Newcastle, for example, the *Interesting Narrative* was one of the 5,416 books that subscribers to R. Fisher's Circulating Library could borrow in 1791 for an annual fee of 12s. *A Catalogue of R. Fisher's Circulating Library, in the High-Bridge, Newcastle. Comprising a Selection of the Best Authors on History, Biography, Divinity, Philosophy, Husbandry, Aerostation, Chemistry; and a Choice Collection of Voyages and Travels, Novels and Romances, Poems and Plays, in the English and French Languages: with a Great Variety of Pamphlets on the Most Interesting Subjects. Which are Lent to be Read, at Twelve Shillings a Year, Three Shillings a Quarter. All New Books and Pamphlets on Interesting or Entertaining Subjects, Will Be Added to the Library as soon as Published* (Newcastle upon Tyne: Printed by M. Angus, Drury-lane, Flesh-market, 1791) lists "The Life of Olaudah Equiano, or Gustavus Vasa the African" among the "Lives. Octavo."

17. Green, "The Publishing History," 367–73, and Akiyo Ito, "Olaudah Equiano and the New York Artisans: The First American Edition of *The Interesting Narrative of the Life of Olaudah Equiano, or Gustavus Vassa, the African*," *Early American Literature* 32.1 (1997), 82–101, discuss the New York edition.

18. Charles Crawford, *Observations upon Negro-Slavery. A New Edition* (Philadelphia: Printed and Sold by Eleazer Oswald, 1790), p. 29. The 125-page 1790 edition was a much-expanded version of the 21-page first edition, printed and sold by Joseph Crukshank in Philadelphia in 1784. Crawford's 1790 edition also quotes part of the letter to Sir William Dolben co-signed by Gustavus Vassa, Cugoano, and others of African descent published in the July 15, 1788 issue of *The Morning Chronicle* (p. 113).

4

KERRY SINANAN

The slave narrative and the literature of abolition

Slave narratives were dynamic, responsive, hybrid writings that evolved within a range of diverse dialogues, debates, and arguments. The interest which they continue to inspire is due, in a large part, to the challenges we face as modern-day readers attempting to bring ourselves closer to the historical moments and discursive practices within which these urgent stories were forged. The responsive nature of the slave narrative means that in order to understand its features and tropes we must explore the literature to which it reacted and by which it was often constituted.

While proslavery debates presented the most racist and virulent arguments to which the narratives had to reply, abolitionist discourse and literature offered representations of slaves and black people, combined with antislavery opinions and views, which became interwoven in the fabric of the slave narratives. This interconnectedness was not always, however, due to an agreement on antislavery strategy or even to a coincidence of perspective: for example, often abolitionist writing could be as racist as proslavery writing, offering negative images of black people as ignorant and morally undeveloped. In *Uncle Tom's Cabin* Harriet Beecher Stowe opposes Eva "the fair high-bred child" and Topsy "the Afric, born of ages of oppression, submission, ignorance, toil and vice," suggesting a racial difference between white and black not to be overcome by the abolition of slavery itself.[1] In his second narrative, *My Bondage and My Freedom*, Frederick Douglass describes his frustration at being used by the abolitionists to repeat his story "month after month": "'Give us the facts,' said Collins, 'we will take care of the philosophy.'"[2] Douglass was clearly reacting against the implication that slaves may not be capable of making the necessary sophisticated antislavery arguments and was aware that the abolitionist drive to secure its political aims often reduced the slaves themselves to mere tellers of stories. Abolitionist literature in circulation and abolitionist strategies often necessitated a response by slaves, thereby affecting the very content and rhetorical thrust of the narratives.

The complex relationship between abolitionism and the slave narrative gave rise to a body of literature that exhibits the signs of exchange, argument, and debate. While their goals may have been the same, white abolitionists and slaves had very different histories and personal experiences. Forged within a fraught history, the slave narratives comprise the agreements and antagonisms both of black and white abolitionists, while ultimately articulating black self-determination and a unifying demand for freedom. We may best understand these dynamics by examining a few selective case studies that exemplify the relationships between abolitionist writing and slave writing.

Ukawasaw Gronniosaw, Olaudah Equiano and abolitionist genres

In his introduction to *African American Slave Narratives* Sterling Bland repeatedly emphasizes the "triangular" nature of the slave narrative genre. In this phrase he captures the tripartite dynamic between slave writers, abolitionists, and the public within which the narratives were produced.[3] However, the triangular nature of the narratives can also be thought of in another equally important way: as reflecting the cultural exchanges of the black Atlantic between Britain, Africa, and America. In this sense, the narratives, by definition, reflect transatlantic relationships, histories, cultures, and ideologies, and need to be approached as nexuses where these congruences and conflicts are manifest. Crucially, this dialectical history of the slave narrative demands that the genre itself be read as fluid and heterogeneous.

While the slave narrative that was to proliferate in the North American abolitionist battle after the 1830s may usefully be related to the slaves' writings that had galvanized the British abolitionist movement, resulting in the 1833 Act of Emancipation, the desire to view this relationship as evidence of a conscious forging of the slave narrative genre must be resisted. Comparing and contrasting the slave writings of Britain and North America highlights their inherent diversity and their capacity to be flexible enough to respond to specific and local arguments while still prioritizing an overall demand for freedom. The narratives do not articulate a fixed black identity essentialized in text, but rather shared histories, conflicts, and goals. The transatlantic, triangular nature of the slave narratives, therefore, emphasizes movement rather than the "sedentary poetics of either blood or soil."[4]

From its beginnings, slave writing strategically drew on available resources. As John Sekora notes, given that the slave narrative genre was not a preexisting model for early black British writers, the question "is to discover and to explain how the genre of the slave narrative emerged from an historical context in which the literary category of 'slave narrative' – name and practice alike – did not exist."[5] In its emergent form the slave narrative drew on the genre of spiritual autobiography. One of the early slave texts in Britain was Ukawasaw Gronniosaw's *Narrative* (1772), dictated to an amanuensis. This slave narrative can most properly be understood as a spiritual autobiography based on John Bunyan's *Grace Abounding* (1666), which was an important text for the evangelical revival of the late eighteenth century. The adaptation of the genre to tell the slave's story enabled the slave to enter the western literary tradition, showing that his life was amenable to the same narratives of transformation and redemption as "everyman's." Gronniosaw is portrayed as a lost sinner and as an innocent "other" who, even while in his African home of "Bournou," is spiritually uneasy: "'Twas certain that I was, at times, very unhappy in myself: it being strongly impressed on my mind that there was some Great Man of power which resided above the sun, moon and stars, the objects of our worship."[6] Gronniosaw's unhappiness is cast as that of the universal sinner whose soul is in need of grace.

The fact that Gronniosaw's *Narrative* went through twelve editions in Britain and three in North America demonstrates the effectiveness and popularity of the slave's spiritual narrative. The text does not engage in a direct attack on slavery and focuses on Gronniosaw's spiritual journey after being captured, enslaved, and brought to New England. The narrator repeatedly refers to his mistress as "good" and mentions the influence of Bunyan on him: "I found his experience similar to my own."[7] In this way Gronniosaw's text registers and co-opts the antislavery possibilities of evangelical Christianity by exploiting the literary form of the spiritual autobiography.

With its teleological plot the spiritual autobiography provided a framework within which to narrate the slave's humanity and potential for Christian salvation. But when used to tell the story of a slave's life, it also constituted a strong response to proslavery interpretations of Christianity, such as Raymond Harris's *Scriptural Researches on the licitness of the Slave Trade, shewing its conformity with the principles of natural and revealed religion* (1788). The eighteenth-century emphasis on rational religion meant that slavery could easily be seen as part and parcel of a utilitarian version of Christianity. In this way, other types of writing in circulation in the late eighteenth century were seized upon by early slave writers, for whom the genre of the slave narrative did not yet exist, to counteract proslavery arguments in pamphlets, letters, and petitions. In his *Thoughts and Sentiments on the Evil and Wicked Traffic of the Slavery* (1787), Ottabah Cugoano combines his life story with a more political approach to Christianity, arguing, in contrast to Harris, that "the righteous laws of Christianity" are incompatible with the "horrible traffic of slavery."[8]

Ensuing British slave writings were written at the same time that the Abolition Society, formed in 1787 by Granville Sharp and the Quakers, published a range of literature designed to undermine justifications for slavery on all fronts. Cugoano's pamphlet and Olaudah Equiano's *The Interesting Narrative of the Life of Olaudah Equiano* (1789) were published alongside the Philadelphian Quaker Anthony Benezet's *Historical Account of Guinea* (1788) and white abolitionist Thomas Clarkson's *An Essay on the Slavery and Commerce of the Human Species* (1786). Contributing their writings to the abolitionist cause was part of a range of activities in which former slaves engaged. Equiano and Cugoano, along with others, formed the Sons of Africa, who published high-profile letters both to antislavery and proslavery proponents. In 1788 they thanked Sir William Dolben in the *Morning Chronicle* and the *London Advertiser* for his "benevolent law" that regulated the ratio of slaves that could be taken on by a slave ship according to its size in order to lessen the mortality rate on board.[9] In these letters the Sons of Africa emphasized the antislavery movement as humane, rational, and Christian. At the same time, they struck a carefully obsequious note epitomized by the Wedgwood antislavery icon of the slave on bended knee, thus responding to an abolitionist culture that saw them as slightly less than equals even while it aimed at freedom: "we trust that we and our whole race shall endeavour to merit, by dutiful behaviour, those mercies, which humane and benevolent minds seem to be preparing us for."[10] While we may well today regard such language as a sign of the oppression of slaves who had to express gratitude for piecemeal amelioration, Robin Blackburn argues that this seeming belittlement of the slave may in contrast be read as an expression of solidarity between slaves and abolitionists: "The African was portrayed, in what seem patronising terms, as a man on his knees; but many abolitionists also felt themselves outcasts and supplicants, labouring under civic or religious disabilities."[11]

Within this multipronged antislavery movement the slave's voice was indispensable, and Equiano's *Interesting Narrative* was to become the most important and effective slave narrative in the history of British abolition.[12] Written by Equiano himself, without any editorial influence, and boasting an illustrious and lengthy list of subscribers, it was forged within the immediate context of British abolitionism in the late 1780s and is a fusion of several types of writing – travel writing, abolitionist and religious tracts, philosophical treatises, the early novel, and the spiritual autobiography. As with Gronniosaw's text, spiritual autobiography is fundamental to the *Interesting Narrative*, for not only does Equiano exploit the teleology of the genre, but he "literally reenacts the basic narrative pattern of the books of Genesis and Exodus, as well as learning, by his conversion or Christian rebirth, to read Israelite history along with his own experience as an allegory of spiritual deliverance."[13] In this way Equiano creates a text that performs the abolitionist belief that the slave's soul could be saved. His *Interesting Narrative* is therefore a powerful melding of abolitionist sources with the slave's life story.

Beyond this generic engagement it is literally composed of a host of other texts, incorporating biblical references, digressional debates that engage with popular ideology, poetry, and quotations from other texts. In the absence of a defined slave narrative genre, Equiano, like a magpie, seizes on a plethora of useful resources. But the content of the *Interesting Narrative* is also forged out of action: Equiano records key incidents as an agent in the abolitionist movement, and so his relationships and interactions with other abolitionists constitute important parts of his story. In 1774 Equiano had first contacted Granville Sharp in relation to the case of John Annis, a free black who was kidnapped by his former owner: "I proceeded immediately to that well-known philanthropist, Granville Sharp Esq. who received me with the utmost kindness and gave me every instruction that was needful on the occasion."[14] Equiano's abolitionist efforts and, in turn, his *Interesting Narrative* were bound up with the movement as a whole, which comprised the efforts of parliamentarians, poets, lawyers, evangelicals, intellectuals, and philosophers. In consequence Equiano's autobiography both responds to and incorporates a range of literary sources and, as in the case of Annis, depicts abolitionist action that challenged legal discourses that defined the slave.

At every turn Equiano's *Interesting Narrative* situates itself within contemporary debates. Anthony Benezet's *Account of Guinea*, itself a compilation of travel writings, histories, and other accounts, has often been cited as a source for much of what Equiano says about Africa. While this may seem to compromise the authenticity of Equiano's own account, it is most useful to read this intertextuality as a necessary responsiveness that strategically amplified the antislavery agenda. Thus we may read Equiano's account of his home Essaka as an Edenic idyll as a deliberate engagement with abolitionist accounts that emphasized the civility and beauty of African regions. As one commentator wrote to Clarkson: "I never saw a happier race of people than those of the kingdom of Benin, seated in ease and plenty, the Slave Trade, and its unavoidable bad effects excepted; every thing bore the appearance of friendship, tranquillity, and primitive independence."[15] It is within a wider culture of reform that Equiano exploits the significations of Africa and Africans for Europe in the opening sections of his *Interesting Narrative*, situating his account of the Ibo within the tensions occasioned by the doubts that a supposedly civilized west was having about itself. These doubts figured Africa as a necessary opposite; was Africa the benighted continent of savages, or did it enjoy an Edenic happiness that was being destroyed by corrupt Europeans? As David Brion Davis points out, the thrust of abolition addressed many of the philosophical, civic, and religious debates that Europe was having about itself: "The Negro represented innocent nature, and hence corresponded, psychologically, with the natural and spontaneous impulses of the reformer."[16] In this way the very figure of the enslaved African embodied, for the abolitionists, their wider concerns about oppression and freedom in civil society.

There is no doubt that Equiano exploits the Rousseauean ideal of the noble savage and extends its significance to his "people" as a whole.

> I was born in the year 1745, in a charming fruitful vale, named Essaka. The distance of this province from the capital Benin and the sea coast must be very considerable; for I had never heard of white men or Europeans, nor of the sea; and our subjection to the king of Benin was little more than nominal; for every transaction of the government, as far as my slender observation extended, was conducted by the chiefs or elders of the place. The manners and government of a people who have little commerce with other countries are generally very simple.[17]

The order described here responds to eighteenth-century Augustan ideals and portrays a balanced, rational, naturally civilized society. Here, Equiano evokes an image of an untouched land with a peaceful existence that is idyllic precisely because of its absolute distance from Europe and its influence. Yet this very representation is possible because of Equiano's intelligent and effective engagement with European literature, including the Bible. Equiano's description of home inevitably represents European concerns, thereby expressing the interconnectedness of African and western destinies, violently yoked together by the history of slavery.

By the time of Equiano's *Interesting Narrative*, then, the slave narrative was a dynamic, hybrid, and effective political tool that testified to the work between black and white abolitionists. Moreover, it had emerged as an impressive genre that seized upon and integrated a range of other types of writing, exploiting the rhetorical and mythical power of the west's own literature.

Frederick Douglass and abolitionist literature

The power of print in the antislavery fight was harnessed in a powerful way in America on January 1, 1831, when William Lloyd Garrison printed the first edition of the antislavery paper *The Liberator*. He established the newspaper following his decision to campaign for the immediate emancipation of all slaves, and he was to be its editor for the next thirty-five years. Garrison was inspired by the radical abolitionism of his British counterparts such as Thomas Pringle, secretary of the Anti-slavery Society in Britain and editor of the *Anti-slavery Reporter*, which had disseminated information vital to the abolitionist struggle. The transatlantic dimension of the American anti-slavery movement at this crucial time is testified to by Garrison's inclusion in his first editorial of Pringle's sonnet on oppression:

> I swear, while life-blood warms my throbbing veins,
> Still to oppose and thwart, with heart and hand,
> Thy brutalising sway – till Afric's chains
> Are burst, and Freedom rules the rescued land, –
> Trampling Oppression and his iron rod:
> *Such is the vow I take*
>   – SO HELP ME GOD! (9–14)

Clearly, Pringle's bold address encapsulated the same commitment felt by Garrison, who cites the poetry of the antislavery activist to express solidarity.

It is important to note the Christian element of this commitment, expressed in Pringle's sonnet, for the renewed activity of the abolitionist movement at this time of American revivalism was intimately connected with an evangelical reconfiguration of slavery as a personal transgression against the will of God:

> Although abolitionists used secular tactics . . . their zeal and their rhetoric resembled nothing so much as a religious crusade. Antislavery could not, in fact, have been what it was after 1830 if there had not been an evangelical Protestant tradition behind it.[18]

Despite this zeal given to abolitionism by the evangelical tradition, *The Liberator* was Garrison's response to his frustration that abolitionism was not working and that many of the churches were entrenched in a slave-owning culture. Religious hypocrisy and inaction were to be urgent concerns in the writings both of slaves and white abolitionists in the American antislavery movement.

In 1833 Garrison became leader of the American Abolition Society, and its Declaration of Sentiments, articulating Garrison's radical stance on slavery and insisting on uncompensated emancipation and the inalienable quality of freedom, included a vow to rally the churches: "We shall enlist the PULPIT and the PRESS" in the cause. However, just as the British abolitionists had needed the slave's voice to strengthen their argument against "nominal Christians," so too did the American abolitionists.[19] Notwithstanding his own considerable output, perhaps Garrison's most enduring contribution to the literature of antislavery was his preface to Frederick Douglass's self-penned *Narrative of the Life of Frederick Douglass, an American Slave* (1845). In his own Appendix, Douglass expresses the same ambivalence as Garrison toward Christianity: "I love the pure, peaceable, and impartial Christianity of Christ: I therefore hate the corrupt, slaveholding, women-whipping, cradle-plundering, partial and hypocritical Christianity of this land."[20] In this way Douglass embeds the core ideals of radical abolitionism within his text, combining political strategy with his considerable rhetorical powers.

In his preface, Garrison notes their first meeting in 1841 at an antislavery meeting in New Bedford at which Douglass spoke and his personal reaction to the fugitive slave's "intellect [and] natural eloquence." Garrison also highlights the effective literary qualities of the *Narrative*: "Compressed into it is a whole Alexandrian library of thought, feeling, and sentiment."[21] Such affirmation may well have been part of the convention by which white abolitionists authenticated the slave's narrative, but by insisting that the literariness of the *Narrative* testifies to Douglass's humanity, Garrison emphasizes that the function of the slave narrative was for "blacks to *write themselves into being*."[22] Douglass's *Narrative* was to become the quintessential expression of black freedom, the "ur-Text of slavery and freedom [which] has informed the Afro-American literary tradition from Douglass's time to the present."[23] Yet its very sophistication and complexity went so far beyond the established conventions of the slave narrative genre that the *Narrative* may also be thought to be "*sui generis*," as Deborah McDowell observes.[24] What such assessments reveal is the *individuality* of Douglass's text which is the perfect vehicle for its core plot, his transformation from a chattel slave into a fully recognized human being, into, as he says himself, becoming "my own master."[25]

Douglass achieves the full construction of individuality in a text that, while it emerges out of abolitionist culture, forges an independent voice: his *Narrative* can therefore be read as simultaneously existing within and going beyond both slave and abolitionist literature. Central to this forging of his individuality through his *Narrative* is the classic scene in which Douglass fights his master.

> I resolved to fight; and, suiting my action to the resolution, I seized Covey hard by the throat; and as I did so, I rose. He held on to me and I to him. My resistance was so entirely unexpected, that Covey seemed all taken aback . . . This battle with Mr. Covey marked a turning-point in my career as a slave. It rekindled the few expiring embers of freedom, and revived within me a sense of my own manhood . . . From this time I was never again what might be called fairly whipped.[26]

Douglass tells his readers that the purpose of his *Narrative* is to chart his development in subject-hood: "You have seen how a man was made a slave, you shall see how a slave was made a man."[27] Thus his scene of resistance is central to his self-realization in the *Narrative*. Crucially, however, it may also be read as a response to ambivalent abolitionist debates about slave resistance and violence. On this matter Garrison was equivocal, advocating pacifist means by which slaves could achieve freedom while also acknowledging the legitimacy of violence: "while Garrison endorsed Christian pacifism, he declared he knew why slaves and abolitionists would be driven to violence."[28] In an "Address to the Slaves of the United States" (1843), Garrison pledged anew his support for slaves but also delineated the limits within which they could legitimately strive for freedom: "it is your duty, whenever you can, peaceably to escape from the plantations on which you are confined, and assert your manhood."[29] It is clear from Douglass's account of his struggle with Covey that the desire for manhood and subject-hood justifies necessary violence against oppressors, and so the fight with Covey also registers tensions within abolitionist debate. Douglass's text, then, is not only a struggle for freedom but, at times, a struggle against the limits of dominant abolitionist discourse.

In his story "The Heroic Slave" (1853), Douglass was to address another prominent abolitionist writer, Harriet Beecher Stowe, whose character Uncle Tom came to epitomize the ideal of the passive, honest, Christian slave. In contrast, Douglass created the rebel Madison Washington, based on and named after a slave who had successfully overthrown the crew of the slave ship the *Creole* in 1841. In this fusion of fact and fiction Douglass represents the rebel slave as embodying "the principles of 1776," the very ideals that won America her own independence.[30] The violence necessary to attain freedom from oppression, Douglass demonstrates, is not merely a moral dilemma for the slave but a moral imperative for individuals and nations alike.

Non-violence was not the only issue on which Douglass and Garrison were to disagree, and their friendship did not survive. In 1847 Douglass established his own newspaper, *The North Star*, which was initially intended to disseminate Garrison's abolitionism westwards. Garrison had never been happy about this move of Douglass's, and by 1851 their opposition over the Constitution's relationship to slavery caused an unbridgeable breach between them. Unlike Garrison, who read the Constitution as "A SLAVEHOLDING COMPACT; it not only tolerates slavery on the soil but sanctions, guards, and strengthens it,"[31] Douglass came to believe that the Constitution could be used to fight slavery: "the constitution of our country is our warrant for the abolition of slavery in every state in the American Union." These crucial arguments with Garrison and his followers were to become part of the content of Douglass's second narrative: *My Bondage and My Freedom* (1855). "Here was a radical change in my opinions, and in the action logically resulting from that change. To those with whom I had been in agreement and in sympathy, I was now in opposition."[32] Just as the title of this second narrative juxtaposes two opposite states, so Douglass shows that conflict and tension form part of the struggle for freedom – even against fellow abolitionists. His freedom, he asserts, is absolutely dependent on being able to think for himself.

Abolitionist fiction and the slave narratives

Not only did slave narratives draw on, incorporate, and debate abolitionist literature and arguments, often abolitionist literature modeled itself on the slaves' narratives. Part of Douglass's agenda in authenticating his own self-penned narrative was to redress the damage that had been done to the antislavery campaign by fictional narratives written by white abolitionists but purporting to be true accounts. In the first American antislavery novel, *The Slave: or Memoirs of Archy Moore* (1836), Richard Hildreth effectively combines many of the established elements of the slave narrative genre with abolitionist argument in a sentimental but powerful plot. Framing the novel as a genuine manuscript, Hildreth uses the preface to allow a fictional editor to proclaim the truth of the ensuing story. The force of this truth-effect is enhanced by the creation of a distance between the editor and the supposed author, Archy Moore:

> I would not be understood, however, as implicitly adopting all the author's feelings and sentiments; for it must be confessed that he sometimes expresses himself with a force and a freedom, which by many will be thought extravagant. Yet, if I am not greatly mistaken, he preserves throughout, a moderation, a calmness, and a magnanimity . . .[33]

Here, the fictional editor creates an air of authenticity by slightly disassociating himself from the fictional author's mode of expression, and so the reader feels that there is a judicious, white, rational, editorial presence from the beginning. In genuine slaves' narratives editorial authority embodied in a preface was necessary either to assert the truth of the story or to comment on the mode of its telling. For example, in the preface to Charles Ball's narrative, the editor lets the reader know that care has been taken "to render the narrative as simple, and the style of the story . . . plain." To that end Ball's "opinions have been cautiously omitted, or carefully suppressed, as being of no value to the reader."[34] In Ball's true story and in Hildreth's fictional one the text's claim to authenticity is established by the editor's judgment about the content and form of the narrative. Such moments inevitably register the hierarchy between white and black abolitionists at the same time as they represent their mutual co-operation.

In his preface to Douglass's *Narrative*, Garrison had to emphasise that this was a real story "essentially true in all its statements" and also that it was free from editorial influence and "entirely his own production."[35] While Hildreth depended on the slave narrative form to construct an imitation, Douglass's true narrative had to respond to such fictions by asserting authorial control over his own story. The repetitive and uniform structures of the slave narratives that often served to authenticate them also meant that, ironically, these formal characteristics could be easily imitated in abolitionist novels, and this mimicry constitutes part of Hildreth's success. As Bland notes, slave narratives use the "escape motif as structuring device."[36] Flight is an inevitable element of slave narrative, since the very existence of the form depends on the successful escape of the narrator. However, while we already know that the slave has escaped, the plot depends on this motif for suspense and as a formal way of conveying the sense of overwhelming oppression from which the slave must run or under which he/she must suffer. In *The Slave* Hildreth uses the structuring trope of escape as a means by which to articulate a common bond between all slaves: "The unhappy slave has but one way of escaping any threatening infliction; – a poor and wretched resource, to which he recurs always at the imminent risk of redoubling his miseries. That remedy is flight."[37] Here the narrative voice of Moore conveys a knowing sense of the universal dilemma of all slaves in a way that convinces us this must be a real slave speaking, and so the fictional text uses the slave narrative's devices to create an air of authenticity.

While his borrowing of stock formal elements of the slave narratives allowed Hildreth to construct a powerful antislavery story, it also gave ammunition to proslavery propagandists who repeatedly questioned the truth of slave narratives. If, they argued, a fiction could be so readily believed, how could readers tell if any narrative was true? Yet this questioning did not necessarily mean that the literary or rhetorical force of the narratives was compromised. Indeed, the very fact that proslavery proponents attacked the truth of the narratives shows that they were aware of how effective these were in mobilizing readers' sensibilities.

Abolitionism had always depended on a wide variety of strategies in its attack on slavery, and blurring the line between fact and fiction was part and parcel of its interrogation of proslavery arguments. Antislavery poetry often gained its force from attempting to voice the imagined feelings of the suffering slave, thereby using a fiction to create empathy. William Cowper's "The Negro's Complaint" (1793), Amelia Opie's "The Negro Boy's Tale" (1811), and Elizabeth Barrett Browning's "The Runaway Slave at Pilgrim's

Point" (1848) are examples of especially powerful poetic "voicings" of the enslaved other within a culture of sentiment. Opie's poem dramatizes the voice of the slave Zambo pleading with the slave trader's daughter for his return to Africa: "'Ah! Dearest missa, you so kind!/ Do take me to dat blessed shore,/ Dat I mine own dear land may find"(21–23).[38] In such poems the lyrical "I" is the slave; in others, such as Sarah Wentworth Morton's poem "The African Chief" (1823), the speaker exploits the rhetoric of sentiment to demand that we feel for the slave: "Has not his suffering offspring clung,/ Desponding round his fettered knee;/ On his worn shoulder, weeping hung,/ And urged one effort free?" (17–20).[39] Such poems undoubtedly speak for slaves within the cult of abolitionist sentiment in ways that potentially bolster views of them as underdeveloped and childlike, and even as savages (albeit noble ones). Yet, in other ways, these acts of imaginative empathy in both poetry and prose attempt to bring us into the slave's world, and the force of abolitionist writing depended on representing the sufferings of the slave figure.

Abolitionist writing, then, was adept at speaking both as and for the slave in a deliberate exploitation of a range of literary genres, including borrowing from the slave narrative itself. This textual hybridity and interdependence meant that when Harriet Beecher Stowe came to write her famous novel *Uncle Tom's Cabin* (1852) she could dispense with the need to deceive her audience about the fictionality of her tale, using her preface, instead, to justify the use of fiction to treat slavery:

> The poet, the painter, and the artist, now seek out and embellish the common and, under the allurements of fiction, breathe a humanizing and subduing influence, favourable to the development of the great principles of Christian brotherhood . . . In this general movement, unhappy Africa is at last remembered.[40]

If Douglass, Equiano, and others gained their individual authority from writing their own true story, then abolitionism could use the form established by the slave narrative to create moving, openly fictional stories that would be an effective complement to them. Stowe's language here is interesting, as it conveys the sense that the abolitionist has deliberately "sought out" the "common" stories of slaves and, by "embellishing" them, is expressing a common humanity born of empathy. She wants her reader to be seduced by the novel's "allurements" and by its special ability to remind Christians of their duty as human beings. Fiction, Stowe claims, can help us negotiate the demands "of interest and passion," offering a mode of mutuality with the slave that stimulates our true feelings. The abolitionist novel emerges, therefore, as a literary genre inspired by the slave's narrative that attempts to go beyond rationalist argument, political prudence, or outraged rhetoric to forge an imaginative response between the white abolitionist and the slave.

Harriet Beecher Stowe and slave narratives

Abolitionist fiction staked its power in the truth-value of its arguments and in the authenticity of feeling stimulated by empathy with the slave. Stowe's novel fully exploits fiction's potential to be an ideal expression of sentiment and so an irresistible motivating influence on the reader. The cabin in which we first find Uncle Tom is an idyll of family contentment and communal co-operation, a bastion of Christian values that contrasts sharply with the brutality and hypocrisy of the "disagreeable business" of slave-trading which dominates the slaves' lives.[41] The voice of the omniscient narrator pushes us to see these contrasts, organizing the plot in an overarching way that is denied to the individual narrator of the slave narrative, who must focus on his own story. We are moved deliberately from the scene of a slave mother committing suicide after her child has been sold, to the contrasting figure of Eliza, who has successfully escaped the same fate by running north and finding refuge with the Quakers:

> Another scene now rises before us . . . and in the chair, gently swaying back and forward, her eyes bent on some fine sewing, sat our old friend Eliza . . . her large dark eye was raised to follow the gambols of her little Harry . . . she showed a depth of firmness and steady resolve that was never there in her earlier and happier days.[42]

This overtly intentional contrast evokes relief in the reader that Eliza, at least, has survived. By openly displaying the props and tropes of her fictional narrative, Stowe enlists our sympathies for the characters she has created and depicts scenes that are transparent about the feelings they are designed to stimulate in us.

This openly deliberate manipulation of the reader is denied to the slave, who must appear as the objective recorder of facts, despite his/her personal investment in the narrative. Arguably, this mode of realistic narration in the slave narrative creates a distance between narrator and reader, for the slave's story is unremittingly outside the white reader's experience. As Karen Sánchez-Eppler notes: "[u]nlike sentimental anti-slavery fiction, the aesthetic strategies of the slave narrative inhibit readerly appropriations, insisting that the bodily meaning of slavery cannot easily be shared."[43] This gap between slave and reader is evident in the first chapter of William Wells Brown's self-penned narrative, when he swiftly introduces us to a disturbing scene in which his mother is whipped for coming late to the field: "As soon as she reached the spot where they were at work, the overseer commenced whipping her. She cried, 'Oh!pray – Oh!pray – Oh!pray' – these are generally the words of the slaves, when imploring mercy at the hands of their oppressors."[44] The deliberate tone of understatement employed by the narrator contrasts with the frantic gaspings of his tortured mother, leaving the reader, like Brown himself, to feel a helpless onlooker of a scene that, despite its horror, we sense has occurred many times before and will be repeated. The narrator's despondency and bleak irony set up a gap between reader and slave, thereby granting the slave speaker authority.

Drawing on the plethora of such scenes in slave narratives, Stowe's use of sentimental fiction allows for a more physical co-option of the reader, evoking their sensual responses through the narrator's pleading:

> The Mississippi! . . . Those turbid waters, hurrying, foaming, tearing along . . . Ah! would that they did not also bear a more fearful freight, – the tears of the oppressed, the sighs of the helpless, the bitter prayers of poor, ignorant hearts to an unknown God – unknown, unseen and silent.[45]

Here, by acknowledging that the slaves' suffering is not ours but is almost invisible, Stowe's sentimental writing "elicits tears, sighs [as] it enrolls the reader's bodily responses in the act of overcoming difference."[46] By amplifying the pathos of the slave's narrative, Stowe effectively invites the reader to *imagine* the plight of slaves in a way that aligns the abolitionist narrator with the reader.

Despite these strategies that emphasized the moral truth of the sentimental antislavery novel, Stowe's work was inevitably open to the very same accusations of exaggeration, invention, and deceit that dogged the slave narratives. The novel spawned a host of responses from the proslavery lobby, including several novels. Other texts included reminiscences and memoirs from the planter class, who in turn asserted the truth of their accounts of slavery: "If what Mrs. Stowe wrote was true, and only that, then our children's children must conclude that their fathers were only half-civilized . . . Slavery was not all bad. It had its evils, God knows; but, on the dark picture, there were many bright spots: our children should be allowed to see them."[47] Ironically, Stowe found herself subject to the very same authenticating process as slave writers, only now slaves had to affirm that what she described tallied with their experience. Demonstrating this reversal of roles, William Wells Brown mentioned Stowe's novel in a speech made in England: "I know that some suppose that the evils of slavery are exaggerated; I have been asked again and again if certain portions of *Uncle Tom's Cabin* were not exaggeration. Of the working of slavery, in my opinion, I don't think anything can exaggerate that infamous system."[48] Brown's words not only demonstrate the reliance of abolitionism on the slaves themselves at all times, they also attest to the transatlantic nature of abolitionist activity and to the international influence of Stowe's novel. Ultimately the truth-value of antislavery texts by slaves and white abolitionists constituted a battleground that engaged both sides in virulent debate.

Eventually Stowe was to produce another text, a supplement to *Uncle Tom's Cabin*, that would "contain all the facts and documents, on which that story was founded."[49] If her sentimental fiction had explicitly appealed to readers' sensibilities, Stowe claimed that gathering and transcribing the material documents of slavery, legal papers, court records, and slave testimonies was even more affecting: "I suffer excessively in writing these things. It may truly be said I write with *heart's blood*."[50] Here, the material reality testified to by slavery's documents provokes a visceral response in the abolitionist perhaps more acute than the sentiment inspired by fiction. *The Key to Uncle Tom's Cabin* (1853) was to unleash further controversy. It must be remembered that the novel was a response by Stowe to the passing of the Fugitive Slave Law (1850) which criminalized those who aided runaway slaves. The fiction emerged from fact. In the *Key* Stowe continues this process, documenting real incidents that corresponded to those in the fictional narrative and demonstrating the novel's dependence on slave narratives, including Frederick Douglass's autobiography. Acknowledging that, despite her intentions, the novel had been "treated as a reality,"[51] she named several slaves whose stories had provided material for it and, in another twist to the fact–fiction debate, unwittingly created a "real-life" Uncle Tom in the figure of Josiah Henson, a slave whose story, Stowe noted, was similar to Tom's.

Stowe's observations were based on Henson's immensely popular first narrative, *The Life of Josiah Henson* (1849). The seed that had been planted in the public's imagination grew when Stowe herself provided the preface to Henson's second autobiography, *Truth Stranger than Fiction* (1858). Although in the preface Stowe made no claims that Henson was a model for Uncle Tom, the title alone invited the reader to read the narrative as a real basis for the fictional character's life. And the title of Henson's third narrative entirely intertwined fact and fiction: *Uncle Tom's Story of his Life* (1877). As Robin W. Winks argues, however, any attempt to chart the exact relationship between Henson and his fictional counterpart is complicated and reveals a series of disclaimers and contradictions: "the sequence is not clear, and Mrs. Stowe seemed incapable of clarifying it, but nothing said publicly by the author of *Uncle Tom* gave real substance to any contention that Josiah Henson and Uncle Tom were one and the same."[52] Henson himself was ambivalent, at times courting the comparison and at others attempting to stifle it: "my name is not Tom, and never was Tom . . . My name is Josiah Henson."[53] What this fascinating interrelationship reveals is the complexity of the interaction between abolitionist writing and slave narratives, and the power of both factual and fictional antislavery stories to feed the popular imagination. Winks's assessment that "[t]he books of Mrs. Stowe and Henson did morally reinforce each other"[54] rightly emphasizes that the goals of antislavery were at the heart of both. Within the fluid dynamics of forged and broken alliances, resonances and divergences, conflicts and reinforcements, the achievement of abolition itself ultimately defines the interconnected nature of abolitionist and slave writing.

Conclusion

In attempting to chart the complex relationship between abolitionist literature and slave narratives we are faced with a dynamic that is characterized by hybridity, fluidity, and exchange. At times the texts emerging both from slaves and white abolitionists chime harmoniously in their aims, at others they clash, but always they respond to each other, feed off each other and exhibit an interdependence that invites us to read them as coterminous. The tensions, cross-currents, co-operations, and rifts were part and parcel of the wider arena of abolitionist activity. And these relationships continue to provide challenges for current scholarship: in particular, the business of identifying factual narratives and fictional narratives reveals the degree to which these genres are mutually intertwined. Previously regarded as "not credible," only in the last twenty years has Harriet Jacobs's *Incidents in the Life of a Slave Girl* (1861) been authenticated as a narrative written by a slave.[55] Letters discovered reveal that, following the popularity of Henson's narrative, Jacobs had hoped that Stowe would act as an amanuensis for her own story. While Stowe had forged a powerful alliance with Henson, she responded to Jacobs with an offer to co-opt her narrative into the *Key*. In a letter to Amy Post, Jacobs expresses alarm at this potential abuse of her narrative, as she saw it: "I wished it to be a history of my life entirely by itself, which would do more good, and it needed no romance."[56] Adding insult to injury, Stowe had asked another abolitionist to vouch for Jacobs's veracity before offering to integrate the narrative into her *Key*: many of the incidents of Jacobs's life fulfilled Henson's maxim that fact is stranger than fiction. Indeed, Stowe's own skepticism has been repeated by the modern academy. Jacobs was to make a much happier connection with the radical abolitionist Lydia Maria Child, who did not wince from editing a narrative that would deal with the sexual exploitation of female slaves: "[t]his peculiar phase of slavery has generally been kept veiled; but the public ought to be made acquainted with its monstrous features."[57]

Notwithstanding Child's commitment to supporting a narrative that would discuss the taboo of sexual abuse in slavery, Jacobs's *Incidents* is tentative in its details, revealing the compromises that had to be made within an ambivalent abolitionist culture. Although abolitionists wanted to highlight their belief that because of slavery "licentiousness pervades the whole land," they also worried that slaves would inevitably be tainted by a culture of immorality and uncivilized behaviour.[58] So, in her narrative Jacobs walks a rhetorical tightrope when relating the sexual realities of her life as a female slave subject to her master's desires: "He told me I was his property; that I must be subject to his will in all things."[59] Jacobs cannot use her narrative to detail sexual abuse without being morally compromised herself, but she can make it known to her reader that it did occur. Through omission and silence, rather than explicit description, she attempts to convey her experience without losing moral or narrative authority. Jacobs's text, then, like all antislavery writing, emerges out of a context marked by negotiation and concession.

Yet slave narratives do not simply derive power and authority from their detailing of real sufferings, from their status as some kind of objective truth: recently Harriet Wilson's *Our Nig; or Sketches From the Life of A Free Black* (1859) has been recognized as an important fictional autobiography that integrates the literary qualities of sentimental abolitionist fiction with the structures and tropes of the slave narrative. While this story was previously dismissed until the discovery of Wilson's death certificate, the text itself remains important because of its literary qualities that fuse fact and fiction. In this novel Wilson forges a literary form that enacts the interdependence of different abolitionist genres. It offers us a paradigm that reminds us to keep these interconnections at the forefront of our minds when examining abolitionist writing and slave narratives.

NOTES

1. Harriet Beecher Stowe, *Uncle Tom's Cabin* (Oxford: Oxford University Press, 1998), p. 254.
2. Frederick Douglass, *My Bondage and My Freedom* (New York and Auburn: Miller, Orton and Mulligan, 1855), p. 361.
3. Sterling Bland, *African American Slave Narratives: An Anthology* (Westport, CT and London: Greenwood Press, 2001), Vol. I, p. 8.
4. Paul Gilroy, *Between Camps: Race, Identity and Nationalism at the End of the Colour Line* (Harmondsworth: Penguin, 2000), p. 111.

5. John Sekora, "Is the Slave Narrative a Species of Autobiography?" in *Studies in Autobiography*. James Olney, ed. (Oxford: Oxford University Press, 1988), p. 100.

6. Ukawasaw Gronniosaw, *A Narrative of the Most Remarkable Particulars in the Life of James Albert Ukawasaw Gronniosaw, An African Prince, Related by Himself* (Bath: 1772), p. 3.

7. Ibid., p. 17.

8. Ottobah Cugoano, *Thoughts and Sentiments on the Evil of Slavery*, ed. Vincent Carretta (London and New York: Penguin, 1999), p. 107.

9. Olaudah Equiano, *The Interesting Narrative and Other Writings, 1789*, ed. Vincent Carretta (London: Penguin, 1995), Appendix E, p. 341. Dolben's Act was passed in 1788.

10. Ibid.

11. Robin Blackburn, *The Overthrow of Colonial Slavery, 1776–1848* (London and New York: Verso, 1988), p. 141.

12. Nine editions of the *Interesting Narrative* were published in Equiano's lifetime, the last one appearing in 1794. It was published by subscription, a common mode of eighteenth-century production, which ensured that it had an audience already committed to purchasing a copy and that a wider audience would be encouraged by the confidence of others willing to subscribe to the book in advance. The first edition had 311 subscribers, including the cream of England's aristocracy, from the Prince of Wales to the Bishop of London. It was published in America in 1791, where it did not enjoy the same degree of success but nevertheless acquired a list of subscribers from the top ranks of New York's elite. The autobiography was popular throughout Britain and in Ireland.

13. Adam Potkay, "Olaudah Equiano and the Art of Spiritual Autobiography," *Eighteenth-Century Studies* 27 (1994), 681.

14. Equiano, *Interesting Narrative*, p. 180.

15. Carretta, *The Interesting Narrative*, p. 241, n.42.

16. David Brion Davis, *The Problem of Slavery in Western Culture* (New York: Oxford University Press, 1966), p. 363.

17. Equiano, *Interesting Narrative*, p. 32.

18. Ronald G. Walters, *The Antislavery Appeal: American Abolitionism after 1830* (Baltimore and London: Johns Hopkins University Press, 1976), p. 37. The relationship between religion and antislavery should not be regarded as a straightforward one, however: Walters notes that many evangelicals supported the project to colonize Africa with freed slaves rather than emancipation itself, and that many religious men continued to be slave owners (pp. 37–53).

19. Equiano, *Interesting Narrative*, p. 61.

20. Frederick Douglass, *Narrative of the Life of Frederick Douglass, an American Slave*, ed. Deborah E. McDowell (Oxford and New York: Oxford University Press, 1999), p. 101.

21. Ibid., p. 8.

22. Charles T. Davis and Henry Louis Gates, Jr., eds., *The Slave's Narrative* (New York: Oxford University Press), p. xxiii.

23. James Olney, "The Founding Fathers – Frederick Douglass and Booker T. Washington" in *Slavery and the Literary Imagination*. Deborah E. McDowell

and Arnold Rampersad, eds. (Baltimore: Johns Hopkins University Press, 1989), p. 8.

24. McDowell, introduction to Douglass, *Narrative*, p. xi.

25. Ibid., p. 75.

26. Ibid., pp. 67–68.

27. Ibid., p. 63.

28. William E. Cain, ed., *William Lloyd Garrison and the Fight against Slavery: Selections from The Liberator* (New York: St. Martin's Press, 1995), p. 19.

29. Ibid., p. 111.

30. Frederick Douglass, "The Heroic Slave" in *Uncle Tom's Cabin*. Jean Fagan Yellin, ed. (Oxford: Oxford University Press, 1998), p. 520.

31. *The Liberator*, April 24, 1846.

32. Douglass, *My Bondage and My Freedom*, p. 396.

33. Richard Hildreth, *The Slave: or Memoirs of Archy Moore* (Boston: John H. Eastburn, 1836), p. i.

34. Charles Ball, *Slavery in the United States: A Narrative of the Life and Adventures of Charles Ball, a Black Man, Who Lived Forty Years in Maryland, South Carolina and Georgia as a Slave* in *I Was Born a Slave: An Anthology of Classic Slave Narratives*. Yuval Taylor, ed. (Edinburgh: Payback Press, 1999), Vol. I, p. 264.

35. Douglass, *Narrative*, p. 7.

36. Bland, *Narratives*, p. 11.

37. Hildreth, *The Slave*, p. 57.

38. Amelia Opie, "The Negro Boy's Tale" in *Poems by Mrs. Opie* (London: 1811; 6th edn.), p. 56.

39. Marcus Wood, *The Poetry of Slavery, An Anglo-American Anthology 1764–1865* (Oxford: Oxford University Press, 2005), p. 457.

40. Stowe, *Uncle Tom's Cabin*, p. 3.

41. Ibid., p. 36.

42. Ibid., p. 139.

43. Karen Sánchez-Eppler, *Touching Liberty: Abolition, Feminism, and the Politics of the Body* (Oxford and Berkeley: University of California Press, 1993), p. 136.

44. William Wells Brown in Yuval Taylor, *I Was Born A Slave: An Anthology of Classic Slave Narratives* (Chicago: Lawrence Hill, 1999). 2 vols. Vol. I, p. 684.

45. Stowe, *Uncle Tom's Cabin*, p. 148.

46. Sánchez-Eppler, *Touching Liberty*, p. 134.

47. J. G. Clinkscales, *On the Old Plantation Reminiscences of his Childhood* (South Carolina: Band and White Publishers, 1916). © This work is the property of the University of North Carolina at Chapel Hill. It may be used freely by individuals for research, teaching, and personal use as long as this statement of availability is included in the text. http://docsouth.unc.edu/clinkscales/clinksc.html

48. Speech by William Wells Brown, delivered at the Town Hall, Manchester, England, August 1, 1854. In C. Peter Ripley, et al., eds., *The Black Abolitionist Papers, Vol. I: The British Isles, 1830–1865* (Chapel Hill, NC: University of North Carolina Press, 1985). Used by permission of the publisher. Originally published in the *Manchester Examiner and Times* (England), August 5, 1854. © This work is the property of the University of North Carolina at Chapel Hill. It may be used freely by individuals for research, teaching, and

personal use as long as this statement of availability is included in the text. http://docsouth.unc.edu/brownw/support5.htm

49. Stowe, *Uncle Tom's Cabin*, p. 460.

50. Ibid., p. 460.

51. Harriet Beecher Stowe, *The Key to Uncle Tom's Cabin; Presenting the Original Facts and Documents Upon Which the Story Is Founded, Together with Corroborative Statements Verifying the Truth of the Work* (Boston: John P. Jewett and Company, 1854), p. 1.

52. Robin W. Winks, "The Making of a Fugitive Slave Narrative: Josiah Henson and Uncle Tom – A Case Study" in Davis and Gates, *The Slave's Narrative*, p. 123.

53. Cited in Robin Winks, 'The Making of a Fugitive Slave Narrative' in Davis and Gates, *The Slave's Narrative*, p. 126.

54. Winks, p. 124.

55. James Blassingame, cited in Jean Fagan Yellin, "Texts and Contexts of Harriet Jacobs' *Incidents in the Life of a Slave Girl: Written by Herself*" in Davis and Gates, *The Slave's Narrative*, p. 278, n.2. In her own edition of Jacobs's narrative, even Yellin herself admits to having previously "dismissed it as a false narrative." See Harriet A. Jacobs, *Incidents in the Life of a Slave Girl: Written by Herself*, ed. Jean Fagan Yellin (Cambridge, MA: Harvard University Press), p. vii.

56. Jacobs to Post, April 4, 1853, cited in Jacobs, *Incidents*, p. 235.

57. Ibid., p. 4.

58. For an overview of the abolitionists' concerns about sexuality and slavery, see Ronald G. Walters, *The Antislavery Appeal: American Abolitionism after 1830* (Baltimore and London: Johns Hopkins University Press, 1976), pp. 70–87.

59. Jacobs, *Incidents*, p. 27.

PART II

The Slave Narrative and Anglo-American Literary Traditions

5

YOLANDA PIERCE

Redeeming bondage: the captivity narrative and the spiritual autobiography in the African American slave narrative tradition

redeem (ri-'dEm) transitive verb.

1) To recover ownership of by paying a specified sum.
2) To set free; rescue or ransom.
3) To save from a state of sinfulness and its consequences.
4) To restore honor, worth, or reputation.

synonym See SAVE

In 1798 Venture Smith, the eldest son of an African prince, dictates the narrative of his life, *A Narrative of the Life and Adventures of Venture, a Native of Africa: But Resident above Sixty Years in the United States of America. Related by Himself*, to Elisha Niles, a Connecticut schoolmaster.[1] Approximately ten years later, in 1810, itinerant preacher George White publishes the story of his life, appropriately titled: *A Brief Account of the Life, Experiences, Travels and Gospel Labours of George White, an African; Written by Himself and Revised by a Friend*. While the two narratives reflect vastly different experiences of bondage, both Smith's and White's autobiographical stories highlight acts of redemption: Smith and White consciously try to recover and restore what is lost and stolen from them by the institution of slavery. By charting the literary influence of the captivity narrative and spiritual autobiography tradition on Smith's and White's narratives, we can see a common rhetorical strategy both men employ: using conventional Anglo-American literary genres to tell unconventional African American stories. To fully understand the genre of slave narrative requires a familiarity with the other literary genres that have influenced the slave narrative form and that have also been transformed by the slave narrative tradition. In exploring the influence of the captivity narrative and the spiritual autobiography on these two texts, we can use Smith's and White's narratives to illuminate the literary interconnections that exist, on a lesser scale, in most all of the texts in the slave narrative tradition.

The captivity narrative

Annette Kolodny writes that "the single narrative form indigenous to the New World is the victim's recounting of unwilling captivity."[2] Judging from the popularity of seventeenth-, eighteenth-, and nineteenth-century published accounts, we can conclude that the captivity narrative form was not only an important literary tradition, but that the use of the captivity narrative was essential in the emerging formation of an Anglo-American identity. Broadly defined, a captivity narrative is an account of an individual, forcibly abducted from his or her home, and taken to a distant and unknown place. The subject of the narrative often endures tremendous suffering at the hands of the captors, particularly as he or she is pressured to conform and to adapt to the beliefs and behaviors of a vastly different culture. Captivity narratives usually feature two completely unfamiliar peoples and two cultures so foreign that the very act of being forced into life with the "other" is itself a type of imprisonment – even if the subject is well treated by the capturing nation. In terms of religious, national, and bodily identity, the captor and the captive are as utterly separate from each other as possible. Captivity narratives often document the deprivation of all that is familiar to the subject and the forcible acceptance of a new way of life. And while many narrators yearn to return home, some accounts record such complete acculturation to the culture of the captors that there is no desire to return home; despite their initial unwilling abduction, some captivity narrators eventually accept, and even embrace, the lifestyles, rituals, and beliefs of their captors.

The captivity narrative genre becomes a New World literary success, particularly because of the popularity of the "Indian captivity narrative."[3] For three centuries, tales of kidnapping and abduction inflicted on "innocent" colonists by the "savage" indigenous American people captivated the Anglo-American literary imagination. These accounts generally featured marauding groups of Indians who kidnap at whim, as well as accounts of their "barbaric" customs of cannibalism, scalping, rape, and torture. The heroes of these stories are the captive men and women who, when exposed to these foreign practices, resist the savagery, attempt to bring religion and civilization to their captors, and otherwise reveal the ignorance of the American Indian way of life and the superiority of the Anglo-American, Christian way of life. Less often, the hero is a "noble savage," one who, although a member of the uncivilized group, is of royal birth and thus able to serve as a link between the cultures of the "savage" and the "civilized." Yet despite the obvious biases of these captivity narratives, these documents provide rare first-hand insight into the language, customs, religious practices, and traditions of the colonial-period American Indian peoples – even as they firmly entrenched the differences between two groups in the emerging white American imagination.

On a social and historical level, these narratives speak to the threat that the indigenous American people represented for the colonists, who needed not only physical force, but rhetorical might to colonize the New World. If the indigenous people are savages who do not abide by God's law, then they are the enemy of God, and their forced removal and elimination is doctrinally sound and morally right. The concept of manifest destiny ensured early Anglo-Americans that the settlement of the entire North American continent was God's will, and the genre of the Indian captivity narrative reinforced the necessity of removing, either peacefully or forcibly, all those who stood in the way of this divine plan. At their core, these captivity narratives are religious documents, modeled along conversion and spiritual narrative forms, replete with Puritan and Calvinist theology. The Indian captivity narrative is a New World *Pilgrim's Progress*, a document of a journey through the metaphorical and literal wilderness, where the spiritual hero triumphs, despite adversities and obstacles.

As stories full both of religious instruction and political indoctrination, the captivity narratives are generally considered the domain of Anglo-American men; but several early American women also wrote captivity narratives. It becomes one of the earliest American literary forms in which women writers are well represented.[4] Yet whether the narrator was male or female, in the captivity narratives we can see the emerging "self-made man" identity common to later American literature. The authors and subjects of these accounts take care to fashion an identity for themselves as independent and autonomous agents, beholden only to divine law, even while they must account for their capture and trials at the hands of a supposedly savage and heathen people. The Indian becomes fully "other" in contrast to this new identity taken on by the narrator: American.

So, if the captivity narrative as written by whites who were captured by Indians helps to define an explicit white American identity in the New World, what do we make of captivity narratives written by the supposedly savage African, who is abducted and tortured by his "civilized" moral and intellectual superiors? Is the captivity narrative, when authored by an African, the beginning of the formation of an African American identity? What happens when Africans, exposed to this genre, begin to write the stories of their own captivities? In several cases, the focus of African-authored narratives is also on the experience of Indian captivity and not primarily on the experience of enslavement under white masters. John Marrant's 1785 *A Narrative of the Lord's Wonderful Dealings with John Marrant, A Black* is the autobiographical story of a free black who converts to Christianity and later helps to convert several Cherokee Indians to the Christian faith. Briton Hammon's 1760 *Narrative of the Uncommon Sufferings and Surprizing Deliverance of Briton Hammon, a Negro Man-Servant* details Hammon's plight in bondage under both Indian and Spanish captivity, with scarce attention paid to his New World status as "slave for life." The autobiographical accounts of both Hammon and Marrant were dictated to white amanuenses, so they may have been unable to reveal their true thoughts on chattel slavery. Yet essential portions of both narratives engage the idea of captivity by the American Indian people, evidence that these men were building upon a by then long-established literary tradition.

Diverging from the traditions of his African literary predecessors, it is Venture Smith who fully exploits, and then transforms, the captivity narrative genre, laying the groundwork for the use of this genre as a tool in the formation of a new African American identity. Smith's captors were not the "savage" indigenous American people, but those "civilized" whites who spread their ironic message of Christian salvation through their participation in the slave trade. Smith uses the various dichotomies set up in a traditional Indian captivity to tell a specifically African American story. Like Marrant and Hammon, Smith's narrative is also dictated to a white amanuensis who claims that nothing is "added in substance" other than what "he [Smith] related himself" (*Narrative*, p. iii). And while we can wonder at what material is not included in Smith's narrative (like a strong indictment against slavery), Smith maintains a high degree of agency in the telling of his tale. We can see the expression of this agency when we note the complete lack of religious content in Smith's narrative – a fact that is almost unfathomable, given the time in which he is writing, his use of a religious editor, and his subject matter. Had Smith merely conformed to the already established conventions of the genre, his narrative would have explicitly engaged prevailing religious sentiment and would most certainly have contained quotations and references to scripture. Yet despite Smith's lack of explicit rhetoric about Christian salvation, he pays the utmost concern to the notion of "redemption" as it applied to him and to all his brothers and sisters in bondage.

Venture Smith

Though the son of a King, he was kidnapped and sold as a slave, but by his industry he acquired money to purchase his freedom.
(Venture Smith's epitaph, 1805)

Born the son of a West African prince, Venture Smith endures a boyhood kidnapping, the arduous Middle Passage, and three decades of chattel slavery, primarily in the New England area. And yet he manages to purchase his own freedom and that of his wife, three children, and three other unrelated enslaved men. He accrues real estate, a shipping fleet, and significant cash savings in his lifetime. Concerning Smith, his editor, Elisha Niles, writes: "this narrative exhibits a pattern of honesty, prudence and industry, to people of his own colour; and perhaps some white people would not find themselves degraded by imitating such an example" (*Narrative*, p. iv). Niles also compares Smith to a "Franklin and a Washington," since Smith, despite his previous status as a slave, exhibits "ingenuity and good sense" (ibid.). Like the heroes of the traditional captivity narratives, Smith is a self-made man who endures the bitter trials of life and somehow still emerges triumphant. Niles respectfully pays tribute to a man who, though "wholly uncultivated, enfeebled and depressed by slavery, and struggling under every disadvantage," is still worthy of comparison to America's greatest forefathers (ibid.). As the narrative shifts from Niles's voice to Smith's story, we begin to see how Smith digresses from the conventions of an established literary form when he locates "civilization" in the middle of the wilderness.

Smith's first act of redemption is to challenge ideas about Africa in the minds of his eighteenth-century audience, for whom the continent of Africa is even more terrifying than the unclaimed American wilderness. Literary critic William Andrews writes: "as the Indian captivity narrative proved, the settlement was a realm of order and security, an outpost of moral values in a land of savagery. Outside the white man's sunny clearings lay darkness, chaos, and destruction, to be warded off only by the merciful hand of providence."[5] If the space a few miles outside of a settlement's walls incites fear in these narratives, then Africa (and its peoples) represents the ultimate form of "other" and "savagery" in the early Anglo-American imagination. But for Smith, Africa – in particular, his home in West Africa – is the site of striking physical beauty, highly organized family structures, and a well-developed and prosperous way of life. Even as Smith dispels notions about the supposedly inferior African continent and people, he also provides valuable historical information about the traditions and customs of African people. Like the Indian captivity narratives, these early African slave narratives are a form of ethnographic record; however, it is Venture Smith, a "Native of Africa," who provides this insight, and not a biased outside observer. Smith's description of the practice of polygamy in his family, for example, redeems it from being yet another example of black hypersexuality. Smith's narrative opens with the scene of his mother leaving his father because he failed to consult her about the decision to take a third wife. Smith defends his mother's actions as appropriate and well within her rights as the first wife. Moreover, he presents polygamy as a form of family structure specifically suited to life in an agrarian setting, with specific rules and regulations for the protection of children and women.

While critics decry Smith's lack of explicit attention to abolition, it is during these scenes of his early childhood that we can see Smith's indictment both of slavery and the general lack of morality of the New World. He describes his father, an African chief, as a highly principled and respected man whose experience as a leader had in no way prepared him to deal with the treachery of slaveholders and colonizing forces. Relying on a promise that his group would be spared attack, Smith's father found out that his white enemies' "pledges of faith and honor proved no better than those of other unprincipled hostile nations" (*Narrative*, p. 9). Living up to the example of honesty and integrity his father provides for him, Smith becomes an ideal and trustworthy servant. Contrary to eighteenth-century sentiment, Smith does not embrace bondage because his African racial ancestry somehow makes him uniquely suited to it. He detests being a slave, but in his mind willful wrongdoing is far worse than enforced captivity. One of Smith's masters notes that "young Venture was so faithful that he . . . should not fear to trust him with his whole fortune, for that he had been in his native place so habituated to keeping his word, that he would sacrifice even his life to maintain it" (*Narrative*, p. 14).

Smith encounters a decided lack of honor and moral decency throughout his dealing as both a slave and a free black in the American colonies, where he is consistently betrayed, cheated, and ill-used. After describing one incident in which he is unfairly prosecuted and fined for another man's economic loss, Smith states:

> Such a proceeding as this, committed on a defenceless stranger, almost worn out in the hard service of the world, without any foundation in reason or justice, whatever it may be called in a christian land, would in my native country have been branded as a crime equal to highway robbery. But Captain Hart was a *white gentleman*, and I a *poor African*, therefore it was *all right, and good enough for the black dog.* (*Narrative*, p. 30)

Smith's second act of redemption dispels the idea that Africans cannot act with honor, even when they are rendered animals, or "black dogs," because of their race and slave status. His narrative demonstrates that decency and integrity are essential components of the African worldview; and these ideals are only stunted by participation in the "civilized" world of their captors. Instead of the Anglo-American settlements and colonies being a haven and place of safety from the savage wilderness, Smith posits the New World as a site of moral degeneration. And despite the widespread notion that enslaving Africans gives them access to Christian doctrine and salvation, Smith asserts that it is exposure to this "christian land" that renders the so-called savage morally bankrupt.

Concerning this incident, William Andrews writes that: "this is the climax of Smith's narrative, this assertion of an idealized African point of reference of defining morality in the face of the arbitrariness of American standards. In this culminating instance of betrayal, the former slave demonstrates a lesson in American sociolinguistics, namely, that all reference is in the service of racism" (*Free Story*, p. 52). Smith's narrative uses italics to contrast "white gentleman" with "poor African," and the final sentence begins with "Captain Hart," which contrasts with the phrase at the end of the sentence: "black dog." Despite his economic success, his "more than one hundred acres of land and three habitable dwelling houses," Smith acknowledges that European racism toward Africans will forever equate his national status as an "African" with his social slave status as a "dog," or other beast of burden. Literary critic Frances Smith Foster argues that in these eighteenth-century narratives, slavery as an institution is not condemned, but immoral behavior is.[6] In fact, Smith does condemn the institutional nature of slavery which renders him, or any African, a "black dog," even as he decries the individual moral behavior of those he encounters. And the immorality of those Smith encounters is psychologically damaging to him, but also creates serious economic repercussions for him – mirroring both the psychic and tangible consequences of bondage for all African peoples.

As was the custom in chattel slavery, Smith's African family name, Broteer, is stripped from him and he is renamed "Venture," by his first slave master, "on account of his having purchased [me] with his own private venture" (*Narrative*, p. 13). Smith is appropriately named, as his narrative details a series of economic ventures, both successes and failures. Despite being cheated by his third master in his efforts to redeem himself from bondage, Smith preserves and purchases his freedom. Concerning this, he dictates: "being thirty-six years old, I left Col. Smith once and for all. I had already been sold three different times, made considerable money with seeming nothing to derive it from, been cheated out of a large sum of money, lost much by misfortune, and paid an enormous sum for my freedom" (*Narrative*, p. 24). Smith takes on his "emancipator's" surname and spends the remainder of his narrative detailing his various business undertakings. Smith seems obsessed with the financial details of economically providing for his family, as well as building an empire. Everything and everyone has a price, a fact of which he reminds his readers again and again. When speaking of the death of his son, he laments that: "[my] son died of the scurvy in this voyage, and the Church has never paid me the least of my wages. In my son, besides the loss of his life, I lost equal to seventy-five pounds" (*Narrative*, p. 26). This sentence seems oddly to conflate both the loss of money with the loss of his son's life, as if the two events are equally tragic. When describing his daughter's illness, Smith notes that he experiences "much trouble and expence" as a result of her illness (*Narrative*, p. 28). Ultimately, tragedy unfolds, and Smith states: "she fell prey to her disease, after a lingering and painful endurance of it. The physician's bills for attending her during her illness amounted to forty pounds" (ibid.). This certainly is an odd sentiment of grief for a father who, through great difficulty, purchases three of his children. Even when lamenting the end of his own life, Smith says: "while I am now looking to the grave as my home, my joy for this world would be full – IF my children, Cuff for whom I paid two hundred dollars when a boy . . . walked in the way of their father" (*Narrative*, p. 31). Again, the reader is left with the notion that the economic aspects of bondage are of greater concern to Smith than the moral ones; his notion of redemption seems to extend only to his ability to recover ownership of his body, family, and property.

Phillip Gould offers that: "Smith . . . constructed identities that culminated in freedom, but did so in a historical period that still generally founded freedom on the possession of property."[7] He argues that essential to Smith's protest of slavery and notion of abolition is the ability to own material wealth. In this vein, Smith fits the mold of the emerging self-made American man; his rags-to-riches story echoes the stories of previous New World autobiographers. Literary critic Rafia Zafar has much harsher words for Smith. She writes: "Smith . . . spends little time on the issue of race: his quarrel with the world is his lack of financial achievement, and the rampant ingratitude of relatives and former servants."[8] I suggest that both Gould and Zafar miss an important element of Smith's text in which he explores the root of why he connects achieving economic wealth with possessing true bodily and psychological freedom:

> My father was closely interrogated respecting his money which they knew he must have. But as he gave them no account of it, he was instantly cut and pounded on his body with great inhumanity, that he might be induced by the torture he suffered to make the discovery. All this availed not in the least to make him give up his money, but he despised all the tortures which they inflicted, until the continued exercise and increase of torment, obliged him to sink and expire. He thus died without informing his enemies of the place where his money lay. I saw him while he was thus tortured to death. The shocking scene is to this day fresh in my mind, and I have often been overcome while thinking on it. (*Narrative*, pp. 10–11)

This pivotal childhood scene, Smith's first encounter with the true horror of bondage, serves both as a harsh lesson about slavery and a brutal introduction to European culture. Smith follows his father's footsteps in valuing personal honor and integrity above all things, even in the face of death: his father refuses to acquiesce to his captors' demands, despite the penalty. The elder Broteer's body is physically broken, but he maintains his dignity and strict moral code in front of his son and other witnesses. While his body is physically enslaved until he is thirty-six years old, Smith never allows the hypocritical culture of slavery to enslave his mind. Because of his formative instruction by his African family, Smith never believes that he is the one who is a savage; he never believes that he is the moral or intellectual inferior of his captors; he never believes that his native home is the uncivilized wilderness, and that his fellow African descendants are destined by God to be slaves for life. Smith's story of survival, despite the significant odds, is a protest not only against the institution of slavery but also the individual immoral deeds he witnesses on a daily basis.

At the same time, the circumstances of his father's death involve money, economic value, and financial loss. From the time he witnesses this scene, until his death, Smith understands the economic realities of the system of slavery. His narrative strips away the religious and the philosophical, both as justification for bondage and as a pretext for telling his story. When eighteenth-century religion and philosophy, and even notions of race, are removed from the operation of chattel bondage, all that is left is the naked truth: slavery exists because it is an economically viable system. So Smith fights fire with fire, combating slavery in the one area in which he can compete, even if on a very uneven playing field: the financial marketplace.

And finally, this primal scene of his father's brutal death propels Smith to acts of personal redemption in which, by accruing property and wealth, he can restore honor to his father's legacy. As his father was the caretaker for an entire village, entrusted with the welfare and the lives of an entire tribal group, Smith recreates his African village in a New World context. His financial empire allows him to employ other Africans; he purchases and frees at least three enslaved men who are not related to him; he leaves property and money to his descendants, ensuring their continued well-being. His relentless pursuit of success in the financial marketplace is not simply a replication of a western value system. Allowed to mature and come of age in his African village, Smith would have assumed the responsibilities and duties of his father. Displaced by the Middle Passage and the institution of slavery, Smith attempts to redeem, to recover, the values, ideals, and ethics of his ancestors.

In his paradigm-shifting story which signifies on the Indian captivity narrative genre, Smith presents us with "savages" who have a greater code of ethics than their captors; an "untamed wilderness" that is more highly ordered than the American settlements; and "exotic" belief systems and ways of life that are as principled as Christian religious doctrine. And most importantly, Smith shatters the myth that thrift, hard work, frugality, and economic success are only "American" values; as he reveals in his narrative, these values reflect his African core and not his acculturation to American society.

Spiritual autobiography

An initial reading of George White's 1810 narrative may convince the reader that, unlike Venture Smith, White's primary desire is to become completely acculturated and accepted into an Anglo-American way of life.[9] White models his narrative after the longstanding tradition of spiritual autobiography, a literary form American writers inherited from their English forebears. And unlike the captivity narrative, which we can argue is a distinctly American literary genre, the spiritual autobiography is a longstanding tradition in many cultures and belief systems. As used within the western Christian tradition, a spiritual autobiography is a written document in which a convert to Christianity details his or her experience in recognizing the true light of Christian doctrine. Most of these stories are loosely modeled after the biblical account of Paul's conversion, where the former persecutor of the early Christian church is miraculously converted into its most ardent advocate. Such writings as Richard Baxter's *Call to the Unconverted* (1657), William Law's *Serious Call to a Devout and Holy Life* (1728), and Philip Doddridge's *On the Rise and Progress of Religion in the Soul* (1745) are some of the more popular spiritual autobiographies in eighteenth-century American culture. Perhaps because of his fame as a minister, Jonathan Edwards's 1738 *Faithful Narrative of the Surprising Work of God* becomes one of the hallmark narratives after which other spiritual autobiographers model their work.

Early black writers, influenced by these popular texts, overwhelmingly adopt the spiritual autobiography form in their accounts of bondage. Writing that we today identify as foundational texts in the slave narrative tradition center on the act of religious conversion.[10] Olaudah Equiano's 1789 narrative, *The Interesting Narrative of the Life of Olaudah Equiano or Gustavus Vassa, the African, Written by Himself*, and Boston King's 1798 narrative, *Memoirs of the Life of Boston King, a Black Preacher, Written by Himself, During his Residence at Kingswood-School*, are just two of the early texts by former slaves that were marketed primarily as spiritual memoirs. Within these works, issues of theology coexist, and are fused, with various social and political messages; which of these aspects takes precedent in the imagination often depends upon the reader. Despite the personal context of each story, the spiritual autobiography serves as a witnessing tool and proselytizing device. Whereas the captivity narrative serves as ethnography, cautionary tale, and political propaganda for its eighteenth-century audience, the spiritual autobiography represents a behavioral guide and an instrument of moral leadership.

If the central message of Christianity is the redemptive work of Christ on the cross, in which the sacrifice of one redeems the sins of all, it is no wonder that enslaved men and women take this message to heart both for their spiritual and earthly needs. The rhetorical message of the Christian faith promises freedom, liberation, and deliverance from bondage, particularly for those wrongly punished. The signs, symbols, and stories of this belief system reinforce the notion that the very least, the most humble, and the most abject are the ones who eventually inherit the kingdom. What other message could provide such hope and offer so many scriptural parallels to the situation of the enslaved African population? In using the spiritual autobiography form to narrate the story both of his religious conversion *and* his life in slavery, George White joins Venture Smith in reworking a conventional literary form to tell an unconventional story.

George White

> I began to think, that as God in his providence had delivered me from temporal bondage, it was my duty to look to him for deliverance from the slavery of sin.[11]

Unlike Smith, George White is born into slavery in the New World, and is eventually freed at the age of twenty-six upon the death of his slave master. He makes a living as a rural laborer and fruit seller, but at the center of his story is his conversion to Christianity, his "call" to preach, and his quest to become an ordained Methodist minister. Denied a preaching license on five separate occasions, White eventually prevails, and becomes one of the first African American ministers with authority to preach both in black and white churches. As in other autobiographies in which the central focus is on the Christian message, the religious aspects of White's narrative seem to consume his personal identity, perhaps even obscuring his intended antislavery message. Because of White's relentless drive to obtain a license to preach, his obsessive focus on clerical politics, and his heavy-handed use of theological language, the reader of his narrative is often unsure as to his specific thoughts concerning the institution of slavery. Even the title of his narrative tells a conflicted story: *A Brief Account of the Life, Experiences, Travels and Gospel Labours of George White, an African; Written by Himself, and Revised by a Friend*. While White does not fail to identify himself as an "African," he mentions his extensive labors for the gospel, but not his forced labor for a slaveholder.

It is in his letter "To the Reader" that we begin to grasp the nuances of White's religious and political project. He writes: "when I consider the station in which I am placed, and the obligations I am under, especially to my African brethren, I rejoice at every opportunity of facilitating their spiritual welfare and happiness" (*A Brief Account*, p. 51). There seems to be a clear identification with the plight of his fellow enslaved, even if it is only to bring the message of the gospel to them. And White makes it clear throughout his narrative that his first and primary mission is as God's messenger to the unsaved masses, black and white.

Because spiritual autobiographers often conform their own life stories to fit a fairly rigid biblical model, literary critic Sacvan Bercovitch argues that these personal stories have serious liabilities: that is, they "serve not to liberate, but to constrict; selfhood appears as a state to be overcome, obliterated."[12] These religious texts often create a generic Christian "Everyman," so that the reader easily identifies with the narrator and so that the gospel message is always front and center.

Even though White frames his life as one of service to God, he does intentionally highlight his selfhood, as he gives voice to his family and community and provides a brief glimpse into early African American life. He is careful to note specific details, allowing a distinct picture of himself to emerge: the ages at which he is sold; the year and place of his birth; the names and ages of family members and friends. These details, which may appear to the modern reader minutiae, represent an exceptional achievement for any former slave who had little or no information about the circumstances of his or her birth and early life. Literary historian Patricia Caldwell remarks that in the traditional Anglo-American spiritual autobiography, writers fail to make reference to these intimate details: "there were certain potentially symbolic aspects of their lives that they did not seem to find pertinent . . . they seldom resorted to talk about children . . . nor allegorized their experience of marriage . . . and none dwelt at length on his occupation."[13] These personal aspects do have a significant place within White's narrative, as he also describes for his readers his life and his struggles as a father, husband, and son.

In 1791 White experiences a profound religious conversion:

> I experienced such a manifestation of the divine power, as I had before been a stranger to: and under a sense of my amazing sinfulness in the sight of God, I fell prostrate on the floor, as one wounded or slain in battle; and indeed I was slain by the law, that I might be made alive by Jesus Christ.
>
> (*A Brief Account*, p. 53)

This moment, according to Christian doctrine, is the point at which the redemptive work of Christ's suffering provides a sinner access to eternal salvation. But this moment provides White with something more: he experiences a "manifestation of power" at a time in which African Americans have no power. Up to this point, the circumstances of White's life have been wholly determined by slavery society. Even when free, White is mistaken for a fugitive slave, arrested, and detained. If his status as a slave allows him no control over his life, his religious conversion is one moment that no other human being (even a slaveholder) can manipulate or control. White redeems, or recovers, personal agency for himself by making an active choice to submit to God's will, as he had no choice but to submit to the will of his earthly master.

After this conversion, White is called to preach, believing that he is hand-selected by God to deliver the message of salvation. Working under the auspices of the Methodist Church, White is given permission to be an exhorter, an individual who encourages the congregation and expounds on the preacher's message. But still feeling constricted in this limited role, White continues for several years his quest to be licensed to preach. The reader of White's narrative may ask why he would pursue his preaching license after being denied five times. The reader may also ask why White is not content with being an exhorter – or why he did not leave the Methodist Church altogether, as did Richard Allen, Absalom Jones, and other eighteenth-century black preachers. White desires the liberty to speak directly from the Bible, because to preach from this sacred text is to speak from a position of authority. As an exhorter, he is not allowed to choose his own scripture; he must merely defer to the textual authority of the presiding minister. To allow a slave or former slave to take bible in hand and speak a message that is applicable to everyone is to give him, an "African," power. White refuses to leave the racially segregated Methodist Church, which confined blacks to the balconies or to the space behind whites in the main sanctuary, and did not allow for the ordination of black ministers. The reason may be that, once ordained by the Methodist Church, White occupies a position of authority to teach and to admonish both in black *and* white pulpits; had he left the Methodist Church for the nascent African Methodist Episcopal Church, White would have been limited to preaching only before all-black congregations. But despite his bi-racial ministry, it is clear that White's primary concern is for the African American community:

> I found in the several towns and villages where I stopped, that religion was in a prosperous way among the coloured, as well as the white people. But the former being my own blood, lay near my heart; so that my chief happiness consisted

in seeking to promote their spiritual welfare, by preaching and exhortations among them; and by instructing them in class meetings.

(*A Brief Account*, p. 70)

White attempts to redeem his brothers and sisters in bondage by helping them become free from sin, as he posits that being enslaved to sin is a worse situation than being enslaved to an earthly master. White accepts the premise of the Pauline doctrine that argues one is either a slave to sin or a slave to righteousness, but every person has a spiritual master. Based on this belief, White's argument is that it is far better for Africans to be enslaved to the righteousness of God. This enslavement to God implies something vastly different from the physical bondage Africans knew all too well; enslavement to heavenly things is in fact a form of freedom. White uses his own life as an example as he attempts to demonstrate to his readers that, because of his religious convictions, he is able to become emancipated from slavery, able to financially support his own family, able to secure a preaching license, and able to learn to read and write. And, as White reminds his readers, these earthly achievements pale in comparison to the eternal rewards he will one day experience.

We can look to one primal scene in White's early years (as we can with Venture Smith) to see why the eternal aspects of religious salvation appeal to him. Removed from his mother as an infant, White eventually experiences a reunion with her during his early adulthood:

The reader will easily imagine the affecting nature and circumstances of the scene . . . a parent lost, and a child unknown; and both in a state of the most cruel bondage, without the means, or even hope of relief. But our joyful interview of mingling anguish, was of but short duration; for my condition, as a slave, would not admit of my prolonging the visit . . . we were obliged to undergo the painful sensations occasioned by a second parting.

(*A Brief Account*, p. 52)

It is no wonder that White is attracted by the message of an eternal existence that could replace the temporal life of slavery and its devastating effects on most natural bonds of kinship. Having endured separation from his mother once, White is again ripped from her loving embrace. Torn from different countries, customs, and religious beliefs, forced to learn new languages, traditions, and ways of life, African descendants like George White embrace a religious framework to redeem the immeasurable losses experienced under chattel slavery. White not only believes in this framework, but he devotes his life to traveling in slave and free states, actively encouraging his brothers and sisters in bondage to undergo religious salvation, with hopes that their early freedom would not be far behind.

The heartbreaking scene of White's separation from his mother also challenges prevailing eighteenth- and nineteenth-century notions that Africans have no natural affection for blood ties and that, like animals, they have no need for normal human bonds of family and friendship. In the traditional spiritual autobiography tradition, the narrator often leaves his family behind in order to experience religious life more fully. White proposes just the opposite, as he transforms the spiritual autobiography form to meet the needs of a "peculiar people." The immorality of slavery that destroys family ties also destroys natural spiritual sentiment. He writes:

> Perhaps nothing can be more conducive to vice and immorality, than a state of abject slavery, like that practiced by the Virginia planters upon the degraded Africans for being deprived by their inhuman masters and overseers, of almost every privilege. (*A Brief Account*, p. 53)

The core of White's message in his narrative is one of Christian salvation and redemption; but the careful reader can have little doubt about White's antislavery sentiment. White provides his own linguistic twist in this passage: while Africans may be degraded, their enslaved status is not innate to them and can be changed. It is slave masters who are vile, immoral, and, moreover, "inhuman," lacking souls and unable to receive Christian redemption.

At the end of Venture Smith's narrative, the reader is left to wonder who is savage and who is civilized, as his work shatters conventions about the captivity narrative. With White, we are left to ponder an even more central question: who has a soul that can be saved? Well into the nineteenth century, proslavery advocates argue that because Africans and their descendants are little more than beasts, they do not possess souls that can experience Christian redemption. At stake is the issue of *humanity* for these first generations of African Americans: are the enslaved fully human, and if they are, are they not entitled to the full rights and privileges of every human being? The narratives of Venture Smith and George White leave little doubt as to the answers to these questions. Rugged individuals, engaged both in personal and community uplift, revising and transforming conventional narrative forms, Smith and White restore honor and worth to the status of "African" in early American culture.

NOTES

1. Venture Smith, *A Narrative of the Life and Adventures of Venture, a Native of Africa: But Resident above Sixty Years in the United States of America. Related by Himself* (New London, CT: C. Holt, 1798). Subsequent page references will be cited parenthetically in the text.

2. See Annette Kolodny, *The Land before Her: Fantasy and Experience of the American Frontiers, 1630–1860* (Chapel Hill, NC: University of North Carolina Press, 1984), p. 6.

3. This narrative form is also commonly referred to as the "Puritan captivity narrative," as well as the "American captivity narrative" or the "Colonial captivity narrative."

4. For a thorough discussion of women's roles in captivity narratives, see Kathryn Zabelle Derounian-Stodola's introduction to *Women's Indian Captivity Narratives* (New York: Penguin Books, 1998).

5. William Andrews, *To Tell a Free Story: The First Century of Afro-American Autobiography, 1760–1865* (Urbana: University of Illinois Press, 1986), p. 39. Subsequent page references will be cited parenthetically in the text.

6. Frances Smith Foster, *Witnessing Slavery: The Development of Antebellum Slave Narratives* (Madison: University of Wisconsin Press, 1979), p. 47.

7. Philip Gould, *Barbaric Traffic: Commerce and Antislavery in the Eighteenth-Century Atlantic World* (Cambridge: Harvard University Press, 2003), p. 123.

8. Rafia Zafar, "Capturing the Captivity: African Americans among the Puritans," *MELUS* 17 (summer 1992), 29.

9. For an extended treatment of White's narrative, see my chapter on him in *Hell without Fires: Slavery, Christianity, and the Antebellum Spiritual Narrative* (Gainesville: University Press of Florida, 2005).

10. You could even argue that because of its focus on distinguishing slaveholding religion from true Christianity, Frederick Douglass's 1845 slave narrative, the quintessential slave narrative, is in fact a spiritual autobiography.

11. George White, *A Brief Account of the Life, Experiences, Travels and Gospel Labours of George White, an African; Written by Himself, and Revised by a Friend* (New York: John C. Trotten, 1810), p. 53. Subsequent page references will be cited parenthetically in the text.

12. See Sacvan Bercovitch, *The Puritan Origins of the American Self* (New Haven: Yale University Press, 1975), p. 13.

13. See Patricia Caldwell, *The Puritan Conversion Narrative: The Beginnings of American Expression* (Cambridge: Cambridge University Press, 1983), p. 26.

6

ROBERT S. LEVINE

The slave narrative and the revolutionary tradition of American autobiography

Is the slave narrative a subspecies or subgenre of autobiography? That is one of the large questions posed by John Sekora in his seminal "Black Message/White Envelope," a study of the crucial role that white abolitionists played in publishing, and indeed helping to shape, the antebellum slave narrative. Arguing that the slave narrative usually presents an account of a life "mandated by persons other than the subject," and that the "black message" of the slave narrative therefore inevitably comes "sealed within a white envelope," Sekora regards slave narratives as the products of a racist cultural process in which "white sponsors compel a black author to approve, to authorize, white institutional power." That process, he says, necessitates the relative silencing of the black voice. Moreover, because the slave narrative, according to Sekora, emphasizes not the "individualized Afro-American life, but rather the concrete detail of lives spent under slavery," he insists that it cannot do what autobiography typically does: creatively work with language and narrative to portray an individual self. Given his skepticism about black narrators' participatory role in the texts that just about always bear their names, Sekora's response to his rhetorically posed question about the status of the slave narrative as autobiography comes as no surprise: "the separately published [slave] narratives are thus not a subspecies of autobiography." In reaching this conclusion, Sekora aligns himself with James Olney, who elaborates a similar argument in "'I Was Born,'" an influential analysis of the formal components structuring a number of slave narratives: the opening announcement of the slave's birth without a known birthday or clear sense of parentage, the accounts of separations from family members, the portrayals of brutal masters and overseers, the attainment of literacy, the escape to the North, and so on. Claiming that, with the exception of Frederick Douglass's 1845 *Narrative*, virtually no slave narrative manages to "rise above the level of the preformed, imposed and accepted conventional," Olney, too, denies the slave narrative the status of autobiographical art.[1]

But these influential negative assessments of the slave narrative as auto-biography, I would suggest, raise more questions than they answer. For instance, is it true that "classic" white-authored autobiography exists apart from the conventional? After all, most autobiographers of the eighteenth and nineteenth centuries rather traditionally describe the course of a life history running from childhood to the defining moments of adulthood that helped to occasion the autobiography. In some respects, there is nothing more conventional than Benjamin Franklin's classic autobiography, which can be read as a secularized updating of the Puritan John Bunyan's spiritual autobiography, *The Pilgrim's Progress* (1684). Moreover, can it really be said that white autobiographers, as opposed to the black narrators of the slave narrative, are able to stand apart from the mediating forces of their culture? In fact, one could make the opposite argument, that precisely because white autobiographers are located more comfortably within their culture, they can assume such mediating forces as a given, and thus remain relatively blind to questions of racial and class hierarchies. In this respect, however subversive they may seem, their autobiographies, much more than the slave narrative, can work in the way of the jeremiad to shore up the dominant culture. Benjamin Franklin, for instance, whose influence on the development of the slave narrative was considerable, presents himself in the second section of his autobiography as responding to Benjamin Vaughan's request to provide the postrevolutionary generation with a model "for the forming of future great men; and . . . improving the features of private character, and con-sequently of aiding all happiness both public and domestic."[2] Accordingly, unlike in the autobiography's first section, his calls for virtue and order can seem relatively traditional efforts at "improving" the status quo.

Vaughan made his request to Franklin in a letter that Franklin included as a preface to the autobiography's second section. Because of the formal similarity of the Vaughan letter to the letters, prefaces, and authenticating appendices that typically frame the slave narrative, the letter raises ques-tions of agency that are also relevant to considerations of the slave narrative in an American autobiographical tradition. Most would agree that, despite the prefatory letter, Franklin retains agency as an autobiographer, for the simple reason that he had the option of using the Vaughan letter for his own purposes. The black narrators of the slave narrative surely did not have the freedom of a Franklin, but does that mean they completely surrendered agency or allowed themselves to be silenced by those who, in the manner of Vaughan, framed their narrative accounts? *Contra* Sekora and Olney, a number of scholars in the field have emphasized the collaborative nature of the slave narrative, the ways in which black "authors" could use both the features of the genre and their seemingly subordinate relation to their sponsors to develop their own voices and perspectives. To take an extreme example of such collaboration in a text that at first glance can seem anything but collaborative (or a slave narrative): In the 1831 *The Confessions of Nat Turner*, in which the condemned slave rebel Turner tells his life history to his white racist inquisitor Thomas Gray, there remains the distinct possibility, Eric J. Sundquist has argued, that Turner *used* Gray to publicize the Americanness of his rebellion (Turner had originally planned the slave conspiracy for July 4, 1831), to adumbrate the Christian spirituality that informed his plot, and to exacerbate white fears of possible black terror to come. From within the double enclosure of his jail cell and the confessional narrative as framed by Gray, Turner, as Sundquist demonstrates, resourcefully found a way to tell his story of black resistance, and thus can be thought of as one of the "authors" of the *Confessions*. In his classic study of what he calls "The First Century of Afro-American Autobiography," William L. Andrews similarly shows how blacks worked with and against their white sponsors in their efforts to tell their own stories on their own terms; and in a recent study of nineteenth-century black women's writings, Xiomara Santamarina highlights the "conflicted collaboration" between black author and white sponsor, finding even in Sojourner Truth's 1850 *Narrative*, which the "illiterate" Truth produced with the help of the white abolitionist amanuensis Olive Gilbert, a black-authored emphasis on the value of her slave labor that conflicted with Gilbert's somewhat naive celebration of Northern market culture.[3]

Truth's skeptical account of black "freedom" in the racist North went against the grain of most antebellum slave narratives, which, despite their depictions of Northern racism, typically charted the movement of the black male narrator from what Frederick Douglass termed "the tomb of slavery, to the heaven of freedom." This movement, or progress, was hailed by sympathetic readers of the time as typically American, a raced version of Benjamin Franklin's archetypal account of the "American" rise from rags to riches. In a lecture of 1849, the abolitionist Unitarian minister Theodore Parker celebrated slave narratives as the most distinctively American literature yet produced in the new nation, the very texts, he asserted, which contained "all the original romance of Americans in them." For Parker, slave narratives offered black voices and perspectives that could not be found "in the white man's novel" and that harkened back to the revolutionary spirit of the nation's founding; clearly, he discerned in these narratives much more than the political desires of their white abolitionist sponsors.[4] The remaining pages of this chapter will focus on what I take to be the distinctive voices and perspectives of the slave narrative – the black voices, or messages, that emerge from their not entirely white "envelopes" and that can be productively examined in relation to a tradition of American autobiography. Central to that tradition is Benjamin Franklin, whose autobiography served as a model for numerous slave narratives to come, even those narratives, as noted at the conclusion of the chapter, authored by formerly enslaved black women.[5]

Franklin's autobiography was written over a nearly twenty-year period (1771–90) and was not published during his lifetime. With its interest in temperance, self-examination, and virtue, the autobiography has important sources in the tradition of the Protestant spiritual autobiography, which charts the individual's struggles against the temptations of the body in the larger context of the slow and uncertain progress toward salvation and grace.[6] As the chapter by Yolanda Pierce in this volume makes clear, the spiritual narrative would continue to have an influence on the slave narrative well into the nineteenth century. In Franklin, the influence of the spiritual narrative tradition can best be discerned in the autobiography's second section, wherein he sketches out his project to achieve perfection. Bearing the impress of the Puritan Cotton Mather's insistence on the regular need for self-examination, this inspiring account of the possibilities of uplift appealed to a number of black autobiographers, especially Frederick Douglass.

But even more influential on the development of the slave narrative was the autobiography's first section, which depicts Franklin's flight from the puritanical constraints of Boston to the apparent freedoms of cosmopolitan Philadelphia (and London). At times, Franklin presents those constraints in language that evokes slavery, as in his descriptions of being regularly beaten by his older brother (in the way of a flogging) during his apprenticeship. In a footnote to those beatings, Franklin conceives of his resistance to his brother in revolutionary terms: "I fancy his harsh & tyrannical Treatment of me, might be a means of impressing me with that Aversion to arbitrary Power that has stuck to me thro' my whole life."[7] Though Franklin hadn't quite committed to the American revolutionary cause in 1771, the year he drafted the first part of the autobiography, James M. Cox nevertheless persuasively argues that there was an intimate connection between the rise of autobiography in what would become the United States and the revolutionary energies of the period, and that such connections are nowhere more apparent than in Franklin's autobiography. As Cox eloquently explains: "What literally happens in the form of Franklin's work is that the history of the revolution, in which Franklin played such a conspicuous part, is displaced by the narrative of Franklin's early life, so that Franklin's personal history *stands in place of the revolution*."[8] The linking of the autobiographical self with the founding revolutionary ideals of the new nation would become central to the numerous slave narratives that drew on key aspects of Franklin's autobiography: the emphasis on the self-made life; the value of capitalist exchange and possessive individualism in the creation of a "free" self; the strategic uses of rhetoric, literacy, and deception in a competitive and inequitable social landscape; and the importance of linking the self to larger ideals of the community. Slave narrators vary in their responses to Franklin, placing different emphases on different aspects of this "American" model and in some cases challenging and subverting the model. Such varied black messages and autobiographical selves can be discerned even despite the putative silencings and maskings of their white sponsors.

The first slave narrative directly influenced by Franklin is Venture Smith's 1798 *A Narrative of the Life and Adventures of Venture*. In the narrative's editorial preface, the white Connecticut schoolteacher Elisha Niles presents Smith as a black Franklin, or "Franklin . . . in a state of nature," particularly in the way Smith "exhibits a pattern of honesty, prudence, and industry." In the remarkable life history that follows, Smith tells of how he was taken from Africa and remanded into slavery, and of how, in the manner of Equiano, he eventually managed to purchase his freedom, along with the freedom of his wife and children. In the manner of Franklin, he would continue his economic rise in the culture, purchasing several homes and a farm, and developing a fleet of sailing vessels that would make him one of the more prominent traders of the day. Though the narrative can at times be chilling with its cold, economic calculus (for example, Smith states about his son who dies at sea that in "the loss of his life, I lost equal to seventy-five pounds"), there is every sense that this economic striver has, with the help of the Franklinian model, developed a strategy for survival in white racist culture. But as much as Franklin may have influenced Smith's thinking about how to present the upward arc of his life history, Smith's autobiographical account also turns away from Franklin and works against Niles's framing preface. For, unlike Niles, Smith also emphasizes the importance of his African youth to the development of his prideful resistance to slavery. Whereas the paternalistic Niles refers to Smith as "an untutored African slave," who, despite his successes, remains something like an animal "in a state of nature," Smith provides in his narrative's opening section an account of the inspiring example of his African father, who sacrifices his life rather than betray his people to their tribal enemies. In Smith's narrative, it is his father, as much as Franklin and other American revolutionaries, who teaches him about the value of "liberties and rights."[9]

With his appeal to liberties and rights, Smith departs from a spiritual narrative like the free black Briton Hammon's 1760 *Narrative*, attempting to instruct possible black readers in particular about the importance of the secular values of self-reliance and industry to their efforts to elevate themselves in market culture. Though Smith depicted both the African and republican sources of his prideful self-reliance, subsequent black autobiographers would place an even greater emphasis on the self-possessive rhetoric of Franklin's autobiography and the related political ideals of what was regularly presented as an unfinished American Revolution – unfinished for the simple reason that equality and liberty were not yet fully available across the color line. In the *Life of William Grimes, the Runaway Slave* (1825), for instance, Grimes regularly remarks on the importance of industrious labor to black uplift. At the same time, he makes clear that blacks face enormous obstacles in attempting to make a Franklin-like rise in the culture because of the pervasiveness of whites' antiblack racism. The story that Grimes ultimately tells about both Northern and Southern culture, then, is one of anger and frustration that builds to an evocative American revolutionary declaration of his plans to will his flogged body to the nation, so that his skin "might be taken off and made into parchment, and then bind the constitution of glorious, happy, and *free* America."[10] In this arresting image, Grimes's scarred skin becomes a text of revolutionary resistance that tells the story of violation but also of the possibilities of a regenerated America. Before reaching the point of bequeathing his skin to the nation, however, Grimes presents himself in the Franklinian mode as attempting to make money and improve his social standing, even if that means becoming a lottery ticket agent in New Haven.

Franklinian uplift is of course central to Frederick Douglass's autobiographical narratives. Although there is much in his great 1845 *Narrative* suggestive of the possible influence of Smith, Grimes, and other "black bourgeois autobiographers,"[11] the *Narrative* can also be thought of in relation to the tradition of spiritual autobiography. In his prefatory letter to the *Narrative*, the white abolitionist William Lloyd Garrison talks of how slavery "entombs the godlike mind of man, defaces the divine image, reduces those who by creation were crowned with glory and honor to a level with four-footed beasts." Douglass gives some credence to that view in his autobiographical account, but he also poses a challenge to Garrison, showing how the slaves' sorrow songs and his own personal story demonstrate blacks' spiritual resiliency. Throughout the *Narrative*, Douglass, in the tradition of the Puritan autobiographer, depicts himself as fighting off the temptation to succumb to the tug and pull of the body, even as he strives to show that the undue attention that he and other slaves pay to the body has much to do with the violations of slavery. Douglass's efforts to teach himself how to read, to establish a Sabbath school, to resist the brutalization of Covey, and to engineer his escape help him to achieve a spiritual progress that, in terms of the imagery of the *Narrative*, has its most poignant expression in his apostrophe to the vessels he discerns at sail on the Chesapeake "robed in purest white." When, at the end of the *Narrative*, Douglass takes up the "severe cross" of leadership, he has made clear to white and black readers alike that he can assume this role because he has achieved a Christ-like or Mosaic spirituality.[12]

But as important as the spiritual narrative may be to the *Narrative*, Douglass seems most indebted to the motifs of uplift, self-making, and possessive individualism central to Franklin's autobiography.[13] Like Franklin, Douglass presents himself at the outset of his autobiographical account as stultified by the arbitrary authority of a culture that attempts to keep him in his "proper" place. The move from the constraints of the Eastern Shore of Maryland to the relative freedoms of Baltimore has important parallels with Franklin's move from Boston to Philadelphia, for the more cosmopolitan city exposes Douglass to greater intellectual and economic possibilities. Like Franklin, he learns by imitation, teaching himself to read and write on his own, and like Franklin, he strategically uses deception and deceit whenever such modes can forward his pragmatic ends. Whereas Franklin rises at a steady pace, Douglass, as a slave, repeatedly confronts the obstacles, or what Franklin terms the "harsh & tyrannical Treatment" and "arbitrary Power," that will forever be in his way in a slave culture. In attempting to overcome those obstacles, he presents himself and his like-minded compatriots as American revolutionaries who "did more than Patrick Henry, when he resolved upon liberty or death." With this conception of himself as an American revolutionary, Douglass appeals to white readers who may be suspicious of slave rebels, highlighting the connections between blacks' fights against slavery and the spirit of 1776. Here is a harmonious relationship between white envelope and black message, for Garrison describes Douglass as akin to "PATRICK HENRY, of revolutionary fame." What Garrison fails to attend to is the racism that will continue to thwart Douglass even after he escapes to the North, including the paternalism of Garrison's and other white abolitionist societies. In the Franklinian mode of Venture Smith and William Grimes, Douglass attempts to continue his rise in the culture once he makes his way to New Bedford, but ultimately faces the racist resistance of white workers who do not seem all that different from the racist workers at the docks of Baltimore's Fells Point. Choosing to join hands with the abolitionists, Douglass presents himself at the conclusion of his *Narrative* as a freedom-fighter in "the cause of my brethren."[14]

In his 1855 *My Bondage and My Freedom*, a major expansion and revision of the 1845 *Narrative*, Douglass explores at greater length the cultural and institutional pressures that, in the racist slave culture of the United States, make it next to impossible for a black man to become a Benjamin Franklin. Having broken with Garrison and the Boston Anti-Slavery Society in the early 1850s, Douglass takes even greater pains in *Bondage* to link himself with his black "brethren." This is a calculated rhetorical shift on the part of Douglass, who for the most part presents himself in the *Narrative*, despite the occasional acknowledgments of his fellow slaves, as a heroic individualist. Douglass deliberately enlarges upon the Franklinian model in *Bondage* by registering a greater sense of his communal ties to other rebellious blacks. In the *Narrative*, Douglass underscores the heroic individualist achievement of his resistance to the slave breaker Covey; in *Bondage*, by contrast, he describes the invaluable assistance he received from other slaves that helped to enable that resistance. Consistent with the black communitarian vision of the 1855 autobiography, Douglass dispenses in this self-published work with the "white envelope," ridding himself of Garrison's and Wendell Phillips's somewhat condescending prefaces, and adding a preface by the black abolitionist James McCune Smith. Significantly, Smith continues to present Douglass in a Franklinian mode as a "Representative American" – an American who, through his initiative, hard work, and self-restraint, managed to raise himself "from the lowest condition in society to the highest." At the same time, McCune Smith follows Douglass's lead in making it clear that the persona of *Bondage* has close connections to black culture and is much more than a shining example of self-elevation. He is also an exemplary American revolutionary with a "special mission" of helping both the free and enslaved blacks to achieve "the exercise of all those rights" from which they have "been so long disbarred."[15]

In Douglass's and many other slave narratives of the antebellum period, the Franklinian model is ultimately put to the service of linking the individual uplift of the black persona to the revolutionary cause of freedom. And yet, as indebted as the slave narrative is to Franklin's autobiography, there remains the fact that most slave narrators cannot do what Franklin does at the outset of his autobiography: provide an authorizing family genealogy. In the *Narrative*, Douglass alludes to his unknown white father; in *Bondage* he focuses more on his black mother. McCune Smith reads Douglass's account of his mother's "deep black, glossy complexion" and "native genius" as an effort to show that "for his energy, perseverance, eloquence, invective, sagacity, and wide sympathy, he is indebted to his negro blood."[16] But ultimately Douglass and McCune Smith can only speculate about the sources, lineage, and trajectories of Douglass's genealogical history. The absence of known genealogies can be taken as a defining feature and subject of most slave narratives of the period, which is why so many of these narratives begin with the words both vague and boldly enunciatory: "I was born." The "I was born" serves as a kind of self-silencing, for the alternative would be to address the fact that many black autobiographers owe their very existence to the rape of the black slave mother. In his *Narrative*, Douglass addresses this reality obliquely by presenting the violation of his Aunt Hester almost immediately after acknowledging the uncertainties of the genealogical line on the paternal side. In this way, Hester serves as a displaced surrogate for his mother. Watching her in effect being raped by the master, the boy Douglass has intimations of the traumatic truths of sexuality on the plantation that are ultimately too painful to bear. In their subsequent autobiographical narratives, William Wells Brown and Henry Bibb attempt to address matters of gender and sexuality more directly and with an even greater sympathy for the plight of the female slave.

Bundled with testimonial letters from the Boston Anti-Slavery Society, William Wells Brown's *Narrative* of 1847 would appear to be heavily indebted to Douglass's *Narrative* of two years earlier, and thus to Franklin's autobiography as well. As in Douglass, Brown implicitly and explicitly invokes American revolutionary ideals when he poses challenges to arbitrary authority, and by the end of his narrative account of his journey from slavery to freedom he underscores the large irony that in order to achieve his freedom he will have to take refuge with the very enemy of the American revolutionaries by "fleeing from a Democratic Republic, Christian government, to receive protection under the monarchy of Great Britain." Given the failure of the United States to live up to its revolutionary ideals, Brown, like Douglass, makes it clear that the slave needs to develop strategies for survival, specifically, by learning how to deceive the masters. It is in his use of deception that Brown most resembles Franklin, though, given that, as Brown says, "slavery makes its victims lying and mean," it is difficult for him to live up to Franklin's famous (and problematic) maxim: "Use no hurtful Deceit." In order to survive, Brown has to work for a slave trader in "blacking" the slaves who are being sold at auction (he colors their hair to make them look younger), and in one of the more memorable scenes in the narrative, he writes about how he escaped from a flogging by giving the written orders for the flogging to an innocent free black, who takes the punishment in Brown's place. Though Brown says that he "deeply regretted the deception I practised upon this poor fellow," it is clear from the overall narrative that his art of deception (as in such later works as Henry "Box" Brown's *Narrative* [1851] and William Craft's *Running a Thousand Miles for Freedom* [1861]) allows him to make his escape, and that the art of deception remains central to his autobiographical art.[17] For in the manner of a Franklinian trickster, Brown rhetorically shapes his stories to fit particular audiences at particular times, and in subsequent autobiographical narratives he tells different versions of the same story, increasingly distancing himself from the narrator who can sometimes seem so callous in the version published by the Boston Anti-Slavery Office in 1847.

In all of his autobiographical narratives, Brown tells the story of the bodily violations that can't quite be told directly, in part because of a hesitancy about violating Victorian norms of propriety (similar issues would come up in Harriet Jacobs's 1861 *Incidents*), but mostly because of what the ex-slave Henry Bibb would describe in his 1849 *Narrative* as the "despair in finding language to express adequately the deep feeling of [the] soul." That story is the sexual violation of his mother and sister. Brown, like Douglass, begins his narrative "I was born," a statement that, despite its seeming simplicity, speaks to the blunt fact of the rape of his mother. Whereas Douglass imagines a version of that rape through the account of the sexual violation of his Aunt Hester, and then seems to leave concerns about his mother and other slave women behind, Brown's *Narrative*, in ways that are barely acknowledged by the "white envelope" abolitionists who preface and publish his work, testifies to his pain and guilt over the fact that not only his existence but ultimately his escape and freedom depend upon the continued enslavement and sexual violation of the women of his family. For this reason, Brown's various autobiographical narratives (*Narrative*, his autobiographical preface to *Clotel* [1853], *Memoir* [1859], and others) regularly stage scenes in which his mother and sister urge him to escape despite their ongoing sufferings. Whether or not these moments actually occurred in Brown's life history is beside the point: these scenes of benediction serve both to vindicate and excuse what Brown himself no doubt felt was his questionable abandonment of those he loved. His sister, who is eventually sold to Natchez and vanishes forever from his life, urges him thus: "If we cannot get our liberty, we do not wish to be the means of keeping you from a land of freedom."[18] Similar urgings by his mother, with whom he tries to escape but whom he eventually sees sold to New Orleans, confess to the pathos of his guilt.

We see a similar emphasis on gender and sexuality in Henry Bibb's complex *Narrative* (1849), a work that, like Brown's, seems to follow the Franklin– Douglass autobiographical model. But as is true for many of the slave narratives that Olney, Sekora, and others regard as driven by convention and silenced by abolitionist interference, Bibb's autobiographical narrative has a distinctive story to tell, which he relates with a creative artistry that, as in Brown, covers up and attempts to rationalize his abandonment of others. Like Douglass, he begins with the "I was born" that points to the vagueness of his genealogical antecedents and then describes the hardships of slavery, his desire for escape, his efforts to run a Sabbath school, and the impact of American revolutionary ideology on his active pursuit of freedom. Alluding to the Declaration, he asserts his belief that "every man has a right to wages for his labor; a right to his own wife and children; a right to liberty and the pursuit of happiness; and a right to worship God according to the dictates of his own conscience."[19]

But the autobiographical focus of Bibb's unique narrative is on his "marriage" to "a mulatto slave girl named Malinda," a woman whom he claims to have loved so profoundly that he was willing to link himself to her via a slave marriage, despite knowing that "such a step would greatly obstruct my way to a land of liberty." Like Brown, he emphasizes that the status of his wife and (later) daughter as property makes them vulnerable to the sexual predations of their legal masters. When Bibb states that "no tongue, nor pen ever has or can express the horrors of American Slavery," it is clear that, in the manner of Brown, he is simply unable or unwilling directly to address the implications of that propertied relationship, beyond stating that he regrets "being a father and husband of slaves." Bibb's efforts throughout the *Narrative* to free himself and his wife and child from slavery enact his own revolution against the patriarchal authority of the master. But the autobiographer who can seem so sympathetic to his non-legal wife, and who is quite open about the fact that his mother and her parents had been sexually violated by slaveholders, nonetheless turns against his wife in unsettling fashion when, at the conclusion of his life history, he refers to the "degradation" of his wife, who, he says, "was living in a state of adultery with her master." Bibb fails to ask important questions about volition, and he uses the news of his wife's putative "fall" to justify his marriage in 1848 to the Boston antislavery activist Mary Miles. Having escaped to Detroit, he says about his former wife from the relative comfort of his situation in a free state: "Poor unfortunate woman, I bring no charge of guilt against her, for I know not all the circumstances connected with the case. It is consistent with slavery, however, to suppose that she became reconciled to it."[20] One of the large arguments of the relatively few slave narratives written by women is that there is no reconciling to such a situation.

Precisely because slave women bear the burden of white patriarchy on their bodies, their narratives have a different story to tell from those of formerly enslaved black men, though there are broad overlaps. Critics have argued that male slave narratives emphasize Franklinian "self-sufficiency and independence," while those authored by black women emphasize "community, interdependence, heritage, and culture."[21] But there are risks in conceiving of these differences in such binary terms. Numerous autobiographies by black male narrators display an interest in community and interdependence (Bibb's *Narrative*, Douglass's *Bondage*, and Samuel Ringgold Ward's *Autobiography* [1855] come to mind as especially compelling examples), and self-sufficiency and independence are crucial to such key texts as Truth's *Narrative* and Jacobs's *Incidents*, despite the fact that both Truth and Jacobs address their roles as mothers in ways that black male narrators obviously could not. As Joanne Braxton demonstrates in her pioneering study of a black women's autobiographical tradition, slave narratives like Jacobs's *Incidents* evolve, in part, "from the autobiographical tradition of heroic male slaves," in which the "use of disguise and concealment" are put to the service of the larger "quest for freedom."[22] To be sure, Truth's *Narrative* and Jacobs's *Incidents* are more focused on matters of sexual exploitation and social interdependencies than most male-authored slave narratives. But these works also display important debts to the Franklinian tradition of American revolutionary autobiography. Sojourner Truth, after all, is a freedom-fighter, and one of the large motifs of the overall narrative is her effort to obtain the freedom of her son after making a "declaration" of independence that she would do just that. Similarly, near the beginning of *Incidents*, Jacobs announces her own revolutionary dictum: "He that is *willing* to be a slave, let him be a slave." In this ideological context, Jacobs's decision to fight back against Dr. Flint, her willingness to match her "might" against that of the master, has more in common with Douglass's fighting back against Covey than most critics have been willing to allow.[23]

Still, matters of sexuality and gender are at the center both of Truth's and Jacobs's autobiographical narratives. Because Sojourner Truth's 1850 *Narrative* was dictated to Olive Gilbert and presented as a third-person account, this particular version of Truth's life history would at first glance appear to be an unlikely source for a frank perspective on such provocative concerns. Moreover, the evidence suggests that the five children Truth gave birth to while a slave in New York State were the children of her slave "husband" Thomas, and that, as indicated by Truth's successful lawsuit in 1827 for the return of a son, she remained empowered as a mother in ways that the Southern black women described in Brown's and Bibb's narratives could not. And yet Truth's *Narrative* does describe sexual rivalries and violations in ways that look forward to similar such descriptions in Jacobs's *Incidents*. For example, Truth initially wished to marry a slave named Robert, but that union was denied by Robert's master. The marriage that followed shortly thereafter thus clearly served the needs and desires of her own master, who then develops an oddly proprietary watchfulness over Truth's children. The master's kind interest in the children is described by Truth (or Truth–Gilbert) as "proof of her master's kindness," but the extent of that kindness raises questions about the master's relationship to those children. As Truth elaborates in her *Narrative*: "If her master came into the house and found her infant crying, (as she could not always attend to its wants and the commands of her mistress at the same time,) he would turn to his wife with a look of reproof, and ask her why she did not see the child taken care of . . . And he would linger to see if his orders were obeyed, and not countermanded."[24] While there is no explicit hinting that the white master is the father of some of the children (and, as I say, the evidence suggests that he was not), this account nonetheless speaks to the sexual rivalry between the white wife and the black slave woman that is nowhere commented on in the framing preface and conclusion, but that is built into the texture of Truth's overall narrative of how her freedom was constrained not only by her labors in the field but also by her vulnerability to white master and mistress alike.

Jacobs's *Incidents*, which is framed by a preface by her white "Editor" Lydia Maria Child and an appendix with testimonial letters from both black and white friends, addresses similar matters of female vulnerability in US slave culture. In her editorial preface, Child states that she may be accused of "indecorum" in presenting a narrative that is so frank about sexuality, but in *Incidents* itself, Jacobs turns the matter of decorum against her white readers, making it clear that the standards for "pure" female behavior simply have no relevance to the exigencies of the life of a slave girl. Her decision to have a child with a white slave owner so that she could avoid sexual relations with her own white master was made, she asserts, "with deliberate calculation," and her later decision to hide out in a crawl space for nearly seven years is also presented as a deliberately conceived act that, when all is said and done, emerged from her motherly concerns for her children and eventually helped them to achieve their freedom. Throughout the narrative there are mentions of the various white and black people, mostly women, who come to Jacobs's aid, but without her Franklin-like independence and deceptiveness, her plots simply would not have succeeded. When she states, for example, with respect to Dr. Flint, "I resolved to match my cunning against his cunning," Jacobs invokes the tradition going back to Franklin that manifests itself in numerous slave narratives, of the need to learn how to master appearances in order to bring about the success of one's ventures (or, in this case, to survive and eventually escape from slavery). By taking refuge in a crawl space for seven years, Jacobs also draws on, or invokes, the Thoreauvian tradition of pursuing spiritual regeneration in one place – a place made sacred by the autobiographical narrator. Or, to put the matter another way, Jacobs's "Loophole of Retreat" has parallels with the Concord jailhouse of Thoreau's "Resistance to Civil Government" (1849). If, for Thoreau, "the true place for a just man is . . . a prison," for Jacobs, the true place for a just woman in a slave culture is a self-imprisonment that serves to liberate her body from the sexual labors and violations of patriarchy. Inspiring Jacobs's incredibly creative stratagems and eventual escape are her desires, consistent with the ideals of the revolutionary Franklin, for "pure, unadulterated freedom" for herself and her children. But her narrative ends, as do most slave narratives, with an understanding that freedom will always remain illusory in the North until slavery is no longer the law of the land. Jacobs thus concludes with a Stowe-like instance of direct address, "Reader, my story ends with freedom," that has the ring of irony given that her freedom is the result of a slave sale – of herself – in "free" New York City.[25]

Jacobs's concluding direct address to her reader speaks to her awareness of the rhetorical constraints on her autobiographical narrative. She is writing to Northern whites who she knows will never completely fathom her experiences and may never be able to see her as anything but a fallen woman. Jacobs presents her experiences from within the "white envelope" that has been fashioned by her sympathetic editor Lydia Maria Child, and yet she is still able to fashion her own version of her story through her rhetorical resourcefulness. There are similar rhetorical constraints on virtually all of the slave narratives that I have examined in this chapter, but also similar signs of agency and rhetorical resourcefulness on the part of black authors, who did what they could to maintain authority over the narratives that bore their names. If some or all of these writers worked in an American revolutionary tradition that had its most influential exemplar in Benjamin Franklin, they did not blindly or un-self-consciously follow in that tradition, and female authors in particular had their own distinctive story to tell about the limits of Franklinian individualism. All of these writers called attention to the lack of freedom in the "free" North and in this way suggested that the challenge that continued to face the nation was to live up to its revolutionary ideals. In post-Civil War autobiographical narratives and in the neo-slave narratives of twentieth-century US fiction, African American writers such as W. E. B. Du Bois and Sherley Anne Williams would re-voice that challenge while honoring the agency and vision of the slave narrators who came before them.

NOTES

1. John Sekora, "Black Message/White Envelope: Genre, Authenticity, and Authority in the Antebellum Slave Narrative," *Callaloo* 32 (1987), 509, 502, 497, 510; James Olney, "'I Was Born': Slave Narratives, Their Status as Autobiography and Literature," *Callaloo* 20 (1984), 64. See also Robert B. Stepto, *From behind the Veil: A Study of Afro-American Narrative* (Urbana: University of Illinois Press, 1979), chapter 1.
2. Benjamin Franklin, *The Autobiography and Other Writings*, ed. Kenneth Silverman (New York: Penguin Books, 1986), p. 80.
3. Eric J. Sundquist, *To Wake the Nations: Race in the Making of American Literature* (Cambridge: Harvard University Press, 1993), p. 21; William L. Andrews,

To Tell a Free Story: The First Century of Afro-American Autobiography,
1760–1865 (Urbana: University of Illinois Press, 1986), p. 1; Xiomara Santamarina, *Belabored Professions: Narratives of African American Working Wom-*
anhood (Chapel Hill: University of North Carolina Press, 2005), p. 40.

4. Theodore Parker, "The American Scholar" (1849), in Parker, *The American*
Scholar, ed. George Willis Cooke (Boston: American Unitarian Association,
1907), p. 37.

5. For an invaluable overview of Franklin's influence on subsequent writers, including African American writers, see Carla Mulford, "Figuring Benjamin Franklin
in American Culture Memory," *New England Quarterly* 72 (1999), 415–43.

6. The classic study is Daniel B. Shea, *Spiritual Autobiography in Early America*
(Princeton: Princeton University Press, 1968).

7. Franklin, *Autobiography,* p. 21.

8. James M. Cox, *Recovering Literature's Lost Ground: Essays in American Auto-*
biography (Baton Rouge: Louisiana State University Press, 1989), p. 16.

9. Venture Smith, *A Narrative of the Life and Adventures of Venture. A Native of*
Africa: But Resident above Sixty Years in the United States of America. Related
by Himself (1798), in *Unchained Voices: An Anthology of Black Authors in*
the English-Speaking World of the Eighteenth Century. Vincent Carretta, ed.
(Lexington: University Press of Kentucky, 1996), pp. 369, 382, 369, 372. For
an excellent reading of Smith's *Narrative,* see Robert S. Desrochers, Jr., "'Not
Fade Away': The Narrative of Venture Smith, An African American in the Early
Republic," *Journal of American History* 84 (1997), 40–66.

10. William Grimes, *Life of William Grimes, the Runaway Slave, Brought down to*
the Present Time, Written by Himself (1825. Rev. edn. 1855), in *Five Black Lives,*
Arna Bontemps, ed. (Middleton, CT: Wesleyan University Press, 1971), p. 120.

11. Andrews, *To Tell a Free Story,* p. 52.

12. Douglass, *Narrative,* pp. 39, 106, 151.

13. On Franklin and Douglass, see Rafia Zafar's excellent "Franklinian Douglass:
The Afro-American as Representative Man" in *Frederick Douglass: New Lit-*
erary and Historical Essays, Eric J. Sundquist, ed. (New York and Cambridge:
Cambridge University Press, 1990), pp. 99–117.

14. Douglass, *Narrative,* pp. 124, 35, 151.

15. Douglass, *My Bondage and My Freedom,* ed. William L. Andrews (Urbana:
University of Illinois Press, 1987), pp. 17, 9, 11, 9.

16. Ibid., p. 22.

17. William Wells Brown, *Narrative of William W. Brown, A Fugitive Slave. Written*
by Himself (1847), rpt. in *Slave Narratives,* William L. Andrews and Henry Louis
Gates, Jr., eds. (New York: Library of America, 2002), pp. 420, 398; Franklin,
Autobiography, p. 92; Brown, *Narrative,* pp. 391, 399.

18. Henry Bibb, *Narrative of the Life and Adventures of Henry Bibb, an Ameri-*
can Slave, Written by Himself (1849), rpt. in Andrews and Gates, eds., *Slave*
Narratives, p. 442; Brown, *Narrative,* p. 386.

19. Ibid., pp. 441, 444.

20. Ibid., pp. 452, 459, 552, 553.

21. Kimberly Drake, "Rewriting the American Self: Race, Gender, and Identity in
the Autobiographies of Frederick Douglass and Harriet Jacobs," *MELUS* 22
(1997), 94, 96. See also Nellie Y. McKay, "The Narrative Self: Race, Politics, and

Culture in Black Women's Autobiography" in *Women, Autobiography, Theory: A Reader*, Sidonie Smith and Julia Watson, eds. (Madison: University of Wisconsin Press, 1998), pp. 96–107.

22. Joanne M. Braxton, *Black Women Writing Autobiography: A Tradition within a Tradition* (Philadelphia: Temple University Press, 1989), pp. 23, 30, 29.

23. *Narrative of Sojourner Truth, a Northern Slave, Emancipated from Bodily Servitude by the State of New York, in 1828* (1850), rpt. in Andrews and Gates, *Slave Narratives*, p. 600; Harriet A. Jacobs, *Incidents in the Life of a Slave Girl: Written by Herself* (1861), ed. Jean Fagan Yellin (Cambridge: Harvard University Press, 1987), pp. 26, 85.

24. *Narrative of Sojourner Truth*, p. 594.

25. Jacobs, *Incidents*, pp. 3, 54, 128, 114; Henry David Thoreau, *Walden and Resistance to Civil Government*, ed. William Rossi (New York: Norton Critical Edition, 1992), p. 235; Jacobs, *Incidents*, pp. 183, 201.

7

CINDY WEINSTEIN

The slave narrative and
sentimental literature

Always it gave me a pain that my children had no lawful claim to a name.
(*Incidents in the Life of a Slave Girl*)

"Monsieur, je m'appelle Ellen M _____"
She stopped short, in utter and blank uncertainty what to call herself;
Montgomery she dared not; Lindsay stuck in her throat.
(*The Wide, Wide World*)

Slave narratives are famously or, more precisely, infamously surrounded by
the voices of white men and women. Their function is to vouch for the
integrity of the narrator and to authenticate the facts of her narrative lest a
suspicious reader think that a slave remembers too much, writes too well,
or has had experiences too romantic to be believed. Ironically, such attesta-
tions of truthfulness seem to be required by narratives whose very plots are
founded upon lies, secrecy, and identity theft. Lydia Maria Child's introduction to Harriet Jacobs's *Incidents in the Life of Slave Girl* (1861) perhaps
most fully embodies this defensive strategy of framing the narrative by anticipating objections to the slave's integrity and honesty. Child frankly states
that she has undertaken the task of making public Jacobs's story of compromised womanhood, at least according to conventional Victorian sexual
norms, "with the hope of arousing conscientious and reflecting women at
the North to a sense of their duty in the exertion of moral influence on the
question of Slavery."[1]

While making the case for the virtuous character of the slave, the truthfulness of her narrative, and the necessity for the reader, in the language of
Harriet Beecher Stowe, to "feel right" and assume an antislavery position,
these introductions, prefaces, appendixes, and testimonials also instruct the
reader on how to read the narrative. Thus, William Lloyd Garrison and Wendell Phillips call attention to the image of the white sails on the Chesapeake
Bay in the *Narrative of the Life of Frederick Douglass* (1845) in order to foreground this moment as one upon which the reader should linger and reflect,
both for the way it measures "the cruel and blighting death which gathers
over [the slave's] soul" and for that "[passage's] pathos and sublimity." In his

introduction to *The Life and Adventures of Henry Bibb: An American Slave* (1849), Lucius Matlack similarly alludes to the slave narrative's "elevated style, purity of diction and easy flow of language." The power of a slave narrative, in other words, is an effect not only of the facts of the individual's story from bondage to freedom, but how the story is told; in other words, its power as a literary artifact.[2]

This might seem an obvious point to make, except that slave narratives have not traditionally been analyzed in terms of the literary contributions that the genre makes to antebellum literature.[3] And with good reason. Supporters of slavery often questioned the authenticity of a slave narrative based on the extent to which it seemed more like a literary performance than a no-nonsense account of the facts. If it were too good, a slave could not have written it. If it were too melodramatic or novelistic, it could not have been true. Jacobs's seven-year imprisonment, for example, seems the stuff of a sentimental novel (in fact, Child's own *Romance of the Republic* comes to mind as the two heroines are sequestered in the Georgia hinterlands by the evil Gerald Fitzgerald, a fictional relative of the villainous Dr. Flint), which is why her story was thought to be a fiction and dismissed accordingly, until Jean Fagan Yellin's groundbreaking work established the authenticity of Jacobs's experiences. Ellen Craft's gender-bending, race-switching escape in *Running a Thousand Miles for Freedom* seems like a plot line taken from E. D. E. N. Southworth's *The Hidden Hand, or Capitola the Madcap*. The kidnapping of Solomon Northup, a free black man living in upstate New York, overlaps so extraordinarily with Mary Hayden Pike's *Ida May*, a novel whose white protagonist is kidnapped into slavery, that Frederick Douglass's *Paper* features a headline, "The arrival of Solomon Northup, and 'Little Ida May.'" Mildred Botts was the real name of the girl upon whom Ida May's story was based, but the *Paper* interestingly chose to use the fictional name, and in doing so, not only brings together the story of a real black adult male with a fictional white young girl, but also links the protagonist of a slave narrative and the heroine of a sentimental novel. The headline thwarts the usual distinctions of genre, as well as the categories of fact and fiction, and invites us to do the same.[4]

To be sure, there are profound thematic resonances between slave narratives and sentimental fictions. The protagonists of both experience the hardships that come with the absence of family ties, the slave because of the institutional assault on the biological family, and the sentimental heroine because parental loss is the novel's point of departure. Both endure a dizzying array of first and last names. The surname of a slave is her owner's, not her own, and virtually every slave narrative includes at least one passage that explains how and why she has the name she does. Sentimental heroines are similarly plagued by an instability in name, as they travel from one adoptive family to the next, never knowing exactly what their real last name is. Also yoking the two genres is the emphasis on sympathy or feeling, whether for the brutal treatment of the slave or the suffering of the heroine. However, as Nina Baym rightly points out in her essential *Woman's Fiction*, "the slave woman's problems were of another order of magnitude than the bourgeois heroine's." In placing their bourgeois heroines in situations analogous to those of the slaves, however, these texts help elucidate the very differing experiences of bondage and of freedom even as they use the analogy. How a white sentimental heroine becomes free, how she experiences her bondage, and how her experience is told is quite distinct from the slave's narrative, even though the slave narrative genre is being deployed as a lens through which to view the sentimental experience.

In what follows, slave narratives are read in dialectical relation with sentimental novels so as to demonstrate how the two genres intersect with, challenge, and speak to one another. I take as an operating principle Anne duCille's claim, "if [William Wells] Brown's text [*Clotel*] talked back to the novels of Harriet Beecher Stowe, Catharine Maria Sedgwick, Lydia Maria Child, and E. D. E. N. Southworth, *all* of these writers also listened to and drew from the Josiah Hensons, Henry Bibbses, Frederick Douglasses, Harriet Jacobses, Mary Princes, and Ellen Crafts of their times." Such an approach not only reveals the differing literary and political effects of this generic hybridization, it also illuminates the constitutive elements of each genre, particularly how the categories of race are produced or challenged, how freedom is attained (or denied or limited), and the narrative assumptions that go along with the telling of the story.[5]

To focus on the ways in which slave narratives imbue the landscape of sentimental fictions like *Ida May*, *The Wide, Wide World*, and the many other texts that deploy, even if temporarily, the narrative arc of the slave narrative is to risk minimizing its political force and its specific power as a representation of slavery told from the point of view of one who has experienced slavery. Yet this need not be the case. In fact, I shall demonstrate that the temporal, epistemological, and ideological complexities of slave narratives are better understood when we do exactly that. Such an interpretive approach borrows from and reverses the racial structure of the slave narrative's frame by using the slave narrative as the primary point of reference through which to examine antebellum sentimental fiction, specifically fictions that take up the issue of slavery. It also reverses the more conventional critical position, best represented by Hazel Carby and Karen Sánchez-Eppler, which views slave narratives as at once appropriating and undermining sentimental conventions in order to get primarily white readers to sympathize with the condition of the slave and to challenge white middle-class norms in the process. Instead, we might ask how sentimental novels might be deploying conventions of the slave narrative. Indeed, what are we to make of the many sentimental novels whose (white) protagonists venture into the territory of the slave narrative only to find their way out and back into the genre to which they belong by racial fiat? What might we learn about the slave narrative genre if Solomon Northup introduces Mary Hayden Pike, or William and Ellen Craft frame Caroline Lee Hentz? What happens to our understanding both of the slave narrative and the sentimental novel when the slave's becomes the primary voice of instruction?[6]

Role reversals

Before beginning such an analysis, however, it is worth focusing upon the editor's preface to *My Bondage and My Freedom*, the second version of Douglass's slave narrative, because it elucidates the potential hazards and possibilities of an approach that combines more typically understood literary considerations with ideological ones. Right from the start, the reader is instructed to read the text for its factual rather than artistic merits: this is not "a mere work of Art," and "[the reader's] attention is not invited to a work of Art, but to a work of Facts." These statements about what the text is not carry the burden of attesting to what it is, which is a truthful account of Douglass's journey to freedom. And yet James McCune Smith's introduction to Douglass's 1855 autobiography, after asserting that "the secret of [Douglass's] power" is that "he is a Representative American man – a type of his countrymen" (p. xxv), takes up precisely the question of the text as "a work of Art": "Memory, logic, wit, sarcasm, invective, pathos and bold imagery of rare structural beauty, well up as from a copious fountain, yet each in its proper place, and contributing to form a whole, grand in itself, yet complete in the minutest proportions" (p. xxviii). Smith finds himself needing to explain what he calls the "intellectual puzzle" (p. xxix) that is the "rare polish" (p. xxix) of Douglass's style. Thus, as much as Smith wants to avoid the thorny issue of Douglass's text as art, "the very marvel of his style" (p. xxx) demands an acknowledgment of the literary feat that is *My Bondage and My Freedom*.[7]

Similarly, Matlack's 1849 introduction strives to position slave narratives in relation to the broader category of literary production. From this perspective, his is one of the most interesting readings of the slave narrative genre: "Naturally and necessarily, the enemy of literature, it has become the prolific theme of much that is profound in argument, sublime in poetry, and thrilling in narrative." Matlack marvels that a system as "obnoxious" as slavery can be transformed into literature, that an institution so "hideous" can be embodied in an "eloquent narrative" (p. 2). He does not argue that slavery is the enemy of literature because slaves are not permitted to read or write, nor does he suggest that the facts of slavery are in any way compromised by the act of composing them into a "thrilling" narrative (that, of course, would be a proslavery contention). Rather, he claims that the experience of slavery itself, which ought to preclude the production of narrative, instead becomes the logical consequence, if not necessity, of those who escape the grasp of the peculiar institution. Slavery paradoxically becomes the foundation of literary production.

This fact was not lost on writers who were not slaves. Indeed, just as slave narratives appropriated certain conventions of sentimental novels, the literary possibilities of the slave narrative were explored by antebellum writers, *Uncle Tom's Cabin* being, of course, the most obvious case in point. Hentz's *The Planter's Northern Bride*, one among many proslavery responses to *Uncle Tom's Cabin*, incorporates slave narratives in order to undermine the entire genre by calling into question its validity and very reason for being. Thus, fugitive slaves turn out to be frauds, and slaves who have escaped their benevolent masters, temporarily lured by freedom in the North which turns out to be no freedom at all, beg to be taken back into slavery. From Hentz's point of view, the slave narrative genre is a fraud, perpetuated and supported by abolitionists who know nothing about slavery and are blinded by their absolute antipathy to all things Southern.

There are other, less politically noxious, examples of this generic crossing. Herman Melville's *Typee*, for instance, develops the plight (and I use the word advisedly given that he has as much food, sex, and leisure time as he might desire) of Tommo in the context of his growing sense that, for all intents and purposes, he is being enslaved by the Typee and must escape. The fact is, however, that what we might call "miniature slave narratives" can be found in a variety of texts, such as Fanny Fern's *Ruth Hall*, Marion Stephens's *Hagar, the Martyr*, and Susan Warner's *The Wide, Wide World*, texts not directly about slavery or captivity. The ties that bind these sentimental protagonists, though, turn out to be much more easily abrogated than those that link master to slave. The former are rescued, the latter must escape.[8]

The great escape: William and Ellen Craft

Running a Thousand Miles for Freedom or The Escape of William and Ellen Craft from Slavery tells the story of the Crafts and their daring journey out of enslavement in Georgia and toward freedom in Boston (relatively speaking, since the Fugitive Slave Law [1850] was already being enforced) and eventually England, where they finally settle. Theirs is a brilliant act of imagination, involving cross-dressing, passing, and all manner of disguise (including invalidism), which concludes in the couple's liberation. But their strategy is more complicated than a simple disguise might suggest, because it also involves the reproduction of the very master–slave relationship that they are trying to escape. Like Babo in Melville's "Benito Cereno," who performs the part of the slave when, in fact, he is Cereno's master, William acts the part of the slave to his wife, who performs the role of master. For example, while purchasing tickets to Philadelphia in the Custom House Office in Wilmington, North Carolina, William is accosted by an officer who inquires, "Do you belong to that gentleman?" to which he "quickly replies, 'Yes, sir' (which was quite correct)."[9] William means that the two belong to one another as husband and wife, while the officer means that William belongs to his master as a master belongs to a slave, but the same response correctly answers both very different and mutually exclusive frames of reference.

As they travel further north and the proximity between themselves and their "real" master decreases, William conveys the ironic humor of the situation in which abolitionists encourage him to run away, and he maintains the guise of the slave. When he is advised to "run away and leave that cripple, and have your liberty," William explains that he cannot do that because "I shall never run away from such a good master as I have at present" (p. 313). At another point, William and Ellen are separated, and onlookers tell him, "he [Ellen] thinks you have run away from him," to which William replies, "No, sir; I am satisfied my good master doesn't think that" (p. 312). It is preposterous that Ellen would think William would run away from her, and yet run away is exactly what he (and she) are doing. The language and the situation are saturated with irony, as William maintains the fiction of his enslavement by speaking the truth, which is that he is a slave.

The Crafts' narrative offers not only an apology for the practical necessity of disguise but its vindication. For fugitive slaves, terrible punishments, in the form of being returned into slavery, come with revelation. Because truth and suffering are so closely allied, the technique of disguise or concealment becomes the fundamental strategy in the slave's quest for freedom.[10] Thus, Ellen pretends to be a white male plagued by ill-health (she not only binds up her right hand in a sling, but puts a poultice in a white handkerchief which covers her chin and cheeks), Jacobs veils her face so that she may not be recognized by those trying to find and return her to Dr. Flint, and Lewis Clarke "took two pocket handkerchiefs, tied one over my forehead, the other under my chin," and when approached by a passer-by who inquires

"Massa sick?" responds in the affirmative (p. 627). In order for the slave to become free (and to write her narrative), the disguise can only be exposed afterwards, which is to say in the act of writing. To be exposed prior to that is never to get to write at all.

The slave narrative is, thus, brought into being by a celebration of concealment and lies – a fascinating fact, given that the prefaces testify to the truthfulness of the narrative. This emphasis could not be more different from that of sentimental novels, which are, for the most part, committed to what we might think of as a logic and ethic of exposure, even as their plots, like slave narratives, are driven by the effects of disguise. Indeed, sentimental protagonists pass for or, more broadly, often pretend to be that which they are not, but the revelation of their true identity is the necessary prelude to their ultimate reward, which is marriage. In this way, the stability of the novelistic world is restored. This is very different from the slave for whom concealment is the necessary condition for their freedom. Exposure means punishment, which means re-enslavement. One might argue that the emphasis on hiding as opposed to revealing is a consequence of the one genre being factual and the other fictional, but there is more to the difference than that. Sentimental novels are committed to restoring a transparency about character and relationships as they try to create, at least in the endings of their novels, a coherent, domestic, middle-class world, where children know who their fathers are and husbands and wives know the make-up of one another's blood type. In the world the slaveholders made, where fathers would not acknowledge the children they had with the slaves, there were to be no such assurances.

Unlike the Crafts' narrative, where their disguises are revealed only after they have attained their freedom, sentimental novels make the revelation of disguise a generic condition of their protagonists' successful narrative journey. The main character of *The Hidden Hand*, for example, cross-dresses in order to get jobs that are reserved for boys. Not only does her disguise not work, but she is arrested, and when, through a series of coincidences typical of sentimental fiction, she is rescued, adopted, and happily dressed in girls' clothes again, she is dutifully ashamed of having transgressed the boundaries of good taste and gender normativity. She begs the man who has adopted her not to discuss her previous life as an impoverished, homeless child with her friend and future husband, Herbert Grayson: "*please* don't tell him, especially of the boy's clothes!" Whereas Ellen and William are ultimately rewarded with freedom by assuming their disguises, Capitola is not only disciplined for becoming a boy, but she is also ashamed of it. Yes, the narrative allows Capitola this transgressive moment of being what she is not, but she must ultimately renounce any pleasures she may take from her performance as a boy, and the female identity that she is concealing must be revealed.[11]

There are many examples to choose from within the sentimental canon, but a particularly illustrative case of disguise, exposure, and renunciation occurs in Hentz's *Marcus Warland*, illustrative because the moment is one of passing. The passing, however, is not the usual black to white but white to black. When reading this scene (and the novel as a whole), it is important to keep in mind that Hentz was an avid defender of the peculiar institution in *The Planter's Northern Bride*. Thus, the fact that Florence Delavel, the future wife of the protagonist, Marcus Warland, pretends to be a mulatta in order to care for Marcus during a serious illness (she could not do so as herself because she would risk her reputation as a modest woman, one who dare not throw herself at the man she loves) and then represents it as "an act of infatuation that I now mourn in dust and ashes" seems in keeping with Hentz's political position.[12] A white heroine who assumes the mask of a slave must not only be exposed but punished, and she nearly loses Marcus as a consequence of her transgression. Although her disguise helps establish the degree of her love for Marcus and even allows him to have feelings for a mulatta that he otherwise would not be permitted to feel, the bottom line is that Florence must experience abjection because of her transgressive performance as a mulatta. Her reward (or marriage) depends upon her rejection of disguise.

How she gets exposed is a complicated story, full of improbabilities typical of the genre, but the fact of exposure is far more significant than the method. Suffice it to say that when she asks her slave, Letty, to "*mulattofy* me again" (p. 275, emphasis in original), she transforms herself, from served to servant, from Florence to Rosa, and, most threateningly, from white to black. This metamorphosis has to be discovered and repudiated in order to realign the temporarily confused racial categories. Interestingly, there is only one other mulatta character in a novel filled with black characters whose complexions are seemingly blacker than black: "clusters of black faces were grouped together; the light reflected from their charcoal surface as from mirrors of polished jet. Dark, shining constellations they looked . . . and at intervals rolled together in an opaque, ebon mass" (p. 195). When Florence asks her servant, "to *mulattofy* her," she says, "I hate to put this ugly stuff on my face any more, but I must" (p. 275, emphasis in original). This awareness of the aesthetics of changing her skin color is an insufficient acknowledgment of her transgression. Not only is she making herself that which she is not, but in taking on the identity of a mulatta, she ushers into the text one of the most horrific aspects of slavery – white on black rape.

Hentz works hard to keep this sexual threat out of her idyllic representation of slavery. In fact, the only other mulatta in the novel, Cora, is killed in a conflagration on her wedding day. When Florence assumes the disguise of Rosa, whose name clearly resonates with Cora's – Marcus even says, "she reminded him of Cora" (p. 204) – she embodies the alleged danger of interracial love. The narrator remarks, she "regarded [Marcus] with emotions he was far from wishing to inspire" (p. 206). Although "she had believed her disguise impenetrable – her secret unrevealed" (p. 225), the novel cannot let her get away with it. The emotions that her disguise elicits are too dangerous. Her future marriage with Marcus, which is the endpoint of this novel, as marriage is in virtually all sentimental texts, depends upon the revelation of her true, which is to say white, identity.

"This is all *sub rosa*" (*Marcus Warland*, p. 271)

What is *sub rosa*, or beneath Rosa, is Florence, the white sentimental heroine. The discovery of the protagonist's biological and, by extension, racial identity is a hallmark of sentimental novels and a virtual dead-end for slave narratives. Douglass writes, "A person of some consequence here in the north, sometimes designated *father*, is literally abolished in slave law and slave practice" (p. 35). Bibb similarly states, "it is almost impossible for slaves to give a correct account of their male parentage" (p. 14). Often, the best a slave could do in terms of naming her father was to refer to a rumor that her father was her master or note that she resembled her master, to the outrage of his wife. The point is that slave narratives are almost always founded upon a fundamental lack of knowledge. Thus, so many of them begin with what is not known. Douglass writes, "like other slaves, I cannot tell how old I am" (p. 35). Bibb asserts his knowledge of his mother's name in this curious way: "My mother was known by the name of Milldred Jackson" (p. 14). Such phrasing leaves open the question of whether or not this is her name. He also knows that she had "what is called the slaveholding blood flowing in her veins," but quickly adds, "I know not how much" (p. 14). And the fact is that he will never know. The mystery will remain unsolved, the knowledge forever out of reach. Whereas what is underneath Rosa is discoverable, what is beneath Bibb is not.

To think about the slave narrative in relation to knowledge that is absent, partial, or deferred illuminates a fundamental fact not only about the experience of slavery, but about how that experience is told. Slave narratives continually remind the reader not only of the remembered and the known horrors of slavery, such as the separation of parents and children, the brutal beatings and rape, but also the experience of not knowing essential parts of one's life. Douglass tells us, "I suppose myself to have been born about the year 1817," which is based on information that he has pieced together "from certain events . . . the dates of which I have since learned" (p. 35). This quotation reveals that even at the moment of writing his slave narrative, the facts of his own life continue to elude him. His is a retrospective narration that foregrounds that narration as a process, forever incomplete, of gathering the material that both is and is not his experience. Yes, his life is his, but the knowledge of some of its most important aspects is achingly out of reach.

J. W. C. Pennington's *The Fugitive Blacksmith* exemplifies this same dilemma. Having escaped from slavery in Maryland, Pennington is given shelter and love from a Quaker family in Philadelphia. After six months with the family of W. W., he no longer feels safe after mistaking the voice of W. W.'s brother-in-law for his master's. He records his anxiety about remaining and subsequent decision to pursue a northward course, after which he remarks, "the following curious fact also came out."[13] The curious fact is that W. W.'s brother-in-law, who has taken lodgings at a hotel, overhears a conversation between "a traveling peddler and several gossipers of the neighborhood" (p. 239) about the search for Pennington. The narrative includes their conversation verbatim (quotation marks and all), a conversation which Pennington clearly was not a party to and could only have known about after the fact either from this brother-in-law or W. W. Although we are told neither the source of the information nor the time Pennington received it, he concludes, "All this happened within a month or two after I left my friend. One fact which makes this part of the story deeply interesting to my own mind is, that some years elapsed before it came to my knowledge" (p. 240). A similar moment when a slave narrative abruptly shifts its temporal frame in order to register knowledge more recently acquired occurs in the Crafts' narrative, when William, who is employed by a cabinetmaker from whom he gets a holiday pass in order to effect his escape, makes this observation: "I have heard since that the cabinetmaker had a presentiment that we were about to 'make tracks for parts unknown'" (p. 294).

What I find so interesting about passages like these is the way they interrupt the temporal flow of the narrative.[14] The shuttling back and forth between time frames is an important element both of the slave narrative's style and its antislavery appeal. The slave's story is primarily told in the past tense, which is then punctured by a different time frame which describes a less remote past, as it were, when the slave gets information that she did not have during the escape itself. Such moments are part of an aftermath that often alludes to the present – the "now," in which the author is writing. Douglass invokes this time of writing when he recalls the slave songs that "even now afflict me" and "still follow me" (p. 263). Jacobs similarly remarks upon a family reunion in which she "had no share in the rejoicings" because "the events of the day had not come to my knowledge" (p. 431).

The most powerful instance of a slave narrative whose time frames refuse to remain discrete is Northup's *Twelve Years a Slave*, which tells the story of a free black in New York who is kidnapped by persons whose names he does not know and who eventually gets his freedom back by means which remain uncertain. Northup's narrative is preoccupied with its own making, and there is a sense in which he is barely able to make his story a coherent one. What signals most clearly the narrative's instability is the designation of time. For example, sometimes "now" refers to the "now" of writing, sometimes to the "now" of slavery. He writes that Ford, one of his earliest masters, is "now a Baptist preacher," but then, when his name is changed, he writes, "I was now known as Platt." Still later, he explains, "I was now in which I afterwards learned was the 'Great Pacoudrie Swamp.'"[15] This last phrase is particularly awkward, though illuminating, because it simultaneously references two time frames: the "now" in which he did not know that he was in the Great Pacoudrie Swamp, and the "afterwards" in which he learned the name of where he was. Such a strained formulation is typical of Northup's narrative style, which is marked by what we might alternately view as temporal clarifications or interruptions. Phrases such as "as I learned afterwards" (p. 21), "as will presently be seen" (p. 93), and "as I have since learned" (p. 48) pervade the narrative, although the most graphic example occurs in the chapter where Northup explains having been sold to a man named Tibeats "in the winter of 1842. The deed of myself from Freeman to Ford, as I ascertained from the public records in New-Orleans on my return, was dated June 23rd 1841. At the time of my sale to Tibeats . . . Ford took a chattel mortgage of four hundred dollars. I am indebted for my life, as will hereafter be seen, to that mortgage" (p. 75). This passage is fascinating because Northup not only narrates the events in "the winter of 1842," but he lurches ahead to a description of his return (as a free man) to New Orleans twelve years later when he gets access to "the deed of myself," which supplies him with the information, in the form of dates, that he did not have at the time of his sale. The deed further clarifies Freeman's initial sale of Northup to Ford, thereby securing the 1841 date, which takes Northup back a year prior to the 1842 event that is the ostensible subject of the passage. Every tense is represented in the space of a few sentences. The wrenching temporality figures the obfuscations that Northup must penetrate in order to get knowledge about his own experience.

And even then, full knowledge remains out of reach, both for Northup and, by extension, the reader, who is, strangely enough, in the same position regarding certain details of Northup's experience as Northup himself. He writes that "those who read these pages will have the same means of determining myself" (p. 16) how he was kidnapped and who did it, which is to say the determination remains ambiguous because the means are ultimately insufficient. About the two men who are the primary suspects, he observes, "their names, as they afterwards gave them to me, were Merrill Brown and Abram Hamilton, though whether these were their true appellations, I have strong reasons to doubt" (pp. 12–13). About his first tormentor, Burch, Northup explains or, more precisely, tries to explain: "His name was James H. Burch, as I learned afterwards – a well-known slavedealer in Washington; and then, or lately, connected in business, as a partner, with Theophilus Freeman, of New Orleans. The person who accompanied him was a simple lackey, named Ebenezer Radburn . . . Both of these men still live in Washington, or did, at the time of my return through that city from slavery in January last" (p. 21). "Then" or "lately," "still" or "did" – it is as if Northup is searching for, but cannot find, a stable temporal position out of which to produce his narrative.

Such a close reading of this temporal arrhythmia in Northup is instructive because it foregrounds his complicated position as a retrospective narrator of an experience that, while it surely happened to him, continually challenges his ability to tell it. The difficulties are profound. He is trying to relate what happened to him during his enslavement, but the content of that experience is one in which he does not know people's names, he does not necessarily know where he is, and, most profoundly, he does not always know who he is. This last fact is demonstrated early on in the text when Northup does not respond to his new name as a slave. When the trader calls out the name of Platt, and there is no answer, he says to Northup, "Your name is Platt – you answer my description. Why don't you come forward?" (p. 116). Northup does not recognize himself as the person designated as "you." Not only is his name now Platt, but the description of who he is doesn't match the one he has heretofore taken himself to be (husband of Anne, father to Elizabeth, Margaret, and Elonzo). He is a set of unrecognizable traits to be assessed and sold. At this point in the narrative, Northup knows that he is not Platt, but as his enslavement continues and his hopes for rescue fade, his relation to himself gets transformed.

There is a bizarre passage in the text where he describes his visit to plantations to entertain people with his fiddle-playing and does not narrate his experience from his position as Northup, but rather as Platt: "'Where are you going now, Platt?' and 'What is coming off tonight, Platt?' would be interrogatories issuing from every door and window, and many a time when there was no special hurry, yielding to pressing importunities, Platt would draw his bow, and sitting astride his mule, perhaps, discourse musically to a crowd of delighted children" (p. 165). The important point is that whereas Northup initially refers to himself as Platt, using quotation marks that designate the fact that he is Platt to others rather than to himself, by the end of the passage, when he should be reinhabiting his identity as Northup, he remains Platt *sans* quotation marks. This narrative moment instantiates what Orlando Patterson has referred to as the "social death" that is slavery.[16] Northup, the father and husband, is dead; only Platt remains.

Northup's story of being separated from his family, having his name changed, and eventually finding a safe haven is a familiar one in slave narratives. It is also the plot of many sentimental novels, where children are routinely cut off from their parents because of death, abandonment, and even kidnapping. Despite these intersecting plot lines, though, the stories of sentimental protagonists differ in many ways, among the most important being that they are usually not beaten (although there are exceptions, as in *Ida May*), never raped, and able to find quickly a community of people waiting to care for and love them. Losing the biological tie is critical (indeed, virtually all sentimental novels begin with this loss), but unlike the slave, like Bibb, for example, who repeatedly wants to reconnect with his biological family, the sentimental protagonist finds a family that is superior to the one into which she was born.

Ida May exemplifies how sentimental novels are governed by a fundamental access to knowledge that is denied in the slave's story. Pike's novel is particularly interesting because the first part of the text has Ida as a slave. She has been kidnapped, blackfaced, beaten, and sold into slavery, but unlike Northup, whose identity as a free man is unrecognizable, Ida physically carries with her traces of her earlier free self. First, the fact that her name is changed (like Northup's) would seem to indicate a loss of her former identity, but that is not completely the case, because her new name is Lizzie White. Her whiteness, and therefore her true identity as free, is never out of reach, because it lies on the very surface of her body, waiting to be discovered, refusing to be denied. Second, the revelation of her whiteness is made possible by a material object similarly waiting to be exposed at precisely the right moment, when everything about who Ida is and what has happened to her will be explained. The object is a "fragment of linen . . . which Venus [her black mammy] had the good sense to save, in hopes it might, at some time, lead to a discovery," and of course it does. Knowledge, rescue, and freedom are never further away than a piece of fabric, conveniently located, with the heroine's name sewn upon it.[17]

A similar fate of racial mistakenness strikes Hagar in *Hagar, the Martyr*. Early on in the novel it is announced that she is the illegitimate child of

Minnie, the quadroon slave of the family, and her father, Alva Martin. A legal clerk appears on the scene and declares, "set spies about the house, intercept all egress from the grounds, and proceed at once to investigate her [Hagar's] birth" (p. 101). Convinced of the truth of this claim, though oddly enough expressing very little emotion toward her newly discovered mother (the first hint that this claim is false), Hagar and Minnie manage to leave the house and embark for freedom, all the while pursued by the villainous Laird. He captures Hagar, while Minnie, to whom "liberty *beckoned*" (p. 102), does nothing to rescue her daughter, which is the second clue that Minnie is not Hagar's biological mother. As "incidents tangle themselves up with incidents" (p. 125), Hagar's real mother eventually arrives on the scene and reveals that Minnie is no blood relation to Hagar and that the man she thought was her father was, in fact, her uncle. With Hagar's ancestry uncovered, she can now marry Walter, the white man of her dreams, with the full knowledge that their children will not be octaroons.[18]

Many critics have been struck by the degree to which sentimental novels bring together in some kind of order every character to whom the reader has been introduced. In Mary Jane Holmes's *'Lena Rivers*, a fourth cousin and extremely minor character saves the day by explicating the kinship relations in the Rivers's family, thereby freeing 'Lena to marry Durward Bellomont. Baym correctly draws our attention to this aspect of sentimental fiction, in general, and specifically alludes to the "absurd" ending of Maria Cummins's *The Lamplighter*, which reunites Gerty Flint with her long-lost father, Philip Amory, allowing Gerty to marry Willie Sullivan, and ties up the loose ends of every other character's life in the last several pages. Such endings are usual fare for a genre in which everyone is connected. The families that have been torn apart by death, geographical separation, or bad choices get resituated (along with all of the other characters in their path) in order to lay the foundation for a new family that, in all likelihood, will be plagued by death, separation, and bad choices.[19]

Indeed, the central problem of the novel and the whole point of the plot are to clarify what that connection is and how it became obfuscated in the first place. Unlike Northup's world, where loose ends cannot be tied up because full knowledge is unavailable, the sentimental gestalt is one in which information, though temporarily hard to get, is ultimately within reach. Their endings, senseless though they may seem in their desire to bring everything and everyone full circle, are meant, paradoxically, to testify to the fact that their fictional worlds make sense. There is another reason that knowledge must be disclosed, in addition to the threat of miscegenation. The heroine cannot marry until the mystery of her parentage is solved, or else she might end up committing incest by marrying her father or brother. Interestingly, as with slave narratives the father's identity is almost always the mystery to be unraveled, but in sentimental novels the father is found, revealed, often exposed as a ne'er do well, and punished accordingly. This is not the case with slave narratives, where incest is committed by fathers who are also masters. And not only are they not punished, but the fugitive slave herself (especially post-1850 and the Fugitive Slave Law) is threatened with being returned into slavery unless she leaves the United States. Is it any wonder that the endings of slave narratives, in contrast to those of sentimental novels, are profoundly troubled?

In conclusion, or "something akin to freedom" (*Incidents*, p. 385)

The co-ordinates of slavery and freedom, black and white, past and present are neatly in place at the end of most sentimental novels. The heroine, whose temporary journey into what Douglass describes as the "arms of slavery" (p. 300), ends up in the arms of her (white) beloved and safely returned to the genre to which she belongs. *Ida May* is especially relevant here, because toward the end of the novel, when she should be making her way down the wedding aisle, she is waylaid by the specter of her earlier kidnapping and mistaken identity as a black slave. Threatened with rape by a man who believes that she is trying to pass, she cannot prove that she is white other than to assert that this is so. As luck (and sentimental convention) would have it, she is rescued at the moment of greatest peril, confirmed (yet again) in her whiteness, and forever free. Here, the analogy between Ida and a slave is being deployed in order to ratchet up the tension and increase the reader's sympathy for Ida in this moment of grave danger. Not only do we understand that we are in the presence of sentimental convention and therefore we know that Ida will not be raped (because then she would not be able to marry Walter), but also we have seen Ida, the child, beaten and abused, and we know what ground zero for suffering is. It is a child, treated as a slave, being violated and having no way out. The fact that she is rescued by Walter just in the nick of time, and that Ida's father reappears with Walter, as well, to certify her white lineage, extinguishes any threat to her future freedom. The words of Ellen Montgomery as John Humphreys rescues her from Mr. Lindsay's "hand of power" (p. 510) could just as easily be Ida's: "This may all be arranged, easily, in some way I could never dream of" (p. 520). Slaves only for a while, these white sentimental heroines need not actively pursue freedom. They are always rescued. For the slave, however, freedom must be pursued, and it is never fully achieved.

Such uncircumscribed freedom, like Ellen's, is not an element of the fugitive slave's inheritance. The closest one can get, in the poignant words of Jacobs, is "something akin to freedom." We see this over and again in slave narratives, whether it is a realization that life in the North has its own set of racist constraints, or the acknowledgment that one's pursuit of freedom must lead one still further from one's place of birth and into Canada or to England, or the sense that one can never fully free oneself of the horrible memories of slavery. Jacobs explains that her body will not let her forget her seven-year concealment in an attic: "my body still suffers from the effects of that long imprisonment, to say nothing of my soul" (p. 467). When she tells the reader, "my story ends with freedom" (p. 513), that freedom is circumscribed in all sorts of ways. Hers is no middle-class sentimental ending. There is neither a "hearthstone of my own," nor is there a marriage (p. 513). More significant, though, is her notion of freedom as a concept that needs to be defined and applied in relative terms. Not unlike Douglass who, in the conclusion to his first narrative, notes that "I spoke but a few moments, when I felt a degree of freedom" (p. 326), Jacobs similarly thinks of freedom in terms of degree: "I and my children are now free! We are as free from the power of slaveholders as are the white people of the north; and though that, according to my ideas, is not saying a great deal, it is a vast improvement in *my* condition" (p. 513). The withering irony of this final sentence, combined with the acknowledgment that she is freer than she once was, captures Jacobs's experience of having achieved "something akin to freedom."

The conclusion to Northup's narrative is, perhaps, even more vexed and oppressive than Jacobs's, as he tries and fails to get justice in a Washington, DC courtroom. Not only is his evidence "rejected solely on the ground that [he] was a colored man" (p. 247), but he is treated to a version of his kidnapping that he knows to be untrue and about which he can do nothing. "I do solemnly declare before men, and before God, that any charge or assertion, that I conspired directly or indirectly with any person or persons to sell myself . . . is utterly and absolutely false" (p. 249). Burch, his first tormentor, and others make this preposterous case, which the court accepts, as the truth is shown to be hopelessly obfuscated and unrecognizable. There is no omniscient narrator, as in the sentimental genre, whose knowledge can put things right – only Northup's faith in a "higher tribunal, where false testimony will not prevail" (p. 251).

The stories of sentimental heroines are at once analogous to and utterly different from those of the narratives of the Crafts, Northup, Douglass, Jacobs, and others, but as Toni Morrison reminds us, "explicit or implicit, the Africanist presence informs in compelling and inescapable ways the texture of American literature . . . even, and especially, when American texts are not 'about' Africanist presences or characters or narrative or idiom."[20] The production of the white sentimental heroine's freedom is intimately linked with the story of the slave's bondage. The endings of sentimental novels assure readers that the past, especially if that past has contained a descent into slavery, will never again threaten to intrude upon the present. To be rescued is to be rescued not only from one's past but even from remembering it. It happened, and now it is over. Time is neatly and categorically separated. So is race. By contrast, fugitive slaves are in a perpetual state of escape. They may escape, but they also may be recaptured. They may have freed themselves from their masters, but they never escape from the past, which is always with them, haunting them physically and psychically. When Ellen Montgomery marries John, when Ida marries Walter, when Florence marries Marcus, they begin a new life, unfettered by the past. They may have had a momentary glimpse of slavery, but surely one of the greatest fictions of the sentimental novel is that the encounter with slavery, no matter how brief and no matter how distanced, can not only be safely separated from the present, but can even be forgotten. By placing slave narratives at the center of our analysis of sentimental fictions, we discover an element of the sentimental genre that the novels both depend upon and work to erase. In an interesting paradox, we can see that though their protagonists must fulfill the requirements of transparency, the genre works to disguise its engagement with the slave narrative. In attending to the ways in which slave narratives are constitutive of sentimental novels, we expose this concealment and see how these "mere work[s] of Art," to return to James McCune Smith's description of Douglass's autobiography, were instrumental in the production of antebellum literature.

NOTES

I would like to thank Audrey Fisch, Cathy Jurca, Robert Levine, and Michelle Hawley for their careful readings of this essay.

1. Here are some examples of this defensive strategy. Joseph C. Lovejoy writes, "His Narrative bears the most conclusive internal evidence of its truth. Persons of discriminating minds have heard it repeatedly, under a great variety of circumstances, and the story, in all substantial respects, has been always the same" (*Narratives of the Sufferings of Lewis and Milton Clarke, Sons of a Soldier of the Revolution, During a Captivity of More than Twenty Years Among the Slaveholders of Kentucky, One of the So Called Christian States of North America. Dictated by Themselves* [Boston: Bela Marsh, 1846]) rpt. in *I Was Born a Slave: An Anthology of Classic Slave Narratives*. Yuval Taylor, ed. (Chicago: Lawrence Hill Books, 1999), Vol. I, p. 606. The Reverend T. Price, DD assures readers that "Moses Roper brought with him to this country [England] several other testimonies, from persons residing in different parts of the States . . . They all speak the same

language, and bear unequivocal witness to his sobriety, intelligence, and honesty" (*A Narrative of the Adventures and Escape of Moses Roper, from American Slavery; with a Preface by the Rev. T. Price, DD* [Philadelphia: Merrihew & Gunn, Printers, 1838]) rpt. in Taylor, *I was Born a Slave*, p. 490. Harriet Jacobs, *Incidents in the Life of a Slave Girl*, in *The Classic Slave Narratives*, ed. and with an introduction by Henry Louis Gates, Jr. (New York: Signet, 1987), p. 338. All further quotations from these slave narratives will be from these editions and will be noted in the text.

2. Frederick Douglass, *Narrative of the Life of Frederick Douglass* in Gates, *Narratives*, pp. 252, 294. Henry Bibb, *The Life and Adventures of Henry Bibb, an American Slave, Written by Himself. With an Introduction by Lucius C. Matlack* (New York: 5 Spruce Street, 1850), p. 1. All further quotations from Douglass's 1845 narrative and Bibb's will be from these editions and will be noted in the text.

3. There are, of course, exceptions. See, for example, Henry Louis Gates, Jr.'s illuminating introduction to Harriet E. Wilson's *Our Nig; or, Sketches from the Life of a Free Black* (New York: Vintage, 1983), Russ Castronovo, *Fathering the Nation: American Genealogies of Slavery and Freedom* (Berkeley: University of California Press, 1995), and Anne duCille's *The Coupling Convention: Sex, Text, and Tradition in Black Women's Fiction* (Oxford: Oxford University Press, 1993), p. 24.

4. March 16, 1855 edition of Douglass's *Paper*.

5. Nina Baym, *Woman's Fiction: A Guide to Novels by and about Women in America, 1820–1870* (Ithaca: Cornell University Press, 1978), p. 286. For a fuller account of my reading of the genre of sentimental fiction, see C. Weinstein, *Family, Kinship, and Sympathy in Nineteenth-Century American Literature* (Cambridge: Cambridge University Press, 2004).

6. See Hazel Carby, *Reconstructing Womanhood: The Emergence of the Afro-American Woman Novelist* (Oxford: Oxford University Press, 1987), and Karen Sánchez-Eppler, *Touching Liberty: Abolition, Feminism and the Politics of the Body* (Berkeley: University of California Press, 1993).

7. Frederick Douglass, *My Bondage and My Freedom*, ed. with a new introduction by Philip S. Foner (New York: Dover, 1969), p. v. All further quotations from the 1855 version of Douglass's narrative will be from this edition and will be noted in the text.

8. For example, in *Ruth Hall*, Ruth's younger daughter, Katy, finds herself captive in the home of her grandparents where she is physically abused and eventually rescued by her mother. In *Hagar, the Martyr*, Hagar finds herself at the mercy of the evil Laird, who threatens to disclose her identity as his slave (which she is not) unless she agrees to marry him. Ellen Montgomery similarly must endure a period of captivity, which she experiences as a form of slavery, as a "net from which she had no power to get free," when she is adopted by her relatives in Scotland who demand that she change her name, break off all former attachments, and submit to their will in all things. Susan Warner, *The Wide, Wide World*, with an afterword by Jane Tompkins (New York: Feminist Press, 1987), p. 520. All further quotations from Warner will be from this edition and will be noted in the text.

9. *Running a Thousand Miles for Freedom or The Escape of William and Ellen Craft from Slavery*, in *Great Slave Narratives*, selected and introduced by Arna Bontemps (Boston: Beacon Press, 1969), p. 301. All further quotations from the Crafts will be from this edition and will be noted in the text.

10. This observation has been made by many readers of the slave narrative. See, for example, William L. Andrews, *To Tell a Free Story: The First Century of Afro-American Autobiography, 1760–1865* (Urbana: University of Illinois Press, 1986), Henry Louis Gates, Jr., *Figures in Black: Words, Signs, and the "Racial" Self* (Oxford: Oxford University Press, 1987), and Ann Fabian, *The Unvarnished Truth: Personal Narratives in Nineteenth-Century America* (Berkeley: University of California Press, 2000).

11. E. D. E. N. Southworth, *The Hidden Hand, or Capitola the Madcap*, ed. Joanne Dobson (New Brunswick: Rutgers University Press, 1988), p. 53.

12. Caroline Lee Hentz, *Marcus Warland; or, The Long Moss Spring. A Tale of the South* (Philadelphia: A. Hart, late Carey & Hart, 1852), p. 265. All further quotations from *Marcus Warland* will be from this edition and will be noted in the text.

13. James W. C. Pennington, *The Fugitive Blacksmith or Events in the History of James W. C. Pennington Pastor of a Presbyterian Church New York, Formerly a Slave in the State of Maryland* in *Great Slave Narratives*, selected and introduced by Arna Bontemps (Boston: Beacon Press, 1969), p. 239. All further quotations from Pennington's narrative will be from this edition and will be noted in the text.

14. On slave narratives and the complexity of temporal representation, see Gates, *Figures in Black* and *The Signifying Monkey, A Theory of African American Literary Criticism* (Oxford: Oxford University Press, 1988), esp. pp. 156–57.

15. Solomon Northup, *Twelve Years a Slave. Narrative of Solomon Northup, a Citizen of New-York, Kidnapped in Washington City in 1841, and Rescued in 1853, from a Cotton Plantation near the Red River, in Louisiana*, ed. by Sue Eakin and Joseph Logsdon (Baton Rouge: Louisiana State University Press, 1968), p. 103. All further quotations from Northup will be from this edition and will be noted in the text.

16. Orlando Patterson, *Slavery and Social Death* (Cambridge, MA: Harvard University Press, 1982).

17. Mary Hayden Green Pike, *Ida May; A Story of Things Actual and Possible* (Boston: Phillips, Sampson and Company, 1854), p. 197. All further quotations from *Ida May* will be from this edition and will be noted in the text.

18. Mrs. H. Marion Stephens, *Hagar, the Martyr; or, Passion and Reality. A Tale of the North and South* (New York: W. P. Fetridge & Co., 1854), p. 101. All further quotations from *Hagar* will be from this edition and will be noted in the text.

19. Baym, *Women's Fiction*, p. 165. See also Elizabeth Barnes's reading of *The Lamplighter* in *States of Sympathy: Seduction and Democracy in the American Novel* (New York: Columbia University Press, 1997). Susan K. Harris argues that the "formulaic" happy endings of sentimental novels are, in fact, "cover[s] for a far more radical vision of female possibilities embedded in the texts" (*19th-Century American Women's Novels: Interpretive Strategies* [Cambridge: Cambridge University Press, 1990], pp. 12–13). Such absurdities were occasionally remarked

upon by antebellum reviewers as well. *The Knickerbocker*, for example, said this about the conclusion of Maria McIntosh's *The Lofty and the Lowly*: "Donald, Charles, Wharton, and Grahame all marry each other's sisters, and produce a family that will puzzle the most learned of genealogists" (Vol. XVI, March 1853, no. 3, p. 265).

20. Toni Morrison, *Playing in the Dark: Whiteness and the Literary Imagination* (New York: Vintage Books, 1993), p. 46. Morrison's fictional response to these issues is *Beloved*. Sethe, the protagonist, "had to do something with her hands because she was remembering something she had forgotten she knew" (New York: Signet, 1987), p. 61.

PART III

The Slave Narrative and the African American Literary Tradition

8

ROBERT F. REID-PHARR

The slave narrative and early Black American literature

There is perhaps no stronger impetus within the study of Black American literature and culture than the will to return, the desire to name the original, the source, the root, that seminal moment at which the many-tongued diversity of ancient West Africa gave way to the monolingualism of black North America. This explains why within the span of no more than fifty years the polite nomenclature that has been used to define "us" has moved decidedly backwards. Colored, Negro, Black and finally African. With each renaming one imagines a people groping ever closer to the mystery of their collective truth, a truth always buried within an always heavily veiled past. Thus it should come as no surprise that our theoretical and historical practices so often work to reiterate a sort of "Big Bang" conception of Black American life and culture. Bang. An organic, if multiform, African whole was assaulted, destroyed, and scattered to the far ends of the globe. And, miraculously, modern Black American culture developed at those many awkward locations at which the broken shards of ancient Africa caught, coalesced, melted, and melded into a new and vibrant people. This is, in fact, the idea that stands behind the notion that black literature presumably became more muddled and less sophisticated as it moved from the "simple truths" articulated with slave narratives and toward the "complicated imaginings" of presumably more creative forms.

I begin by re-articulating this central conceit within the study of Black American literature not to suggest that the work of historical recovery has somehow been miraculously accomplished. Nor do I wish to deny the deep connections that exist between Black America and West Africa, ancient and otherwise. Instead, I would suggest that we are seriously handicapped by our over-utilization of linear and singular conceptions of the development of Black American culture. Of course we are all aware that Black Americans have from the seventeenth century forward utilized an amalgam of practices and aesthetics emanating from African, European, and (aboriginal) American sources to produce our distinctive New World cultural forms.

Moreover, we should be equally aware, at this late date, that even when one says "Africa," "Europe," or "America" one has hardly settled the debate. In truth, the African cultures that were encountered by Dutch, French, Spanish, Portuguese, and English slavers were just as complex (one almost wants to say cosmopolitan) as were the European societies that "discovered" them.

Thus if we take literature produced in colonial, early national, and antebellum America to represent basic structures of Black American experience, then we will have to read these texts for the ways in which they represent an intricacy that is belied by notions of a devastated African culture seeking to re-establish itself within American contexts. We should pay close attention, then, to a number of significant realities: the fact that early Black American literature was primarily written within urban contexts, that it was heavily influenced by extremely well-established traditions of abolitionist and religious literature, and that it both debunked and reiterated the many stereotypes of Black American persons, slave and free, extant within early American society. Moreover, the forms of early Black American writing – slave narratives, poetry, novels, newspapers, and essays – required just as much stylistic and conceptual complexity from Black American authors as they did from their white counterparts.

We might begin to bring some of these ideas into focus by dwelling for a moment on the difficulty posed by one of the most cherished originating texts within the Black American literary canon, Olaudah Equiano's pseudonymous *Interesting Narrative of the Life of Gustavus Vassa, the African.* This work, originally published in 1789, is now available in a number of handsome editions that are widely read and taught in the United States. Moreover, the secret of its appeal is undoubtedly the remarkably clear picture that Equiano provides of the traditional West African culture in which he was nurtured until his capture at about age ten. The great difficulty for a Black American reading public, however, may be the fact that this glimpse into a bucolic African past is evidence that Vassa may not, in fact, be "one of us." Obviously all black writers and black texts were oddities in the eighteenth- and nineteenth-century Anglo-American world. This notion of the black writer's outsider status (no matter the location of that writer's birthplace) was, therefore, a constant theme within the literature. Still, that Equiano was born in West Africa, that he first published the *Interesting Narrative* in London, that he traveled extensively, and that he married and eventually settled in Britain while continuing to edit the text over the course of his lifetime all work together to make it difficult to claim Vassa and his work as specifically Black American. This is all exacerbated by the many supporting documents that attend the *Interesting Narrative*, documents that attest to the hybrid or, better put, multivocal nature of Equiano's efforts. Vassa (who eventually became something like a respectable English gentleman) does not provide in his narrative the clearly articulated bridge to the African past that so many in Black America sought. Instead, the text itself becomes evidence of the rather profound manner in which Black American literature can always be said to be mediated and mediating, always returning home but never quite arriving.

Of course, as Frances Foster reminds us, black texts, particularly slave narratives, had from the beginning to conform to the demands of eighteenth- and nineteenth-century reading publics.[1] A significant portion of early Black American literature, including work by American-born authors, was published in London for white audiences sympathetic to abolitionist thought and rhetoric but profoundly racist nonetheless. At the same time, many texts attempted the difficult work of shuttling back and forth between these readers and a minority of literate Black Americans who were eager to see the contradictions of their experience and thought represented on the page.

One of the greatest of these contradictions was the simple fact that though most slave narratives gestured toward rural, agricultural societies, the authors and audiences of these texts were most often urban and, as I have suggested of Vassa, cosmopolitan. By 1830 there were some 125,000 free blacks in the Northeast of the United States. One of the ways in which antebellum America looked significantly different from colonial and early national America was that with the close of slavery in the North one no longer found the black population scattered throughout the region. Instead, Black Americans congregated in just a handful of population centers, particularly New York and Philadelphia, locations that I have referred to as "the uncontested pinnacles of black publishing."[2]

In this regard, it is important to note that the first newspaper published by Black Americans, *Freedom's Journal* (1827), was produced in New York City almost immediately after the end of slavery in the state. In 1829 the paper changed its name to *The Rights of All*. This was followed in 1837 by *The Weekly Advocate*, later renamed *The Colored American*. Then came the *Elevator* (1842), the *Anglo-American* (1843), *Rising Sun* (1847), Frederick Douglass's famed *North Star* (1847), the *Daily Creole* (1856), and the *New Orleans Tribune* (1864). In all, some two dozen periodicals were published by blacks before the close of the Civil War.[3]

All of these papers and magazines were heavily dependent upon the patronage and largesse of black urban populations in the Northeast, Southeast and Middle West. Thus, given that a vibrant journalistic tradition developed alongside the tradition of slave narratives and novels, we are wrong when we narrate a Black American writing tradition that developed spontaneously from the cotton and tobacco fields of the slave South. Indeed there was an impressive amount of cross-fertilization between different genres of black writing in early national and antebellum America. One might easily find that the same person who wrote a moving slave narrative was also a journalist, a poet, a playwright, and even a novelist.

This was true of William Wells Brown, who wrote the first Black American novel, *Clotel, or the President's Daughter* (1853). Further, one of the finest novels produced by a Black American prior to the close of the Civil War, Martin Delany's *Blake, or the Huts of America*, was first serialized in the *Anglo-African* magazine between 1859 and 1861. Therefore, though students of early Black American literature and culture very often bemoan the loss of our earliest artifacts, we should not forget that the Black American community developed within the context of the highly developed print cultures of colonial and early national America. The earliest traditions and techniques of Black American intellectuals, most particularly those established within the novels, newspapers, political tracts, and poetry of eighteenth- and nineteenth-century Black American authors, may not have been so much lost as ignored.

Black newspapers and, more importantly, the urban environments in which they were published did not provide unique physical and social apparatuses for the development of a specifically Black American literature. It is important to remember how unsettled notions of black community and black culture were prior to the Civil War. Not only were many of the most significant Black American intellectuals and activists former slaves – Olaudah Equiano, Frederick Douglass, William Wells Brown, Sojourner Truth, and Harriet Jacobs among many others – but also many of these individuals had traveled great distances, geographical, social, and mental, to establish themselves in the "free" North. Once there, they were met by other Black Americans, many of them fugitives, all of whom were busily engaged in piecing together new forms of community and kinship. Perhaps more important still, these individuals attempted this difficult work within urban contexts where they necessarily operated cheek by jowl with individuals who represented a great variety of ethnicities, social classes, religions, and political tendencies. Therefore, early Black American literature had necessarily to represent a complex, some would say hybrid, conception of history and community.

The feminist cultural and literary critic Hazel Carby has argued that "no language or experience is divorced from the shared context in which different groups that share a language express their differing group interests."[4] It follows that, as literary production is, in fact, a social activity, what one discovers in any published text is a give and take (at the very least between author and audience) in which competing versions of "reality" are recognized, if not always reconciled. This is precisely what Bakhtin is attempting to get at when he speaks of "polyglossia" within the modern novel. He suggests that the novel always speaks with many voices. Thus the job of the novelist is not to discipline his work into some sort of clumsy singularity but instead to orchestrate the often contradictory elements of the work that he is attempting to produce into a lucid and coherent whole. The rare artist who is successful at this endeavor may end up producing a piece of literature whose effect is, as Bakhtin would have it, carnivalesque.[5] That is to say, though novels are always produced and organized, they are never fully under the control of either the novelist or his community. Like carnival celebrations, they represent both societal norms as well as the many ways those norms are contested.

We have, thus, laid the groundwork for a sympathetic reading of early Black American literature, particularly novels. First, our discussion of travel, cities, newspapers, and the literary activities that they supported reconstructs the complicated and contradictory contexts in which early Black American literature was produced. Second, the work of Carby and Bakhtin reminds us that this literature cannot – and should not – be extricated from these same contexts. Instead, the work of the artist is always to negotiate these contradictions, not to deny them.

The simple procedures above allow us to approach a work like William Wells Brown's *Clotel, or the President's Daughter* in a manner that might help us to remove the veil of hostility through which far too many critics have looked at this important text. *Clotel*'s many faults are immediately apparent. It treats what at the time was taken to be an ugly piece of gossip – that Thomas Jefferson fathered several children with his slave concubine, Sally Hemmings. Moreover, by doing so the text initiates the Black American novelistic tradition with a mixed-race, fair-skinned character whom many have taken as evidence of some sort of internalized racism on the part of Brown. Still others have suggested that Brown, along with many other early Black American authors, populated their works with fair-skinned characters in order to pander to their mainly white readership. To make matters worse, Brown borrows heavily from a minstrel tradition in which dark-skinned black slaves provided comic relief with their continual malapropisms and clownish antics. Take, for example, the character Pompey, who reappears in a number of Brown's texts: "Pomp, as he was usually called . . . was of real Negro blood, and would often say, when alluding to himself, 'Dis nigger am no counterfeit, he is de ginuine artikle. Dis chile is none of your haf-and-haf, dere is no bogus about him."[6]

These many "difficult" aspects of Brown's work have been read far too often as proof that early black literature is by necessity bad black literature.

Many have assumed that in making the transition from the slave narrative to the novel, Black American intellectuals stumbled almost immediately into the terrain of cliché and unquestioned antiblack racism. Indeed, one can find a wealth of cliché, stereotype, and amateurish writing in the work of early Black American novelists, poets, journalists, essayists, and playwrights. The presence of these elements, however, particularly within a novel like *Clotel*, does not suggest that Black American intellectuals were ill-equipped to move from the supposed realism of the slave narrative to the fantasy and farce of the novel.

As Henry Louis Gates, Jr. reminds us, slave narrators often took great liberties in the telling of their presumably distinct and peculiar stories of bondage and escape. Even, and especially, a writer with the fantastic gifts of Frederick Douglass was extremely careful to mold his own life story in such a manner as to produce the greatest political and emotional effect. "Frederick Douglass took wide liberties with the order and narrating of the 'facts' about his experiences as a slave," Gates argues, "and that . . . reinforces a more subtle re-evaluation of Douglass as a language-using, social, historical, and individual entity."[7] Stated more simply still, Frederick Douglass was certainly not above dissimulation. One might argue, in fact, that Douglass's careful molding of his own life story, his production of himself as a peculiar individual imbedded within a social, political, and literary universe with specific rules of engagement, if you will, was absolutely necessary if Douglass was to achieve the public presence that he was after and that indeed we continue to celebrate today.

Slave narrators, in other words, were just as susceptible to the coercion of markets and audiences as were other early Black American writers. Indeed, all our literary and intellectual forebears had to negotiate existing cultural forms in the production of their art. Thus it is not fair to dismiss an author like William Wells Brown because he turned to images he had seen on the minstrel stage in order to produce *Clotel*. Brown was in fact very clever in his negotiation of these ugly antiblack stereotypes. As we have seen, Pomp says, "'Dis nigger am no counterfeit, he is de ginuine artikle. Dis chile is none of your haf-and-haf, dere is no bogus about him.'"[8] The careful reader of Brown's text will understand the intense irony that is on display here. Not only is Pompey a character who has been specifically created to feed the desires of an American audience, he is also one who, Brown informs us, works to prepare slaves for the auction block by darkening their skin and removing gray whiskers. It seems clear, then, that Brown is winking at his audience when he presents us with a character who is, on the one hand, expert at occluding the truth but who, on the other, speaks with such force about so-called black authenticity.

While Brown presumably cheapens his novel by dwelling on gossip about Thomas Jefferson and Sally Hemmings, he also reminds us of the fact that informal modes of conveying information are often much more reliable than official channels. Given that it is only within the last decade that the Jefferson family finally admitted to the relationship between the third president and his slave, it becomes clear that what Brown does is to create space for Black American literature precisely by avoiding the wide leafy avenues down which writers like Franklin, Emerson, and Jefferson himself traveled, and instead attending to the back alleys overflowing with minstrelsy and gossip but full of useful information and great artistic promise nonetheless.

In this way, we can resist the positivistic tendencies that still continue to hold sway within the study of Black American literature and culture. We are wrong to place Black American literature, early or otherwise, on some poorly imagined historical grid in which one might track the continual improvement of so-called Black letters. With my discussions of travel, cities, (literary) dissimulation, and audience I have worked to debunk what I have called the "Big Bang Theory" of Black American literature. The earliest texts produced by Black Americans were neither the worst nor the most naive within the tradition. This indeed is why I began with consideration of a figure as complicated as Equiano, an individual who lacked everything but talent, but who nonetheless produced a text that in terms of rhetorical sophistication and cosmopolitan content rivaled the best works of its time.

Again the work of Hazel Carby is instructive. She writes that the mulatta figure, continually present in nineteenth- and early twentieth-century Black American literature:

> allowed for movement between two worlds, white and black, and acted as a literary displacement of the actual increasing separation of the races. The mulatta figure was a recognition of the difference between and separateness of the two races at the same time as it was a product of a sexual relationship between black and white.[9]

Carby's straightforward analysis of the mulatta character in American fiction goes a long way toward allowing us to move beyond the tendency to dismiss the efforts of early Black American writers like William Wells Brown – a tendency that is still very much alive within the study and criticism of Black American literature. That said, we should be careful not to assume that all of our eighteenth- and nineteenth-century forebears were as "racially progressive" as Carby's comments might have one believe.

Indeed, one of the things that has long stood in the way of our truly appreciating early Black American literature is the simple fact that it has taken us so very long to read early works within the contexts suggested by the authors themselves. That is to say, there are a number of important Black American works that were largely ignored when they were first published and that continue to be treated as anomalies, false starts, or straight-out failures. Such is the case with Frank Webb's important, if underexamined, 1857 novel, *The Garies and Their Friends*. This text tells the story of Clarence Garie, a (white) Georgia planter who marries his beautiful slave concubine, Emily, and moves with her and their children, Clarence and Emily, to Philadelphia. There they are befriended by the Ellises, "a highly respectable and industrious coloured family," composed of a mother, father, and their three children: Esther, Caddy, and Charlie. By the end of the novel both Mr. and Mrs. Garie are dead. Mr. Garie is killed during a race riot by his neighbor and distant relative, Mr. Stevens, while Mrs. Garie dies in the family's woodshed delivering her stillborn child, the very sign of the couple's thwarted attempts to establish new forms of family and civility. For his part, Mr. Ellis is severely wounded during the riot, paving the way for the ascendency of a new generation of Black American moderns as represented by the three important families that form out of the ashes of the older community. The valiant black real-estate speculator, Mr. Walters, marries the Ellis's older daugher, Esther. Charlie marries young Emily Garie. Finally, the irascible Kinch, a comical dark-skinned character who almost perfectly references William Wells Brown's Pompey, marries Caddy Ellis. And in keeping with the novel's theme of extreme tidiness, young Clarence Garie dies near the end of the text, never relinquishing his claims on whiteness or his desire for the (white) girl next door.

Immediately one is struck while reading *The Garies* by how closely this text hews to the "Big Bang Theory" of Black American culture. It seems, in fact, that the horrific tragedy of the race riot, with its murders, rapes, thefts, and profound displacements, was necessary if the modern Black American community was to come into existence. Indeed, one of the things that Frank Webb does with great finesse is to demonstrate that imbedded within the idea that the Black American community has lost access to its past because of the horrific violence visited upon it by others is a certain unspoken (black) hostility to that same past. We see in *The Garies* the half-formed idea that a difficult figure like Clarence Garie is nonetheless (like the Africans referenced by Equiano) not quite "one of us." Thus, though I applaud the efforts of Hazel Carby to resuscitate the mulatta figure, it is important that we own the profound hostility and ambiguity that such a figure evokes.

The will to deny the profound ambiguity and contradiction that defined the culture of colonial, early national, and antebellum America is not simply a tendency among Black Americans. An example here is Harriet Beecher Stowe's well-known distaste for so-called race-mixing. Even as we assume that American culture has tended to diminish notions of racial distinctiveness, exactly the opposite may be true. Indeed, instead of taking the decidedly American desire to return to our "origins" as a natural outgrowth of our country's traditions of immigration and slavery, we should recognize this articulation of desire as a primary mode in our efforts to organize and discipline cultural memory.

Let us, with this idea in mind, approach Harriet Wilson's fine novel, *Our Nig or, Sketches From the Life of a Free Black, In a Two-Story White House, North* (1859). Therein, Mag Smith, a destitute white woman living alone in a small New England town, marries a black man, Jim, and bears him two children. When Jim dies, Mag begins a relationship with another black man, Seth, who eventually leaves with her and one of the children while the second, Frado, is deposited with a local white family, the Bellmonts. Once established in the Bellmont home Frado is worked like a slave, "Our Nig," and beaten unmercifully by Mrs. Bellmont and her daughter, Mary. Of course, the ideological work that the beating does is to reassure the Bellmont family and presumably the larger white community that though this young, attractive, "yellow" girl lives under the same roof as the Bellmonts, she indeed does not belong. The punches, the pinches, the slaps, the pieces of wood wedged into her mouth reiterate "the fact" of Frado's African origins, her separateness from the metaphorical American family represented by the Bellmonts. Further, at the most basic level the violence preempts the type of gossip that surrounded even a figure as respected and prominent as Thomas Jefferson. A girl so abused could not possibly be the progeny of the master of the household. Frado is no lost daughter brought home by a repentant Mr. Bellmont. Thus there is no question as to lovely Mary's own racial purity, nor that of any of the other "white" members of the Bellmont family.

The game being played here is one quite a bit different from the enactment of racial antipathy that generations of Americans have so glibly narrated as a natural aspect of our shared culture. Instead, what we see is a wholesale denial of the possibility that the national drama did *not* begin with pure Africans coming into contact with pristine Europeans, but rather with our realization and negotiation of the always already mixed nature of our origins and traditions. Just as the most distinguished, if not the most gifted, of American historians vehemently denied that Jefferson, the greatest of our forefathers, could possibly have sired yellow and brown children, so too the Bellmonts deny that Frado possesses even the slightest family resemblance. Of course, both these claims are belied by the brave, difficult work of historians like Martha Hodes, who remind us that so-called miscegenation was actually quite common in colonial and early national America.[10] Moreover, racial panic in the antebellum period was a result not so much of the sudden recognition that the United States was a multiracial nation but, on the contrary, the even more pressing recognition that, left to their own designs, Americans, bluebloods all, were as happy as anyone to leave their children with a touch of the tarbrush.

There is a way in which the revisionist nature of my comments forces me to ignore some of the more obvious aspects of early Black American literature. To the extent that the slave narrative can be said to have been the dominant form prior to the American Civil War, one has to take into account both the extreme efforts made on the part of enslaved persons to become literate (a theme that has been developed quite ably by Robert Stepto) as well as the incredible journeys that many persons undertook in order to attain their freedom.[11] The story of Henry "Box" Brown, who mailed himself North, or William and Ellen Craft, who "cross-dressed," she as an ill white man, he as a trusted servant, to "run a thousand miles for freedom" come readily to mind. And there is perhaps no better-wrought story of flight than that of Henry Bibb, who negotiated swamps, slave hunters, and wild animals in his efforts to free himself and his family. Still, what we often take to be the "truth" of the slave fugitive – the daring late-night run, the desperate flight just ahead of dogs and trackers, the retreat into forests, the unexpected help of white and black conductors on the underground railroad – may not be the fugitive's *only* story, but instead *a* story that has come to stand in for all others. Further, this displacement was accomplished through the careful manipulation of culture by Americans of every hue.

Understanding this simple fact might help us better appreciate Martin Delany's fantastic novel, *Blake, or the Huts of America*, a work that helped establish many of the images of the fugitive with which we are now so familiar. The work tells the story of Henry "Henrico" Blacus, who attempts to reunify a family that has been torn apart by a deceitful and lascivious master. That is to say, Delany transforms the narrative of the gallant slave fugitive fighting for freedom and family, the same narrative that we witnessed earlier with Bibb, into a metaphor for nascent Black American nationalism.[12] In this sense, the fugitive acts as an almost perfect example of what Benedict Anderson has described as a sociological organism, that character who allows the reader to see and understand his profound connections to a larger community.[13] Blake travels throughout the slave South, Africa, the Indian territories, and finally Cuba in search of his wife and child. In the process, he works to demonstrate the contours of Black America. Thus he acts as the very thread that draws together many disparate peoples into a sort of Black American whole.

This procedure is accomplished much more easily and straightforwardly by a traveling subject. Indeed, part of the reason that early works by black female writers like Harriet Wilson's *Our Nig* or Harriet Jacobs's *Incidents in the Life of a Slave Girl* were marginalized in the Black American literary canon was the fact that these texts treated of characters who were trapped in particular (and peculiar?) domestic spaces.[14] As we saw above, Wilson's Frado was kept as a virtual prisoner in the household of the white Bellmonts, while Jacobs's Linda retreated to the crawl space in her grandmother's attic for seven years. The result was that while these texts were surprisingly articulate regarding questions of black interiority and the slave's intimate relations with white masters, they were nonetheless often ignored precisely because they lacked utility within the nationalist projects that have dominated Black American literary and cultural life since the antebellum period. That is to say, they did not reproduce that all-important "bang."

In closing, let us consider one more Black American author who, like Olaudah Equiano, produces considerable difficulties for students of Black American literary history. Early in 2002 Henry Louis Gates, Jr. published Hannah Craft's *The Bondwoman's Narrative*, an act that immediately threw critics and historians into fits of anxiety and frustration. Of course, there was the matter of origins. For if this text was indeed written in 1851, it would predate *Clotel* by two years and would become, as Gates suggests, the first novel written by a fugitive slave. This matter is complicated by the fact that *The Bondwoman's Narrative* was first published in 2001. One might properly expect, then, a sort of chicken-and-egg debate over the two novels for some time to come. There is also the subject of the novel's provenance. Who was the living individual standing behind the name "Hannah Craft"? This question remains unsettled, though a number of historians and genealogists are in hot pursuit of the answer.

The even greater difficulty, however, is that the novel borrows so heavily and so unapologetically both from classic British literature (especially Dickens and the Brontës) and the narratives of other escaped slaves. These are all mixed, gumbo-style, with the author's own poignant observations. That is to say, this is a novel in which there is very little effort to disguise the polyglossia that Bakhtin describes. Instead, as Gates argues in his introduction, the text is rather shockingly naive in its deployment of the devices used by one author to obscure her reliance on another.

Craft is not a sophisticated writer, in a lot of ways, and she clearly did not have a well-developed sense of authorship and ownership. She threw all of herself into this book, but she threw in others, too. There's almost a sense of a person educating herself in what she considers to be a proper literary style. To read the book is to witness this process of self-education. Craft's unorthodox pattern of lifting passages from other novels and dropping them into her own, often quite arbitrarily, is one of several reflections of her status as an uneducated former slave, obviously unaware of the conventions and rules governing paraphrase, citation, and attribution. It is highly unlikely that a middle-class white author would have made such naïve errors.[15]

Gates's comments and the literary historical tendencies they represent accuse Craft of naiveté. In contrast, we can instead read the author's naive relationship to citation and attribution and her lack of fussiness in relation to (literary) origins as the only viable mode of production available to slaves, ex-slaves, and their descendants. This type of clumsy pastiche is precisely the type of relationship to culture and history that has enabled the undisputed sophistication of Black American cultural production. In fact, it would be difficult to imagine a serious treatment of early Black American music and musicianship that worried in this way about the "parroting" of white European forms. What we see with Gates, then, is again the anxiety that no matter how diligently we examine the archive, we may never find that first truly exceptional black author whose simple efforts led to the multiform complexities of contemporary Black American writing. Instead of "Bang, it all begins" we must be content with "A little of this, a little of that, and keep stirring."

It is time for students of early Black American literature to give up on discovering African or European origins and to focus instead on what we already know or can know about our culture. I have focused, then, on those aspects of early Black American history that have been extremely important to the development of Black American literature: travel, cities, newspapers, cross-fertilizations, and the anxieties that attend them. My own conceit is that Black American culture represents a new start within modern history not because we have produced forms that are distinct from all others but instead because we have seen fit to borrow promiscuously, clumsily, and naively from the many traditions within our considerable reach. It is widely understood and accepted that the Black American has vigorously resisted the lie of race and nation in search of the knowledge and insight necessary for our community's unlikely survival. What may be more difficult to accept is the reality that we have been none too careful in covering our tracks in the process.

Indeed, the first and perhaps only right of the slave, stripped of nation and culture, home and tradition, is the right to assume that he – or more likely she – is always a beginning, an origin, an unlikely source. I take great pride in those many moments within early Black American literature in which authors break the rules, in which they refuse to establish proper allegiances to the presumably sophisticated modes and methods of Europe, Africa, *or* America.

This messy, parodic, over-determined, promiscuous, multiform, and naive tradition represents the best part of the fantastic legacy that has been left to us by Craft, Bibb, Brown, Douglass, Delany, Wilson, Webb, Jacobs, Equiano, and the many other early Black American intellectuals whom they represent. And if this is not a bang, then it is so very much more than a whimper.

NOTES

1. Frances Smith Foster, *Witnessing Slavery: The Development of the Ante-Bellum Slave Narratives* (Westport, CT: Greenwood Press, 1979).
2. Robert F. Reid-Pharr, *Conjugal Union: The Body, the House and the Black American* (New York: Oxford University Press, 1999). See also Jane H. Pease and William H. Pease, *They Who Would be Free: Blacks' Search for Freedom, 1830–1860* (Urbana: University of Illinois Press, 1974).
3. See Penelope Bullock, *The Afro-American Periodical Press, 1838–1909* (Baton Rouge: Louisiana State University Press, 1981); Frankie Hutton, *The Early Black Press in America, 1827–1860* (Westport, CT: Greenwood Press, 1993).
4. Hazel Carby, *Reconstructing Womanhood: The Emergence of the Afro-American Woman Novelist* (New York: Oxford University Press, 1987), pp. 16–17.
5. Mikhail M. Bakhtin, *The Dialogic Imagination: Four Essays*. Translated by Michael Holquist and Caryl Emerson. (Houston: University of Texas Press, 1981); *Rabelais and His World*. Translated by Helene Iswolsky. (Cambridge: MIT Press, 1968).
6. William Wells Brown, *My Southern Home: or, the South and its People* in *From Fugitive to Free Man: The Autobiographies of William Wells Brown*. William L. Andrews, ed. (1880. Rpt. New York: Mentor, 1993), pp. 191–92.
7. Henry Louis Gates, Jr., *Figures in Black: Words, Signs and the "Racial" Self* (New York: Oxford University Press, 1987), p. 115.
8. Brown, *My Southern Home* in Andrews, *Free Man*, pp. 191–92.
9. Carby, *Reconstructing Womanhood*, p. 90.
10. Martha Hodes, *White Women, Black Men: Illicit Sex in the Nineteenth Century South* (New Haven: Yale University Press, 1997).
11. See Robert Stepto, *From behind the Veil: A Study of Afro-American Narrative* (Urbana: University of Illinois Press, 1979).
12. Henry Bibb, *Narrative of the Life and Adventures of Henry Bibb, an American Slave, Written By Himself* 3rd edn, (1850. New York: Negro Universities Press, 1969).
13. See Benedict Anderson, *Imagined Communities: Reflections on the Origin and Spread of Nationalism* (New York: Verso, 1983).
14. See "Black, White, and Yeller," in Robert F. Reid-Pharr, *Conjugal Union: The Body, the House and the Black American* (New York: Oxford University Press, 1999).
15. Henry Louis Gates, "Preface to the Trade Edition," in Hannah Craft, *The Bondwoman's Narrative* (New York: Warner Books, 2002), p. xix.

9

DEBORAH E. McDOWELL

Telling slavery in "freedom's" time: post-Reconstruction and the Harlem Renaissance

Summarizing the condition of Southern blacks following the Civil War and Reconstruction's end, W. E. B. Du Bois was uncharacteristically terse: "The slave went free; stood a brief moment in the sun; then moved back again toward slavery."[1] In Du Bois's compressed account of African American history, one phase blurs so easily into the other that the distance separating slavery from freedom is difficult to fathom. The phase during which the "slave went free" and then passed that liquid "moment in the sun" could seem to augur not just the transformation of socio-political circumstances for African Americans, but also the expansion of aesthetic options beyond the realm of personal testimony and the slave narrative. For generations, African American writers had been duty-bound to the conventions of these forms, which had been instrumental in the protracted campaign to end the Atlantic slave trade and to abolish slavery. But inasmuch as the abolition of chattel slavery did not make real Emancipation's proclamation that all former slaves would be "henceforth and forever free," the slave narrative continued to play a dominant role in African American letters from the end of the Civil War until well into the 1920s.[2] But to observe that the slave narrative remained a viable form well into the 1920s is not to say that African American writers accepted uncritically its salient tactics or conventions. Even as they advanced the genre's political drives, along with its fervent commitments to forging social change, African American writers continually grappled with the generic conventions of the slave narrative. At one level, that grappling offers us an excursion into the dynamics of continuity and change observable in the historical development of any literary genre, but the struggle of African American writers with this distinguished form went beyond generic matters: it bespoke a vexed relationship to the institution of slavery itself.

The writers covered in this essay, which spans the post-Reconstruction era to the Harlem Renaissance, all confronted the challenges of representing slavery in "freedom's" time. How could they treat the subject of slavery when the urgencies of abolitionism had passed? Much of the work produced during this stretch (roughly 1892–1928) might be seen to explore, directly or indirectly, the question David Brion Davis posed succinctly in *The Problem of Slavery in Western Culture*: Was the past a "seedbed of the future, or . . . a rotting husk that threatened to impede healthy growth?"[3]

Although vestiges of slavery perpetually haunted the hopes and future prospects of African Americans, especially following Reconstruction's end in 1877, the generation of writers emerging in its aftermath attempted to soften those horrors. If the fugitive slave narrative had underlined slavery's horrors iconicized in "bullwhips and iron chains and auction blocks, and slave coffles and empty stomachs and broken hearts," post-bellum narratives, both fiction and non-fiction alike, were dedicated to the "proposition that something positive, something sustaining, could be gleaned from that past."[4] Ron Eyerman agrees, noting that African American writers of the post-Reconstruction era were "shaped by the promise of Emancipation" and thus "looked expectantly toward the future, not the past." For them, slavery was "treated not as the ultimate evil it was in abolitionist literature, but as a tragic condition which brought hardship and misery to black people, but which also provided grounds for racial uplift" and the promise of a brighter future.[5]

The promises of Reconstruction

"There is light beyond the darkness"
(Frances E. W. Harper, *A Brighter Coming Day*)

For Frances E. W. Harper, among the most popular African American writers of the late nineteenth century, such a future could be but faintly glimpsed, even during the seemingly promising days of Reconstruction. As she had indicated in a July 1867 speech, the South of Reconstruction was actually "unreconstructed," a "sad place . . . rife with mournful remains and sad revelations of the past." Interestingly, in setting her 1892 novel, *Iola Leroy*, during the Civil War and early Reconstruction, Harper illustrates a complex view of history, one that necessitated looking simultaneously toward the future and the past. Such a dual perspective held clear implications for her narrative choices. Long a lecturer on the abolitionist circuit, Harper, both during and after Reconstruction, displayed in her work alliances with the antislavery literary tradition, even as she tweaked the generic conventions of the fugitive slave narrative, particularly its catalogue of slavery's horrors and abuses. For example, while emphasizing the separation of families and the threat of sexual violation, *Iola Leroy* "does not simply rehearse the outrages of slavery."[6] Nor, for that matter, does it replace slavery's outrages with those committed against blacks during and after Reconstruction when mob violence and lynching reigned supreme. Harper did not gloss over these evils but, never one to dwell on doleful matters, she prophesied that even though slavery's "shadows" obscured the hopes of Reconstruction, the "promise of a brighter coming day" remained.[7] That Harper repeated this image in the poem that closes *Iola Leroy* says much about her forward-looking inclinations. In the rhyming stanzas typical of her poetry, Harper writes,

> There is light beyond the darkness,
>   Joy beyond the present pain.
> There is hope in God's great justice
>   And the Negro's rising brain.
>
> Though the morning seems to linger
>   O'er the hilltops, far away
> Yet the Shadows bear the promise
>   Of a brighter coming day.[8]

Considering the gloomy historical setting of *Iola Leroy*, one could question its surface optimism and pious sentiments, especially as they seem tied to Christian doctrine. But Harper's projected brighter future does not reflect blind and passive faith, for the future for Black Americans is tied not just to "God's great justice" but also to the "Negro's rising brain." Here, Harper, who expressed a desire to "grasp the pen and wield it as a power for good," stresses that link between knowledge and power, between aesthetics and politics, associated so strongly with the slave narrative. But importantly, Harper understood the power of literacy to liberate or enslave by turns, which point she dramatizes in the many scenes of instruction, both in and out of formal classrooms, that crop up in *Iola Leroy*. Students must learn to manipulate language and literacy in ways that fall outside conventional bounds and escape the ken of former slaveholders. In one of many scenes of stolen knowledge that call to mind the fugitive slave narrative, one character in the novel "sold his cap for a book"; another "made the beach of the river his copybook, and thus he learned to write" (p. 45), while yet another "tore up a book, greased the pages, and hid them in his hat" (p. 44).

Although Harper stakes African American future prospects to the acquisition of literacy, thus maintaining her connection to the abolitionist tradition, she understood that such an emphasis effectively discounted the vital role that illiterate former slaves, as well as their descendants, had played and could continue to play in a future Black America. If literacy, as well as assumptions about black progress, was all too often presumed to be the exclusive province of that elite corps of intellectuals whom W. E. B. Du Bois would later term "The Talented Tenth," Harper constructs a more democratic constituency that includes the literate and illiterate alike. But, more important, she demonstrates that those illiterate former slaves were practiced in the arts of "reading" beyond the book. In other words, Harper distinguished between "reading" as deciphering marks and letters and "reading" as interpreting an arcane set of signs and symbols, a coded language developed by illiterate slaves. Significantly, the book opens on this coded language through which those enslaved "convey[ed] in the most unsuspected manner news to each other from the battle-field" (p. 9). Even bed sheets could be hung in different ways to signal the enemy's movements to soldiers encamped near Rebel lines. The narrative's play on "sheets" is not its only riff on reading, for it makes repeated references to the face as page or script or book. Aunt Linda cannot "read de newspapers, but ole Missus' Face is newspaper nuff for me" (p. 9). Similarly, while the parents of Iola's pupils are "ignorant of books, human faces were the scrolls" they'd read for ages (p. 146).

Harper expands her concerns with "face reading" to accommodate her critique of the paradoxes of "race" as well as the irrationalities of color prejudice in the United States. She channels this critique through the mulatto figure, who functions in *Iola Leroy* much as it did in abolitionist slave narratives and fiction: to embody the sexual exploitation of black women by white men. But writing in an era when racial separatism was legalized throughout the Jim Crow South and "whiteness" became a valuable "property" which blackness could not claim, Harper deployed the mulatto as the flashpoint for the US cultural debate on "blood," bloodlines, and the origins of the "human family." Much like her contemporaries – Pauline Hopkins in *Of One Blood* (1903) and Charles W. Chesnutt in *The House behind the Cedars* (1900) and *The Marrow of Tradition* (1901) – Harper used the mulatto in a bid to shift definitions of race from biology to culture, from an ocular-driven means of understanding race (that which depends on visually recognizing the "signs" of blackness) to one that makes seeing (and thus "knowing") race distinctly unreliable. Even so, while *Iola Leroy* may underscore that racial identity is unstable, the novel is fully invested in an idea of race associated with "kinship" and synonymous with "family."

If the slave narrative of the abolitionist era focused on the separation of families, judging it one of slavery's greatest sins, narratives during and after Reconstruction focused on reunions. These decidedly matrifocal reunion plots point to divergent strands in Harper's literary legacies, strands distinctly gendered. The plot of family reunion so central to *Iola Leroy*, as well as to Pauline Hopkins's *Contending Forces* and *Of One Blood*, might be seen as a legacy of Harriet Jacobs's *Incidents in the Life of a Slave Girl* (1861), a text widely regarded as counterpoint to the individualistic template of the slave narrative, set perhaps most strongly by Douglass's *Narrative* (1845). Jean Fagan Yellin is correct in noting that, in Jacobs's hand, "the slave narrative is changed from the story of a hero who single-handedly seeks freedom and literacy to the story of a hero tightly bound to family and community who seeks freedom and a home for her children."[9]

This equation of "freedom" with family constitutes not only a break with that class of slave narratives that presented the stories of independent "self-made men" but also a release from that commitment to facticity or historicity demanded of abolitionist writing even in fictive forms. That release afforded African American writers the freedom to experiment with a variety of literary subgenres, which, for Harper, included trying her hand at utopian fiction. From the Greek *outopia*, meaning "no place," and *eutopia*, meaning "good place," utopia refers to a non-existent reality to an ideal place, in a future time, hovering faintly on the horizon. As that "brief moment in the sun" of Du Bois's description, Reconstruction died while barely born, leaving former slaves, freed men and women, to imagine a different Southern space (in Harper's words) "for those who had passed from the old oligarchy of slavery into the new commonwealth of freedom" (p. 271).

"Up" from the slave narrative

"The School of American Slavery"
(Booker T. Washington, *Up From Slavery*)

Harper's reference here to "the new commonwealth of freedom" could only be interpreted as utopian, given the dystopian reality – slavery in form if not in fact – that defined 1890s America. As the century turned, African Americans confronted what W. E. B. Du Bois famously termed "the problem of 'the color line.'" That invisible but powerful social divide structured to "separate" the races, the color line was policed so violently in turn-of-the-century America even as (undoubtedly because) crossing it had mainly proved the custom of the country. Amid this climate of inter-racial sexual violence and intimidation, economic exploitation, and political disenfranchisement, Booker T. Washington came to prominence and dedicated himself to making Tuskegee Institute, the school he established in 1881, a "Black Utopia."

Washington's "utopia" was not projected in a distant future or set in fantasy's domain, but rather in that very violent Black Belt of the South. It was here that Washington urged African Americans to "cast down their bucket[s]," the familiar refrain of his controversial "Atlanta Exposition Address" (1895).[10] Earlier that year Frederick Douglass had died. Perhaps abolitionism's most strident voice and Black America's most revered and preeminent leader, Douglass had come to prominence picturing slavery's horrors and calling for black resistance to slavery's oppressive force. Douglass's death can be seen to have left a vacuum in black leadership, and Washington was primed to step into the breach. Although Washington idolized Douglass (he even wrote a biography of the leader) and devoutly desired to become his heir apparent, he "offer[ed] himself and his autobiographies as correctives or replacements for Douglass's life and works" and for the antebellum slave narrative more generally.[11]

Up from Slavery signaled a "new wave of revisionism in post-bellum Afro-American literature," insofar as representations of slavery were concerned. No longer needing to denounce slavery to white America, turn-of-the-century slave narrators cast slavery in pragmatic perspective.[12] Whereas Douglass had likened slavery to a "tomb," Washington likened it to a "school," writing in Up from Slavery, "Notwithstanding the cruelty and moral wrongs inflicted upon us, the black man got nearly as much out of slavery as the white man did" (p. 37). He reassured his readers that the "members of my race entertain no feelings of bitterness against the [Southern] whites" (pp. 35, 37).

Critics have typically read these early passages as evidence of Washington's subservience, and, to be sure, his overall portrayal of slavery in Up from Slavery softened its horrors, much as did his portrayal of the post-Reconstruction-era South. At critical moments, however, Washington exhibited duplicity toward slavery. This duplicity informed his narrative strategies throughout Up from Slavery, perhaps nowhere more explicitly than in the quaint anecdotes of homemade caps and ginger cakes, and of spoons of molasses trickling from the "big house." Among these ingratiating anecdotes, Washington's account of boyhood Sunday mornings at the plantation stands out. Significantly, Washington incorporates this memory in a larger account, "The Secret of Success in Public Speaking," which directly follows "The Atlanta Exposition Address." The passage from Up from Slavery must be quoted in full:

> I rarely take part in one of these long dinners that I do not wish that I could put myself back in the little cabin where I was a slave boy, and again go through the experience there – one that I shall never forget – of getting molasses to eat once a week from the 'big house.' Our usual diet on the plantation was corn bread and pork, but on Sunday morning my mother was permitted to bring down a little molasses from the 'big house' for her three children, and when it was received how I did wish that every day was Sunday! I would get my tin plate and hold it up for the sweet morsel, but I would always shut my eyes while the molasses was being poured out into the plate, with the hope that when I opened them I would be surprised to see how much I had got. When I opened my eyes I would tip the plate in one direction and another, so as to make the

molasses spread all over it, in the full belief that there would be more of it and that it would last longer if spread out in this way. So strong are my childish impressions of those Sunday morning feasts that it would be pretty hard for any one to convince me that there is not more molasses on a plate when it is spread all over the plate than when it occupies a little corner – if there is a corner in a plate. At any rate, I have never believed in 'cornering' syrup. My share of the syrup was usually about two tablespoonfuls, and those two spoonfuls of molasses were much more enjoyable to me than is a fourteen-course dinner after which I am to speak. (p. 162)

This charming memory of the child's Sunday morning treat enables Washington to perform an oblique analysis of the economics of slavery and the politics of food, through the seemingly benign and "innocent" filter of childhood consciousness. Washington's repeated reference to "corner" (the last to "cornering") simultaneously describes the "tin plate," tipped to disguise his meager portion, and underscores the economic disparities between those in the slave cabin and those in the "big house." But Washington makes this point obliquely, hitting, in the language of the African American vernacular, a "straight lick with a crooked stick."

In this narrative that pulled itself up from the slave narrative, Washington avoided the genre's straightforward rehearsal of slavery's wrongs, producing a counter-narrative which seemed aglow with optimism at a time when the noose of disenfranchisement was tightened literally and figuratively around the necks of Black Americans. But as I've suggested, Washington's stance toward slavery in this revisionist slave narrative is far from simple. If he seemed to some all too eager to downplay slavery's scourges so as to curry the favor and approval of his financial backers while marking his own upward progress, he may actually have "slipped the yoke" in *Up from Slavery*, offering, in the process, but one example of the myriad strategies African American writers devised in response to the shifting trends and expectations in the literary marketplace of America. Any effort to discuss post-bellum responses of African American writers to slavery and the slave narrative must take account of the broader literary trends and market forces of post-bellum America. Many African American writers were caught in the crosshairs of these trends and forces, and perhaps none more so than Charles W. Chesnutt.

Unlike Booker T. Washington, Chesnutt aspired "to be an author," as he put it. Like Washington, he confronted slavery at a moment when the antebellum slave narrative was no longer the most viable literary template for African American writers, but more important, at a moment when dominant cultural memories of slavery, circulating in nineteenth-century popular fiction, had become idyllic and benign. Such works as George Washington

Cable's *Ole Creole Days* (1879), Thomas Nelson Page's *In Ole Virginia* (1887), and Joel Chandler Harris's *Uncle Remus: His Songs and Sayings* (1881) conformed to the nostalgic formulae of the "plantation" fiction of the day which pastoralized slavery and idealized the antebellum South. It is largely against this increasingly popular trend that Charles W. Chesnutt reacted.

Beyond the plantation tradition

In a letter to fellow writer and correspondent George Washington Cable, Chesnutt served notice that he would not bow to any reader expecting his work to conform to the nostalgic formulae of "plantation" fiction, especially not to its stereotypic treatment of former slaves. Their "chief virtues," Chesnutt argued, were evident in "their doglike fidelity to their old masters, for whom they have been willing to sacrifice almost life itself. Such characters exist . . . but I can't write about these people, or rather I won't write about them."[13] No matter the strength and tenor of his resolve, Chesnutt's literary choices were not his alone to make, for the literary marketplace of late nineteenth-century America offered him a limited set of options. On one side lay the plantation fictions and on the other the rabid, racist fiction of Thomas Dixon, from whose novel *The Clansman* D. W. Griffith adapted his infamous film *Birth of a Nation* (1915). For Chesnutt, the "lesser evil" might seem to lie within the plantation formula while exploding its assumptions.

Chesnutt's early stories, especially those collected in *The Conjure Woman* (1899), seemed to take this route, exploiting the "frame story," standard fare in the era's literary magazines. A "new formula for the literary production of Southern-ness," the frame story featured an old black retainer from slavery who plied a white auditor with tales of bygone days.[14] In Chesnutt's conjure tales, that "black retainer" is the wily Uncle Julius, and his auditors, John and Annie, a Northern white couple who have purchased the old North Carolina plantation on which Julius was a slave. Highly successful, Chesnutt's conjure stories eventually brought him national attention and acclaim, but he chafed at the thought that he was identified mainly as one who wrote quaint tales of "bygone" days.

Indeed, Chesnutt seemed to have tired of the formula even before it began to bring his name and work to the attention of an enthusiastic public. As early as 1889, ten years before the conjure stories were collected, he wrote to Albion Tourgee, enclosing a copy of "Dave's Neckliss," a story interestingly not included among the previously published stories that made up *The Conjure Woman*, though Chesnutt thought it "the best" of his stories. "Dave's Neckliss" was meant to mark the start of a new literary direction for Chesnutt beyond the frame device of the conjure tales, but more important, it was meant to mark his break with the "old Negro." As he put it, "I think I have used up the old Negro who serves as mouthpiece, and I shall drop him in future stories, as well as much of the dialect." He continued, "I tried in this story to get out of the realm of superstition into the region of feeling and passion." In that same letter to Tourgee Chesnutt mentioned a forthcoming "Southern story," one "not of slavery exactly, but showing the fruits of slavery." For Chesnutt, the "fruits of slavery" were the "sins of the fathers," the slaveholders, whose children were robbed of their birthrights (often used to liquidate their "father's" debts) and relegated to the margins of society.[15]

The realm of "feeling and passion" that Chesnutt attempted to explore in "Dave's Neckliss" and beyond did not endear him to the critics. As he abandoned the seeming simplicities of the conjure tales his audience declined, as did the support he had first enjoyed from members of the American literary establishment. William Dean Howells, editor of *The Atlantic Monthly*, the prestigious literary magazine in which some of Chesnutt's early work appeared, reviewed *The Marrow of Tradition* (1901), Chesnutt's best-known novel, judging it a "bitter, bitter" book, marked "more [by] justice than mercy."[16]

Perhaps the deepest roots of Howell's rejection lay in Chesnutt's insistent investment in exploring "stories of the color line," particularly those concerned with miscegenation, racial passing, and the wages of "whiteness." Like so many of his African American contemporaries, Chesnutt sought to "disrupt the literary economy of whiteness at the turn of the century." He wrestled with a difficult and central question, notes Mason Stokes: "How is it possible to intervene in the literary economy of whiteness without simultaneously becoming invested in that economy?" After all, "one isn't either in or out of whiteness; rather, one always exists in some relation to it."[17] No one understood this more profoundly than did W. E. B. Du Bois, and never more so than in his famous "double-consciousness" formulation.

The world inside the veil

For a great many students of African American letters, considerations of Du Bois's life and work must begin there in "Of Our Spiritual Strivings," the first chapter of *The Souls of Black Folk* (1903), where he describes the "Negro," who inhabits a "world which yields him no true self-consciousness," a world that condemns him to "double-consciousness," this "sense of always looking at [him]self through the eyes of others" (those others being whites).[18] But no sooner has Du Bois begun this disquisition on the psychic lives of Black

Americans than he interrupts himself to pass again on slavery, which he termed the "sum of all villainies, the cause of all sorrow, the root of all prejudice" (p. 12). Although he never experienced slavery first-hand – he was born on free soil in Great Barrington, Massachusetts – Du Bois was nonetheless acutely sensitive to slavery "both as an institution in American history and as an idea," argues Arnold Rampersad. Slavery was the subject of his Harvard doctoral thesis, *The Suppression of the African Slave-Trade to the United States of America* (1896), and slavery figured prominently in his corpus overall. But of all of Du Bois's writings on slavery, perhaps none has exerted more power and influence than has *The Souls of Black Folk*.

Many have read *The Souls* as a direct challenge to post-bellum representations of slavery, particularly Booker T. Washington's *Up from Slavery*, but also as a challenge to the forms and assumptions of the slave narrative. Whereas, you will recall, Washington had portrayed slavery's benignant side, likening it to a school, Du Bois found slavery a social evil, the germ of a range of intractable social ills amounting to a form of neo-slavery. Whereas Washington's tone in *Up from Slavery* was characteristically optimistic, *The Souls* was mournful and melancholic. In "The Apology" chapter of his *Dusk of Dawn* (1940), for example, Du Bois indicated that *The Souls* was "written in tears," was "a cry at midnight thick within the veil, when no one rightly knew the coming day."[19]

The Souls is a catalogue of losses – grand and small, public and private – for which Du Bois grieves in fits and starts. But the book takes a particular and panoramic view of the losses African Americans had suffered historically, beginning with the rupture of the Middle Passage: "slave-ship[s] . . . groan[ing] across the Atlantic" carrying "faint cries [which] burdened the Southern breeze" (p. 135). Slavery, Du Bois writes, was "the cause of all sorrow" (p. 12), and when it ended, it left the "weeping freedmen" "without a cent," "without a home," "without land, tools, and savings" (pp. 28, 14). He likened the death of the Freedmen's Bureau to "the passing of a great institution" (p. 33), and in his running descriptions of its aftermath, Du Bois refers repeatedly to images of death and grief and ruin. Taken together, these images could clearly suggest that the conventional trajectory of the slave narrative – from slavery to freedom, from South to North, ill-suited Du Bois's purposes in *The Souls*, for as he put it, writing at the dawn of the twentieth century, forty years after Emancipation, "the freedman has not yet found in freedom his promised land" (p. 12).

If the "slavery to freedom" arc of the antebellum slave narrative did not entirely suit Du Bois's purposes, its peripatetic structure did, for among its varied functions, the slave narrative symbolically challenged the spatial limitations that slavery imposed. But even so, *The Souls* reverses that which

Robert Stepto terms "the seminal journey in Afro-American narrative": toward the North.[20] Starting from Great Barrington, Massachusetts and moving to various Southern points, Du Bois's reverse migration returns his readers to the ground of constriction, of confinement, the former site of slavery, thus establishing his resistance to ideologies of progress, even those vaguely implied by the conventional forward movement of the slave narrative.

We might argue that, from its very first incarnation, Briton Hammon's *Narrative of the Uncommon Sufferings and Surprising Deliverance of Briton Hammon* (1760), the slave narrative, as Hammon's title suggests, has been devoted to chronicling the "uncommon sufferings" and then "surprising deliverance" of black captives.[21] For Du Bois, however, there was to be no "deliverance," certainly not executed by "the kind Providence of a good God" (Hammon, *Narrative*, p. 523). There was no "North Star" to follow, no refuge from the wilderness of slavery to be found anywhere on US soil in Du Bois's melancholic view.

Not only did *The Souls* abandon the developmental logic of the antebellum slave narrative (the arc from "slavery to freedom," from "captivity to deliverance"), it helped to inaugurate an "inward" turn, a shift to the psychic, the spiritual realm in which Black Americans lived and moved. In asking in *The Souls* at the outset, "How does it feel to be a problem?" (p. 9), Du Bois announced his interest in this inner landscape even as he understood the psychic and the social to be thoroughly intertwined. While the antebellum slave narrative had excelled at cataloguing the physical and material realities of slaves, especially as made manifest in bodily abuses of various kinds, it mainly drew a veil across what Du Bois would term, in the chapter titled "Of the Sons of Master and Man," the realm of "thought and feeling" (p. 115).

Not only does Du Bois unveil this realm in appealing to sentiment and emotion throughout *The Souls*, he represents himself as a man of feeling, prepared to "sweep the Veil away and cry" (p. 141). In attempting to capture the "storm and stress," the "ferment of feeling" among Black Americans in the post-Reconstruction South, Du Bois saw himself as representing phenomena mainly "outside of written history" (p. 115), but in the process he provided his readers a written history of his own interior landscape, particularly in the prose elegies "Of Alexander Crummell" and "The Passing of the First-Born." In this sense, *The Souls* not only opened channels often sealed in the antebellum slave narrative, it helped to pave the way for alternative models for subsequent African American writers, models associated with at least two objectives of modernism: to represent human consciousness and emotion, and to question, if not reject, preexisting modes of representation.

In his enigmatic novel, *The Autobiography of an Ex-Colored Man*, James Weldon Johnson showed his indebtedness to Du Bois, even appropriating his famous "double-consciousness" trope. That Johnson ends the *Autobiography* focused on the "inner life" of an isolated character who has the luxury of "analy[zing] his feelings," as opposed to "publicly fighting the cause of [the] race," partly indicates the distance African American narrative had traveled since the slave narrative, ante- and post-bellum.[22] First published anonymously in 1912, then re-published in 1927 under Johnson's name, the *Autobiography* has sometimes seemed to echo the slave narratives even as its revises the genre's salient tropes. Among the text's most obvious connections to the slave narrative, at least those written by men, is its treatment of the relation between genealogy and racial identity. Never acknowledged by his white father, Johnson's narrator fills his life with father substitutes, most notably the wealthy white patron, with whom he forms a relationship more reminiscent of that of master to slave. Hired to play piano at the patron's parties, he must agree not to "play any engagements . . . except by his instructions" and when he "'loaned' me to some of his friends" (pp. 120–21). But while these and other isolated aspects of the novel may recall the slave narrative, *The Autobiography* clearly abandons that genre's project, especially pertaining to ideas of self, identity, cultural belonging, and racial responsibility.

Donald Goellnicht is right to argue that "The *Ex-Colored Man*'s narrative calls into question the validity of the idealism and the certitude of identity expressed in many autobiographies of (ex)-slaves."[23] While the narrator gestures toward the high ideals of these "race men" and women, who advanced the cause of black liberation through art and once had dreams of "bringing glory and honour to the Negro race" (p. 46), he ultimately makes a mockery of these ideals by passing as a white man and devoting himself to realizing a "white man's success": making money (p. 193). Forsaking the activist legacies of "race men," Johnson's narrator lacks even the fiber to make the conscious choice to cross the color line, writing: "I finally made up my mind that I would neither disclaim the black race nor claim the white race; but that I would change my name, raise a moustache, and let the world take me for what it would" (p. 191).

As Giulia Fabi notes, "In contrast to turn-of-the-century characters such as Iola Leroy . . . who embark on a series of learning experiences . . . motivated by race loyalty [that] lead to race consciousness," for Johnson's narrator "'becoming' black is just the first of many temporary metamorphoses." Further, the act of passing does not create for him "psychological torture" but is, rather, an attempt to escape such torture.[24] It is after witnessing a lynching that he decides to leave the South. As he looks on the "scorched post," the "blackened bones, charred fragments" and catches the "smell of burnt flesh," he is overcome with "humiliation and shame . . . shame that I belonged to a race that could be so dealt with, and shame for my country, that it, the great example of democracy to the world, should be the only civilized, if not the only state on earth, where a human being would be burned alive" (p. 188). In fleeing the South, Johnson's narrator is presumably fleeing a form of slavery in "modern" guise – the threat of lynching and the realities of caste that racial segregation imposed – but, importantly, he is also fleeing the psychological and emotional effects of his tangled genealogy, most notably shame. While passing may have liberated him from economic anxieties and social persecution, it burdens him with an all-consuming dread. He embodies that restlessness and anomie explored in much modernist fiction, that sense of psychic crisis and despair, that skepticism toward the idea of a grounded human subject at "home" in the world. In creating a peripatetic character whose restless movement enables him to shed the burden of race, rather than find his psychic grounding in it, Johnson implied a clear critique both of the prerogatives of the antebellum slave narrative and the late nineteenth-century project of racial uplift. In this sense he is best seen as a transitional figure linking the nineteenth century to the Harlem Renaissance, the "old" Negro to the new.

The idea of a Renaissance in Harlem

"Out From the Gloomy Past"
(James Weldon Johnson, "Lift Every Voice and Sing")

What distinguished "The New Negro" from the "old" would become a matter of some contention. For Alain Locke, "The New Negro" represented, first and foremost, a "vibrant . . . new psychology," a "spiritual emancipation," "buoyancy from within." In his titular essay to *The New Negro* (1925), the volume credited with launching the Harlem Renaissance, Locke saw that spirit exemplified in Langston Hughes's poem "Youth," which he ran in the body of the essay:

> We have tomorrow
> Bright before us
> Like a flame.
>
> Yesterday, a night-gone thing
> A sun-down name.
> And dawn today
> Broad arch above the road we came.
> We march![25]

Its images of dawn and movement, of a sun gone down on yesterday, gave the poem, like Locke's essay, a millennialist inflection, that is, the tone of heralding a new, more perfect age. This "self-willed beginning," as Henry Louis Gates, Jr. describes the trope of the "new Negro," depended fundamentally upon "self-negation, turning away from the . . . labyrinthine memory of black enslavement."[26] Although Locke never mentions slavery by name, its spectral presence is evident in his references to the "'aunties,' 'uncles' and 'mammies,'" to "Uncle Tom and Sambo," all of whom have "passed on."

Zora Neale Hurston registered her relation to slavery much more forthrightly in her frequently anthologized essay, "How it Feels to be Colored Me" (1928):

> Someone is always at my elbow reminding me that I am the granddaughter of slaves. It fails to register depression with me. Slavery is sixty years in the past. The operation was successful and the patient is doing well, thank you. The terrible struggle that made me an American out of a potential slave said "On the line!" The Reconstruction said "Get set!"; and the generation before said "Go!" I am off to a flying start and I must not halt in the stretch to look behind and weep. Slavery is the price I paid for civilization.[27]

Vaguely analogous to Booker T. Washington's metaphor of slavery as school, Hurston's image of slavery as successful operation has exasperated generations of scholars, who cannot square that characterization with Hurston's more radical views on race and African American history, or with her later depiction of the institution in *Their Eyes Were Watching God* (1937). But here in "How it Feels to be Colored Me" Hurston separates herself from the "sobbing school of negrohood who hold that nature somehow has given them a lowdown dirty deal and whose feelings are all hurt about it." While they are "weep[ing] at the world," she is "busy sharpening [her] oyster knife" (p. 152).

Here, Hurston's references to slavery, along with Locke's to "Uncle Tom," to mammies and sambos, are among the few literal references to slavery in the writings of the Harlem Renaissance, for the outward spirit of the movement seemed incompatible with the crucible that was slavery. At least some writers of the period seemed to indicate that that tortured past could be erased with rhetorical flourish and fiat, with the mere proclamation of "the new." And even if those who could see slavery's legacies in the current socio-political circumstances of African Americans, then so be it; they need not allow "social discrimination to segregate [them] mentally"; they could take their writing to a different place.[28] Indeed, the writing could itself, in time, prove socially liberating, or so many thought, which notion amounted, argues David Levering Lewis, to a belief in Civil Rights by copyright.

Much of Locke's heady optimism can be attributed to the post-World War I zeitgeist of progressivism, but perhaps, more compellingly, to the promises of the Great Migration. The exodus of masses of African Americans into the urban centers of the USA was inspired by faith in the possibility of a community outside the South, beyond the grip of slavery and segregation's scourge. Harlem was one such ideal community, a utopia that could be realized. Harlem was fast becoming what James Weldon Johnson called the "culture capital" in the essay he contributed to Locke's *New Negro* anthology. The overweening optimism, the emancipatory energies, the preoccupation with "newness" reflected in Locke and Johnson's contributions to *The New Negro* were far from being representative of the spirit and tone of the Harlem Renaissance. Indeed, other selections in the volume sound more sobering notes, both as regards the future possibilities of Harlem, as well as its relation to the Southern past.

Of course, not everyone associated with the Harlem Renaissance was equally invested in newness and youth or scornful of the Southern past. Notably, Jean Toomer, like Zora Neale Hurston, saw the values of African American culture rooted in the South. In *Cane* (1923), he attempted to capture the spirit of what he termed the "song-lit race of slaves" before the "epoch's sun declines."

> An everlasting song, a singing tree,
> Caroling softly souls of slavery,
> What they were, and what they are to me,
> Caroling softly souls of slavery.[29]

In other words, for Toomer, slavery constituted a "usable past" epitomized in the music that slaves and their descendants produced – the spirituals, the folk melodies. By the time Toomer moved to Sparta, Georgia, where he prepared himself to write *Cane* by "listening to the old folk melodies that Negro women sang at sun-down" (p. 148), he observed that these songs were dying out. Casualties of what he termed "mechanical civilization," they were also succumbing to black ambivalence about the slave past. "I learned," Toomer wrote, that the "Negroes of the town objected to them. They called them 'shouting.' They had victrolas and player-pianos . . . So I realized with deep regret, that the spirituals, meeting ridicule would be certain to die out" (p. 142).

It would clearly oversimplify the matter to counter-pose the elegiac spirit of Jean Toomer's *Cane* to the manifestoes cum birth announcements of the Harlem Renaissance. After all, three years before Alain Locke and others began to herald a "new" art spawned from a transformed racial consciousness, Toomer had produced in *Cane* a book that realized, particularly in its spatial structure, the modernist demand to "make it new."

Despite the emancipatory proclamations, the Harlem Renaissance, like artistic movements generally, was an amalgam of continuity and change. The insistent pronouncement that a new day had dawned/was dawning for African Americans seemed at times to be more fantasy than fact. A mere sixty years in the distance, slavery's legacies, even its psychic legacies, could not be so easily exorcised. Indeed, it could be argued that underneath the optimistic claims and declarations of independence from the past lay not only slavery's spectral presence, but also perhaps the intimation that slavery was a source of shame. It is striking to note the frequency with which shame appears in writings of the period, even in the manifestoes of the new. Langston Hughes ends his famous essay "The Negro Artist and the Racial Mountain" with the assertion that "We younger Negro artists who create now intend to express our individual dark-skinned selves without fear or shame."[30] And Nella Larsen's *Quicksand* offers a portrait of Helga, a character (significantly, an artist-figure) who is gripped by shame, paralyzed by "nameless, shameful impulse[s]."[31] Prior to rejecting the marriage proposal of a white man, while invoking "race and shame" (p. 88), Helga had broken her engagement to a black man, because the knowledge that only sex bound him to her "filled her with a sensation amounting almost to shame" (p. 8). It is not only the shame of sex that leads to her undoing, but the fact of her existence as a "despised mulatto" (p. 18), who compulsively "recall[s] the shames and . . . absolute horrors of [Black American] existence in America" (p. 82).

For a brief period, many writers of the Harlem Renaissance created the illusion that they could forget that shame and horror, epitomized for many by slavery and its legacies. And if the past could not be simply willed away, then it could be hidden beneath the clang and glitter of the Jazz Age and the modernist drumbeat of the new. But the Depression brought an end to the future of this illusion. Interestingly, slavery, only sixty years gone, then re-emerged as a compelling topic for artistic and intellectual exploration. It is tempting to argue that W. E. B. Du Bois's *Black Reconstruction* may have helped to set the stage for its re-emergence with his thumbnail history of Reconstruction: "The slave went free; stood a brief moment in the sun; then moved back again toward slavery" (p. 30). Published in the middle of the 1930s, this book suspended, at least for its over 700 pages, all talk of the future, all talk of the "new." The very next year, Arna Bontemps published his novel *Black Thunder*, a treatment of Gabriel Prosser's 1800 slave revolt in Richmond, Virginia. As Bontemps puts it, "the gloom of the darkening Depression [was] settling all around us," and in that context, he continues, "I began to ponder the stricken slave's will to freedom." The question "Don't you want to be free?," repeated throughout the novel, resounded beyond the historical moment of Bontemps's recreation, for, as Arnold Rampersad notes, Bontemps had "discovered a link between the slave narratives and the revolutionary social and political goals" of the 1930s.[32]

The decade of the 1930s closed on a large-scale reclamation of narratives of slavery in the form of the over 2,000 interviews with ex-slaves compiled by the Works Progress Administration between 1936 and 1938. While scholars continue to debate their value and reliability and point to the difficulties they present for historical accuracy and scholarly interpretation, the sheer volume of these accounts establishes nothing more profoundly than that, sixty years removed from slavery, the institution was still alive, if only on the friable and often unreliable chords of memory.

NOTES

1. W. E. B. Du Bois, *Black Reconstruction in America* (New York: Russell and Russell, 1962 [1935]), p. 30.
2. William L. Andrews, "Reunion in the Post-Bellum Slave Narrative: Frederick Douglass and Elizabeth Keckley," *Black American Literature Forum* (spring 1989), 14.
3. David Brion Davis, *The Problem of Slavery in Western Culture* (Ithaca: Cornell University Press, 1966), p. 425.
4. Marion Wilson Starling, *The Slave Narrative: Its Place in American History* (Boston: G. K. Hall, 1982), p. 176; Andrews, "Reunion," p. 14.
5. Ron Eyerman, *Cultural Trauma: Slavery and the Formation of African American Identity* (Cambridge: Cambridge University Press, 2001), p. 45.
6. William L. Andrews, *The African American Novel in the Age of Reaction* (New York: Penguin, 1992), p. x.
7. Frances Smith Foster, ed., *A Brighter Coming Day: A Frances Ellen Watkins Harper Reader* (New York: The Feminist Press, 1990), p. 121.
8. Frances E. W. Harper, *Iola Leroy* (Boston: Beacon Press, 1987 [1892]), p. 282. All further quotations from this book will be from this edition and will be noted parenthetically within the text.
9. Harriet Jacobs, *Incidents in the Life of a Slave Girl*, ed. Jean Fagan Yellin (Cambridge: Harvard University Press, 1987), p. 34.
10. Booker T. Washington, *Up from Slavery* in *Three Negro Classics*. John Hope Franklin, ed. (New York: Avon, 1965), p. 146. All further quotations from this book will be from this edition and will be noted parenthetically within the text.
11. David Dudley, *My Father's Shadow: Intergenerational Conflict in African American Men's Autobiography* (Philadelphia: University of Pennsylvania Press, 1991), p. 31.
12. See William L. Andrews, "The Representation of Slavery and Rise of Afro-American Literary Realism, 1865–1920" in *Slavery and the Literary Imagination*. Deborah E. McDowell and Arnold Rampersad, eds. (Baltimore: Johns Hopkins University Press, 1989).

13. Joseph McElrath and Robert Leitz, eds., *"To Be an Author": Letters of Charles W. Chesnutt* (Princeton: Princeton University Press, 1997).
14. Richard Brodhead, *Culture of Letters: Scenes of Reading and Writing in Nineteenth Century America* (Chicago: University of Chicago Press), p. 196.
15. McElrath and Leitz, *"To Be an Author,"* p. 44.
16. William Dean Howells, "A Psychological Counter-Current in Recent Fiction," *The North American Review* 173 (December 1901), p. 882.
17. Mason Stokes, *The Color of Sex: Whiteness, Heterosexuality and the Fictions of White Supremacy* (Durham: Duke University Press, 2001), p. 109, 110.
18. W. E. B. Du Bois, *The Souls of Black Folk* (New York: W. W. Norton, 1999 [1903]). All further quotations from this book will be from this edition and will be noted parenthetically within the text.
19. W. E. B. Du Bois, *Dusk of Dawn* (New Brunswick: Transaction Publishers, 1992 [1940]), pp. xxix–xxx.
20. Robert Stepto, *From Behind the Veil: A Study of Afro-American Narrative* (Champaign-Urbana: University of Illinois Press, 1979), p. 67.
21. In Dorothy Porter, ed., *Early Negro Writing* (New York: Beacon Press, 1995), pp. 522–38.
22. James Weldon Johnson, *The Autobiography of an Ex-Colored Man* (New York: Penguin, 1990 [1927]), p. 211. All further quotations from this book will be from this edition and will be noted parenthetically within the text.
23. Donald Goellnicht, "Passing as Autobiography: James Weldon Johnson's *The Autobiography of an Ex-Colored Man.*" *African American Review* 30 (spring 1995), 25.
24. Giulia Fabi, *Passing and the Rise of the African American Novel* (Urbana: University of Illinois Press, 2001), pp. 95, 98.
25. Alain Locke, *The New Negro* (New York: Simon and Schuster, 1992 [1925]).
26. Henry Louis Gates, Jr. "The Trope of the New Negro and the Reconstruction of the Image of the Black," *Representations* (fall 1988), 132.
27. In Alice Walker, ed., *I Love Myself When I Am Laughing* (New York: The Feminist Press, 1979), p. 153.
28. Locke, *The New Negro*, p. 9.
29. Jean Toomer, *Cane* (New York: W. W. Norton, 1988 [1923]).
30. In David Levering Lewis, ed., *Harlem Renaissance Reader* (New York: Viking, 1994), p. 95.
31. Nella Larsen, *Quicksand* (New Brunswick: Rutgers University Press, 1986 [1928]), p. 95.
32. Arna Bontemps, *Black Thunder* (Boston: Beacon Press, 1992 [1936]), pp. xxvi, xii.

10

VALERIE SMITH

Neo-slave narratives

The critical context

The institution of slavery in the United States was a site of unimaginable physical, emotional, and spiritual cruelty, justified by greed and racism, and sanctioned by religion, philosophy, and the law. Written into the nation's founding documents, its very existence betrayed the contradictions at the heart of national identity and consciousness. It is thus little wonder that it has compelled a rich, challenging, and demanding body of cultural products, from sorrow songs and work songs, to the antebellum narratives written by individuals who had emerged from a system that denied them literacy, to an extraordinary genre of retrospective literature about slavery that exploded in the last decades of the twentieth century and shows no signs of abating.

According to conventional wisdom, the term "neo-slave narratives" originated with Bernard W. Bell's 1987 study *The Afro-American Novel and Its Tradition*. Bell described "neo-slave narratives" as "residually oral, modern narratives of escape from bondage to freedom,"[1] although over time that definition has expanded to include a more diverse set of texts than Bell's initial description could have anticipated. This genre, which includes some of the most compelling fiction produced in the last fifty years, has evolved to include texts set during the period of slavery as well as those set afterwards, at any time from the era of Reconstruction until the present. They approach the institution of slavery from a myriad perspectives and embrace a variety of styles of writing: from realist novels grounded in historical research to speculative fiction, postmodern experiments, satire, and works that combine these diverse modes. Their differences notwithstanding, these texts illustrate the centrality of the history and the memory of slavery to our individual, racial, gender, cultural, and national identities. Further, they provide a perspective on a host of issues that resonate in contemporary cultural, historical, critical, and literary discourses, among them: the challenges of representing trauma and traumatic memories; the legacy of slavery (and other atrocities) for subsequent generations; the interconnectedness of constructions of race and gender; the relationship of the body to memory; the agency of the enslaved; the power of orality and of literacy; the ambiguous role of religion; the commodification of black bodies and experiences; and the elusive nature of freedom. The twentieth- and twenty-first century writers of these works of literature possess a measure of creative and rhetorical freedom unavailable to the freed and fugitive slaves who wrote narratives during the antebellum period. Moreover, the contemporary authors write from a perspective informed and enriched by the study of slave narratives, the changing historiography of slavery, the complicated history of race and power relations in America and throughout the world during the twentieth century, and the rise of psychoanalysis and other theoretical frameworks. They are therefore free to use the imagination to explore the unacknowledged and elusive effects of the institution of slavery upon slaves, slaveholders, and their descendants.

The diversity of the neo-slave narratives has inspired a rich array of critical studies. Works such as Ashraf Rushdy's *Neo-Slave Narratives: Studies in the Social Logic of a Literary Form* (1999) and *Remembering Generations: Race and Family in Contemporary African American Fiction* (2001), Caroline Rody's *The Daughter's Return: African American and Caribbean Women's Fictions of History* (2001), Angelyn Mitchell's *The Freedom to Remember: Narrative, Slavery, and Gender in Contemporary Black Women's Fiction* (2002), and Arlene R. Keizer's *Black Subjects: Identity Formation in the Contemporary Narrative of Slavery* (2004), as well as innumerable articles, have advanced a range of theories that expand Bell's initial definition, situate the genre in contemporary cultural politics, and analyze the ideological work these texts perform.

For instance, in *Neo-Slave Narratives* Rushdy defines the genre as "contemporary novels that assume the form, adopt the conventions, and take on the first-person voice of the antebellum slave narrative."[2] He reads the works on which he focuses in light of the social, political, and cultural changes that emerged out of the Black Power and Black Arts movements. Rushdy's later book, *Remembering Generations*, concentrates on a subcategory in the genre, a body of texts he calls "palimpsest narratives," works in which a late twentieth-century African American is haunted by a family secret that involves an antebellum ancestor. Here, Rushdy is particularly concerned with how texts such as Gayl Jones's *Corregidora* (1975), Octavia Butler's *Kindred* (1979), and David Bradley's *The Chaneysville Incident* (1981) "all represent the processes of transmitting and resolving family secrets as a way of showing the perduring effects of slavery on contemporary subjects."[3]

Preferring the term "liberatory narratives" to "neo-slave narratives," Angelyn Mitchell explores how *Kindred*, Sherley Anne Williams's *Dessa*

Rose (1986), Toni Morrison's *Beloved* (1987), J. California Cooper's *Family* (1991), and Lorene Cary's *The Price of a Child* (1995) problematize the meaning of freedom. As she puts it: "the liberatory narrative is self-conscious thematically of its antecedent text, the slave narrative; is centered on its enslaved protagonist's life as a free citizen; and is focused on the protagonist's conception and articulation of herself as a free, autonomous, and self-authorized self."[4]

Caroline Rody and Arlene Keizer expand our perspective on the genre by exploring how writers across the African diaspora engage with the history of slavery. In *The Daughter's Return*, Rody considers the disparate ways in which African American women writers (such as Octavia Butler, Lucille Clifton, Julie Dash, Jewelle Gomez, Paule Marshall, Gloria Naylor, Phyllis Alesia Perry, and Alice Walker) and Caribbean women authors (such as Jamaica Kincaid, Jean Rhys, Michelle Cliff, and Maryse Conde) map revisions of narratives of New World slavery onto feminist allegories of "a daughter's recuperation of a severed mother–daughter relationship."[5] Arlene Keizer argues that works such as *Beloved*, Charles Johnson's *Oxherding Tale* (1982), *Middle Passage* (1990), and "The Education of Mingo" (1977), Paule Marshall's *The Chosen Place, The Timeless People* (1969), Derek Walcott's play, *Dream on Monkey Mountain* (1972), and Carolivia Herron's *Thereafter Johnnie* (1991), which she calls "contemporary narratives of slavery," theorize about "the nature and formation of black subjects, under the slave system and in the present, by utilizing slave characters and the condition of slavery as focal points."[6]

Early texts

Most accounts of the neo-slave narrative as a genre begin with Margaret Walker's *Jubilee* (1966), a magisterial historical novel which draws on Walker's meticulous research to extend the reach of her grandmother's stories of her life in slavery and freedom. While it is true that neo-slave narratives began to appear in earnest after the mid-1970s, no discussion of the genre is complete without some mention of *Black Thunder* by Arna Bontemps (1936). Although it was published during the Depression rather than during the late twentieth century, *Black Thunder* is a compelling novel that anticipates much of the cultural work that later texts in the genre perform.

First, like *Chaneysville*, *Beloved*, Michelle Cliff's *Free Enterprise* (1993), Louise Meriwether's *Fragments of the Ark* (1994), *The Price of a Child*, and so many others, *Black Thunder* uses a real historical event, in this instance the Gabriel Prosser Revolt of 1800, as the point of departure from which to explore a host of complex issues: the meaning of freedom; the ideological connections between the French Revolution, the Haitian Revolution, and the spirit of rebellion among slaves in the United States; the diversity of black male experiences and identities within the institution of slavery; and the complex interaction of Anglo-American and African-derived traditions in the production of black culture, particularly religious practices.[7] Second, as both Hazel V. Carby and Eric J. Sundquist note, Bontemps (who would later edit *Great Slave Narratives*, published in 1969) anticipated the writers and social historians of the 1960s and afterwards by drawing on the slaves' own testimony in order to describe their inner lives. Third, as later writers in this tradition create a subtle conversation between stories based in slavery and contemporary cultural politics, Bontemps likewise turns to the past to illuminate the persistence of injustice and resistance throughout history. In the words with which he begins and ends the foreword to the 1968 edition of the novel, he asserts that time "is not a river. Time is a pendulum" (pp. xxi, xxix). It is thus little wonder that he would be drawn to the story of a slave insurrection at a time when his attention was captivated both by Mahatma Gandhi and the struggle for independence in India, and by the trials of the "Scottsboro Boys."[8]

Black Thunder focuses on the period immediately preceding and following Gabriel Prosser's unsuccessful attempt to emancipate more than a thousand slaves in Virginia. The narrative moves through a variety of perspectives, including those of Gabriel (the fierce and charismatic leader), Pharaoh (a cowardly and insecure field hand of mixed racial origins), Old Ben (a retainer torn between his desire for freedom and his devotion to his master), Mingo (a bold freedman and saddle-maker), Criddle (the brave but dim-witted stable boy), Melody (a freed woman who shares her sexual favors with white men), Juba (the passionate and fearless slave woman who is Gabriel's lover), and two white men who sympathize with the slaves' desire for freedom, M. Creuzot, the French printer, and Alexander Biddenhurst, the lawyer from Philadelphia. Perhaps most strikingly, through the use of interior monologue, the novel also incorporates the collective consciousness of the slave community.[9] In scenes that depict burial rituals, clandestine practices of communication, and discussions of root working, this unattributed group voice conveys the ways in which blacks maintained community within the context of the brutal and dehumanizing conditions of enslavement.

In this novel, versions of the rhetorical question "Don't you want to be free?" recur in conversations between and among black people. The answer to this question proves to be anything but self-evident; through the array of characters, the novel problematizes the very notion of freedom. Mingo and Melody may be free in name, but they are subject to the whims of whites as long as they live in a slaveholding state.[10] Old Ben is not sure that he wants to be free if freedom means leaving his comfortable life with Moseley Sheppard, the white man he has served for many years. And for Gabriel, true freedom is more than a solitary escape. He might well have been able to escape on his own, but his personal freedom is meaningless while others are left behind in slavery. As he puts it: "A man is got a right to have his freedom in the place where he's born. He is got cause to want all his kinfolks free like hisself" (*Black Thunder*, p. 210). In the process of redefining freedom, the text also prompts readers to think what it means to consider the revolt a failure. Gabriel meets his execution with such courage and fortitude that his death testifies to the triumph of the human capacity to conquer oppression.

The neo-slave narratives published during the latter decades of the twentieth century represent slavery from a variety of perspectives and with a broad range of emphases. Satires like Ishmael Reed's *Flight to Canada* (1976) and Charles Johnson's *Oxherding Tale* (1982) use techniques such as humor, hyperbole, and anachronism to underscore the absurdity of the institution itself and of its representations, as well as its links to contemporary practices that commodify black bodies and cultural forms. The subgenre that Rushdy calls "palimpsest narratives" includes works such as *Corregidora*, *Kindred*, and *Chaneysville* in which late twentieth-century characters are haunted by their enslaved ancestors. In *Kindred*, Butler (like Phyllis Alesia Perry in her 1998 novel *Stigmata*) mines the possibilities of the supernatural in order to capture the inextricable ties between the past and the present. Butler's protagonist, Dana, is a young African American woman who lives in California with her white husband, Kevin, in 1976. She finds herself ripped back into antebellum Maryland whenever the life of her white ancestor, Rufus Weylin, is in jeopardy. Thus she agonizes over the fact that although she empathizes with the subjection that Hagar (the enslaved black woman who is also her ancestor) endures, her very existence depends upon her ability to keep Rufus alive long enough to rape and impregnate Hagar.

Set in the context of the bicentennial of US independence, *Kindred* underscores the extent to which American national consciousness depends upon the sexual violation of black women. The fact that Dana confronts her own identity as the product of a coercive relationship between Rufus and Hagar highlights the interdependence of constructions of black and white identities. Finally, during the scenes when Kevin accompanies Dana back to Maryland, they confront the history of white supremacy and racial exploitation that underlies the "color-blind" surface of their post-Civil Rights era inter-racial marriage. For their own safety, Kevin has to "pass" as Dana's master, and he falls into that role all too easily. This experience thus suggests the proximity and connection between slavery and contemporary racial relations.

Many of the works in this genre turn to the story of slavery as a lens through which to examine contemporary issues of gender and sexuality. *Corregidora* considers how the history of an enslaved woman's sexual abuse has become inscribed in the sexuality of her female descendants in the twentieth century. *Dessa Rose* imagines not only the erotic tension of stolen moments of intimacy among slaves, but also the sexual competition and the possibility for collaboration between enslaved black women and free white women in the antebellum South. Works such as *Flight to Canada* and *Oxherding Tale*, like *Black Thunder*, examine how black masculinity is both compromised and asserted within the institution of slavery. David Bradley's *The Chaneysville Incident* considers the weight of this legacy upon a young black man in the twentieth century.

Chaneysville was inspired by the story of a group of thirteen slaves, en route to freedom on the Underground Railroad, who chose to die when they realized that they were about to be recaptured in Bedford County, Pennsylvania. The novel focuses on a young black man's search for the meaning of his father's life and death. The protagonist, a Philadelphia-based professor of history named John Washington, does not know that he is after his father's story when he returns home to western Pennsylvania to nurse (and then to bury) his ailing surrogate-father, Old Jack Crawley. Jack's death prompts him to visit his parents' home and study the exhaustive collection of manuscripts and journals that his late father, Moses Washington, left behind. This research helps him to understand that the meaning of his father's suicide is deeply connected to the slaves' decision to die years before. Moreover, as he creates a coherent account out of these disparate materials to share with Judith, the white psychiatrist with whom he is romantically involved, he comes to understand the role of the imagination in the making of historical narrative.

Chaneysville features two consummate raconteurs, Old Jack and John. Jack, a mangy shoe-shiner who spent his life in an isolated cabin, was one of Moses' closest friends. He assumed responsibility for instructing John in the ways of the woods after Moses' sudden death, teaching him to drink, hunt, fish, and build a fire. Moreover, he spun for John countless yarns about his own escapades with Moses and their mutual friend, Josh White. John's return home triggers flashbacks of his own childhood and adolescent adventures, and recalls a series of the old man's stories.

John appears to have inherited his talent for recording history from Jack, the storyteller, and from Moses, the keeper of documents, although he has difficulty reconciling his analytic and narrative abilities. In the early sections of the novel, he tends to fall into extended, pedantic stories about sociological phenomena and historical events. Indeed, Judith upbraids him for hiding his feelings by talking in lectures. But John learns to transform facts imaginatively when he discovers the store of journals and manuscripts on which his father was working at the time of his death. The data Moses had accumulated means nothing to John until he can reconstruct the minds of his father and of the thirteen slaves. When he can explain what motivated the fugitives to give up their lives, he can also understand his father's reason for taking his own.

Beloved

Based on the true story of Margaret Garner, a slave woman in Boone County, Kentucky, who killed her own child rather than allow her to be sold, Toni Morrison's *Beloved* remains one of the most celebrated contemporary novels of the slave experience and one of the most highly acclaimed novels of the twentieth century. In writing *Beloved*, Morrison confronted, like other writers of neo-slave narratives, the challenge of recovering the lived experience of enslavement given the paucity of available materials from the slaves' perspective. As she remarks in an interview with Marsha Darling, the process of writing the book required her to supplement historical research with the resources of the imagination; only then could she get at the story of the infanticide of a slave child from the child's perspective:

> I did research about a lot of things in this book in order to narrow it, to make it narrow and deep, but I did not do much research on Margaret Garner other than the obvious stuff, because I wanted to invent her life, which is a way of saying I wanted to be accessible to anything the characters had to say about it. Recording her life as lived would not interest me, and would not make me available to anything that might be pertinent. I got to a point where in asking myself who could judge Sethe adequately, since I couldn't, and nobody else that knew her could, really, I felt the only person who could judge her would be the daughter she killed.[11]

Although *Beloved* is based on a real-life incident, Morrison deliberately altered the original account for strategic purposes. Her protagonist left her husband in slavery, escaped to freedom, and remained free with her living children. In contrast, as she remarks to Darling:

> Margaret Garner escaped with her husband and two other men and was returned to slavery . . . [Garner] wasn't tried for killing her child. She was tried for a *real* crime, which was running away – although the abolitionists were trying very hard to get her tried for murder because they wanted the Fugitive Slave Law to be unconstitutional. They did not want her tried on those grounds, so they tried to switch it to murder as a kind of success story.

They thought that they could make it impossible for Ohio, as a free state, to acknowledge the right of a slave-owner to come get those people . . . But they all went back to Boone County and apparently the man who took them back – the man she was going to kill herself and her children to get away from – he sold her down river, which was as bad as was being separated from each other. But apparently the boat hit a sandbar or something, and she fell or jumped with her daughter, her baby, into the water. It is not clear whether she fell or jumped, but they rescued her and I guess she went on down to New Orleans and I don't know.[12]

Set in Cincinnati in 1873, eight years after the end of the Civil War, *Beloved* is nevertheless a novel about slavery. The characters have been so profoundly affected by the experience of slavery that time cannot separate them from its horrors or undo its effects. Indeed, by setting the novel during Reconstruction, Morrison invokes the inescapability of slavery, for the very name assigned to the period calls to mind the havoc and destruction wrought during both the antebellum era and the Civil War years.

A novel as complex as *Beloved* does not lend itself easily to summary. It is a work that explores, among other topics, the workings and the power of memory; to represent the persistence of the past, Morrison eschews linear plot development for a multidirectional narrative into which the past breaks unexpectedly to disrupt the movement forward in time. The novel begins at 124 Bluestone Road, in the household that Sethe, a former slave, shares with her daughter Denver and the ghost of the daughter she killed. Number 124 had once been home also to Baby Suggs, Sethe's mother-in-law, and Howard and Buglar, Sethe's two sons, but Baby Suggs has died and the two boys have run away from the baby ghost.

The trajectory of the plot begins when Paul D, one of Sethe's friends from the Sweet Home plantation, arrives unannounced at her home. In short order they renew their friendship, become lovers, and decide to live together. Paul D tries to rid the house of the presence of the baby ghost, but his attempt at exorcism only triggers her return in another form, as a ghost made flesh and in the form of a young woman.

Sethe and Paul D are both haunted by memories of slavery that they wish to avoid. Sethe tries to block out the experience of being whipped and having her breast milk stolen by the nephew of Schoolteacher (her master's cruel brother-in-law); of killing her daughter to prevent her from being taken back into slavery; and of exchanging sex for the engraving on that same daughter's tombstone. Paul D wants desperately to forget having seen the physical and psychological destruction of the other black men who worked on the Sweet Home plantation; having been forced to wear a bit; and having endured the hardships of the chain gang.

The former slaves' desire for forgetfulness notwithstanding, the past will not be kept at bay. The slightest sensation triggers memories that overwhelm them. Moreover, the novel turns on the embodiment and appearance of Beloved, the daughter Sethe killed in order to prevent her return to slavery. In the intensity of their connections with each other, and in their various encounters and engagements with Beloved, the characters explore what it means for them to confront their past suffering and to move beyond that past. Additionally, through the use of the incarnate ghost, the novel considers the place of black bodies in the construction of narratives of slavery.

Early in her life in freedom, Baby Suggs ministers to the black fugitive and former slaves outside Cincinnati. Her message, which transforms the Christian doctrine of self-abnegation and deliverance after death, is meant to heal the broken and suffering bodies of those who endured slavery. As she herself, with legs, back, head, eyes, hands, kidneys, womb, and tongue broken by slavery, has resolved to use her heart in the service of her vast congregation, she yearns to restore the bodies and spirits of the former slaves through her sermons:

> 'Here,' [Baby Suggs] said, 'in this here place, we flesh; flesh that weeps, laughs; flesh that dances on bare feet in grass. Love it. Love it hard. Yonder they do not love your flesh. They despise it. They don't love your eyes; they'd just as soon pick 'em out. No more do they love the skin on your back . . . So love your neck; put a hand on it, grace it, stroke it and hold it up. And all your inside parts that they'd just as soon slop for hogs, you got to love them. The dark, dark liver – love it, love it, and the beat and beating heart, love that too. More than eyes or feet. More than lungs that have yet to draw free air. More than your life-holding womb and your life-giving private parts, hear me now, love your heart. For this is the prize.'[13]

Readers may be inclined to read Baby Suggs's use of the word "heart" metaphorically, to assume that by "heart" she means compassion. But in the context of this litany of broken body parts, one is reminded that the word "heart" points to an organ as well as to an emotional resource. In this context, it becomes more difficult to make the leap from the corporeal referent to the metaphysical; such an erasure of the corporeal would be all too close to the expendability of black bodies under slavery.

The focus on bodies in the novel is clear both in the predominance of scenes of physical suffering and scarred bodies and also in the characters' sensory experience of their past. During their lives as slaves, Sethe, Paul D, and Baby Suggs know psychological and emotional humiliation. For instance, Paul D is shamed by the knowledge that the barnyard rooster possesses more autonomy than he himself does. Sethe is humiliated by Schoolteacher's efforts to measure and quantify her own and her fellow slaves' racial characteristics. And Sethe and Baby Suggs are acutely sensitive to the power that slavery has over the bonds between kin. Yet despite the recognition of these sorts of philosophical and emotional deprivations, *Beloved* seems especially engaged with the havoc wrought upon black bodies under slavery: the circular scar under Sethe's mother's breast and the bit in her mouth; the bit in Paul D's mouth; Sethe's stolen breast milk and the scars on her back; the roasting body of Sixo, one of the Sweet Home men, to name but a few.

Notwithstanding her attempts to forget her enslavement, Sethe's memories come to her through her body; sensory perceptions set flashbacks in motion. When washing stinging chamomile sap off her legs, the scent and the sensation propel her back into the past:

> The plash of water, the sight of her shoes and stockings awry on the path where she had flung them; or Here Boy lapping in the puddle near her feet, and suddenly there was Sweet Home rolling, rolling, rolling out before her eyes, and although there was not a leaf on that farm that did not want her to scream, it rolled itself out before her in shameless beauty. (p. 6)

Sethe's body is also linked to the past by virtue of the hieroglyphic nature of the scars on her back. She wears on her body the signs of her most arduous ordeal at the Sweet Home plantation. The story of the brutal handling she endured as a slave – the stealing of her breast milk and the beating that ensued – is encoded in the scars on her back. Their symbolic power is evident in the variety of ways that others attempt to read them. For Baby Suggs, the imprint of Sethe's back on the sheets looks like roses of blood. And Paul D, who cannot read the words of the newspaper story about Sethe's act of infanticide, reads her back as a piece of sculpture: "the decorative work of an ironsmith too passionate for display" (p. 17). Paul D further reads the suffering on her body with his own:

> He rubbed his cheek on her back and learned that way her sorrow, the roots of it; its wide trunk and intricate branches . . . [He] would tolerate no peace until he had touched every ridge and leaf of it with his mouth, none of which Sethe could feel because her back skin had been dead for years. (pp. 17–18)

Paul D registers in an incessant trembling the humiliation he felt before Brother, the rooster, and the indignity of being forced to wear leg irons and handcuffs. No one knew he was trembling, the narrator tells us, "because it began inside":

A flutter of a kind, in the chest then the shoulder blades. It felt like rippling – gentle at first and then wild. As though the further south they led him the more his blood, frozen like an ice pond for twenty years, began thawing, breaking into pieces that, once melted, had no choice but to swirl and eddy.

(pp. 106–07)

Insofar as the characters feel suffering through their bodies, they are healed through the body as well. Sethe is cured three times by healing hands: first Amy Denver's (the young white woman who helps deliver Denver), then Baby Suggs's, and finally Paul D's. Indeed, one might read Beloved's sexual relations with Paul D as a bodily cure. Paul D refuses to speak too fully the pain of his suffering in slavery. This refusal reflects his sense that his secrets are located in what remains of his heart: "in that tobacco tin buried in his chest where a red heart used to be. Its lid rusted shut" (pp. 72–73). However, when Beloved, ghost made flesh, compels him to have sexual relations with her, she tells him, in language that recalls Baby Suggs's earlier speech, "to touch her on the inside part" (p. 117). The description of this scene suggests that the act of intercourse with Beloved restores Paul D to himself and restores his heart to him:

She moved closer with a footfall he didn't hear and he didn't hear the whisper that the flakes of rust made either as they fell away from the seams of his tobacco tin. So when the lid gave he didn't know it. What he knew was that when he reached the inside part he was saying, 'Red heart. Red heart,' over and over again.   (p. 117)

In a number of ways, then, Morrison calls attention to the suffering that bodies endured under slavery. The novel, much like Baby Suggs, seeks to reclaim those bodies and to find a way to tell the story of the slave body in pain.

In her essay "Unspeakable Things Unspoken," Morrison writes that she hoped that from the opening lines of Beloved her readers' experience of the novel would approximate the slaves' sense of dislocation.[14] Of course, however evocatively Morrison renders human suffering in Beloved, finally the reader experiences only narrative representations of human suffering and pain. To speak what is necessarily, essentially, and inescapably unspoken is not to speak the unspoken; it is rather only to speak a narrative or speakable version of that event.

Beloved thus points to a paradox central to any attempt to represent the body in pain: one can never escape narrative. The figure of Beloved herself most obviously calls into question the relationship between narrative and the body. As a ghost made flesh, she is literally the story of the past embodied. Sethe and Denver and Paul D therefore encounter not only the story of her sorrow and theirs; indeed, they engage with its incarnation. Beloved's presence allows the generally reticent Sethe to tell stories from her past. Once Sethe realizes that the stranger called Beloved and her baby Beloved are one, she gives herself over fully to the past, and to Beloved's demand for comfort and curing. Indeed, Sethe is so devoted to making things right with Beloved, she is almost consumed by her. Without Denver's and her neighbors' and Paul D's interventions pulling her back into the present, she would have been annihilated.

The very name "Beloved" interrogates a number of oppositions. Simultaneously adjective and noun, the word troubles the distinction between the characteristics of a thing and the thing itself. To the extent that the title of the book is an unaccompanied modifier, it calls attention to the absence of the thing being modified. Additionally, the word "beloved" names not only the girl baby returned: in the funeral service the word addresses the mourners of the dead. The word thus names at once that which is past and present, she who is absent, and those who are present.

Finally, the word "beloved" calls attention to the space between written and oral, for until readers know the context in which her name appears, we do not even know how to speak that name: with three syllables or two. In the terms the novel offers, Beloved might be understood to exemplify what Sethe calls "rememory," something that is gone yet remains. Recalling both "remember" and "memory," "rememory" is both verb and noun; it names simultaneously the process of remembering and what is being remembered.

The reader confronts the unnarratability, indeed the inadequacy of language, perhaps most powerfully in the passages of interior monologue told from Sethe's, Denver's, and Beloved's points of view. After telling Paul D about Sethe's murder of her daughter, Stamp Paid, the man who conveyed the family to freedom, is turned away from 124 Bluestone Road by the "undecipherable language . . . of the black and angry dead" (p. 198). Mixed in with those voices were Sethe's, Denver's, and Beloved's thoughts – "unspeakable thoughts, unspoken" (p. 199). In the four sections that follow, we read the unspeakable and unspoken thoughts of the three women, first separately, then interwoven. Here, from Sethe's perspective, are her memories of killing her daughter, of being beaten, of being abandoned by her mother. Largely addressed to Beloved, Sethe's words convey recollections she could never utter to another. Likewise, in her section, Denver expresses her fear of her mother and her yearning to be rescued by her father, anxieties that, for the most part, had previously been suppressed.

Beloved's is, however, the most riveting and most obscure of the monologues. For here is represented the preconscious subjectivity of a victim of infanticide. The words that convey the recollections and desires of someone who is at once in and out of time, alive and dead, are richly allusive. The linguistic units in this section, be they sentences, phrases, or individual words, are separated by spaces, not by marks of punctuation. Only the first-person pronoun and the first letter of each paragraph are capitalized. This arrangement places all the moments of Beloved's sensation and recollection in a continuous and eternal present.

From the grave, Beloved yearns to be reunited with her mother: "her face is my own and I want to be there in the place where her face is and to be looking at it too" (p. 210). But in addition to her feelings and desires from the grave, Beloved seems also to have become one, in death, with the black and angry dead who suffered through the Middle Passage: "in the beginning the women are away from the men and the men are away from the women storms rock us and mix the men into the women and the women into the men" (p. 211). In the body of Beloved, then, individual and collective pasts and memories seem to have become united and inseparable.

By representing the inaccessibility of the suffering of former slaves, Morrison reveals the limits of hegemonic, authoritarian systems of knowledge. The novel challenges readers to use their interpretive skills, but finally turns them back upon themselves. By representing the inexpressibility of its subject, the novel asserts and reasserts the subjectivity of the former slaves and the depth of their suffering. *Beloved* reminds us that, our critical acumen and narrative capacities notwithstanding, we can never know what they endured. We can never claim and possess a full understanding of lives lived under slavery. To the extent that *Beloved* returns the slaves to themselves, the novel humbles contemporary readers before the unknown and finally unknowable horrors the slaves endured.

Recent interventions

Among recently published narratives of slavery, several merit at least brief mention here. Alice Randall's *The Wind Done Gone* (2001), a reimagination of the world of Margaret Mitchell's *Gone with the Wind* from the point of view of a mixed-race woman, and Nancy Rawles's *My Jim* (2005), told from the point of view of Sadie Watson, the wife Jim left behind when he goes off on the raft with Mark Twain's Huckleberry Finn, suggest how the genre has been used to speak back to conventional practices of representing the lives of the enslaved. While earlier neo-slave narratives address this issue by incorporating white or black writer-figures (*Chaneysville*, *Beloved*, and *Dessa Rose*, to name but a few), these works confront the politics of representation more directly by invoking the omissions and inclusions of some of the best-known works of American fiction.[15]

With its focus on Mercer Gray, a fugitive slave who lives in a community of freed blacks in Philadelphia, Lorene Cary's *The Price of a Child* reflects upon the meaning of freedom and of identity for those living under the shadow of the Fugitive Slave Law. Based on a true incident involving a slave named Jane Johnson, Mercer, formerly known as Ginnie, walks away from her master with the help of prominent real-life abolitionists William Still and Passmore Williamson. Although she is able to keep the two children who are traveling with her, the price of her freedom is her third child, the one she was forced to leave behind in Virginia. The novel evokes her experience as a woman forging a sense of herself as an individual, a mother, and a citizen within a multifarious community of free black people and the integrated abolitionist movement. *The Price of a Child* provides a rare window into emergent black identities in the context of fierce legal battles, the vexed politics of the antislavery lecture circuit, and the competitive dynamics of the free black community.

Edward P. Jones's *The Known World* (2003) takes this meditation on the meaning of freedom one step further, offering a nuanced reflection on the epistemological, moral, ethical, legal, economic, and spiritual implications of owning and trafficking in human life. By de-coupling the condition of slave ownership from whiteness and the condition of enslavement from blackness, the text offers a multivalent perspective on the construction of race and the elusiveness of freedom for blacks in the United States during the antebellum period. A richly plotted novel filled with fascinating, complicated, morally ambiguous characters, *The Known World* lacks a protagonist toward whom our attention might naturally gravitate.

The novel centers on the world that surrounds Henry and Caldonia Townsend, free black slave owners in antebellum Virginia. Besides an assortment of free and enslaved blacks, Native Americans, and white owners and workers, that world includes Henry's parents, Mildred and Augustus; their former master, William Robbins; Henry and Caldonia's former teacher and close friend, Fern Elston; Moses, Alice, Elias, and Celeste (several of Henry and Caldonia's slaves); and John Skiffington, the local sheriff, his Northern-born wife, and his treacherous, Southern cousin, Counsel. Through persistent foreshadowing and a riveting yet meandering narrative line, Jones signals both the unpredictable ways in which lives are connected and the inescapable consequences of even the most insignificant actions.

One might assume that in a novel about black slave owners, the villains and the victims would be clear. But one of the great achievements of *The Known World* is Jones's use of this subject to explore the nature of moral ambiguity. Henry, Caldonia, and Fern, the black masters, are smart, generous, and loving individuals who believe that they are more compassionate than their white counterparts. All of them make moral compromises in order to justify their collusion with the system of slave ownership. When Anderson Frazier, the Canadian journalist, interviews Fern in 1881 for his pamphlet on "free Negroes who had owned other Negroes," he remarks that were he in her position, he would consider slave ownership to be "like owning my own family, the people in my family."[16] The repetitions that erupt in Fern's response convey the extent to which her reliance on "fictions of law and custom" have overridden her sense of morality:

> 'Well, Mr. Frazier, it is not the same as owning people in your own family. It is not the same at all . . . You must not go away from this day and this place thinking that it is the same, because it is not . . . All of us do only what the law and God tell us we can do. No one of us who believes in the law and God does more than that. Do you, Mr. Frazier? Do you do more than what is allowed by God and the law? . . . We are like in that way. I did not own my family, and you must not tell people that I did. I did not. We did not. We owned . . . We owned slaves. It was what was done, and so that was what we did . . . We, not a single one of us Negroes, would have done what we were not allowed to do. (pp. 108–09)

Mildred and Augustus are outraged that Henry, the son they worked so hard to free, would purchase slaves to help him build his estate. They believe that they have failed in some fundamental way to teach him that the very condition of slave ownership is a moral contaminant that the owner cannot avoid. This interior monologue, following two brief yet pointed questions, captures the intensity of Mildred's self-reproach:

> 'Henry, why?' she said. 'Why would you do that?' She went through her memory for the time, for the day, she and her husband told him all about what he should and should not do. No goin out into them woods without Papa or me knowin about it. No stepping foot out this house with them free papers, not even to go to the well or the privy. Say your prayers every night.
> 'Do what, Mama? What is it?'
> Pick the blueberries close to the ground, son. Them the sweetest, I find. If a white man say the trees can talk, can dance, you just say yes right along, that you done seen em do it plenty of times. Don't look them people in the eye. You see a white woman ridin toward you, get way off the road and go stand behind a tree. The uglier the white woman, the farther you go and the broader the tree. But where, in all she taught her son, was it about thou shall own no one, havin been owned once your own self. Don't go back to Egypt after God done took you outa there. (p. 137)

The final sentence of this passage alludes to the familiar parallel between the enslavement of blacks in the United States and the enslavement of the Jews in Egypt as recounted in the Old Testament. The sentence also equates the position of the slaveholder with that of the slave; as Mildred and Augustus see it, by purchasing Moses, Henry has compromised his own freedom and returned to the system of enslavement. Like Fern, Henry sees the situation differently; he too retreats behind a fiction of custom, when he says: "'Papa, I ain't done nothing I ain't a right to. I ain't done nothing no white man wouldn't do'" (p. 138).

Henry and Augustus come to blows over the issue of slave ownership, but the two generations make peace with each other over time. Augustus refuses to stay in Henry and Caldonia's house when he visits them, but he and Mildred are happy to stay in an unoccupied cabin on the property and visit with the other slaves. After she is widowed, Caldonia decides to keep, rather than free, the slaves she inherited from Henry. She begins an intimate relationship with Moses, and then asks herself if miscegenation laws apply to sex between a free black woman and her slave: "His words caused her to wonder if Virginia had a law forbidding such things between a colored woman and a man who was her slave. Was this a kind of miscegenation? she wondered" (p. 292).

The moral ambiguity at the heart of the text is mirrored by its aesthetics. The textured characterizations, detailed descriptions, spellbinding plot, and elegant prose provide a luxurious reading experience. But these qualities constitute the medium through which readers are seduced into contemplating the outrages and ambiguities at the heart of the system of slavery: the meaning of trafficking in human property, the erotics and sexual protocols of the master–slave relationship, the implications of buying one's own children out of slavery and therefore owning one's own offspring, the tenuous position of freed people. Moreover, the presence in the text of imagined twentieth-century scholars who have made their careers out of their research on slavery suggests a link between historical and contemporary commodification of black labor and bodies.[17]

Given the limits of space, I can only begin in this essay to capture the range and complexity of this genre of writing. While some of these texts have already inspired a rich and illuminating body of critical writing, very little has been written about most of them. Moreover, there is every indication that black writers will continue to wrestle with the legacy of slavery in contemporary culture. With the steady stream of historiographical research on New World slavery and the transatlantic slave trade, the emergence of new editions of little-known slave narratives, and persistent questions about reparations for the descendants of former slaves, new perspectives on the institution of slavery are certain to emerge. Indeed, the publication of Francis Bok's *Escape from Slavery* (2003) and Mende Nazar's *Slave* (2005), two accounts of the authors' experience of slavery in Sudan, remind us that slavery as an institution is not an obsolete historical practice. Regrettably, the notion of the neo-slave narrative may need to be expanded to include slave narratives by former slaves written (and not merely reprinted) in the twenty-first century.

NOTES

I wish to thank Clarence E. Walker for his help with this essay.

1. Bernard W. Bell, *The Afro-American Novel and Its Tradition* (Amherst: University of Massachusetts Press, 1987), p. 289.
2. Ashraf Rushdy, *The Neo-Slave Narrative: Studies in the Social Logic of a Literary Form* (New York: Oxford University Press, 1999), p. 3.
3. Ashraf Rushdy, *Remembering Generations: Race and Family in Contemporary African American Fiction* (Chapel Hill: University of North Carolina Press, 2001), p. 33.
4. Angelyn Mitchell, *The Freedom to Remember: Narrative, Slavery, and Gender in Contemporary Black Women's Fiction* (New Brunswick, NJ: Rutgers University Press, 2002), p. 4.
5. Caroline Rody, *The Daughter's Return: African-American and Caribbean Women's Fictions of History* (New York: Oxford University Press, 2001), p. 10.
6. Arlene R. Keizer, *Black Subjects: Identity Formation in the Contemporary Narrative of Slavery* (Ithaca, NY: Cornell University Press, 2004), pp. 1–3.
7. For a discussion of the ways in which Bontemps altered the facts of the account, see Arnold Rampersad, "Introduction to the 1992 Edition," *Black Thunder* (Boston: Beacon Press, 1992). Other especially compelling readings of the novel include Hazel V. Carby, "Ideologies of Black Folk: The Historical Novel of Slavery" in *Slavery and the Literary Imagination*, Deborah E. McDowell and Arnold Rampersad, eds. (Baltimore, MD: Johns Hopkins University Press, 1989), pp. 125–43, and Eric J. Sundquist, "'A Son without Words': *Black Thunder*" in *The Hammers of Creation: Folk Culture in Modern African-American Fiction* (Athens, GA: The University of Georgia Press, 1992), pp. 92–134.
8. The trials of the "Scottsboro Boys," as they came to be known, involved nine black teenagers who were falsely accused of raping two young white women on March 25, 1931 on a Southern Railroad freight train. Sundquist explores this connection at some length in "'A Son without Words.'"
9. Interior monologue refers to a technique by which an author represents a character's (or group of characters') thoughts directly, in his or her (or their) idiom and syntax. Here, for example, is the passage where Old Bundy's burial is described:

> Down, down, down: old Bundy's long gone now. Put a jug of rum at his feet. Old Bundy with his legs like knotty canes. Roast a hog and put it on his grave. Down, down. How them victuals suit you, Bundy? How you like what we brung you? Anybody knows that dying ain't nothing. You got one eye shut and one eye open, old man. We going to miss you just the same, though, we going to miss you bad, but we'll meet you on t'other side, Bundy.

Arna Bontemps, *Black Thunder* (New York: The Macmillan Company, 1936. Rpt. Boston: Beacon Press, 1992), p. 52.

10. After the passage of the Fugitive Slave Law in 1850 black people were not really free in the "free" North either.
11. Marsha Darling, "In the Realm of Responsibility: A Conversation with Toni Morrison," *The Women's Review of Books* 5 (March 1988), 5.
12. Ibid., 6.
13. Toni Morrison, *Beloved* (New York: Knopf, 1987), pp. 88–89. Subsequent references will be cited parenthetically in the text.
14. Toni Morrison, "Unspeakable Things Unspoken: The Afro-American Presence in American Literature," *Michigan Quarterly Review* 28.1 (winter 1989), 1–34.
15. These texts also bring to mind Ishmael Reed's parodic references not only to such historical figures as Abraham Lincoln and Jefferson Davis, but also to such literary figures as Harriet Beecher Stowe, Lord Byron, and Edgar Allan Poe in *Flight to Canada*.
16. Edward P. Jones, *The Known World* (New York: Amistad, 2003), p. 107. Subsequent references will be cited parenthetically in the text.
17. In interviews, Jones admits that while he collected shelves of books about slavery, he actually did only minimal research on the topic before he began to write the novel; he "just didn't want to fill [his] head with all that stuff." See, for example, Robert Birnbaum. "Author of *The Known World* Converses with Robert Birnbaum" *identitytheory.com* 21 January 2004. <http://www.identitytheory.com/interviews/birnbaum138.php>

PART IV

The Slave Narrative and the Politics of Knowledge

11

STEPHANIE A. SMITH

Harriet Jacobs: a case history of authentication

Introduction: the question of authenticity

In 1987 Harvard University Press published a newly authenticated slave narrative, titled *Incidents in the Life of a Slave Girl.*[1] Jean Fagan Yellin was the editor of this admirable new edition, because unlike other historians and scholars – such as the historian John Blassingame and scholar Robert Stepto – she believed the author, "Linda Brent" (Harriet Jacobs), and the original editor, Lydia Maria Child, when they said that the narrative was true. Searching through various archives, Yellin was able to find solid documentary evidence, in the form of letters, newspapers, and official state papers, as to the truth: that the incidents recounted in *Incidents* had actually occurred.[2]

By proving that Harriet Jacobs had indeed composed the narrative, and that the events in it were more or less true, Yellin had single-handedly changed the book's status and the shape of what could be understood more broadly as "authentic" slave narrative, which I will discuss later in this essay. Indeed, although *Incidents* had been known to scholars and historians for years (it had, indeed, never really been lost), few regarded it as genuine; its value as a slave narrative was questioned or doubted, and for a host of reasons. Most critics who worked with slave narratives had labeled *Incidents* fiction. Indeed, Yellin herself had originally accepted "received opinion" and had "dismissed it as a false slave narrative" (*Incidents*, p. vii). Why?

Slave narrative, received opinion, and the archive

Why did scholars and critics resist believing that the events in *Incidents* were true? One reason had to do with the way in which the slave narrative itself had been defined. In 1977 the influential, indeed groundbreaking, African American historian John Blassingame published an important and unprecedented collection of papers titled *Slave Testimony: Two Centuries of Letters,*

Speeches, Interviews and Autobiographies.[3] By 1977 Professor Blassingame, the first acting chair of Yale's fledgling African American Studies Program in 1971–72, had established a reputation as a first-rate historian who had almost single-handedly established the importance of African American writing – especially the slave narrative – as historically crucial.

But, as previously noted, Blassingame (like the literary critic Robert Stepto) insisted that *Incidents* was not, nor could be, an authentic slave narrative. Given how important Professor Blassingame's work was (and still is), his judgment, especially in the 1970s, would have been difficult to question: he recovered numerous texts, laid the groundwork for African American studies, and his work was acclaimed because he did away with stereotypical, racist histories of slavery and replaced them with complex portraits of how slaves, former slaves, and freedmen formed social bonds and cultural practices.

However, it should be recalled here that the slave narrative *itself* had suffered its own rocky road to being valued as "literature."[4] Although once hailed by such figures as William Lloyd Garrison as the only truly *American* form of literature – because only in America, during slavery, could such an account be written – since the turn of the nineteenth century the slave narrative's value, too, came into question. As anything like true racial equality faded into history with the "success" of Jim Crow and segregation, slave narratives became quaint, historical documents about a (sometimes regrettable) past. Plantation life became a memory, and for a time the horrors of race slavery were replaced, at least in popular culture, by racist misrepresentations such as *Birth of a Nation* or *Gone with the Wind*.

So although Frederick Douglass is now regarded as one of the greatest American voices of nineteenth-century America, in the mid-twentieth century this was not so, except perhaps for historians, and even then histories of the Civil War themselves suffered from the poisonous effects of legalized racism. In fact, it would not be until the Civil Rights Movement and the social upheavals of the 1960s, events that brought racial politics back into the majority public eye, that the slave narrative became valuable as American and African American literature – and John Blassingame could pursue his study as a legitimate one, because, as many scholars note, academia itself changed radically during these years, as federally mandated integration challenged all-white schools to desegregate, up through the university level. This, along with the foundation of programs like African American, Native-American, Asian-American, and Women's studies, came re-evaluations and recoveries of always present but also muted voices, voices that were never lost but culturally silenced, like both Lydia Maria Child's and Harriet Jacobs's.

The double negative

But there were other contributing factors with respect to Harriet Jacobs in particular. As critic Rafia Zafar writes, the text represents a problem that is both literary and sociological: "faced with the 'double negative' of black race and female gender, like Wheatley before her and Hurston after her," Jacobs "had to contend with a skeptical readership that said her work could not be 'genuine' because of her emphasis on the domestic, her 'melodramatic' style, and her unwillingness to depict herself as an avatar of self-reliance."[5] And, as Trudy Mercer quite succinctly notes, the two primary reasons that scholars continued to ignore Jacobs were:

> (1) Jacobs chose to use Linda Brent as a pseudonym and to mask the names of people mentioned in her narrative. While this is understandable for the period in which she wrote, the need to protect people being paramount, the use of pseudonymous names by an author of a single published book for which no manuscript exists requires a textual scholar to authenticate the work, whether the author was an ex-slave or not. That Jacobs's powerful use of language and literary conventions led critics to cast doubt upon whether she, as a former slave, was capable of such a work only adds cultural weight to the need for authentication. (2) Lydia Maria Child was known for works of fiction that treated interracial relationships.[6]

Thus, this narrative not only presented textual problems that Yellin's archival research at last resolved – i.e. that Harriet Jacobs was indeed the same person as Linda Brent, and that even if novelist and abolitionist Lydia Maria Child had edited the work (sometimes aggressively), Jacobs was the author, and she was recounting her own life's story – it also challenged fixed racist and sexist preconceptions that scholars had about women held as slaves. However, once presented with Yellin's archival facts, critics and historians had to re-examine, and indeed redefine, the parameters of the slave narrative altogether.

So let's see how this redefinition happened, since the problems that *Incidents* faced, as I've said above and discussed elsewhere, had everything to do with what scholars considered to be credible fact, since a slave narrative had to be a true narrative: could a slave woman truly have been able to confound her master by usurping his so-called right to her body? In other words, could a slave woman choose to have children with a man she actually had feelings for?[7] Could a slave hide, for years, in what amounted to a crawl space, in order to fool her master into thinking she'd fled north? And as numerous critics have noted, one of the oft-cited (racist) questions was: could a slave have the cultural ability to manipulate sentimental tropes, to play upon her audience's sensibilities, as it were, with such skill?[8]

Joanne Braxton took note that "Marion Starling, a black woman, had argued for the authenticity of the Jacobs narrative as early as 1947, but male critics like Sterling Brown and Arna Bontemps contested that authorship."[9] Frederick Douglass's 1845 *Narrative of the Life of Frederick Douglass* was regarded as the most accomplished text in the genre, and, as I have also argued elsewhere, most scholars valued this, his first and, as some critics argue, his most "muscular" narrative, over and above the later versions of the same narrative, titled *My Bondage and My Freedom* and *The Life and Times of Frederick Douglass*. Each succeeding version is more sentimental, more tear-inducing than its predecessor, which did not fit the prevailing vision of masculine triumph (*Conceived by Liberty*, pp. 134–59). Thus, there was no critical groundwork upon which to build or framework within which to value or even adequately comprehend the sort of cultural "work" that *Incidents* does as a slave narrative with respect to race, slavery, and gender.

Moreover, as a number of feminist critics have argued, most (male) critics of the slave narrative, because they regarded the text as a sort of overblown nineteenth-century female sentimental fiction, favored the idea that the work was probably concocted by Lydia Maria Child, whose own writings, such as her remarkable first novel *Hobomok*, were undervalued for some of the same reasons that *Incidents* was ignored.[10] Any tale of domestic womanhood written by a woman had been, at least since the mid-twentieth century (if not earlier), consigned to something like the literary trash-bin. Despite the fact that during the nineteenth century women took up the pen in unprecedented numbers, by the early 1940s, if a student could find a class about "American" literature, which would have been doubtful, that student would have been sorely hard-pressed to find a single woman, black or white, discussed favorably, if noted at all. It would not be, as I've stated, until the social unrest of the 1960s that the very present, well-known, and not as well-known voices of nineteenth-century womanhood would be heard again. Still even now, in 2007, the aesthetic question, "But is it any good?" – a question that Jane Tompkins in *Sensational Designs* certainly could not resolve – haunts these texts, Jacobs's included, given that present standards for "good" writing remain essentially the same as modernist standards. Even for today's critics and writers, sentimentality, so much a part of a nineteenth-century aesthetic, is that which signifies 'weak' – which is often conflated with feminine – writing.

Feminism and restoration

Despite the weight of critical opinion against taking *Incidents* seriously, the story still raised questions for some, like Jean Fagan Yellin, particularly questions that Deborah Gray White's important study *Ar'n't I a Woman? Female Slaves in the Plantation South* raised as well, which is to say the central historical observation that slavery had had different consequences and effects for a woman. Would not a woman's experience of slavery have to be narrated in a very different way than a man's? Jean Fagan Yellin clearly agreed, and the story of her archival search for corroborating documents that would prove previous scholars had been mistaken about *Incidents* is in many ways a truly representative feminist tale.

Later in her career, and "schooled by the women's movement," Yellin "was struck by [*Incidents'*] radical feminist content" (*Incidents*, p. vii) and set off to find out for herself whether or not *Incidents* was in fact a true account of a slave woman's life. As Yellin recalls in her preface to the 1987 edition, she came to the conclusion that if Lydia Maria Child said she was the editor, not the author, of the narrative, then she was, and that if Mrs. Child attested to its authenticity, given the politics of the abolitionist cause in which false slave narratives had been written and used to discredit the abolitionists, then Mrs. Child was telling the truth. Following her belief in Child's veracity, Yellin went first to the editors of the Child papers, who put her "in touch with archivists at the University of Rochester who had recently acquired Harriet Jacobs's letters to the abolitionist-feminist Amy Post" (*Incidents*, p. vii). These letters make it quite clear that Harriet Jacobs is Linda Brent, and that she wrote the narrative after much soul-searching, and after being very badly treated by Harriet Beecher Stowe; these are indeed remarkable, personable letters from one friend to another, and from one abolitionist to another, in which Jacobs worries about her inability to live as a Christian woman ought to have lived – her inability to remain chaste, in slavery – and about her status as what we would call today a single mother. Jacobs is by turns modest and frank, humorous and sweet.

Yellin, employing the help of a number of archives across the country and the willing research of numerous archivists, but in the end essentially reviewing archival material that had been languishing under the noses of any number of researchers, was able to piece together the facts that subtend the narrative, discovering the identities of all the "characters" in Linda Brent's (Harriet Jacobs's) life: Dr. Flint was James Norcom, Emily Flint was Mary Matilda Norcom, Mr. Sands was Samuel Tredwell Sawyer, and so on. Looking at these documents from the perspective that slavery, for women, must have entailed far more sexual exploitation than had been previously recorded or discussed, Yellin was able to substantiate, without much archival doubt, that Harriet Jacobs's story was a true story, if also highly stylized with respect to the literary conventions of her day, and with respect to standard abolitionist rhetoric. Yet "what finally dominates," wrote Yellin, "is a new voice. It is the voice of a woman who, although she cannot discuss her sexual past without expressing deep conflict, nevertheless addresses this painful personal subject in order to politicize it, to insist that the forbidden topic of the sexual abuse of slave women be included in the public discussions of the slavery question" (*Incidents*, p. xiv).

History and narrative

Since the 1980s there has been an explosion of interest in Harriet Jacobs and her narrative. As scholar and editor Rafia Zafar recounts in her "Introduction: Over-Exposed, Under-Exposed: Harriet Jacobs and *Incidents in the Life of a Slave Girl*," solid critical scholarship on the narrative was virtually invisible until Yellin's research was first published in 1981 ("Introduction," pp. 4–5). That is, even though the first modern reprint of the 1861 text was published in 1969, still only a few considered it an important document, and "Jacobs was either decried as inauthentic or dismissed as atypical" ("Introduction", p. 4).

In order to try to appreciate this silencing of *Incidents in the Life of a Slave Girl* before Jean Fagan Yellin set the facts straight, it is useful at this juncture to examine how the story came to be, and to be repudiated, and how, precisely, it was authenticated by Jean Fagan Yellin to go on to become one of the most widely taught slave narratives outside of Frederick Douglass's.

To start, a brief textual history is in order. As Trudy Mercer points out, there is no extant manuscript version of this narrative, only the 1861 published version ("*Inquiry*"). Without a manuscript or proofs, one can only conjecture about how the original text was shaped, how much influence others exerted over Jacobs or her manuscript, and what types of change appeared in the proof version that may or may not have ended up in the final, published version.

Such questions alone are problematic for any text, but for autobiography and for slave narratives, problems of revision and transmission only muddy already muddy water because the material is presumed by the audience to be true or real. As Mercer rightly points out, despite semiotics and postmodernism, most readers still believe or expect that the published text will be what the author intended it to be. Given the political nature of slave narrative – that it was used as propaganda by abolitionists to further their cause, and that the genre is now central to African American literary studies, American studies and Women's studies – the demand for the true, the real, and the authentic becomes paradoxically urgent. I say paradoxically because the demand that a text, any text, be entirely true to experience is an illogical demand. Representation is mediation. No representation can ever completely capture experience. Further, since readers also require a fiction to feel real, how precisely is a fictionalized account unreal? Indeed, the demand for authenticity seems almost pathological, since anything written is subject to interpretation. Still, the audience's demand for authenticity remains with us.

In the case of *Incidents*, as I've said earlier, several charged political questions about authenticity clouded critical judgment. First, as Mercer notes, Harriet Jacobs took great pains to conceal her identity in order to protect herself, her family, and her children, and, as Mercer writes, "the use of pseudonymous names by an author of a single published book for which no manuscript exists requires a textual scholar to authenticate the work, whether the author was an ex-slave or not" (*"Inquiry"*). Second, Lydia Maria Child was Jacobs's editor, and given that Child had already written novels about slavery, inter-racial love and passion, how much she edited and how much she wrote herself is a question (both before Yellin's research and even to some extent after it). Third, the slave narrative, at least as defined by such influential scholars as John Blassingame, was supposed to follow the slave from captivity to enlightenment to (manly) resistance and finally escape. But although Jacobs's story includes such a tale (of Uncle Benjamin's escape), according to the way Jacobs narrates this escape it is "as if he'd been sold down river to a Georgia trader" (*Conceived by Liberty*, p. 142), because Benjamin loses precisely what *Incidents* values more than anything: family bonds. "Although she rejoices that her uncle has escaped the condition of white man's property, Brent shows that Benjamin still loses what the slavocracy insisted a slave had no real cognizance of . . . a family" (ibid.).

Valuing family ties over the breaking of bondage, *Incidents* is far more concerned with domesticity and inter-relations than any other slave narrative, and thus presented (male) critics with a (feminine) tale unlikely to be valued as real or authentic. Add to this features of the narrative that were sentimental (all that loving! all those tears!), unbelievable (nobody could stay in a crawl space for seven years), and downright audacious (she's a slave and she chooses to have children – not property – by Mr. Sands, a white Senator? She successfully avoids being raped by her master? Are you kidding me?), the text was deemed a fiction, and as a fiction of no worth because it did not tell a true (slave narrative) tale. Given that other (women's) fictions of that ilk – most famously, perhaps, Harriet Beecher Stowe's *Uncle Tom's Cabin* – had been deemed both bad writing and sentimental tripe (even if historically important with respect to the Civil War), it is hardly surprising, really, that *Incidents*, with all of its dubious textual problems and obvious political agenda, fell by the wayside.

As a number of critics also point out, *Incidents* was published in 1861, just as the Civil War began, and so its political use as propaganda was no doubt limited, especially considering how much, during those first few years, the White House insisted that the war was about secession, not slavery. Abolitionists appreciated the story, and it did circulate, but as Child herself noted, the kind of horrific and sexualized degradation Jacobs describes would have strained the *average* white, Northern, middle-class female reader's credulity. Many Northerners simply did not want to know what slavery was like, and the slavocracy preferred it that way; and certainly, after the bloody mess that was the Civil War ended, stories such as Jacobs's must have seemed, at least to a white, middle-class readership, rather obsolete, even if the conditions of racial violence, race hatred, and prejudice remained in place.

Meanwhile, literary standards in the United States were changing as well; during the latter half of the nineteenth century the movement among editors and artists toward literary realism and naturalism made anything sentimental less "real" than it had once been received by readers.[11] When what is now called the modernist aesthetic, with its emphasis on spare, economical language, novelty, and formal experimentation, began to change how a text was written and valued, anything regarded as traditional or sentimental was buried under disdain, at least with respect to its literary worth. For example, although Willa Cather was a powerful editor, and a well-regarded writer, in the early part of the twentieth century younger writers like Ernest Hemingway saw her more traditional storytelling as old-fashioned and out of date. The slave narrative, which depended on arousing an emotional response, a direct call to moral outrage, traveled from the literary to the historical pretty quickly. Thus, for most of the twentieth century, the slave narrative was seen, if seen at all, as historical documentation of a bygone era.

Although it would be fascinating indeed to trace out a complete critical picture of how literary aesthetics changed between 1850 and 1950, and thus the popular view of what the purpose of literature is, I do not have the time or space to do so here; but I would like to offer one telling example of how the many voices of nineteenth-century America became the few heard. In 1941 F. O. Matthiessen authored a groundbreaking book, *American Renaissance*. In it, he argued that there was something specifically identifiable as American – as opposed to English – literature, and that it had seen a "renaissance" in the mid- to late nineteenth century.[12] Infamously, perhaps, Matthiessen's argument prepared the critical groundwork for Cold War American canon formation. Importantly, none of the writers for whom he argued were of any color (except white), and the fact that American women had written scads and scads in this same time period had utterly vanished. How appreciative Hawthorne would have been! Not only does Matthiessen canonize Hawthorne (as had Henry James, years before), but in one critical move Matthiessen had also wiped out "that damned mob of scribbling women" whom Hawthorne so loathed. According to the *American Renaissance*, Fuller, Stowe, Child, and Jacobs were even less than negligible. They didn't exist at all.

Certainly neither slave narratives nor any of the other works by notable African American authors written in the nineteenth century, whether written by a man or a woman, were in Matthiessen's critical sight. And while one could wish otherwise, it is easy to see why: post-World War II America was still a legally segregated America. Racism (sexism, and a deadly homophobia, which Matthiessen knew personally) was the social climate. To be fair to Matthiessen, however, I must take note that Henry James is also missing from the *American Renaissance*, which might seem odd but isn't, because Matthiessen's standard of value had to do with whether or not the author or work upheld the cultural promises of democracy, something James really could not have cared less about. On the other hand, as many later African American critics were quick to point out, if the promise of democracy is of value, Douglass (and Jacobs!) certainly fits the bill. But Matthiessen could not see or hear Douglass, either.

By the latter half of the 1950s African American citizens grew weary of their second-class citizenship. The National Association for the Advancement of Colored People (NAACP) had been agitating for some time, particularly (but not exclusively) because African American, as well as Native American, men had served their country and been wounded or died during World War II. In 1954 Rosa Parks refused to relinquish her bus seat to a white man; and the resulting outrage gave the Civil Rights movement a boost. Of course, by 1968 the country was in deep sociological and political turmoil, what with the failures of Vietnam, the Women's Liberation Movement, and the civil disobedience of the Civil Rights Movement changing, among young people, into outright resistance or into the violent tactics employed by groups like the Weathermen. Out of those conflicts sprang an academic response with respect to a reconsideration of discipline, aesthetics, and politics. Although the New Criticism of the 1940s and 1950s, as a critical practice, had consigned to "outside" the text influences like biography and politics, the critical fray that ensued during the 1960s through today, with permutations, highs, and lulls, has at least called into question how literary worth or value is adjudicated in the academy. Again, I don't have the time here in this essay to examine all of the ways in which these battles were fought, although Alice Walker's timely resurrection of Zora Neale Hurston's work and Jane Tompkins's *Sensational Designs* (a book which attempts to re-value nineteenth-century sentimentality) come to mind as crucial.

Meanwhile, during the same years that Yellin was doggedly pursuing what others might have seen as a wild goose chase, African American women writers found the audience that had always been there but that (male) critics (such as Ishmael Reed) and the publishing industry had often refused to see or hear. It is hard, now, in the midst of what Ann duCille has called the "traffic jam . . . that black feminist studies has become" (as quoted in "Introduction," p. 4) to recall that before the late 1960s, the African American woman writer was more or less an unknown voice. For example, until Alice Walker brought her back to us, Zora Neale Hurston, despite her Guggenheim, had vanished as surely as if a Florida swamp had opened up; Nella Larsen had likewise been forgotten. Lorraine Hansberry was still in the general public's mind perhaps, but it wasn't until the late 1960s that African American women's writing began to gain high visibility and finally, during the 1980s, to take literary center stage. A staggeringly large readership has made the voices of women such as Alice Walker, Gayl Jones, Toni Morrison, Toni Cade Bambera, Angela Davis, Octavia Butler, Gloria Naylor, Margaret Walker, and Sherley Anne Williams heard. And in many cases, these writers returned to the same themes and questions that Harriet Jacobs had explored nearly two centuries ago: how to live with dignity, as a woman, a mother, and a citizen in a sexist, racist, often violently antiblack, antiwoman American society.

Conclusion

In the wake of Jean Fagan Yellin's remarkable discovery, made all the more remarkable for the way in which such archival evidence can be "lost" in the archive or ignored, what can we learn? Certainly that racism and sexism, both causal reasons for the loss of *Incidents* to the academy for so long, have hardly vanished, no matter how many speeches to the contrary have been delivered. On the other hand, Yellin's work points to the rich historical record that we do have but often make scant use of. But further, this case history should serve as a cautionary tale about aesthetic value and literary politics, about memory and truth, interpretation and prejudice. What constitutes great literature is and should be up for debate rather than set in the stone of a canon; memories can be lost and, with them, truths. To accept what Yellin called "received opinion" without skepticism, or to read without doing the work of interpretation, may blind us to the complexity of our histories and to the courage of those who do not assent to the status quo when they feel it to be unjust, which only impoverishes everyone. In today's academia, if not in the larger social domain, to be a forceful, formidable woman is still often popularly regarded as unseemly, unwomanly, or worse, despite lip service to the contrary. A woman can become a US Senator or a Supreme Court Justice, but only by dint of the same remarkably resourceful stubbornness and pride that the voice of Linda Brent reveals. American race slavery may be almost two centuries in the past, but its lingering effects still haunt us, as the loss and re-birth of Harriet Jacobs's *Incidents in the Life of a Slave Girl* only too clearly demonstrate.

NOTES

1. Harriet A. Jacobs, *Incidents in the Life of a Slave Girl, Written by Herself*, ed. Jean Fagan Yellin (Cambridge, MA: Harvard University Press, 1987). Further references to this text appear in the body of the essay as *Incidents* with page numbers in parentheses.
2. Jean Fagan Yellin's first article authenticating Jacobs's authorship appeared in 1981 as "Written by Herself: *Harriet Jacobs's Slave Narrative*" in *American Literature* 53.3 (November 1981): 479–86.
3. See John Blassingame, *Slave Testimony: Two Centuries of Letters, Speeches, Interviews and Autobiographies* (Baton Rouge: Louisiana State University Press, 1977).
4. Numerous critics have discussed the long years of African American silence in literary studies; see, for example, Houston Baker, *The Journey Back: Issues in Black Literature and Criticism* (Chicago: University of Chicago Press, 1980).
5. Rafia Zafar, "Introduction: Over-Exposed, Under-Exposed: Harriet Jacobs and *Incidents in the Life of a Slave Girl*" in *Harriet Jacobs and Incidents in the Life of a Slave Girl: New Critical Essays*. Deborah Garfield and Rafia Zafar, eds. (Cambridge and New York: Cambridge University Press, 1996), p. 4. Further references to this text appear in the body of the essay as "Introduction" with page numbers in parentheses.
6. Trudy Mercer, "An Inquiry into the Text Transmission of Harriet Jacobs' *Incidents in the Life of a Slave Girl*" at http://www.drizzle.com/~tmercer/ Jacobs/history.shtml. Further references to this source appear in the body of the essay as "*Inquiry.*"
7. Stephanie A. Smith, *Conceived by Liberty: Maternal Figures and Nineteenth-Century American Literature* (Ithaca: Cornell University Press, 1995), pp. 134–59. All further references to this text will appear in the body of the essay as *Conceived by Liberty* with page numbers in parentheses.
8. See the essays in Garfield and Zafar, *Harriet Jacobs*.
9. Joanne Braxton, "Harriet Jacobs' *Incidents in the Life of a Slave Girl*: The Re-Definition of the Slave Narrative Genre," *Massachusetts Review* 27.2 (summer 1986), 382.
10. See Jane Tompkins, *Sensational Designs: The Cultural Work of American Fiction, 1790–1860* (New York: Oxford University Press, 1985). See also Lydia Maria

Child, *Hobomok, and Other Writings on Indians*, ed. Carolyn L. Karcher (New Brunswick: Rutgers University Press, 1986).

11. See Amy Kaplan, *The Social Construction of American Realism* (Chicago: University of Chicago Press, 1988).

12. F. O. Matthiessen, *American Renaissance: The Art of Expression in the Age of Emerson and Whitman* (Chicago: University of Chicago Press, 1941, 1990).

12

JOHN STAUFFER

Frederick Douglass's self-fashioning and the making of a Representative American man

Frederick Douglass was the most famous African American of the nineteenth century and one of its greatest writers and intellectuals. Over the course of his long life from 1818 to 1895, he published three autobiographies, one novella, and a dozen or so speeches in pamphlet form. He delivered thousands of lectures and was one of America's best orators, at a time when public speaking was a major form of entertainment. For sixteen years, he edited, under three different names, the longest-running black newspaper in the nineteenth century. And thousands of photographs and engravings of him were in circulation, in forms that ranged from frontispiece engravings to daguerreotypes, ambrotypes, *cartes de visite*, and cabinet cards. He sat for his portrait at least as much as Walt Whitman, who was famous for visually creating and re-creating himself. As early as 1860, his "likeness" was familiar to virtually every American.[1]

Douglass became an American icon through art. He brilliantly used the power of the word, voice, and image to write himself into public existence and remake himself while seeking to reform his nation. He was widely called "a Representative Man": his close friend, the black abolitionist and physician James McCune Smith, referred to him as a "Representative American man" because he continually transformed himself; he "passed through every gradation of rank comprised in our national make-up and bears upon his person and his soul everything that is American."[2] Lincoln said something similar; he met with Douglass at the White House three times and called him "one of the most meritorious men, if not the most meritorious man, in the United States." For Douglass, "true" art could break down racial barriers and enable people to remake themselves and their society. "True" art meant accurate and authentic representations of himself and other blacks, rather than caricatures such as blackface minstrelsy. Art was truthful when it expressed the essential humanity of all people and sought to fulfill the nation's democratic ideals.[3]

Of the three forms Douglass used to represent himself and critique American society, he felt most comfortable as a public speaker. He believed that oratory was the most effective tool for an activist and his greatest accomplishment as an artist. "I hardly need say to those who know me," he wrote near the end of his life, "that writing for the public eye never came quite as easily to me as speaking to the public ear."[4] He had a rich baritone voice, was a brilliant mimic (especially of slaveholders), which drew howls of laughter, and he coupled irony and sarcasm with pathos and sentimentality in his performances. And he was beautiful to look at, "majestic in his wrath," as one sympathetic admirer noted.[5] In 1841, soon after Douglass began his public-speaking career, the abolitionist editor Nathaniel Rogers extolled his talents by saying:

> As a speaker he has few equals. It is not declamation – but oratory, power of debate. He has wit, arguments, sarcasm, pathos – all that first rate men show in their master efforts. His voice is highly melodious and rich, and his enunciation quite elegant, and yet he has been but two or three years out of the house of bondage.[6]

The following year, a reporter for the Salem, Massachusetts, *Register* compared his oratory to that of famous statesmen:

> He seemed to move the audience at his will, and they at times would hang upon his lips with staring eyes and open mouths, as eager to catch every word, as any "sea of upturned faces" that ever rolled at the feet of [Edward] Everett or [Daniel] Webster, to revel in their classic eloquence.[7]

In 1855 a well-known Whig editor and politician (and no friend of abolitionists), after hearing Douglass speak, told a white friend: "I would give twenty thousand dollars if I could deliver that address in that manner" (*My Bondage*, p. lii).

Douglass considered a speech to be a more authentic and immediate form of protest and self-representation than writing. More than the pen, a speech penetrated the heart and soul of its listeners, inspiring people to act on their visions of reform. The pen could be powerful, but proslavery advocates used the pen "with considerable impunity," as Douglass noted: "ink and paper have no sense of shame." While proslavery advocates refuted abolitionists' writings, Douglass said they were afraid of abolitionist speeches and seldom ventured into their meetings. When they did, they sought to silence speakers rather than challenge them with their own speeches.[8]

Douglass's oratory led directly to his 1845 *Narrative*. In 1841, three years after fleeing north from slavery, he became a paid lecturer for William Lloyd

Garrison's American Anti-Slavery Society. He already felt comfortable lecturing, for while still a slave in Baltimore, he had joined a secret debating club with some free black friends. Even as a slave he had enormous faith in the power of the word to remake himself. During one debating session he declared that he did not intend to stop advancing in social rank until he was a United States Senator. It was a revolutionary declaration in his slave republic, and it betrayed his boundless hope and confidence in the power of the word to change society.[9] As a paid lecturer he was doing what he loved – working with words. He received a regular salary for the first time in his life, and abolitionist friends helped him purchase a home in Lynn, Massachusetts. In his new job he traveled around the Northern states, preaching to audiences about the horrors of slavery. The most effective way for him to do that was to tell the story of his life. He talked about other things as well: the fate of other slaves, who had fared far worse than him; Northern racism; and current political conditions. But the focal point of these early speeches was his story. His *Narrative* was an artistic synthesis of the speeches he had been delivering for over three years.[10]

The immediate impetus for writing his *Narrative* was his success as a speaker. Douglass was so good that some of his colleagues advised him to tone down his rhetorical flourishes. "People won't believe you ever were a slave, Frederick, if you keep on this way," Stephen Foster, a Garrisonian colleague told him (*Life*, p. 218). "Better have a little of the plantation speech than not," another abolitionist lecturer, John Collins, advised; "it is not best that you seem too learned" (*Life*, p. 218). While Douglass chafed at such paternalism and despised these attempts to control what he said and how he said it, he also recognized that "these excellent friends were actuated by the best of motives and were not altogether wrong in their advice," as he noted (*Life*, p. 218; *My Bondage*, p. 216).

In many respects, Foster's warning proved prophetic: people began doubting that he had ever been a slave. He did not talk or act like a slave, and he avoided certain facts, like where he was from, who his master was, and his former name (Frederick Bailey), to avoid exposing his whereabouts to slaveholders. As he walked down the aisles of churches in which antislavery meetings were held, he began hearing people say, "He's never been a slave, I'll warrant you" (*Life*, p. 218; *My Bondage*, p. 216). In August 1844, after speaking in Philadelphia, he learned that

> many persons in the audience seemed unable to credit the statements which he gave of himself, and could not believe that he was actually a slave. How a man only six years out of bondage, and who had never gone to school a day in his life, could speak with such eloquence – with such precision of language and power of thought – they were utterly at a loss to devise.[11]

In response to such claims, he began writing his *Narrative*. Published under the auspices of the American Anti-Slavery Society, it authenticated his identity as a former slave. The preface, with letters by William Lloyd Garrison and Wendell Phillips, two of the best-known white abolitionists, further verified Douglass's identity as an ex-slave, orator, and the author of his narrative. In it he named names and characterized in rich and accurate detail his former masters and overseers. But exposing himself in such a way put him in danger of being recaptured. When Wendell Phillips read the manuscript, he said that if he were Douglass he would "throw it into the fire" (*My Bondage*, p. 217). Not even the state of Massachusetts could protect him, Phillips said. His narrative put his liberty in jeopardy, and two months after publishing it he went abroad, in part to seek refuge "from republican America in monarchical England," as he put it (*My Bondage*, p. 218).

Douglass's *Narrative* was an immediate bestseller and made him internationally famous. It was published in June, 1845, priced at fifty cents, and by the fall it had sold 4,500 copies. Three European editions soon followed, with translations in French and German. By 1848 11,000 copies had been published in the United States alone, and it had gone through nine editions in England. By 1850 30,000 copies had been sold. The reviews were overwhelmingly positive. The reviewer for the Lynn, Massachusetts newspaper compared Douglass to Daniel Defoe and called his *Narrative* "*the most important*" (emphasis in original) book "the American press ever issued." In England and Ireland, reviewers lauded "its native eloquence" and its effectiveness at converting readers to the antislavery cause. One editor said that through his *Narrative*, Douglass "stands up and rebukes oppression with a dignity and a fervor scarcely less glowing than that which Paul addressed to Agrippa." Another reader wrote: "Never before have I been brought so completely in sympathy with the slave."[12] While Douglass felt more comfortable as a public speaker, his voice reached a limited audience. His *Narrative* struck a chord with the masses.

In many respects, Douglass's *Narrative* adheres closely to the tradition of slave narratives. It sets out to condemn slavery and convert readers to the abolitionist cause. It narrates the life of an ex-slave and begins with his unknown birthdate and paternity and ends at the moment of freedom. It exposes the crimes and cruelties of his former masters, overseers, and other slaveholders, highlighting the essential inhumanity of slavery. It emphasizes the natural love of freedom common to all humans and emphasizes the importance of literacy as a means to achieve it. Douglass draws on his memory and history to dismantle some of the dualisms that existed in antebellum America: slavery and freedom, man and brute, black and white, oppressor and oppressed, sacred and profane, Christian redemption and slaveholding churches.[13]

But in other respects, the *Narrative* was virtually unique in its time. Douglass had a brilliant ear for language and an understanding of such literary devices as plot, characterization, scene, and pacing. With the *Narrative* he creates one of the great "I"-narratives of American literature.[14] The narrator is an Emersonian self who embraces sacred self-sovereignty and an indwelling God – one who is present within the self and in the world. (Douglass read and often quoted Emerson in the 1850s and acknowledged his influence.) The narrator is also a confident, defiant, sarcastic performer who controls his story while seeking control over his life. Other characters, also memorable, are juxtaposed with him. They illuminate his performative self-sovereignty. Edward Covey, "the snake" against whom Douglass defines himself, is one of the great villains in literature, and their fight is cast as a theatrical performance. His Aunt Hester, who suffers pain and pornographic subjection at the hands of her master, stands in opposition to the narrator's dignity and quest for self-reliance and control. These characters are also accurate historical representations, even when, as in the case of Hester (Esther) and the overseer "Severe" (Sevier), the names are spelled phonetically, since Douglass had only heard them.[15]

The *Narrative* enacts language itself as a mode of liberation, as David Blight and other scholars have noted, "first as a source of hope, later as a strategy of escape and a form of power."[16] Understandably, one of the turning points in the *Narrative*, and in Douglass's life, is when the narrator discovers *The Columbian Orator*, a popular elocution manual for boys that was published by George Bingham and helped shape the male American mind. Its teaching strategies are everywhere in the *Narrative*, from instructions on how to achieve lyricism and narrative "reversals" to the "action" established between narrator and reader.[17] The reversals, from ignorance to knowledge and slave to free man, reflect a self that is in a state of continual evolution and flux. Such fluidity is conveyed in the frontispiece, over which Douglass sought as much control as over the narrative itself. It is an unfinished portrait; there are no details below Douglass's shoulders, as though to illustrate that his persona was not fixed, still being formed. In this sense the portrait echoes the *Narrative*, for Douglass writes in a pictorial mode, another rhetorical strategy suggested by *The Columbian Orator*. He creates visual portraits with his characters and settings, and in many scenes achieves ekphrasis – creating a picture with words in order to achieve sympathy between narrator and reader and motivate the reader to abolitionist action.[18]

Douglass brilliantly describes the liberating role of language when he addresses the ships sailing down the Chesapeake toward the sea. This apostrophe to the ships occurs shortly before his famous fight, while working as a field hand for Covey. Covey worked Douglass relentlessly, whipped and beat him frequently, and succeeded in "breaking" him: "I was broken in body, soul, and spirit," Douglass wrote. "My natural elasticity was crushed, my intellect languished, the disposition to read departed," and he found himself "transformed into a brute!" But the Chesapeake Bay was only about twenty yards away, and he described the powerful effect of seeing the ships, "robed in purest white," sailing from every quarter of the globe:

> You are loosed from your moorings, and are free; I am fast in my chains, and am a slave! You move merrily before the gentle gale, and I sadly before the bloody whip! You are freedom's swift-winged angels, that fly round the world; I am confined in bands of iron! O that I were free! O, that I were on one of your gallant decks, and under your protecting wing! Alas! Betwixt me and you, the turbid waters roll. Go on, go on. O that I could also go! Could I but swim! If I could fly! O, why was I born a man, of whom to make a brute! The glad ship is gone; she hides in the dim distance. I am left in the hottest hell of unending slavery. O God, save me! God, deliver me! Let me be free! Is there any God? Why am I a slave? I will run away. I will not stand it. Get caught, or get clear, I'll try it. I had as well die with ague as the fever. I have only one life to lose. (*Narrative*, p. 84)

This famous passage highlights Douglass's narrative power. It relies heavily on the Bible and is at once a Job-like lament, a prayer for deliverance, and a cry of assurance based on the Negro spiritual "Better Days Are Coming."[19] It is a declarative statement, underscored by the thirteen exclamation points, in which the narrator "becomes a godlike authority over the world of his text and seeks to extend his authority to the world outside his text" by defying the rules that govern normal discourse.[20] And it shows how language leads to the willingness to die for freedom. In describing the ships, Douglass identifies with them; his very description inspires him to become like the ships and run away. He begins by defining himself in opposition to the ships – they are free, he is a slave – and then dismantles the dualism, becoming one in freedom with them. Douglass begins with an apostrophe to the ships and ends with an apostrophe to himself and, implicitly, the reader. He heeds his own declaration. The ships, like the narrator, are fluid, moving, in continual flux. The passage necessarily foreshadows his fight with Covey, which leads to his spiritual, psychological, and eventually his physical freedom. And like the ships, he cannot reverse course, cannot return to a brutish state and beast-like stupor. To do so would be to disrupt or fragment the momentum of his narrative. The rhetorical reversal in the passage renders impossible a reversion to the state of bondage. "I will run away" clarifies his future.

Douglass's declaration to run away and his faith in progress connect his personal story to the nation's destiny. The ships, "freedom's swift-winged angels," are metaphors of providence, progress, and commerce. The path of the ships parallels the plight of the nation, sailing to a heaven on earth defined by the millennium. All that stands in the way of the new age are the Edward Coveys and Thomas Aulds, representatives of the nation's reality of slavery, much as Douglass is a representative of the nation's ideal of freedom and self-making. The Coveys and Aulds divert the material and spiritual paths of progress, which are twinned; but the angels of the Lord, whether in the form of ships or slaves, continue sailing before God's gentle gale. By connecting himself with the ships and "freedom's swift-winged angels," Douglass also enables – indeed encourages – readers past and present to find in such passages their own stories and their own barriers that require declarations and faith.[21]

There is one other aspect of Douglass's apostrophe to the ships that sets him apart from other slave narrators: his attempt to grapple with the psychology of slavery. It would remain a major intellectual concern for the rest of his life, and few people captured the psychology of slavery better than Douglass. Such declarative statements as "I *will* run away" depended on his faith in providence and his future and served as a counter-balance to the psychology of slavery. As he later stated:

> The thought of only being a creature of the *present* and the *past*, troubled me, and I longed to have a *future* – a future with hope in it. To be shut up entirely to the past and present, is abhorrent to the human mind; it is to the soul – whose life and happiness is unceasing progress – what the prison is the body; a blight and mildew, a hell of horror. (*My Bondage*, p. 156)

Slavery was for Douglass tantamount to apostasy – a spiritual death with no possibility of an afterlife. It was also a social death, an extreme form of alienation and uncertainty, that denied the slave a future and cut him off from "wife, children, and friends of kindred tie," as he noted (*My Bondage*, p. 95).

******

Douglass continued to transform himself after publishing his 1845 *Narrative*. As a result, the book that catapulted him to fame soon became outdated. In fact his *Narrative* went out of print in the 1850s.[22] Slave narratives, like other forms of autobiography, portray a life from the perspective of the present; they seek to understand and explain the present self.[23] Ten years after publishing his *Narrative*, he was a totally different person. In 1845 he was still quite young – 27 years old, not yet an intellectual, and comparatively immature. Two years later he noted that he had only been out of slavery for nine years, and "in point of mental experience, I was but nine years old" (*My Bondage*, p. 237). His comparative immaturity is reflected in how he defined himself in terms of age: he celebrated September 3, 1838 – the day he fled north to freedom – as the marker of his birth, in place of his unknown birthday. His friend James McCune Smith suggested something of his radical self-transformation when he noted that Douglass had changed more in the eight years from 1846 to 1854 than he had from 1838 to 1846, during his eight-year rise from slavery to internationally acclaimed orator and writer. As a result, he published a second autobiography, *My Bondage and My Freedom*, in 1855 as a way to update his public persona.[24]

In many respects *My Bondage and My Freedom* is a deeper, richer book than Douglass's better-known *Narrative*. While the *Narrative* is shorter and more lyrical, *My Bondage* is more complex, over four times as long, and politically and intellectually more compelling. When it was published, it was even more of a success than the 1845 *Narrative*. It sold about 15,000 copies in the first two months of publication, and one reviewer, writing for the prestigious *Putnam's Monthly*, called Douglass "a genius," *My Bondage* "profoundly touching," and said the book was better than *Uncle Tom's Cabin*. Throughout *My Bondage*, Douglass explores the psychology of slavery and freedom in a way that he is unable to do in his *Narrative*.[25]

The changes in *My Bondage* reflect the changes in Douglass's life. When Douglass published his *Narrative*, he was still legally a slave and often defined himself as such. In 1844, while lecturing on the abolitionist circuit, he emphasized that he was not a "fugitive from slavery," as advertisements for his lectures stated, but a fugitive in slavery – a fugitive and a slave. And in 1849 he referred to himself as a "fugitive slave," even though British sympathizers had purchased his legal freedom in 1847. He was not yet ready to define himself as a free man both in fact and in form.[26]

Douglass's reluctance to define himself as a free man stemmed in part from his association with William Lloyd Garrison and the American Anti-Slavery Society. The Society was committed to the principles of non-resistance (non-violence and non-voting), considered politics and government corrupt, and relied on moral suasion to bring about the immediate abolition of slavery. While he gained crucial experience and confidence working for Garrison and the society, Douglass also felt frustrated. He received less pay than white agents, even though he drew the largest crowds and brought more attention to the society than any other member except perhaps Garrison himself. When he challenged a white colleague, he was more often than not rebuked. Garrison and most other members treated him as a son or dependant rather than an equal, and when he asserted his role as a leader, they became incensed.[27]

Douglass moved to Rochester, New York, in 1847, following a successful eighteen-month British speaking tour. While in England, admirers had raised enough money for him to purchase his freedom and start his own newspaper, *The North Star* (which became *Frederick Douglass' Paper* in 1851). In becoming an editor and independent entrepreneur, he declared his independence from his former employer geographically, intellectually, and emotionally. James McCune Smith suggested the import of Douglass's move to Rochester by telling Gerrit Smith: "You will be surprised to hear me say that only since [Douglass's] Editorial career has he begun to become a *colored man.*" With his move, Douglass liberated himself from the white paternalism of Garrison and the American Anti-Slavery Society.[28]

Douglass chose Rochester for a number of reasons. First, he did not have to compete for business with the American Anti-Slavery Society, which had newspapers in Boston (Garrison's *Liberator*) and New York City (the *National Anti-Slavery Standard*). Second, as a black man Douglass felt more comfortable in Rochester than in Boston. Rochester had a vibrant black and abolitionist community, and African Americans felt less alienated there than in Boston. Compared with Boston, Rochester was still young, racial hierarchies had not yet hardened, and there were few Irish immigrants, the most antiblack group in the North. Finally, Rochester, like Syracuse and Madison County in upstate New York, was a hotbed of political abolitionism, and Douglass (like most other blacks) had lost sympathy for Garrison's doctrines of non-voting and non-violence. Political abolitionists interpreted the Constitution as an antislavery document; and they believed that the government and citizens should intervene in slaveholding regions, using force if necessary, to end the evil. The American Anti-Slavery Society had an opposite understanding of government. Garrison publicly burned the Constitution, calling it "a covenant with death, an agreement with hell" for countenancing slavery. He advocated "disunion," which meant separating from the United States and relying wholly on moral suasion as the means to free the slaves. Douglass had never felt entirely comfortable with non-violence; after all, the turning point in his life as a slave centered around an act of violence – his famous fight with Covey.[29] By 1855, when Douglass published *My Bondage and My Freedom*, he was a political abolitionist, a temperate revolutionary, and an intellectual. A few months before publishing *My Bondage*, he became a founding member of the Radical Abolition party, a militant offshoot of the Liberty party, and in late June 1855 he attended its inaugural convention in Syracuse, New York. The Radical Abolitionists embraced the immediate abolition of slavery; full suffrage for all Americans regardless of sex or skin color; the redistribution of land so that no one would be poor and no one rich; and violent intervention against the growing belligerence of proslavery advocates. They also relied on "pentacostal visitations" (messages from God) to aid them in their fight against slavery. Their goal was nothing short of an immediate end to all evil.[30]

In the Radical Abolitionists, Douglass found mentors he could trust: he became close friends with Gerrit Smith and James McCune Smith, also founders of the party. The wealthy Gerrit Smith helped fund his newspaper and convinced him of the efficacy of political action; Douglass dedicated *My Bondage* to him. McCune Smith, the most learned African American of his day, greatly influenced Douglass's intellectual development; he wrote the Introduction to *My Bondage*.[31]

In many respects *My Bondage* resembled the inaugural convention of the Radical Abolitionists. Both "performances" sought to fulfill the ideals of the Declaration of Independence. It was a moment of exhilarating hope for the nation. Another memorable "performance" occurred at precisely the same time: one week after the inaugural convention of the Radical Abolitionists, and one month before the publication of *My Bondage*, Walt Whitman introduced, in entirely different form, a remarkably similar vision of America. On July 4, 1855 he self-published his first edition of *Leaves of Grass*. These three visions – political, poetic, and autobiographical – represent remarkable examples of faith in the possibility of individual and national liberation in the face of increasing oppression. In their articulation of a new age of democracy, they were *sui generis*.[32]

My Bondage represents Douglass's declaration of black independence from slavery and racism. It announces the presence of a confident black intellectual who borrows from white literary culture to shape his black aesthetic and insists on having his book read alongside classic white literature. Throughout the book, Douglass quotes or paraphrases famous white writers: Coleridge, Sir Walter Scott, Shakespeare, Lord Byron, Aristotle, Milton, Martin Luther, William Cowper, Longfellow, and Whittier; and there are at least thirty-five separate biblical references. These references reveal not only Douglass's growing intellectual powers, they highlight his efforts to break down the color line. He anticipates W. E. B. Du Bois, who declared in *The Souls of Black Folk* (1903): "I sit with Shakespeare and he winces not." Like Du Bois, the Douglass of *My Bondage* seeks to become a "co-worker in the kingdom of culture," dwell above the veil of race, and merge his double self – a black man and an American – into a better and truer self.[33]

Douglass declares his independence from racism and oppression in the opening pages of the book. The frontispiece depicts him elegantly dressed but with his hands clenched in fists as though ready for a fight. It sends a message that is repeated throughout the book: one of artful defiance. And like the portrait in his 1845 *Narrative*, it is unfinished, the details absent below the waist, as if to visualize his continual self-evolution. Following the frontispiece is his elaborate dedication to Gerrit Smith. Spread out over an entire page in ornate type, the dedication attempts to make visual Douglass's praise of Smith for "ranking slavery with piracy and murder" and denying its constitutional existence. At the outset of his book, then, Douglass distinguishes himself from his 1845 self, as reflected in the *Narrative*, and from his association with Garrison and the pacifist American Anti-Slavery Society. Slavery represented a state of rebellion or war, which needed to be vanquished with physical force if necessary in order to preserve the peace. McCune Smith's introduction also represented a sharp break from the structure of the 1845 *Narrative* and the tradition of slave narratives. While two white men presented Douglass to the public in the 1845 *Narrative*, bearing witness to his authentic status as a slave, a black intellectual writes the introduction to *My Bondage*, implying that Douglass refused to be mediated by whites and instead embraced his black identity.

Douglass divides *My Bondage and My Freedom* into two parts: his "life as a slave" and his "life as a freeman." In the first part he represents himself as a slave who continually seeks his freedom. By learning to read and write, believe in his deliverance, and stand up to his masters, he acquires degrees of freedom. Throughout the text he performs his freedom. His fight with Edward Covey, for example, is even more of a performance than in the 1845 *Narrative*, a staged and ritualized battle in which he becomes a free man "in *fact*" even while remaining a slave "in *form*" (*My Bondage*, p. 140).

But the second part gives Douglass considerable trouble. Representing himself as a free man seemed to induce in him a crisis of language and aesthetics. He begins "life as a freeman" by stating: "There is no necessity for any extended notice of the incidents of this part of my life" (*My Bondage*, p. 199). His description of becoming free a few lines later reveals a similar frustration with the inadequacy of words:

> It was a moment of joyous excitement, which no words can describe. In a letter to a friend, written soon after reaching New York, I said I felt as one might be supposed to feel, on escaping from a den of hungry lions. But, in a moment like that, sensations are too intense and too rapid for words. Anguish and grief, like darkness and rain, may be described, but joy and gladness, like the rainbow of promise, defy alike the pen and pencil. (*My Bondage*, pp. 199–200)

The power of words, acquired in part by studying *The Columbian Orator*, had fueled Douglass's desire for freedom and enabled his rise to fame. But now words could not represent the sensation of freedom.

Part of Douglass's problem was that there was no precedent for representing oneself as a free man while embracing immediate emancipation and a sharp break from the past. Douglass had no one to turn to for help, and in writing *My Bondage*, he created a new genre that follows the form previously reserved for white men: a narrative that describes a life in freedom, rather than ending at the moment of freedom, as all previous slave narratives had done.[34]

The teleology of slave narratives centered around the moment of freedom. Narrators saw in one divine event the end of doubt and disappointment; freedom represented a new age, and they worshiped it with unwavering faith, as Du Bois later noted. But since narratives ended at the moment of freedom, they could not articulate this new dispensation. The struggle to develop an aesthetic of freedom perhaps helps to explain why African American literary works published in the 1850s greatly exceeded those works published between 1867 and 1876, a period in which only two novels were published and slave narratives dwindled to a trickle.[35]

In light of Douglass's hesitation about representing himself in freedom, he devotes seventy pages to his "life as a freeman," plus an additional sixty pages of an "Appendix" in small print that contains excerpts of six speeches and one public letter. That is a lot of prose to describe something Douglass suggests cannot be described with words. He resolves the conundrum by emphasizing his continued subaltern status and struggle for freedom in the face of Northern racism. He notes, for example, that after entering Garrison's ranks as a lecturer, he was treated as a commodity, or text, of white abolitionists, rather than having the autonomy to represent himself:

> I was generally introduced as a "*chattel*" – a "*thing*" – a piece of southern "*property*" – the chairman assuring the audience that *it* could speak. . . . "Give us the facts," said Collins, "we will take care of the philosophy." . . . It was impossible for me to repeat the same old story month after month, and to keep up my interest in it. . . . [T]o go through with it every night was a task altogether too mechanical for my nature. "Tell your story," would whisper my then revered friend, William Lloyd Garrison. . . I could not always obey, for I was now reading and thinking. (*My Bondage*, pp. 215–16)

The slave as "thing" could not acquire life and humanity because Garrisonians sought to control Douglass's creative self-fashioning. It was another form of bondage. Douglass's attack on Garrison is subtle but sharp: his *then* revered friend made him feel like a mechanical thing; he yearned for liberty, and could not always obey.

It is significant that Douglass ends his "life as a freeman" at the moment he severs his ties with Garrison. Then he begins his Appendix and radically alters his narrative framework. In struggling to create a new genre and find an appropriate style for representing himself as a free man, Douglass presents himself as a performer – a successful black orator – unadorned, as it were, unmediated by a narrator. He arranges the speeches chronologically, so that readers can glimpse the fragmented evolution of this public persona. The last speech in the Appendix brings us to Douglass's present, in early 1855, with a lecture on the antislavery movement that prophesies the new age. Unlike the *Narrative*, which ends with Douglass parodying the slaveholding hymn, "Heavenly Union," *My Bondage* ends with Douglass connecting himself to God:

> Old as the everlasting hills; immovable as the throne of God; and certain as the purposes of eternal power, against all hinderances, and against all delays, and despite all the mutations of human instrumentalities, it is the faith of my soul, that this anti-slavery cause will triumph.   (*My Bondage*, p. 292)

Douglass is a prophet: the "faith of [his] soul" is as old as God's world and as immovable as God's throne; and he is certain of God's power – he knows that God will help him vanquish slavery.[36]

Many readers of *My Bondage and My Freedom* skim through or even skip the Appendix, and it is almost never discussed in criticism. But it contains some of Douglass's most powerful writings, including "What to the Slave is the Fourth of July?" and "The Slavery Party," the latter which anticipates Lincoln's "House Divided" speech of 1858 in its description of the Slave Power and in its rhetorical power. The speeches are well chosen and edited and imply a continuation of Douglass's persona. But unlike the narrative proper, the focus is on politics and national regeneration. The performative slave has become a political persona. Taken together, the speeches contrast the present sinful society with the coming millennium. The fragmented and episodic nature of the speeches is appropriate to the millennial history that is conveyed.

Even more than his 1845 *Narrative*, *My Bondage* is a testament to Douglass's belief that "true" art could dissolve social barriers and bring life and power to a slave. Speaking, writing, and images work together in the book to create a powerful portrait of an intelligent, authentic, black performer and prophet. By refashioning himself as a performer, or art object, Douglass hoped to confer upon his persona and his readers – especially his white readers – a new life, which would link them together and dissolve social barriers. As a slave – a "thing," – Douglass acquires life and humanity by representing himself as a performer. He hopes that the reader will acquire new life by perceiving that "thing" as human.

The nature of Douglass's art stemmed from his efforts to dissolve the boundaries between black and white, rich and poor, sacred and profane, heaven and earth, and art and politics. These cultural dichotomies had long served as a source of order and hierarchy in western culture. Although Douglass was not always successful in collapsing them, he went further than most of his peers. By attacking the belief that some people were born to be slaves and others masters, he was led to question other social divisions, as opposed to more conservative reformers and artists, who legitimated the status quo by separating slavery and art from politics and other institutions.[37]

In striving to break down social barriers, Douglass continually remade himself at the same time he sought to reform the country. The self-evolution in his 1845 *Narrative* and 1855 *My Bondage* exemplifies his belief in "identity" as constantly changing and highly subjective, dependent upon time, place, and circumstance. The idea of "whiteness" as a sign of superiority and a justification for racial oppression was based in part on an understanding of character that was fixed and unchanging. Douglass first grappled with this notion of fluidity in his *Narrative* and developed it in *My Bondage* by brilliantly attacking "whiteness." While the *Narrative* focuses on forms of bondage and alienation, *My Bondage* foregrounds race and the problems of transition from bondage to freedom.

The dramatic changes in Douglass's persona from 1845 to 1855 reflect his appellation as a "Representative American man." Of course, his trajectory had never been representative. He represented what was possible, but his life was never a synecdoche of the black condition. In describing his continual self-evolution, he necessarily leaves out many things, most noticeably the women who helped him escape from slavery and become an independent newspaperman. The most glaring omission is of his wife, Anna Murray, a free black who enabled him to escape by giving him money, and who supported herself and their children by working as a domestic while he lectured abroad for almost two years. She is referred to as an afterthought. In his 1845 *Narrative*, Douglass casually notes that "Anna, my intended wife, came on" after he arrived safely at New York City (*Narrative*, p. 113). Aside from this and a brief mention of his marriage, his only description of her takes the form of an asterisked footnote: "She was free" (ibid.). There is even less space (one sentence) devoted to her in *My Bondage*. But much like the other classic male "I"-narratives of the era, from Melville's *Moby-Dick* and Thoreau's *Walden* to Whitman's *Leaves of Grass*, self-transformation and emancipation came at the expense of family and domestic life, and the role of father and husband.

NOTES

1. John Stauffer, *The Black Hearts of Men: Radical Abolitionists and the Transformation of Race* (Cambridge, MA: Harvard University Press, 2002), pp. 45–56; Henry Louis Gates, Jr., *Figures in Black: Words, Signs, and the "Racial" Self* (New York: Oxford University Press, 1987), pp. 98–124.

2. James McCune Smith, "Introduction" to Frederick Douglass, *My Bondage and My Freedom*, ed. John Stauffer (1855. Rpt. New York: Modern Library, 2003), p. xlix. Subsequent quotations from *My Bondage* will be from this edition and cited by page number parenthetically within the text.

3. Philip S. Foner, *The Life and Writings of Frederick Douglass, Vol. III: The Civil War, 1861–1865* (New York: International Publishers, 1952), p. 45; Helen Douglass, ed., *In Memoriam: Frederick Douglass* (Philadelphia: J. C. Yorston and Co., 1897), pp. 70–71; Stauffer, *Black Hearts of Men*, pp. 50–51.

4. Frederick Douglass, *Life and Times of Frederick Douglass, Written by Himself* (1892. Rpt. New York: Collier Books, 1962), p. 511. Subsequent quotations from the *Life* will be from this edition and cited by page number parenthetically within the text.

5. John Blassingame, "Introduction," *The Frederick Douglass Papers, Series One, Vol. 1: 1841–46* (New Haven: Yale University Press, 1979), pp. xxi–lxix; Elizabeth Cady Stanton, quoted from *Majestic in His Wrath: A Pictorial Life of Frederick Douglass*, ed. Frederick S. Voss (Washington, DC: Smithsonian Institution Press, 1995), p. v.

6. Nathaniel Rogers, quoted from Philip S. Foner, *Frederick Douglass* (1964. Rpt. New York: The Citadel Press, 1969), p. 47.

7. *Salem [MA] Register*, quoted from Foner, *Douglass*, p. 55.

8. Frederick Douglass, "From the Editor," *The North Star*, November 23, 1849.

9. Dickson J. Preston, *Young Frederick Douglass: The Maryland Years* (Baltimore: Johns Hopkins University Press, 1980), pp. 148–49.

10. David W. Blight, "Introduction," *Narrative of the Life of Frederick Douglass, an American Slave, Written by Himself*, 2nd edn. (Boston: Bedford/St. Martins, 2003), p. 6. Subsequent quotations from Douglass's *Narrative* will be from this edition and cited by page number parenthetically within the text.

11. *The Liberator*, August 30, 1844, quoted in Foner, *Douglass*, p. 59.

12. William S. McFeely, *Frederick Douglass* (New York: W. W. Norton, 1991), pp. 116–17; Foner, *Douglass*, pp. 59–60, quotations from reviewers on p. 60 (emphasis in original).

13. Gates, *Figures in Black*, pp. 80–97; Stauffer, *Black Hearts of Men*, pp. 7, 14–20; Blight, "Introduction," p. 21; James Olney, "'I Was Born': Slave Narratives, Their Status as Autobiography and as Literature" in *The Slave's Narrative*. Charles T. Davis and Henry Louis Gates, Jr., eds. (New York: Oxford University Press, 1985), pp. 148–74.

14. William L. Andrews, "Introduction" to Douglass's *My Bondage and My Freedom* (Urbana: University of Illinois Press, 1987), pp. xi–xxviii.

15. According to the historians Dickson Preston and David Blight, Douglass's aunt was Hester (not Esther) Bailey, the eighth child of Betsey Bailey, born in 1810. When Douglass changed "Hester" to "Esther" in *My Bondage and My Freedom*,

he was relying on the oral tradition. See Preston, *Young Frederick Douglass*, p. 221, n.1; Blight, *Narrative*, p. 45, n.6.

16. David Blight, "Introduction," *The Columbian Orator* (New York: New York University Press, 1998), p. xviii; William L. Andrews, *To Tell a Free Story: The First Century of Afro-American Autobiography, 1760–1820* (Urbana: University of Illinois Press, 1986); Gates, *Figures in Black*, pp. 98–124.

17. Blight, *Columbian Orator*, pp. 5–26, quotation from p. 7.

18. Ibid., pp. 7–11; Stauffer, *Black Hearts of Men*, pp. 6–7; W. J. T. Mitchell, *Picture Theory* (Chicago: University of Chicago Press, 1994), pp. 151–54, 162–63, 183–98.

19. Blight, *Narrative*, p. 84, n.43.

20. Andrews, *To Tell a Free Story*, p. 105.

21. Blight, "Introduction," p. 17. See also Robert G. O'Meally, "Frederick Douglass' 1845 Narrative: The Text Was Meant to be Preached" in *Afro-American Literature: The Reconstruction of Instruction*. Dexter Fisher and Robert B. Stepto, eds. (New York: Modern Language Association, 1979), p. 210; Andrews, *To Tell a Free Story*, pp. 97–138.

22. Blight, "Introduction," p. 19.

23. Ibid., p. 21; James Olney, *Metaphors of Self: The Meaning of Autobiography* (Princeton: Princeton University Press, 1972), p. 264; Waldo Martin, Jr., *The Mind of Frederick Douglass* (Chapel Hill, NC: University of North Carolina Press, 1984), pp. 253–80.

24. Frederick Douglass, *My Bondage and My Freedom*, pp. 257–58; James McCune Smith, "Frederick Douglass in New York," *Frederick Douglass' Papers*, February 2, 1855; Stauffer, *Black Hearts of Men*, p. 160.

25. Stauffer, "Foreword," *My Bondage*, pp. xix–xx.

26. Nathaniel P. Rogers, "Southern Slavery and Northern Religion," February 1, 1844, reprinted in Blight, *Narrative*; Douglass, "A Tribute for the Negro," *North Star*, April 7, 1849, reprinted in Philip S. Foner, ed., *The Life and Writings of Frederick Douglass, Vol. 1: Early Years, 1817–1849* (New York: International Publishers, 1950), p. 380.

27. Stauffer, *Black Hearts of Men*, pp. 158–62; William H. Pease and Jane H. Pease, "Boston Garrisonians and the Problem of Frederick Douglass," *Canadian Journal of History* 2 (Sept. 1967): 29–48; Benjamin Quarles, "The Breach Between Douglass and Garrison," *Journal of Negro History* 23 (April 1938): 144–54.

28. James McCune Smith to Gerrit Smith, July 28, 1848, Gerrit Smith Papers, Syracuse University; Stauffer, *Black Hearts of Men*, pp. 158–63.

29. William E. Cain, ed., *William Lloyd Garrison and the Fight against Slavery: Selections from The Liberator* (Boston: Bedford Books, 1995), pp. 27–36, 101–05, 112–15, 141–43, quotation from p. 36; Stauffer, *Black Hearts of Men*, pp. 158–68; McFeely, *Frederick Douglass*, pp. 50–57; John R. McKivigan, "The Frederick Douglass–Gerrit Smith Friendship and Political Abolitionism in the 1850s," *Frederick Douglass: New Literary and Historical Essays*, ed. Eric J. Sundquist (Cambridge: Cambridge University Press, 1990), p. 208.

30. Stauffer, *Black Hearts of Men*, pp. 8–44, quotation from p. 12.

31. Ibid., p. 160.

32. Ibid., pp. 9, 39–42.

33. W. E. B. Du Bois, *The Souls of Black Folk* (1903. Rpt. New York: Penguin Books, 1989), pp. 5, 90; John Stauffer, "Frederick Douglass and the Aesthetics of Freedom," *Raritan* 25.1 (summer 2005): 122.

34. In 1856, in part inspired by *My Bondage*, Austin Steward published a slave narrative that devoted more space to his life in freedom than to that in slavery. See Austin Steward, *Twenty-Two Years a Slave and Forty Years a Freeman* (1856. Rpt. Reading, MA: Addison-Wesley Publishing Company, 1969).

35. Stauffer, "Douglass and Aesthetics of Freedom," p. 127; Henry Louis Gates, Jr., "The Trope of a New Negro and the Reconstruction of the Image of the Black," *The New American Studies: Essays from Representations*, Philip Fisher, ed. (Berkeley: University of California Press, 1991), p. 321.

36. Stauffer, "Douglass and Aesthetics of Freedom," pp. 127–29.

37. Stauffer, *Black Hearts of Men*, pp. 19–20.

13

JOHN ERNEST

Beyond Douglass and Jacobs

Not very long ago, students taking a standard Survey of American Literature course that covered the years up to the Civil War would have encountered just one slave narrative, *The Narrative of the Life of Frederick Douglass, an American Slave*, first published in 1845. These days, students in that course are likely to encounter two slave narratives – or rather, one complete narrative and about one-seventh of another. Both *The Norton Anthology of American Literature, 1820–1865* and *The Heath Anthology of American Literature – Early Nineteenth Century: 1800–1865* include exactly six of the forty-one chapters of Harriet Jacobs's *Incidents in the Life of a Slave Girl*.[1] The *Heath Anthology* also includes the work of four other African American writers, all collected together with Douglass and Jacobs in the section entitled "Race, Slavery and the Invention of the 'South.'" In this volume of the *Norton Anthology*, Douglass and Jacobs are the only African American writers represented. Students who continue in the survey might encounter one or two other narratives – perhaps Booker T. Washington's *Up From Slavery* (1901), for example. Most students interested in American literary history, then, and many of their teachers, will encounter fewer than a handful of narratives that will represent a genre that includes an estimated 6,000 texts – including books, periodical publications, and oral histories and interviews. Even in courses not burdened by the constraints of historical coverage that makes any survey course a challenge, Douglass's 1845 *Narrative* and Jacobs's *Incidents* (read in its entirety) are often the only slave narratives assigned; similarly, a great deal of scholarship on American literary and cultural history includes significant discussions only of Douglass (most often) or of Jacobs, or of the two together.

Douglass's first narrative (of the three he published) and all or part of Jacobs's *Incidents*, then, have some serious representative work to do. But what is being represented, and how should we understand that representation, and are the *Narrative* and *Incidents*, classics though they are, adequate for this work? Douglass, who in his own time was often viewed as *the* representative of all African Americans, understood well the cultural politics of black representative identity in a white supremacist nation. In an 1865 speech at the inauguration of a school named for him, Douglass complained that "the public, with the mass of ignorance . . . has sternly denied the representative character of our distinguished men. They are treated as exceptions, individual cases, and the like." "When prejudice cannot deny the black man's ability," Douglass noted, "it denies his race, and claims him as a white man. It affirms that if he is not exactly white, he ought to be," and that "he owes whatever intelligence he possesses to the white race by contract or association."[2] In his own time, Douglass's mixed-race status sometimes did indeed play a role in his public recognition; in more recent times, Douglass has often been presented, implicitly and sometimes explicitly, as an exceptional figure in that his *Narrative* has been recognized not only as an important slave narrative but also as a unique literary achievement, one deserving of attention alongside of white writers of his time. Jacobs's *Incidents*, on the other hand, was long ignored or devalued *because* it was an exception, both because it represents a woman's perspective and because scholars suspected that white writers were involved in the production of the narrative. As Rafia Zafar has noted, "for breaking from [the] recognized pattern of male slave narrators – Harriet Jacobs is alone among antebellum female writers of book-length secular autobiographies – Jacobs was either decried as inauthentic or dismissed as atypical."[3] *Incidents* was long assumed to be either the product of a white writer or, later, the achievement of a talented and tactful white editor. Subsequently, Jacobs has become the exceptional-representative woman to balance Douglass's exceptional-representative man.

Of course, there are reasons why Douglass and Jacobs are considered to be both exceptional and representative. As Zafar notes, Jacobs is alone among US women who published a book-length slave narrative before the Civil War. Accordingly, although *Incidents* is not the only slave narrative that addresses the condition and situation of enslaved women, Jacobs's is the only US book from this period that can represent the slave narrative genre from a woman's perspective, making the book representative, in effect, by default. Jacobs's success in presenting that perspective and transforming the conventions associated with this male-dominated genre is among the qualities that make *Incidents* such a stunning literary achievement. Douglass's *Narrative*, on the other hand, was one of many book-length slave narratives authored by men, though Douglass is noted for his memorable representation of the masculine struggle with enslavement. But even in its own time, before most readers thought to question gendered perspectives, Douglass's achievement in his *Narrative*, published shortly before he traveled to Great Britain to promote the antislavery movement, was celebrated as a particularly eloquent and powerful example of the developing genre. As David W. Blight has noted, the *Narrative* "quickly became a best-seller. Much anticipated among abolitionists, it sold five thousand copies in the first four months of publication."[4] Once abroad, "Douglass helped finance his British tour by selling the *Narrative*, which went through nine editions and sold eleven thousand copies between 1845 and 1847. By the eve of the Civil War in 1860, approximately thirty thousand copies of the *Narrative* had been sold on two continents, and the book had been translated into both French and German editions" (*Narrative*, p. 16). "Indeed," Blight observes, "along with his public speeches, the *Narrative* made Frederick Douglass the most famous black person in the world" (ibid.). Jacobs – who had once worked in an antislavery reading room located above Frederick Douglass's offices in Rochester, New York – long resisted requests that she write her story, and when she published *Incidents* in 1861, interest in slave narratives and the antislavery movement was being eclipsed by the Civil War. Unlike Douglass, and reflecting the significant difference between the public perception of a man's story of former degradation and a woman's, Jacobs did not place her name prominently on her book's title page, and the book did not support a European speaking tour, though it did secure her a reputation in the abolitionist community that led to her career of aiding and educating the formerly enslaved during and after the Civil War.

Douglass was viewed as an exceptional-representative in his own time; Jacobs's similar reputation came much later, when both *Incidents* and Douglass's *Narrative* entered into the canon of American literary history – Douglass's narrative firmly, and Jacobs's more tentatively. Of course, the literary canon and what counts as public memory are both subject to the prerogatives of a racialized culture in which importance is measured mainly by one's recognition in the white mainstream. As David Blight has noted of Frederick Douglass, and Sandra Gunning and Rafia Zafar have noted of Jacobs, black scholars had for some time read and studied the work and lives of Douglass and Jacobs, long before these nineteenth-century activists were "discovered" by white scholars and teachers, and in Douglass's case long before the *Narrative* was reprinted for twentieth-century readers.[5] It is not surprising, then, that both the *Narrative* and *Incidents* received increasingly *official* attention – that is, new editions of the texts, scholarship noted by such national organizations as the Modern Language Association, and inclusion in mainstream literary anthologies – only after the Civil Rights Movement and the Black Studies Movement began to force the issue of the need to recover the texts of African American intellectual, cultural, and literary history. As Blight has noted, Douglass's *Narrative* was out of print "for more than a century, from the 1850s to 1960" (*Narrative*, p. 17). "By the 1950s," Blight continues, "a genuine Douglass revival may be said to have begun among literary scholars, and through the civil rights revolution and the rediscovery of black history during the following decade, at least three new editions of the *Narrative* were published by 1968" (*Narrative*, p. 18). As Zafar notes, "one hundred and twelve years were to elapse between the anonymous publication of *Incidents in the Life of a Slave Girl* and the first modern reprint edited by Walter Teller," and "a century and a quarter would pass before Jacobs's autobiography received a comprehensive, scholarly treatment by Jean Fagan Yellin" ("Introduction," p. 4). *Incidents* received increasing attention after the publication of Yellin's authoritative edition and eventually was included (one-seventh of it, anyway) in anthologies of American literary history, where Douglass's *Narrative* had been holding the fort for African American literary self-representation for some time.

Rather quickly during its rise to prominence, *Incidents* was presented in scholarship and classrooms alike as the necessary corrective or counterbalance to the story of masculine struggle that Douglass presents in his *Narrative*. As Valerie Smith has argued, "by representing themselves as isolated heroic subjects, male slave narrators also defined their humanity in the terms of prevailing conceptions of American male identity."[6] In telling a different story, and also in telling similar stories differently, *Incidents* served as a text that could expose the assumptions that guided not only Douglass's experience but also his narration of his experience. In many ways, this was an important and appropriate part of the value of *Incidents* when it was first made widely available. Indeed, as is revealed by the selection of the six chapters of *Incidents* included in either the *Norton Anthology* or the *Heath Anthology*, Jacobs's representation of an enslaved woman's experience remains one of the most important considerations for many who read *Incidents* (thus limiting a woman's perspective, in the process, to those moments when she is addressing most directly experiences that are gender-specific). As Deborah E. McDowell has noted, scholars and teachers have long "privileged and mystified Douglass's narrative" by having it serve a "double duty: not only does it make slavery intelligible, but the 'black experience' as well."[7] "It is this choice of Douglass as . . . 'representative man,'" McDowell argues, "as the part that stands for the whole, that reproduces the omission of women from view, except as afterthoughts different from 'the same' (black men)."[8] Jacobs's one-seventh representative status in anthologies suggests that the situation McDowell describes still prevails. But even when Jacobs is allowed fuller representation, her representative status can too easily be read against her intentions for her narrative. As Frances Smith Foster has argued, "rather than use her experiences as representative of others," as Jacobs intended, "too many scholars and critics have used the experiences of others to invalidate those that Jacobs recounted. Their interest revolves exclusively around Harriet Jacobs as both author and subject and around how her victories and her values contrast with prevailing theories and opinions of slave life."[9]

Foster's comments, along with the role of *Incidents* as truncated supplement to Douglass's *Narrative*, raise serious questions about how and why we read slave narratives. What do these narratives and their authors represent, and how on earth can we know, given that attention to this history in our educational system is sketchy at best? As Foster indicates, readers generally bring a set of questions directed toward an insistent curiosity about the details of the lives of the enslaved. At times, these questions move quickly from the particular to the general, making Douglass's *Narrative*, for example, a brief history of slavery – all one needs to know in roughly one hundred pages. Douglass stands in for all of the enslaved, and the *Narrative* is reduced to a list of horrors, a generalized tale of struggle. At times, as Foster suggests, these questions move from the general to the particular, as Jacobs's narrative is tested against "prevailing theories and opinions of slave life" and her narration thereby judged either reliable or unreliable accordingly. Often, that is, teachers and students alike bring to the classroom (and even scholars sometimes to their studies) a set framework for understanding and responding to slave narratives, and a small and very general body of knowledge about slavery that they apply directly to individual narratives. The narrative, in effect, must say what readers expect it to say.

This was the case, in fact, when those who were once enslaved first published their stories or spoke at antislavery events. One text, for example, *Louisa Picquet, the Octoroon: or Inside Views of Southern Domestic Life*, features an extensive series of questions and answers between Picquet and Hiram Mattison, a white abolitionist. In his interview with Picquet, Mattison presses for details about sexual violations or other physical and mental abuse. Noting Mattison's "prurient obsession" in this interview, Anthony G. Barthelemy has commented on the delicate tensions between Mattison and Picquet. "Responding to Mattison's questions," Barthelemy observes, "Picquet tells us something of her life in slavery and freedom. Mattison, however, was interested in the institution of slavery itself and in its attendant moral corruption. The minister failed to recognize Picquet as an individual; rather, she and her experiences served to substantiate his argument and to justify his self-righteousness and moral indignation."[10] In his approach to understanding both Picquet and the system of slavery, Mattison himself becomes something of a representative figure; many white readers, then and today, resemble Mattison more than they might care to acknowledge. With such approaches in mind, the historian Robin Winks has called slave

narratives "the pious pornography of their day,"[11] stories of intimate violations that white Americans could read while still feeling that they were
engaged in a benevolent exercise. In our day, reading a slave narrative
for particular horrors and generalized outrage can enable readers to keep
the story of slavery neatly generalized, safely individualized, or otherwise
contained.

As we ask, then, whether it is enough to read just one of Douglass's narratives and all or part of Jacobs's, we need to ask as well *how* we read these and
other narratives. What demands do we face when we encounter one or more
of these texts, say, in a literature course? Often, as I've suggested already,
slave narratives in literature courses are studied primarily for their content –
the story told about slavery, the story of physical and psychological abuse,
and the story of a brave escape from slavery. Read in this way, what makes
these narratives count as *literature* is that the style shows conspicuous skill
or that the authors demonstrate familiarity with the literary conventions and
standards of their day, and especially those conventions and standards associated with white American literary history. What makes a particular narrative
stand out is that a particular author (most often, Douglass or Jacobs) can
write in such a way as to utilize those conventions while surpassing those
standards – in terms, say, of stylistic grace or rhetorical skill. Certain episodes
seem especially vivid – for example, Douglass's account of the whipping of
Aunt Hester that was for him "the blood-stained gate, the entrance to the
hell of slavery."[12] Certain phrases seem to capture especially well either the
experience of slavery or the determination required to resist it. Many readers
have commented, for example, on Douglass's provocative statement, "You
have seen how a man was made a slave; you shall see how a slave was made a
man" (*Narrative*, p. 75). Many readers have noted as well the significance of
Jacobs's comment on the conclusion to her narrative: "Reader, my story ends
with freedom; not in the usual way, with marriage."[13] Here Jacobs's invocation of the conventions of sentimental novels, which usually ended with marriage, is especially purposeful, for readers are pressed to realize that Jacobs
has used literary conventions associated with courtship and marriage stories
so as to emphasize the extent to which her condition removed her from the
world in which many of her white female readers lived – thus emphasizing the extent to which hers is a story about both slavery and racism. Such
moments have made Douglass's *Narrative* and Jacobs's *Incidents* the leading
slave narratives in many courses – both in courses where the narratives are
read as literature and in history courses where they are read to give vivid
personal testimonies to the realities covered in scholarly studies of slavery.

For these reasons and others, Douglass's 1845 *Narrative* and Jacobs's *Incidents* are justly valued as great achievements – but students who read only

these texts are not at all in a position to appreciate (or question) the terms of this valuation. Certainly, most readers have no trouble understanding that these narratives tell important stories, for it is impossible to read them without a profound sense of the seriousness and complexity of their subject. Most readers would agree, then, that it would be a rather serious violation to read these narratives as literary achievements and say nothing about the content, or to treat the subject of slavery as just the occasion for these literary achievements. But it would be a serious violation as well to consider literary achievement as a separate category – that is, to consider rhetorical skill and stylistic grace simply as a remarkable sign of individual achievement, simply as the ability of Douglass or Jacobs to rise from their former enslaved position to such a level of education and literacy that they are able to fashion from their experience an extraordinary rhetorical performance. In fact, though, this is often the case. It is not unusual for readers of Douglass's *Narrative* and Jacobs's *Incidents* alike to express surprise that two people born in slavery, first, could write at all and, second, could write so well. Their skill as writers is celebrated, in effect, as an exceptional achievement – so that these writers who are asked to represent the slave narrative genre are considered as not representative at all but exceptional in their talent, and therefore in the position to represent the realities of enslavement. For many, what makes Douglass and Jacobs representative are the conditions under which they lived; what makes them remarkable is that they have reached a level of achievement that meets the standards even of those who have enjoyed the benefits of education and a privileged life. The style and art of slave narratives, then, are implicitly considered to be a measure of the narrator's success in transcending the world of slavery. As most slave narratives begin with slavery and end in freedom, so, too, is the distinction between content (slavery) and style (not just literacy, but rhetorical talent) viewed as a journey *away* from slavery.

The problem with this approach is that to separate style from content is to undermine the authority of the slave narrative *as a text* and of the writers of slave narratives *as authors*. Certainly, Douglass, Jacobs, and many others were justly proud of their achievements – but their approach to writing was not simply an attempt to encourage a doubting public (many of whom did not believe them capable of such writing) to admire their talent. They wrote not to display the extent to which they had escaped slavery; rather, they wrote to *get into the realities of slavery*, and to force their readers to recognize that, in fact, there *was* no escape from slavery, not for African Americans born into it, and not for white Americans in the North who had never experienced it. Authors of slave narratives did not write simply to celebrate their escape; they wrote because so many others remained enslaved, a condition that would not change for many until the nation addressed the economic, political, social, and legal structures that supported slavery and the racial assumptions that extended from slavery. Both Douglass and Jacobs crafted their narratives to make exactly this point, but readers are in a position to fully appreciate the complexity and depth of this point only when they can recognize the complexity and depth of the *craft* of these narratives. It is difficult, however, to evaluate or even to recognize the craft of slave narratives if one knows little about the system of slavery and little about African American literary, political, and intellectual traditions. In short, how are we to read Douglass's *Narrative* and Jacobs's *Incidents* as representative slave narratives if we do not know anything about the genre of slave narratives that they are asked to represent? And given that Douglass and Jacobs are sometimes the only antebellum African American writers that students will encounter, how can those students come to a just and informed understanding of antebellum African American literature if they are encouraged to think that what is most African American about these texts is the subject – oppression experienced under slavery – and not the rhetorical response to that subject?

To appreciate the style of slave narratives, then, one must understand the challenges that Douglass, Jacobs, and other writers of slave narratives faced in trying to represent the system of slavery. Representing the system of slavery, as part of a larger effort to promote antislavery sympathy and activism, involved more than simply pointing to physical abuse or dramatic injustices. As Saidiya V. Hartman has observed, "the most invasive forms of slavery's violence lie not in . . . exhibitions of 'extreme' suffering or in what we see but in what we don't see. Shocking displays too easily obfuscate the more mundane and socially endurable forms of terror."[14] The simple fact of enslavement, in other words, and the daily experience of that fact, was a form of terror that cannot be easily revealed by a strict narration of events or experiences, but the fact itself should have been enough for a nation that had fought a revolution for the abstract ideal of liberty. Slave narrators, who had survived and escaped not just episodic but daily experiences of the abuses of slavery, were constantly in the position of having to make an argument that should have been unnecessary. In a famous speech, Frederick Douglass asserted, "I submit, where all is plain there is nothing to be argued." What argument should be necessary, Douglass wondered, to establish the injustice of slavery? Through a series of pointed questions, he emphasized the absurdity of his position: "Must I undertake to prove that the slave is a man?"; "would you have me argue that man is entitled to liberty?"; "must I argue that a system thus marked with blood, and stained with pollution, is *wrong*?"[15] Such arguments, Douglass asserted, should not be necessary in a nation whose founding document was the Declaration of Independence.

And yet, as Douglass and others recognized, such arguments were precisely the point of slave narratives.

For Douglass and others, what was wrong about slavery was its very existence as a systemic operation of laws, customs, and philosophy that threatened the stability and undermined the integrity of all of American culture. "The system of slavery," wrote the great black abolitionist William Wells Brown, himself a fugitive slave, "is a system that strikes at the foundation of society, that strikes at the foundation of civil and political institutions."[16] Indeed, the system of slavery affected every aspect of American culture, corrupting every institution, degrading every ideal, and touching every life. Even after slavery was abolished in the Northern states, it was still a strong economic and political presence, shaping Northern culture as well as national political life. African American abolitionists knew very well that true anti-slavery efforts would be those directed at fundamental systemic reform, addressing the rights of the nominally free as well as "freeing" those who were enslaved. As Frederick Douglass proclaimed in the same speech from which I've quoted above, "The existence of slavery in this country brands your republicanism as a sham, your humanity as a base pretense, and your Christianity as a lie."[17] How can one hope to tell such a story? To tell it rightly would be to tell a story that reached to the "foundation of civil and political institutions"; to tell it rightly would be to question some of the most fundamental assumptions behind the larger story of American progress and political ideals. It is not surprising, then, that the stories that audiences, then as now, wanted most to hear were generally more manageable, more individual, focusing either on horrors that one can easily denounce or on struggles for freedom that one can heartily celebrate.

African American abolitionists knew that such expectations could not be ignored. In virtually all slave narratives, readers will encounter the kind of stories they expect to encounter – the "exhibitions of 'extreme' suffering" that Hartman discusses. I've noted, for example, Douglass's account of his "entrance to the hell of slavery" through the "blood-stained gate" of abuse. Similarly, William Wells Brown, in his 1847 *Narrative of William W. Brown, A Fugitive Slave*, writes of a time when his mother was whipped: "Though the field was some distance from the house, I could hear every crack of the whip, and every groan and cry of my poor mother."[18] In his *Narrative of the Life and Adventures of Henry Bibb, an American Slave* (1849), Bibb tells of losing a wife and child to slavery, and of his wife losing her honor to her owner. In the *Narrative of the Life of Henry Box Brown* (1851), Henry "Box" Brown even addresses the relative absence of such episodes in his narrative, speaking knowingly to his readers when he prefaces his narrative with the comment, "The tale of my own sufferings is not one of great interest to those who delight to read of hair-breadth adventures, of tragic occurrences, and scenes of blood."[19] In virtually all slave narratives, more-over, readers encounter stories of the journey to relative freedom in the North that quickly became part of the popular legends of the Underground Rail-road, and many readers looked to these stories for brave escapes and heroic adventures. Indeed, in our own time, when the Underground Railroad has developed into an extremely popular story, it is instructive to think about the comments of an early scholar, Albert Bushnell Hart, who in 1899 wrote that those involved in the Underground Railroad were "enjoying the most roman-tic and exciting amusement open to men who had high moral standards." "The Underground Railroad," Hart continued, "was the opportunity for the bold and adventurous; it had the excitement of piracy, the secrecy of bur-glary, the daring of insurrection; to the pleasure of relieving the poor negro's sufferings it added the triumph of snapping one's fingers at the slave-catcher; it developed coolness, indifference to danger, and quickness of resource."[20] As Hart describes it, the story of the Underground Railroad allows Ameri-cans to largely avoid the realities of slavery as a system of daily terror, turning their attention instead to a world of adventure, heroism, and justice – and to the brave and benevolent efforts of individual, heroic white people.

Writers of slave narratives were well aware of the interests and assump-tions of their white readers, but they had a different story to tell – for they knew the realities of the system of slavery, and they knew as well the reali-ties of racism in the North. They faced the challenge, then, of telling stories that few readers wanted to hear – and the art of telling the story that read-ers *want* to read so as to draw them into the story that they *need* to hear was the true art of the slave narrative. Accordingly, the style of the telling is very much a part of the story to be told, and those readers who read these books only to draw out the "facts" of slavery or of lives lived under oppres-sion will miss the complexity of and artistry behind the stories these writers make of their experiences. The phrase "written by himself" or "written by herself" appears in the titles of many narratives, and this phrase draws our attention to the *act* of composing these stories and not just to the stories themselves. As James Olney has noted of Douglass's *Narrative*, "there is much more to the phrase . . . than the mere laconic statement of a fact: it is literally part of the narrative, becoming an important thematic element in the retelling of the life wherein literacy, identity, and a sense of freedom are all acquired simultaneously, and without the first, according to Douglass, the latter two would never have been."[21] Although not all writers of slave narratives learned how to read and write before they escaped from slavery, all would agree that literacy and liberty are complexly connected, and they used their various styles to tell stories that extended beyond the bare facts of enslavement and escape. Some of these styles are seemingly rough, some are deceptively simple, some are quite direct, and some seem frustratingly indirect, before one realizes the point of the approach – but all seem designed to force the reader to look beyond the particular to the systemic, beyond the dramatic to the mundane, and beyond the fact of slavery in the South to the realities of racism in the North. In his approach to writing, for example, Douglass challenged the white antislavery consciousness that expected from him the rough and quaint style of a stereotypical slave, and in his balance of emotional restraint and outbursts of high eloquence, Douglass indicates that the story we are reading is not half the story that he could tell. Jacobs, as I've suggested, uses the conventions of sentimental literature to both relate to readers accustomed to such literature and to underscore the injustices of her situation. Bibb blends freely an energetic narrative style with what would be recognized as standard antislavery discourse (the kind of rhetoric and familiar phrasings that one would encounter regularly on the antislavery lecture circuit and in various antislavery publications). In all of these narratives, readers encounter familiar antislavery or sentimental rhetoric, but usually with a disturbing twist; they encounter adventure and heroism, but the narrative turns back to more recognizable terrors or more intimate threats (the threatened loss of one's child, for example); they encounter evils to denounce, but discover that those evils threaten the security of their own homes (for example, in the commentary on a corrupted Christianity common in most antebellum slave narratives). Slave narrators used style, in other words, to weave their experiences in and around the worlds in which their readers lived and to ask the reader to look at slavery from many different angles and not just through a single narrative perspective.

Just as there is no single position from which one can understand the realities of the system of slavery, so it is difficult to understand the complex cultural dynamics that are part of the historical "truth" of any slave narrative unless one is deeply versed in what Dwight A. McBride has called "the complex cognitive and narrative negotiations involved in telling the 'truth' about slavery."[22] The history of slavery includes not only slaveholders and slaves in the South and the North but also everyone who was invested in the system – economically, politically, and professionally as well as personally. The history of the antislavery movement includes not just heroic stories and brave fugitives but also the racist assumptions of seemingly benevolent white people and the limited understandings of antislavery sympathizers. To get a sense of that complex history – of the mundane, systemic terrors of slavery and of racial oppression – one needs to read a variety of narratives. The narratives themselves – including those written by former slaves, those reported to white writers, famous stories told again in print, or obscure stories told for the first time – provide a context for understanding the narratives. Mattison's curiosity about Picquet might lead one to question the nature of one's interest in other narratives, for example. The differences between Solomon Northup's *Twelve Years a Slave* (written by a white man) and the *Narrative of William W. Brown* (written by Brown himself) can raise important questions about where and when various aspects of slave culture are described in a narrative. The differences between the various versions of Josiah Henson's life (largely influenced by white writers, and in which Henson is increasingly identified with Harriet Beecher Stowe's character Uncle Tom), and the various versions of Douglass's life (as he increasingly redefined himself over time) can raise serious questions about the possibilities and limitations of black public identity in the nineteenth century. Together, these and other narratives – representing different regions, different experiences, different perspectives, and different levels of public recognition and interest – provide an entrance into an unwritten history, a history that, as William Wells Brown put it in 1847, "has never been represented" and that "never can be represented."[23] But this history, and this literary tradition, cannot be represented by just two prominent writers, and those writers, no matter how accomplished, cannot adequately represent themselves or their subjects in a vacuum.

Noting a similar problem in literary studies generally, Trudier Harris has expressed her concern about "the lack of training . . . in blacks, whites, and other folks who profess proficiency in the study of African American literature."[24] Such scholars, Harris notes, are likely to "locate a few 'points of entry' into the literature, identify selected writers and works for focus, and ignore the bulk of the literature and the culture."[25] "You will notice," Harris continues, "that some of the same writers and titles keep popping up because . . . these are the strands of hair on the head of the literature. These are the popular 'points of entry' for folks coming to the literature to begin their explorations."[26] Of course, everyone must begin somewhere, as Harris recognizes, but while "beginning at these points is *not* the problem," she emphasizes, "*staying there is.*"[27] Although students cannot be expected to begin by reading everything, if the entrance to slave narratives is always limited to one of Douglass's narratives and one (or one-seventh) by Jacobs, then students are more likely to encounter settled instruction on how to understand these narratives, and they are less likely to anticipate not only how much there is to understand but also how much of this historical presence, so neatly gathered under the term *slavery*, resists a settled understanding. To canonize just a couple of narratives (or fragments of narratives) is to present a dangerously simplified view of the past. Students who turn to *The American Heritage College Dictionary* for a definition of the word *canon* will find that the word refers to "a group of literary works generally accepted as representing a field," and that it also refers to "an established principle" and "a basis for judgment." In the case of slave narratives, they will often encounter texts that have risen to representative status over a period of time when the field – not only slave narratives but the history of slavery – was obscured by inadequate knowledge or even misrepresentations. What, then, is the basis for judgment, and what or whom is being judged? Against the settled knowledge represented by the canon, it is important that students encounter a variety of texts that raise questions about a still unsettled and unsettling history. Only if we are reading our way into a world in which the questions overwhelm the answers and in which we find ourselves re-examining our most basic assumptions about US history and about our own practices as readers are we actually reading slave narratives.

NOTES

1. Nina Baym et al. eds., *The Norton Anthology of American Literature, Volume B, American Literature, 1820–1865*, 6th edn. (New York: W. W. Norton, 2003); Paul Lauter et al. eds., *The Heath Anthology of American Literature, Volume B, Early Nineteenth Century, 1800–1865* (Boston: Houghton Mifflin, 2006). The *Norton Anthology* also includes three chapters from Douglass's second narrative, *My Bondage and My Freedom*, along with his most famous speech, "What, to the Slave, Is the Fourth of July?"; the *Heath Anthology* includes that same speech and one of Jacobs's letters.

2. "The Douglass Institute, Lecture at Inauguration of Douglass Institute, Baltimore, October, 1865," in Philip S. Foner, *The Life and Writings of Frederick Douglass, Volume IV: Reconstruction and After* (New York: International Publishers, 1955), p. 179.

3. Rafia Zafar, "Introduction: Over-Exposed, Under-Exposed: Harriet Jacobs and *Incidents in the Life of a Slave Girl*," in *Harriet Jacobs and Incidents in the Life of a Slave Girl: New Critical Essays*. Deborah Garfield and Rafia Zafar, eds. (Cambridge: Cambridge University Press, 1996), p. 4. Subsequent references will be cited parenthetically in the text.

4. David W. Blight, "Introduction: 'A Psalm of Freedom,'" in David W. Blight, ed., *The Narrative of the Life of Frederick Douglass, an American Slave, Written by Himself* (Boston: Bedford, 1993), p. 15. Subsequent references will be cited parenthetically in the text.

5. See Blight, *Narrative*, p. 18; see Rafia Zafar (who quotes a private correspondence with Gunning), "Introduction," in Garfield and Zafar, *Harriet Jacobs*, p. 5.

6. Valerie Smith, "Introduction," *Incidents in the Life of a Slave Girl* (New York: Oxford University Press, 1988), p. xxvii.

7. Deborah E. McDowell, "In the First Place: Making Frederick Douglass and the Afro-American Narrative Tradition," in *African American Autobiography: A Collection of Critical Essays*. William L. Andrews, ed. (Englewood Cliffs: Prentice Hall, 1993), pp. 38–39.

8. Ibid., p. 56.

9. Frances Smith Foster, "Resisting *Incidents*," in Garfield and Zafar, *Harriet Jacobs*, pp. 66–67.
10. Anthony G. Barthelemy, "Introduction," in *Collected Black Women's Narratives* (New York: Oxford University Press, 1988), p. xxxix.
11. Quoted in William L. Andrews, *To Tell a Free Story: The First Century of Afro-American Autobiography, 1760–1865* (Urbana: University of Illinois Press, 1986), p. 243.
12. *The Narrative of the Life of Frederick Douglass, An American Slave, Written by Himself* (Boston: Bedford, 1993), p. 42. Subsequent references will be cited parenthetically in the text.
13. Harriet A. Jacobs, *Incidents in the Life of a Slave Girl, Written by Herself*, ed. Jean Fagan Yellin (Cambridge, MA: Harvard University Press, 2000), p. 201. All subsequent references will be cited parenthetically in the text.
14. Saidiya V. Hartman, *Scenes of Subjection: Terror, Slavery, and Self-Making in Nineteenth-Century America* (New York: Oxford University Press, 1997), p. 42.
15. Frederick Douglass, "What, to the Slave, Is the Fourth of July?" in *Lift Every Voice: African American Oratory, 1787–1900*. Philip S. Foner and Robert James Branham, eds. (Tuscaloosa: The University of Alabama Press, 1998), pp. 256–57.
16. William Wells Brown, *A Lecture Delivered before the Female Anti-Slavery Society of Salem, at Lyceum Hall, Nov. 14, 1847* (Boston: Massachusetts Anti-Slavery Society, 1847), p. 4.
17. Frederick Douglass, "What, to the Slave, Is the Fourth of July?" in Foner and Branham, *Lift Every Voice*, p. 265.
18. William Wells Brown, *Narrative of William W. Brown, A Fugitive Slave. Written by Himself* (Boston, 1847), p. 15.
19. Henry "Box" Brown, *Narrative of the Life of Henry Box Brown, Written by Himself* (Oxford: Oxford University Press, 2002), p. 4.
20. Albert Bushnell Hart, "Introduction," in Wilbur H. Siebert, *The Underground Railroad from Slavery to Freedom* (New York: Macmillan, 1899), pp. viii–ix.
21. James Olney, "'I Was Born': Slave Narratives, Their Status as Autobiography and as Literature," in *The Slave's Narrative*. Charles T. Davis and Henry Louis Gates, Jr., eds. (Oxford: Oxford University Press, 1985), p. 156.
22. Dwight A. McBride, *Impossible Witnesses: Truth, Abolitionism, and Slave Testimony* (New York: New York University Press, 2001), p. 12.
23. Brown, *Lecture*, p. 4.
24. Trudier Harris, "Miss-Trained or Untrained? Jackleg Critics and African American Literature (Or, Some of My Adventures in Academia)," in *African American Literary Criticism, 1773 to 2000*. Hazel Arnett Ervin, ed. (New York: Twayne, 1999), p. 462.
25. Ibid.
26. Ibid., p. 466.
27. Ibid.

14

XIOMARA SANTAMARINA

Black womanhood in North American women's slave narratives

> Slavery is terrible for men; but it is far more terrible for women. Superadded to the burden common to all, *they* have wrongs, and sufferings, and mortifications peculiarly their own.
>
> (Harriet Jacobs, *Incidents in the Life of a Slave Girl*)

Formerly enslaved women, like formerly enslaved men, were active participants in eighteenth- and nineteenth-century abolition movements. They participated as fugitives helping other fugitives; as speakers; as organizers and fundraisers; and as the writers of slave narratives. Slave women seeking to represent their experience for their audiences shared some of the problems slave men encountered when telling their stories. In an era in which citizenship was limited to white men, representations of the often humiliating experiences of slave men and women potentially exacerbated former slaves' vulnerability in their readers' eyes. If male slave narrators who sought readers' sympathy for themselves and abolition had to contend with feminizations of slave men as "sambo," as well as depictions of oversexed and violent men, formerly enslaved women had to contend with similar disparaging stereotypes. De-gendered in the eyes of middle-class readers because they performed field and manual labor (where they were often in the majority), yet also viewed as oversexed because of their sexual vulnerability, slave women faced especially contradictory circumstances when they entered the spheres of antislavery publicity. Whether as a "mammy," a "Jezebel," or as a masculinized non-woman, when slave women offered first-hand accounts of slavery they were exposed to an intense scrutiny that conflicted with cultural norms that insisted on the privacy of "woman." Slave women consciously shaped their narratives in direct response to these problematic contexts, as writers and as narrators.[1]

Slave women's entry into the realm of abolitionist publicity posed often unrecognized problems to them: if those hostile to abolition, or proslavery, could be expected to question these slave women's credibility and virtue, antislavery languages that publicized or "outed" slave women's vulnerability – especially slave women's sexual vulnerability – also exposed these women in ways that were antithetical to nineteenth-century formulations of womanhood. We can find an example of this in the narrative of Mary Prince, published in London in 1831 by abolitionist Thomas Pringle. *The History of Mary Prince* is the slave narrative of a West Indian woman who was then living in London. Born in Bermuda in 1788, Prince was the slave of Mr. and Mrs. John Wood of Antigua. After having traveled with the Woods to England in 1830, she argued with them and abandoned the family. While technically not a slave in England, Prince wanted to return to her family and husband in Antigua as a free woman, so she began seeking her emancipation. Pringle, her employer, published Prince's narrative to mobilize public opinion against Wood and to pressure him into selling her. Following publication of the narrative, however, the public debate that emerged in the courts and in antislavery media focused solely on Prince's character and sexual history, and hence on her credibility.

Prince's narrative is a remarkable "as told to" account which offers us the earliest insights into the harsh experiences of Caribbean slave women. It bears many of the hallmark characteristics of slave narratives: several prefatory documents that establish the authenticity of the account as well as the credibility of the narrator; the circumstances under which the account was related and transcribed by amanuensis Susan Stringland; and the claim that Prince's "exact expressions and peculiar phraseology" were retained "as far as was practicable."[2] Pringle's concern with Wood's charge of Prince's illicit sexuality is evident in his editor's preface and supplementary materials. The latter speak to the investment Prince's readers were assumed to have in ascertaining whether this slave woman, susceptible to sexual exploitation, could uphold norms for proper femininity. Despite Pringle's best efforts, however, *The History of Mary Prince* reaffirmed the central role of slave women's sexuality to the proslavery lobby and abolitionists: slave women were henceforth confined to claiming legitimacy on very narrow grounds – as sexually "virtuous" – that obscured the realities of slave women's exploitation.

Prince's slave testimony negotiated this very narrow frame with claims to femininity that appealed to other gendered discourses about sentiment and work beyond those of sexual purity. Through her narrative, she participates in earlier, eighteenth-century discourses about virtue in which virtue was associated with male sentiment or "feeling," telling her readers that they should want to hear from a slave "what a slave had felt and suffered" (p. i). This emphasis on feeling forms the basis of Prince's appeal to her readers' sympathy, principally in the first part of the narrative in which she describes the female-populated spheres of her childhood and the end of these affectionate relationships through her sale (along with siblings) away from her mother. "Oh, that was a sad sad time! I recollect the day well. Mrs. P. came to me and said, 'Mary, you will have to go home directly; your master . . .

means to sell you . . . to raise money.' Hearing this I burst out a crying, – though I was then far from being sensible of the full weight of my misfortune, or of the misery that waited for me" (p. 3). Prince's metaphor of choice is the heart, one she uses liberally to model her own empathy for the pain other slaves experience as a basis for her readers' own. Prince's language becomes more literal, however, when she describes the harsh regimes of labor she endures in the salt marshes of Turk's Island; after she relates this and subsequent experiences she emphasizes overcoming pain and working to earn her freedom. Her industriousness becomes a means for resisting and transforming her slave status, without running away. In this way, Prince shows her capacity for freedom to skeptical readers; her work and industry serve as an alternative basis for credibility to the expectations of virtue uppermost in these readers' minds.

Most significantly, Prince's narrative shows how slave women used their narratives to represent themselves as women in relation to more than just their sexuality. Harriet Jacobs was right to counter abolitionists' focus on slave men's experiences by alerting her readers to the special, yet unrecognized, gendered nature of slave women's domination when she stressed that slavery was "far more terrible for women." But modern readers are wrong to assume that slave women's sexuality was the only significant dimension of their experiences as gendered beings. Slave women asserted their womanhood by appealing to a variety of cultural narratives about gender that included narratives of motherhood, labor, entrepreneurship, spirituality, and collective responsibility. They used their narratives to broaden the nation's limited understanding of how slave women asserted their femininity, despite their nationally disadvantaged status. This should not surprise us, given the range of slave women's experiences in the western hemisphere, and it should also forestall easy generalizations about how slave women experienced their gender. As Nellie McKay has formulated, black women's texts instantiated notions of black womanhood as multidimensional; for black women, womanhood was not "static or a single ideal."[3]

This multidimensionality is especially evident in the narrative of a Northern slave woman who resisted slavery as well as her exploitation in the "free" North after her emancipation. Sojourner Truth (1797–1883) is perhaps the best known of slave women, in her day and ours, for her activism on behalf of abolition and women's rights. Born Isabella Baumfree in upstate New York, Truth worked as a slave until age thirty, when she was emancipated in 1827 under New York State's emancipation laws. A famous and charismatic speaker, Truth is well known for her 1851 Akron, Ohio "Aren't I a Woman?" speech that marked her entry, twenty-four years after her emancipation, into the antebellum public realm. Her long career as a charismatic speaker and the fact that she was unlettered her whole life have restricted scholarly interest in Truth to her speeches and sidelined consideration of her 1850 *Narrative of Sojourner Truth*. Though the critical tradition of the slave narrative includes other familiar "as told to" accounts (including Nat Turner's and Mary Prince's), this narrative has only recently begun to receive the interest it merits. A close look at it reveals that despite Truth's illiteracy, she did influence its transcription enough to warrant being described as a narrator. More importantly, however, the narrative speaks to the literary origins of Truth's egalitarian speaking persona and how, on account of this persona, Truth was simultaneously popular and problematic in her day and in ours.[4]

Truth did not become an abolitionist until some twenty years after her emancipation, when she met abolitionists in Northampton, Massachusetts, where she had settled after leaving New York City (in 1843), changing her name to "Sojourner Truth" and taking up itinerant preaching. Truth may have settled in this intentional community (like a commune) because she had decided to abstain from participating in the competitive market culture of the "free" North. It was here that Truth met Olive Gilbert, an abolitionist with whom Truth collaborated on the narrative which was produced to enable Truth (through its sales) to buy a home in her old age. With her simultaneous entry into abolitionist activism and the publication of her slave narrative in 1850, Truth became an important (though often marginalized) figure in the abolitionist movement.

Perhaps because Truth was middle-aged at the time she became an abolitionist, her sexual history was not foregrounded in her narrative. While Gilbert makes a brief reference to certain "hard things that crossed Isabella's life," it is clear that Truth herself recognizes how complete frankness about slavery's lack of sexual mores would seem "so unreasonable" to her readers that it was liable to backfire: "'Why no!' she says, 'they'd call me a liar! they would, indeed! and I do not wish to say anything to destroy my own character for veracity, though what I say is strictly true.'"[5] With that statement she forcefully closes the door on any consideration of sexuality and slavery. Ironically, Truth's strict honesty – a trait her mother had inculcated in her – and her strong work ethic potentially jeopardized her womanhood for her amanuensis, Olive Gilbert, who sought to justify some of Truth's actions to her readers. When Truth relates her refusal to steal food for her children, Gilbert remarks on the irony of the slave mother's adherence to biblical injunctions against stealing when she herself was "stolen" property. Gilbert suggests that slavery blinded Truth's interest in her children, but Truth's relationship with her mother (whose own loss of her children early taught Truth the suffering that slave mothers experienced) and the fact that her honesty, ironic or not, "made her true to her God," speak against Gilbert's belittling of Truth's motherhood. The former slave's successful suit to reclaim her son from slavery after his illegal sale out of state also testifies to the lengths the former slave was willing to go to assert her motherhood against enormous odds.

If Gilbert betrays a grudging admiration for Truth's unorthodox religious views, she is much more ambivalent and even dismissive of Truth's work ethic and the fact that, as a valued farm laborer, Truth maintained a relatively good relationship with her last owner, Mr. Dumont. Despite her long history as a manual laborer at a time when manual labor was increasingly stigmatized, when she became an abolitionist Truth emphasized the earlier farm labor she had performed as a slave as the basis for her claim to civic entitlement. At a time when women's rights activists were striving to make middle-class women's domestic and clerical labor respectable, the former slave's pride in what was viewed as disparaged and unwomanly labor was remarkable. Both in the Akron speech and in *The Narrative of Sojourner Truth*, Truth's work is central to how she positioned herself as a contributor to the nation and as a figure of yeoman republicanism. Gilbert, like most abolitionists, found it difficult to account for a hard-working slave woman who had not been totally degraded and made "lazy," "ignorant," or masculinized by slavery. For her, like most white readers, Truth's pride in degrading labor signaled the former slave's suspect status as a "white man's nigger," a slave who was seen as collaborating with slave owners in order to obtain special privileges.

A close look at these women's "conflicted collaboration" illustrates the source of many of these conflicts in the unrecognized fact that in her narration Truth drew from textual sources and rhetorical goals that exceeded, and even preceded, the narrow parameters of the 1850 slave narrative. *The Narrative of Sojourner Truth* was not Truth's first foray into the North's print sphere, yet its textual antecedents remain overlooked by many who assume that Truth's illiteracy precluded her from intervening in the public sphere. Truth's contributions to an 1835 book about a religious community in which she had participated, *Fanaticism*, dramatize how an unorthodox "author" could seek to manipulate publicity from which she was considered excluded. This slim volume represents an unprecedented and provocative instance of Truth's early, pre-abolition desire to innovate a juridical, racially legitimating form of publicity that was not bound by the imperatives of the slave narrative. In it, Truth positions her work history as an important, rather than incidental, component to her publicity efforts, an emphasis that would later conflict with Olive Gilbert's abolitionist agenda. This history was problematic insofar as Truth was a hard-working slave when the abolitionist imperative for resistance dictated that she run away or resist this labor. Furthermore,

Truth's open disillusionment with the North's competitive "free" labor system at a time when this labor system was viewed as the only legitimate mode of production – in Truth's words, in the North, "the rich rob the poor, and the poor rob each other" – suggested the North's exploitation of its workers was more similar to slavery than antislavery Northerners liked to think. Ironically, though she saw her womanhood and labor as inextricably linked and crucial to her civic entitlement, the competitive North compromised both. Her labor in the "free" North posed an ethical quandary that she could only evade with her itinerant preaching. As a result, Gilbert and Truth's incompatible agendas produced a conflicted narrative that remains problematic in our day.

Olive Gilbert was sympathetic to Truth, thus her quandary – how do you represent an enslaved woman farm worker as a "woman"? – suggests how pro- and antislavery audiences alike could be expected to doubt whether a female slave could really be a "woman"; or, in the words of the era's phrase, a "true woman." To make matters even more difficult, abolitionists' efforts to generate sympathy for slave women often relied on these women's iconic (and silent) status as "victims," a status that ironically made those slave women who chose to speak out about their experiences suspect. In an era that equated women's modesty with silence, it was one thing for male ex-slaves to describe the beating and violation of slave women, as Frederick Douglass did when he described his Aunt Hester's cruel whipping in his narrative; it was another thing entirely for readers to encounter a slave woman's own description of her physical and sexual humiliation. Furthermore, while resisting women may appear heroic to modern readers historically and rhetorically, a woman who resisted, verbally or physically, could also potentially compromise her womanhood and jeopardize her readers' sympathy.

The two narratives of former slaves Ellen Craft and Louisa Picquet show the different ways former slave women asserted their womanhood and their resistance to slavery for their readers. *Running a Thousand Miles for Freedom, or the Escape of William and Ellen Craft from Slavery* was published in London in 1861 by Ellen's husband, William. That same year in New York, a white minister, Hiram Mattison, published *Louisa Picquet, the Octoroon: or Inside Views of Southern Domestic Life*. In *Running a Thousand Miles for Freedom*, Craft related the story of the remarkable escape his wife and he effected in December 1848 from a Georgian plantation. With the light-complected Ellen "passing" as a sickly white gentleman accompanied by her "servant," William, the two traveled together to Philadelphia and to freedom. Louisa Picquet's narrative also described the troubles of a light-skinned heroine, but unlike Ellen Craft, who had escaped in part to preserve her virtue, the protagonist, Picquet, had had to succumb to sexual exploitation as the long-time concubine of a slave owner. When she collaborated with Mattison to produce her story, she took the risk of describing her highly sexualized history for the purpose of buying her mother's freedom. These narratives testify to the public's ongoing concern with the virtue and credibility of slave women, while also dramatizing how abolitionists commonly deployed mulattas to foreground slavery's illicit sexuality. The narratives illustrate the contradictions that existed between abolitionists' insistence on slave women's pollution and their virtue, even as they show how these women countered the threats that slavery and abolitionism posed to their femininity. Principally, these women refused to enact the part of the "tragic mulatta" who dies as the victim of slavery's moral contamination, instead taking on responsibility for their own survival, taking on the risks this entailed, and emerging as subjects who eke out a slim measure of agency from within the coercions of slavery and abolitionist publicity.

In *Running a Thousand Miles*, Ellen's husband, William, serves as her amanuensis. Their intimate relationship produces a singular narrative insofar as it speaks directly to former slave men's investment in supporting the respectable racialized masculinity and femininity of former slave men and women. William openly adopts a protective (and patriarchal) pose relative to Ellen, as well as to other family members: while William is not able to save other family members, including his sister, from sexual exploitation, his escape with Ellen speaks to his ability and will to enact the role of protector that was central to masculinity norms. "Oh! If there is any one thing under the wide canopy of heaven, horrible enough to stir a man's soul, and to make his very blood boil, it is the thought of his dear wife, his unprotected sister, or his young and virtuous daughters, struggling to save themselves from falling a prey to such demons."[6] Craft's emphasis on womanly virtue places Ellen, famous for her disguise as a white male, in a contradictory dilemma: how can she assert her womanhood to her readers when she escaped slavery dressed as a man? The engraving that circulated before and alongside the narrative (as its frontispiece), in which Ellen appears in her disguise as a white male, potentially only exacerbates this dilemma.

Ellen's dilemma as ambiguously raced and gendered appears in tension with the other mulattas who populate the narrative, some of whom die or succumb to slavery's sexualization; she survives, virtue intact, because of her willingness to temporarily trespass on white men's privileged mobility in order to enter that femininity. Portrayed as modestly reluctant at first – "she thought it was almost impossible for her to assume that disguise" and "my wife had no ambition whatever to assume this disguise" (p. 35) – her understanding of slavery's logic eventually enables her to assume the disguise. "She saw that the laws under which we lived did not recognize her to be a woman, but a mere chattel, to be bought and sold" (p. 30). In such a contradictory position, Ellen reasons that it is slavery's own gender-bending nature, not her own, that she will overcome through her disguise. If slavery prevents her from realizing her womanhood, then by literally enacting this de-gendering she can emerge on the other side as a proper woman.

Notwithstanding Ellen's doubts about assuming the disguise, her performance is so effective that in William's description of their escape he calls his wife "my master" and "he." Throughout his relation of their escape, William maintains this disguise, further blurring Ellen's ambiguous status as woman/man. They surmount many obstacles during the escape – Ellen could not write, and other white proslavery men felt threatened by this invalid white man's relaxed attitude to taking a slave north – testifying to Ellen's quick wits. But once they arrive at an abolitionist boarding-house in Philadelphia, Ellen throws off her disguise and resumes her newly secured identity as the "wife" rather than as the master of a fugitive slave. This identity is short-lived, however, since the passage of the 1850 Fugitive Slave Law makes the Crafts vulnerable again, especially when their master appeals to the US President to remand the well-known fugitives back to slavery. With the whole nation now in the grip of slavery, Ellen again disguises herself as a white woman and the Crafts endure another nerve-wracking escape from the USA through Nova Scotia to England. Their exile, like the one at the end of William Wells Brown's popular 1853 novel, *Clotel*, signals the United States' hostility to black masculinity and femininity and highlights the de-gendering properties of US racial prejudice, not just slavery. Though they are exiled in England, the narrative's ending vindicates Ellen's gender-bending and well-deserved assumption of proper femininity.

While the Crafts' story was a well-known one in its time, the openly sensationalistic and often prurient agenda of Picquet's amanuensis, the Reverend Hiram Mattison, has understandably kept *The Octoroon* on the margins of women's slave narratives. The narrative was transcribed by Mattison in Buffalo, New York, where he met Picquet during a fundraising tour to purchase her mother's freedom (Picquet succeeded in buying her mother's freedom in October, 1860). Picquet's history of concubinage and eventual emancipation were certainly not unique for the time; rather, Picquet's survival as a respectable, married, "Christian" woman who was admired and supported by blacks and whites familiar with her history make her narrative stand out. Notwithstanding the editor's often salacious rendering of details, as in Sojourner Truth's narrative, Picquet's responses, interactions, and narrations succeed in asserting this woman's integrity to her readers and her amanuensis in the face of her sexual history as slave and concubine. Despite the editor's emphasis on the South's "moral corruption" and the threat this emphasis poses in totally sexualizing Picquet and all slave women, Picquet emerges in this account as a loving daughter and mother committed to her family's integrity, notwithstanding slavery's depredations.[7]

In her story, as she related it to Mattison, Picquet (who was born in South Carolina but lived in Georgia and New Orleans before settling in Cincinnati as a free, married woman) tells of her early life and resistance to her slave owners' efforts to rape her. After having been hired out at age fourteen and separated from her mother, Picquet tells of how she confided in and recruited white and black women in her efforts to keep her master away. Her story is not that of the lone female, abandoned and hopelessly victimized; she inserts herself in a women's network that helps briefly mitigate her sexual vulnerability. With this network, Picquet and her supporters manage to foil the efforts of her first master, Mr. Cook, to rape her, even after he gave her the "worst whippin' [she] ever had."[8] Subsequently, however, when Picquet is sold and arrives at New Orleans she must comply with her third (and last) master's demand for concubinage. By that point in her story, however, she has made it clear that slavery's systematic patriarchal authority victimizes all women, not just herself. In this way, Picquet's narrative bespeaks a collectively gendered dimension – a form of inter-racial "sisterhood" – that simultaneously exists within, and is imperiled by, slavery. If her first master's mistress orders Picquet to be sold as a baby because of her intolerable family resemblance, another mistress helps her avoid her master's attempted rape.

Picquet's description of her period as a widower's "housekeeper" is filled with continual conflicts. Piquet never appears resigned to her status as "fallen woman," despite her six years' cohabitation. Instead, she focuses on her master's jealousy, his threats of violence, and her conversations with him about the sin in which they both live. Far from being the corrupt slave concubine, Picquet is the resisting victim who has no doubt about occupying the moral high ground, both in relation to her master and to her amanuensis. When she relates how her faith helped her through this period, she speaks of how she "pray[ed] that he might die." When she sees, after he recovered from an illness, that "there was a change in him," she amends, "I began to get sorry, and begin to pray that he might get religion first before he died. I felt sorry to see him die in his sins" (p. 22). Picquet's prayers are answered: her master eventually dies. Picquet is emancipated at his death and inherits enough money to move north with their children. Despite the master's recommendation that she pass for white in the North, when Picquet arrives in Cincinnati she marries a former slave. Picquet's post-emancipation history is remarkable for the many individuals, black and white, that befriend her and help her assume her new life. The potentially de-legitimating meaning of this slave woman's sexual exploitation is displaced by the accounts of her religious conversion and of the many friends (including other former slaves from Georgia) who help her find her feet and, eventually, locate her mother, still enslaved in Texas. Without much of a backward glance, and notwithstanding her amanuensis's almost single-minded emphasis on the criminality of her sexuality (Picquet's whiteness clearly represents to her amanuensis a major factor in this criminality), Picquet focuses her story on what she (and her husband) can do to reunite with her mother. For this reason alone – to raise money to buy her mother – and not to serve an abolitionist purpose (though Picquet did assist in the escape of several fugitive slaves), Picquet publishes her story. In this way, Picquet's seemingly futile search for her mother and her eventual success in finding her clearly overcome Mattison's narrow rhetorical agenda. This is made clear with Picquet's inclusion at the end of her narrative of the notice she sent to a Cincinnati newspaper announcing the purchase of and reunion with her mother. This final flourish in her narrative illustrates how Picquet, like other former slaves, asserted the value and integrity of familial connections among slave mothers and daughters, despite slave owners' efforts to dehumanize slave women.

Picquet's narrative dramatizes how slave women overcame the many obstacles entailed in their engagements with abolitionist publicity. The combined burdens of childrearing and familial obligations made fugitive slave women who could pen their own stories a very small population. For that reason, we have few "written by herself" narratives and a majority of "as told to" narratives. Though obviously we should attend carefully to the mediated nature of those narratives transcribed by amanuenses so we can trace the (often white) amanuensis's biases, it is also the case that we should not assume the transparent or non-mediated nature of those narratives slave women did write themselves. Lettered women who wrote their experiences also had to negotiate prevailing assumptions about slave women; they faced the constraints and obstacles that all these slave women encountered when they sought entry into a white, male-dominated public sphere, whether they wrote their stories or not. This entails exploring how women who related and/or wrote their stories specifically crafted them in response to how they expected their stories were going to be framed. Just as we recognize that the unlettered Sojourner Truth, Mary Prince, Ellen Craft, and Louisa Picquet encountered and attempted to ameliorate the obvious biases of their amanuenses, it is equally important that we recognize how women who wrote their own narratives anticipated and responded to the biases of their readers. In this way, we keep former slave women's rhetorical negotiations with their amanuenses and their readers at the center of our explorations into how the writings of black women addressed often skeptical and, sometimes, hostile audiences.

The best-known of those former slave women to negotiate with their readers' expectations and biases was Harriet Jacobs, a former slave from Edenton, South Carolina. In her narrative, Jacobs emphasized the strength of slave family connections and in particular the strength of slave motherhood. Since 1981, when scholar Jean Fagan Yellin authenticated Jacobs's identity and authorship, the remarkable *Incidents in the Life of a Slave Girl, Written by Herself* (1861) has become the best-known and most widely read of female slave narratives. The narrative's importance stems in part from the rarity of "written by herself" narratives, but also from its successful integration of abolition with sentimental femininity. In *Incidents*, Jacobs made a remarkable and savvy appeal to white women readers: "Rise up, ye women that are at ease! Hear my voice, ye careless daughters!" Relating her many years' effort to evade her master's rape, Jacobs's narrative tells the absorbing story of a young slave woman who risked alienating readers with a relatively frank discussion of her sexual relationship, while a slave, with a single white man by whom she had two children ("Mr. Sands" in real life was Samuel Tredwell of Edenton, South Carolina, who later married and was elected to Congress). In her narrative, Jacobs describes how she negotiated her master's threat of rape by entering into a sexual relationship with "Sands" that frustrated her master's effort to appropriate her sexuality. However, in keeping with the efforts of other slave women to move their readers beyond their concerns over slave women's sexuality, Jacobs directs the narrative's focus after the birth of her children to the story of their rescue from slavery; instead of a story in which she is the principal protagonist rescued from slavery, Jacobs frames the story as one of imperiled (and eventually triumphant) motherhood centered around the rescue of her children.

Despite what Jacobs's readers would have seen as the clear racial and sexual illegitimacy of her children, it is as a slave mother who overcomes immense odds that Jacobs succeeds in establishing her rhetorical authority. Combined with the obvious risks she assumes in publishing her history, Jacobs's authority as a mother embeds her text in a selfless and activist vein that links her individual history (with all its flaws) to the greater, collective cause of abolition. Whereas other slave women had published their stories for the purpose of raising funds for themselves (like Prince and Truth), or to recover enslaved relatives (like Craft and Picquet), Jacobs stood to gain the least (her children by this time were free) and lose the most (her respectability) from publishing what many would have viewed as a scandalous sexual history. Like the slave mother hiding in her grandmother's attic for years, Jacobs is willing to risk all, even to incur public censure, in the name of her children and other slave mothers. As such a slave mother, Jacobs persuasively revises antebellum norms for womanhood so as to include a formerly enslaved woman and position herself as her readers' equal rather than as their social inferior. While Jacobs clearly maintains the difference between herself and her (likely) married readers by telling them, "Reader, my story ends with freedom; not in the usual way, with marriage," by yoking motherhood, a central trope for sentimental femininity, to abolition and the cause of racial reform, *Incidents* consolidated the significant role and collective dimension that slave (and black) women's experiences offered to African American struggles for civil rights. The slave mother willing to risk losing her character by publishing her story for the greater good emerges as the prototype for the post-bellum "race woman" (a phrase connoting the respectability of activist women) whose domestic labor, usually invisible, becomes visible and is transformed into a collective and raced form of activist labor.

In contrast to *Incidents*, in which motherhood is central to slave women's self-representation (and subsequently to representations of racial legitimacy), Elizabeth Keckley's *Behind the Scenes, or Thirty Years a Slave, and Four Years in the White House* (1868) perfectly symbolizes how slave women strove to establish their credibility on other terms. Keckley, a talented dressmaker for elite white women while enslaved and later emancipated, saw her work as central to representing her investment in, and contributions to, elite femininity. Where Jacobs appealed to her white readers through their shared motherhood, Keckley (herself also a mother) claimed a role in *fashioning* white women's elite image. That is, Keckley did not see herself as ancillary or marginal to these women's femininity because she dressed them as "ladies." Though Keckley recounts her sexual exploitation while a slave and the birth of her child, her sexuality and motherhood are incidental, rather than central, to her description of her labor's importance to white women. This may appear paradoxical to readers today who are familiar with black women's exclusion from national racialized (as white) norms for womanhood; but Keckley's narrative illustrates how slave women nonetheless felt that their work was important, even if the nation (and not just slave owners) refused them this hard-earned recognition. In this way, Keckley, whose central motif is that she was "worth her salt," harkens back to the labor ideals of the older and Northern-born Sojourner Truth.

Keckley's labor ideals make *Behind the Scenes* a hybrid text that is part slave narrative and part political memoir, but which might be best described as a work narrative. When Keckley represented herself as an industrious and in-demand dressmaker, she inserted herself in national post-bellum debates over the potential citizenship of newly emancipated slaves. If there was any question (and resentful Southerners raised many doubts) as to whether former slaves were competent, entrepreneurial, and self-respecting, Keckley proved them wrong. As a popular dressmaker, Keckley had raised herself from the rank of slave in the South, to dressmaker and valued confidante in the Lincoln White House. *Behind the Scenes* relates the story of her mobility, but with a remarkable added dimension. Keckley claimed she published her narrative in large part "to defend" Mary Lincoln, after the former First Lady became involved in the political scandal known as the "Old Clothes Scandal" of 1867.[9] Despite her claims of seeking to place Mary Lincoln "in a better light," however, *Behind the Scenes* provoked public outrage that its author could not have predicted: when Keckley described her work for Mrs. Lincoln and other elite white women (including Mrs. Jefferson Varina Davis), she counted on the public to respect the trust her employers and "friends" had placed in her. But the reading public refused to grant her this trust, describing her instead, in the words of one scandalized review, as "an angry negro servant," a catch-all phrase of derision. This demotion in status for a deferential slave woman who had refused to escape from slavery (she bought her freedom) indicates that Keckley erred in assuming others would "credit" her representations of her labor. Though her employers clearly esteemed her, she mistakenly assumed she could vouch for herself, or, in other words, provide herself as a "reference."

Where did she go wrong? Keckley failed to recognize how her competent labor compromised her clients' elite femininity: given that white femininity was rooted in typically invisible racial and class privilege (because a "true woman" ideally transcended, rather than signaled, class differences), when the black female worker appears "on stage," she dispels the illusion of status and racial privilege that can best be produced "behind the scenes." Despite her close bond with Mrs. Lincoln and her professions of loyalty, when Keckley describes how indispensable she was to Mary Lincoln, she reveals the former First Lady's weaknesses. Keckley's insistence on the value of her work, then, and her stated loyalty to Mrs. Lincoln are rhetorically incompatible. From this perspective, silence rather than speech – no matter how positive – was the only recognizable form of loyalty. When Keckley made her work for Mary Lincoln visible, she breached black labor's subordinate status and appeared center stage, not "behind the scenes": it was the public appearance of this intimacy that worked against Mary Lincoln's image and not, as some averred, Keckley's malicious, or "kiss-and-tell" intentions. Consequently, even as this narrative typifies the wide-ranging and multidimensional forms of women's slave narratives, the reception of *Behind the Scenes* also dramatizes the limits of slave narratives and autobiography in overcoming US cultural logics for race, class, and gender.

Notwithstanding these obstacles, formerly enslaved women helped shape ideas about womanhood in ways that modern readers are beginning to recognize. These women's creativity in responding to the problematic contexts they encountered as writers and as narrators offers us a rich archive about race and gender that demonstrates the multidimensionality of black women's lives. Even if today some narratives are more popular than others, it is important to recognize that these slave narratives do not comprise a monolithic tradition, and that they speak to the importance of labor and race, of sisterhood and motherhood, and of social reform and entrepreneurship to slave women, their families, and their culture.

NOTES

1. Frances Smith Foster, "'In Respect to Females . . .': Differences in the Portrayals of Women by Male and Female Narrators" (1981), reprinted in her book *Witnessing Slavery: The Development of Ante-Bellum Slave Narratives* (Westport, CT: Greenwood Press, 1979).
2. Mary Prince, *The History of Mary Prince, a West Indian Slave, Related by Herself* (London: 1831), p. i. Subsequent page references to this text will appear in parentheses. See Sandra Pouchet Paquet, "The Heartbeat of a West Indian Slave" in her book, *Caribbean Autobiography: Cultural Identity and Self-Representation* (Madison, WI: University of Wisconsin Press, 2002), pp. 28–50, for an interesting account of Prince's narrative.
3. Nellie McKay, "The Narrative Self: Race, Politics, and Culture in Black American Women's Autobiography," in *Women, Autobiography, Theory*. Sidonie Smith and Julia Watson, eds. (Madison, WI: University of Wisconsin Press, 1998), pp. 96–107.
4. Xiomara Santamarina, "Race, Work and Literary Authority in *The Narrative of Sojourner Truth*" in *Belabored Professions: Narratives of African American Working Womanhood* (Chapel Hill, NC: University of North Carolina Press, 2005), pp. 35–63.
5. Sojourner Truth (with Olive Gilbert), *The Narrative of Sojourner Truth* (1850. Rpt. ed. Margaret Washington. New York: Vintage Books, 1993), p. 46.
6. William Craft, *Running a Thousand Miles for Freedom or the Escape of William and Ellen Craft from Slavery* (London: 1861), p. 8. Subsequent page references to this text will appear in parentheses.
7. DoVeanna Fulton, "Speak Sister, Speak: Oral Empowerment in Louisa Picquet the Octoroon," in *Legacy* 15.1 (1998), pp. 98–103.
8. H. Mattison, *Louisa Picquet, the Octoroon: or Inside Views of Southern Domestic Life* (New York: 1861), p. 15. Subsequent page references to this text will appear in parentheses.
9. For a full account of the scandal, see Frances Smith Foster, *Written by Herself: Literary Production by African American Women, 1746–1892* (Bloomington: Indiana University Press, 1993).

GUIDE TO FURTHER READING

This is a select bibliography of academic work about the slave narrative. Space constraints preclude listing many important texts. Specialists will certainly notice omissions, but the hope is that this select bibliography will be a useful starting point for students and scholars of the slave narrative.

Anthologies of African American slave narratives

Numerous other excellent single- and multiple-author editions of slave narratives exist, many with fine bibliographic materials and scholarly introductions. Students of the slave narrative are also encouraged to consult "Documenting the American South," a major digital publishing initiative, sponsored by the University of North Carolina, Chapel Hill, in which William L. Andrews has compiled a comprehensive bibliography of slave narratives with links to full-text electronic versions for most citations at http://docsouth.unc.edu/neh/index.html

Andrews, William L., ed. *North Carolina Slave Narratives: The Lives of Moses Roper, Lunsford Lane, Moses Grandy, and Thomas H. Jones*. Chapel Hill: University of North Carolina Press, 2003.
　　ed. *Sisters of the Spirit: Three Black Women's Autobiographies*. Bloomington: Indiana University Press, 1986.
　　ed. *Six Women's Slave Narratives*. Schomburg Library of Nineteenth-Century Black Women Writers. New York: Oxford University Press, 1988.
Bland, Sterling Lecater Jr., ed. *African American Slave Narratives*. 3 vols. Westport, CT: Greenwood Press, 2001.
Blassingame, John W., ed. *Slave Testimony: Two Centuries of Letters, Speeches, Interviews, and Autobiographies*. Baton Rouge: Louisiana State University Press, 1977.
Brooks, Joanna and John Saillant, eds. *"Face Zion Forward": First Writers of the Black Atlantic, 1758–1798*. Boston, MA: Northeastern University Press, 2002.
Carretta, Vincent, ed. *Unchained Voices: An Anthology of Black Authors in the English-Speaking World of the Eighteenth Century*. Lexington: University Press of Kentucky, 1996.
Edwards, Paul and David Dabydeen, eds. *Black Writers in Britain 1760–1890: An Anthology*. Edinburgh: Edinburgh University Press, 1991.

Ferguson, Moira, ed. *Nine Black Women: An Anthology of Nineteenth-Century Writers from the U.S., Canada, Bermuda and the Caribbean.* New York: Routledge, 1998.

Gates, Henry Louis, Jr., ed. *The Classic Slave Narratives.* New York: New American Library, 1987.

and William L. Andrews. *Slave Narratives.* New York: The Library of America, 2000.

Kitson, Peter J. and Debbie Lee, eds. *Slavery, Abolition and Emancipation: Writings in the British Romantic Period.* Vol. I. London: Pickering and Chatto, 1999.

Krise, Thomas W., ed. *Caribbeana: An Anthology of English Literature of the West Indies, 1657–1777.* Chicago: University of Chicago Press, 1999.

Potkay, Adam and Sandra Burr, eds. *Black Atlantic Writers of the Eighteenth Century: Living the New Exodus in England and the Americas.* London: Palgrave, 1995.

Taylor, Yuval, ed. *I Was Born a Slave: An Anthology of Classic Slave Narratives.* 2 vols. Chicago: Lawrence Hill, 1999.

General studies of slavery

Berlin, Ira. *Generations of Captivity: A History of African-American Slaves.* Cambridge, MA: Harvard University Press, 2003.

Blackburn, Robin. *The Making of New World Slavery: From the Baroque to the Modern, 1492–1800.* London: Verso, 1997.

Blassingame, John W. *The Slave Community: Plantation Life in the Antebellum South.* New York: Oxford University Press, 1979.

Escott, Paul D. *Slavery Remembered: A Record of Twentieth-Century Slave Narratives.* Chapel Hill, NC: University of North Carolina Press, 1979.

Franklin, John Hope and Loren Schweninger. *Runaway Slaves: Rebels on the Plantation.* New York: Oxford University Press, 1999.

Genovese, Eugene D. *Roll, Jordan, Roll: The World the Slaves Made.* New York: Pantheon Books, 1974.

Johnson, Walter. *Soul by Soul: Life inside the Antebellum Slave Market.* Cambridge, MA: Harvard University Press, 2000.

Kolchin, Peter. *American Slavery: 1619–1877.* London and New York: Penguin, 1995.

Miller, Joseph C., ed. *Slavery and Slaving in World History: A Bibliography.* Armonk, NY: M. E. Sharpe, 1999.

Stampp, Kenneth M. *The Peculiar Institution: Slavery in the Ante-Bellum South.* New York: Knopf, 1956.

Stuckey, Sterling. *Slave Culture.* New York: Oxford University Press, 1987.

White, Deborah Gray. *Ar'n't I a Woman: Female Slaves in the Plantation South.* New York: W. W. Norton, 1985.

General studies of the slave trade

Curtin, Philip D. *The Atlantic Slave Trade: A Census.* Madison: University of Wisconsin Press, 1969.

Eltis, David. *Economic Growth and the Ending of the Transatlantic Slave Trade.* New York: Oxford University Press, 1987.

Reynolds, Edward. *Stand the Storm: A History of the Atlantic Slave Trade.* London: Allison and Busby, 1985.

Walvin, James. *Black Ivory: A History of British Slavery.* London: Blackwell, 2002.

General studies of abolition

Anstey, Roger. *The Atlantic Slave Trade and British Abolition 1760–1810.* London: Macmillan, 1975.

Bender, Thomas, ed. *The Antislavery Debate: Capitalism and Abolitionism as a Problem in Historical Interpretation.* Berkeley and Oxford: University of California Press, 1992.

Blackburn, Robin. *The Overthrow of Colonial Slavery 1776–1848.* London: Verso, 1988.

Bolt, Christine and Seymour Drescher, eds. *Anti-Slavery, Religion and Reform: Essays in Memory of Roger Anstey.* Folkestone: William Dawson and Sons, 1980.

The Problem of Slavery in the Age of Revolution, 1770–1823. Ithaca: Cornell University Press, 1976.

Davis, David Brion. *The Problem of Slavery in Western Culture.* Ithaca: Cornell University Press, 1966.

Duberman, Martin, ed. *The Antislavery Vanguard.* Princeton, NJ: Princeton University Press, 1965.

Goodman, Paul. *Of One Blood: Abolition and the Origins of Racial Equality.* Berkeley: University of California Press, 1998.

Stauffer, John. *The Black Hearts of Men: Radical Abolitionists and the Transformation of Race.* Cambridge, MA: Harvard University Press, 2002.

Stewart, James B. *Holy Warriors: The Abolitionists and American Slavery.* New York: Hill and Wang, 1997.

Neo-slave narratives

Compiled by Valerie Smith

Bok, Francis. *Escape from Slavery: The True Story of My Ten Years in Captivity and My Journey to Freedom in America.* New York: St. Martin's, 2003.

Bontemps, Arna. *Black Thunder; Gabriel's Revolt: Virginia, 1800.* New York: Macmillan, 1936; rpt. Boston: Beacon, 1968, 1992.

Bradley, David. *The Chaneysville Incident.* New York: Harper and Row, 1981.

Briscoe, Connie. *A Long Way from Home.* New York: HarperCollins, 1999.

Butler, Octavia. *Kindred.* New York: Doubleday, 1979.

Cary, Lorene. *The Price of a Child.* New York: Knopf, 1995.

Chase-Riboud, Barbara. *Sally Hemings: A Novel.* New York: Viking, 1979.

Cliff, Michelle. *Free Enterprise: A Novel of Mary Ellen Pleasant.* New York: E. P. Dutton, 1993.

Clifton, Lucille. *Generations: A Memoir.* New York: Random House, 1976.

Cooper, J. California. *Family.* New York: Doubleday, 1990.

In Search of Satisfaction. New York: Doubleday, 1994.

D'Aguiar, Fred. *The Longest Memory*. New York: Pantheon, 1995.
Gaines, Ernest. *The Autobiography of Miss Jane Pittman*. New York: Doubleday, 1971.
Herron, Carolivia. *Thereafter Johnnie*. New York: Random House, 1991.
Johnson, Charles. *Middle Passage*. New York: Atheneum, 1990.
   Oxherding Tale. Bloomington: Indiana University Press, 1982.
Jones, Edward P. *The Known World*. New York: Amistad, 2003.
Jones, Gayl. *Corregidora*. New York: Random House, 1975.
Killens, John Oliver. *Great Gittin' Up Mornin'*. New York: Doubleday, 1972.
Meriwether, Louise. *Fragments of the Ark*. New York: Washington Square Press, 1994.
Morrison, Toni. *Beloved*. New York: Knopf, 1987.
Nazer, Mende. *Slave*. New York: PublicAffairs, 2004.
Perry, Phyllis Alesia. *A Sunday in June*. New York: Hyperion, 2004.
   Stigmata. New York: Hyperion, 1998.
Phillips, Caryl. *Crossing the River*. New York: Knopf, 1994.
Randall, Alice. *The Wind Done Gone*. Boston: Houghton Mifflin, 2001.
Rawles, Nancy. *My Jim*. New York: Crown 2005.
Reed, Ishmael. *Flight to Canada*. New York: Random House, 1976.
Walcott, Derek. *Dream on Monkey Mountain*. New York: Farrar, Straus, and Giroux, 1979.
Walker, Margaret. *Jubilee*. Boston: Houghton Mifflin, 1966.
Williams, Sherley Anne. *Dessa Rose*. New York: William Morrow, 1986.

Collections of critical essays on African American slave narratives

Space constraints preclude listing the individual titles for the essays in these collections.

Andrews, William L., ed. *African American Autobiography: A Collection of Critical Essays*. Englewood Cliffs: Prentice Hall, 1993.
   Critical Essays on Frederick Douglass. Boston: G. K. Hall, 1991.
Bloom, Harold, ed. *Frederick Douglass's Narrative of the Life of Frederick Douglass*. New York: Chelsea House, 1988.
Carey, Brycchan, Markman Ellis, and Sara Salih, eds. *Discourses of Slavery and Abolition: Britain and its Colonies, 1760–1838*. Basingstoke: Palgrave Macmillan, 2004.
Carretta, Vincent and Philip Gould, eds. *Genius in Bondage: Literature of the Early Black Atlantic*. Lexington: University Press of Kentucky, 2001.
Davis, Charles T. and Henry Louis Gates, Jr., eds. *The Slave's Narrative*. New York: Oxford University Press, 1991.
Fisher, Dexter and Robert B. Stepto, eds. *Afro-American Literature: The Reconstruction of Instruction*. New York: MLA, 1979.
Garfield, Deborah M. and Rafia Zafar, eds. *Harriet Jacobs and Incidents in the Life of a Slave Girl: New Critical Essays*. Cambridge: Cambridge University Press, 1996.
Hall, James C., ed. *Approaches to Teaching the Narrative of Frederick Douglass*. New York: MLA, 1999.

McDowell, Deborah E. and Arnold Rampersad, eds. *Slavery and the Literary Imagination*. Baltimore: Johns Hopkins University Press, 1989.

Sekora, John and Darwin T. Turner, eds. *The Art of Slave Narratives: Original Essays in Criticism and Theory*. Macomb: Western Illinois University Press, 1982.

Sundquist, Eric, ed. *Frederick Douglass: New Literary and Historical Essays*. Cambridge: Cambridge University Press, 1991.

Books on the slave narrative or with substantial discussions of slave narratives

Andrews, William L. *To Tell a Free Story: The First Century of Afro-American Autobiography, 1760–1865*. Urbana: University of Illinois Press, 1986.

Frances Smith Foster, and Trudier Harris, eds. *The Oxford Companion to African American Literature*. New York: Oxford University Press, 1997.

Beaulieu, Elizabeth Ann. *Black Women Writers and the Neo-Slave Narrative: Femininity Unfettered*. Westport, CT: Greenwood Press, 1999.

Bell, Bernard W. *The Afro-American Novel and its Tradition*. Amherst: University of Massachusetts Press, 1987.

Blackett, R. J. M. *Beating against the Barriers: Biographical Essays in Nineteenth-Century Afro-American History*. Baton Rouge: Louisiana State University Press, 1986.

Bland, Sterling Lecater, Jr. *Voices of the Fugitives: Runaway Slave Stories and Their Fictions of Self Creation*. Westport, CT: Greenwood Press, 2000.

Braxton, Joanne M. *Black Women Writing Autobiography: A Tradition within a Tradition*. Philadelphia: Temple University Press, 1989.

Bruce, Dickson D., Jr. *Black American Writing from the Nadir: The Evolution of a Literary Tradition, 1877–1915*. Baton Rouge: Louisiana State University Press, 1989.

The Origins of African-American Literature, 1680–1865. Charlottesville: University Press of Virginia, 2001.

Carby, Hazel. *Reconstructing Womanhood: The Emergence of the Afro-American Woman Novelist*. New York: Oxford University Press, 1987.

Carey, Brycchan, *British Abolitionism and the Rhetoric of Sensibility: Writing, Sentiment, and Slavery, 1760–1807*. Basingstoke: Palgrave Macmillan, 2005.

Carretta, Vincent. *Olaudah Equiano, the African: Biography of a Self-Made Man*. Athens, GA: University of Georgia Press, 2005.

Coleman, Deirdre. *Romantic Colonization and British Anti-Slavery, 1770–1800*. Cambridge: Cambridge University Press, 2004.

Costanzo, Angelo. *Surprizing Narrative: Olaudah Equiano and the Beginnings of Black Autobiography*. New York: Greenwood Press, 1987.

Edwards, Paul. *Unreconciled Strivings and Ironic Strategies: Three Afro-British Authors of the Georgian Era: Ignatius Sancho; Olaudah Equiano; Robert Wedderburn*. Edinburgh: Edinburgh University Press, 1991.

Ernest, John. *Liberation Historiography: African American Writers and the Challenge of History, 1794–1861*. Chapel Hill, NC: University of North Carolina Press, 2004.

Resistance and Reformation in Nineteenth-Century African-American Literature: Brown, Wilson, Jacobs, Delany, Douglass, and Harper. Jackson, MI: University Press of Mississippi, 1995.

Eyerman, Ron. *Cultural Trauma: Slavery and the Formation of African-American Identity.* New York: Cambridge University Press, 2001.

Fabi, M. Giulia. *Passing and the Rise of the African-American Novel.* Urbana: University of Illinois Press, 2001.

Ferguson, Moira. *Subject to Others: British Women Writers and Colonial Slavery, 1670–1834.* London: Routledge, 1992.

Fisch, Audrey A. *American Slaves in Victorian England: Abolitionist Politics in Popular Literature and Culture.* New York: Cambridge University Press, 2000.

Fleischner, Jennifer. *Mastering Slavery: Memory, Family, and Identity in Women's Slave Narratives.* New York: New York University Press, 1996.

Foster, Frances Smith. *Written by Herself: Literary Production by African American Women, 1746–1892.* Bloomington: Indiana University Press, 1993.

Witnessing Slavery: The Development of Antebellum Slave Narratives. 2nd edn Madison: University of Wisconsin Press, 1994.

Gikandi, Simon. *Maps of Englishness: Writing Identity in the Culture of Colonialism.* New York: Columbia University Press, 1996.

Gilroy, Paul. *The Black Atlantic: Modernity and Double Consciousness.* Cambridge, MA: Harvard University Press, 1993.

Gould, Philip. *Barbaric Traffic: Commerce and Antislavery in the Eighteenth-Century Atlantic World.* Cambridge, MA: Harvard University Press, 2003.

Hartman, Saidiya V. *Scenes of Subjection: Terror, Slavery, and Self-Making in Nineteenth-Century America.* New York: Oxford University Press, 1997.

Innes, C. L. *A History of Black and Asian Writing in Britain, 1700–2000.* Cambridge: Cambridge University Press, 2002.

Jackson, Blyden. *A History of Afro-American Literature.* Vol. I: *The Long Beginning, 1746–1895.* Baton Rouge: Louisiana State University Press, 1989.

Judy, Ronald A. T. *(Dis)Forming the American Canon: African-Arabic Slave Narratives and the Vernacular.* Minneapolis: University of Minnesota Press, 1993.

Keizer, Arlene R. *Black Subjects: Identity Formation in the Contemporary Narrative of Slavery.* Ithaca: Cornell University Press, 2004.

Lee, Debbie. *Slavery and the Romantic Imagination.* Philadelphia: University of Pennsylvania Press, 2002.

Levine, Robert S. *Martin Delany, Frederick Douglass, and the Politics of Representative Identity.* Chapel Hill, NC: University of North Carolina Press, 1997.

McBride, Dwight A. *Impossible Witnesses: Truth, Abolitionism, and Slave Testimony.* New York: New York University Press, 2001.

Mitchell, Angelyn. *The Freedom to Remember: Narrative, Slavery, and Gender in Contemporary Black Women's Fiction.* New Brunswick: Rutgers University Press, 2002.

Paquet, Sandra Pouchet. *Caribbean Autobiography: Cultural Identity and Self-Representation.* Madison: University of Wisconsin Press, 2002.

Pierce, Yolanda. *Hell without Fires: Slavery, Christianity, and the Antebellum Spiritual Narrative.* Gainesville: University Press of Florida, 2005.

Plasa, Carl and Betty J. Ring, eds. *The Discourse of Slavery: Aphra Behn to Toni Morrison.* London: Routledge, 1994.

Reid-Pharr, Robert F. *Conjugal Union: The Body, the House and the Black American.* New York: Oxford University Press, 1999.

Rody, Caroline. *The Daughter's Return: African-American and Caribbean Women's Fictions of History*. New York: Oxford University Press, 2001.

Rushdy, Ashraf. *The Neo-Slave Narrative: Studies in the Social Logic of a Literary Form*. New York: Oxford University Press, 1999.

Sánchez-Eppler, Karen. *Touching Liberty: Abolition, Feminism, and the Politics of the Body*. Oxford and Berkeley: University of California Press, 1993.

Sandiford, Keith A. *Measuring the Moment: Strategies of Protest in Eighteenth-Century Afro-English Writing*. Cranbury, NJ: Susquehanna University Press, 1987.

The Cultural Politics of Sugar: Caribbean Slavery and Narratives of Colonialism. Cambridge: Cambridge University Press, 2000.

Santamarina, Xiomara. *Belabored Professions: Narratives of African American Working Womanhood*. Chapel Hill, NC: University of North Carolina Press, 2005.

Sharpe, Jenny. *Ghosts of Slavery: A Literary Archaeology of Black Women's Lives*. Minneapolis: University of Minnesota Press, 2003.

Smith, Stephanie A. *Conceived by Liberty: Maternal Figures and Nineteenth-Century American Literature*. New York: Cornell University Press, 1995.

Starling, Marion Wilson. *The Slave Narrative: Its Place in American History*. Boston: G. K. Hall, 1982.

Stepto, Robert B. *From Behind the Veil: A Study of Afro-American Narrative*. Urbana: University of Illinois Press, 1979.

Sundquist, Eric J. *To Wake the Nations: Race in the Making of American Literature*. Cambridge, MA: Harvard University Press, 1993.

Thomas, Helen. *Romanticism and Slave Narratives: Transatlantic Testimonies*. Cambridge: Cambridge University Press, 2000.

Weinstein, Cindy. *Family, Kinship, and Sympathy in Nineteenth-Century American Literature*. Cambridge: Cambridge University Press, 2004.

Winter, Kari Joy. *Subjects of Slavery, Agents of Change: Women and Power in Gothic Novels and Slave Narratives, 1790–1865*. Athens, GA: University of Georgia Press, 1992.

Woodard, Helena. *African-British Writings in the Eighteenth Century: The Politics of Race and Reason*. Westport, CT: Greenwood Press, 1999.

Xiomara Santamarina. *Belabored Professions: Narratives of African American Working Womanhood*. Chapel Hill, NC: University of North Carolina Press, 2005.

Yellin, Jean Fagan. *Women and Sisters: The Anti-Slavery Feminists in American Culture*. New Haven: Yale University Press, 1989.

Articles on the slave narrative in journals and book collections

Anderson, Douglas. "The Textual Reproductions of Frederick Douglass." *CLIO: A Journal of Literature, History, and the Philosophy of History* 27.1 (1997): 57–87.

Andrews, William L. "The Changing Moral Discourse of Nineteenth-Century African American Women's Autobiography: Harriet Jacobs and Elizabeth Keckley." *De/Colonizing the Subject: The Politics of Gender in Women's Autobiography*. Eds. Sidonie Smith and Julia Watson. Minneapolis: University of Minnesota Press, 1992. pp. 225–41.

"The Changing Rhetoric of the Nineteenth-Century Slave Narrative of the United States." *Slavery in the Americas.* Ed. Wolfgang Binder. Würzburg, Ger.: Honighausen and Neumann, 1993. pp. 471–86.

Barrett, Lindon. "African-American Slave Narratives: Literacy, the Body, Authority." *American Literary History* 7.3 (fall 1995): 415–42.

"Hand-Writing: Legibility and the White Body in *Running a Thousand Miles for Freedom.*" *American Literature* 69 (June 1997): 315–36.

Bartholomaus, Craig. "'What Would You Be?': Racial Myths and Cultural Sameness in *Incidents in the Life of a Slave Girl.*" *CLA Journal* 39.2 (Dec. 1995): 179–94.

Becker, Elizabeth C. "Harriet Jacobs's Search for Home." *CLA Journal* 35.4 (June 1992): 411–21.

Brawley, Lisa. "Frederick Douglass's *My Bondage and My Freedom* and the Fugitive Tourist Industry." *Novel: A Forum on Fiction* 30.1 (fall 1996): 98–128.

Braxton, Joanne M. and Sharon Zuber. "Silences in Harriet 'Linda Brent' Jacobs's *Incidents in the Life of a Slave Girl.*" *Listening to Silences: New Essays in Feminist Criticism.* Eds. Elaine Hedges and Shelley Fisher Fishkin. New York: Oxford University Press, 1994. pp. 146–55.

Burnham, Michelle. "Loopholes of Resistance: Harriet Jacobs' Slave Narrative and the Critique of Agency in Foucault." *Arizona Quarterly* 49.2 (summer 1993): 53–73.

Carey, Brycchan. "'The Extraordinary Negro': Ignatius Sancho, Joseph Jekyll, and the Problem of Biography." *British Journal for Eighteenth-Century Studies* 26.2 (spring 2003): 1–13.

Carretta, Vincent. "Defining a Gentleman: The Status of Olaudah Equiano or Gustavus Vassa." *Languages Sciences* 21 (2000): 385–99.

"Questioning the Identity of Olaudah Equiano, or Gustavus Vassa, the African." *The Global Eighteenth Century.* Ed. Felicity Nussbaum. Baltimore: Johns Hopkins University Press, 2003. pp. 226–38.

Carson, Sharon. "Shaking the Foundation: Liberation Theology in Narrative of the Life of Frederick Douglass." *Religion and Literature* 24.2 (summer 1992): 19–34.

Casmier-Paz, Lynn A. "Footprints of the Fugitive: Slave Narrative Discourse and the Trace of Autobiography." *Biography* 24:1 (winter 2001): 215–25.

"Slave Narratives and the Rhetoric of Author Portraiture." *New Literary History* 34:1 (winter 2003): 91–116.

Cassuto, Leonard. "Frederick Douglass and the Work of Freedom: Hegel's Master–Slave Dialectic in the Fugitive Slave Narrative." *Prospects: An Annual Journal of American Cultural Studies* 21 (1996): 229–59.

Castronovo, Russ. "'As to Nation, I Belong to None': Ambivalence, Diaspora, and Frederick Douglass." *American Transcendental Quarterly* 9.3 (Sept. 1995): 245–60.

Connor, Kimberly Rae. "To Disembark: The Slave Narrative Tradition." *African American Review* 30:1 (spring 1996): 35–57.

Cruz, Jon D. "Historicizing the American Cultural Turn: The Slave Narrative." *European Journal of Cultural Studies* 4:3 (Aug. 2001): 305–23.

Cutter, Martha J. "Dismantling 'The Master's House': Critical Literacy in Harriet Jacobs' *Incidents in the Life of a Slave Girl.*" *Callaloo* 19.1 (winter 1996): 209–25.

Dalton, Anne B. "The Devil and the Virgin: Writing Sexual Abuse in *Incidents in the Life of a Slave Girl.*" *Violence, Silence, and Anger: Women's Writing as Transgression.* Ed. Deirdre Lashgari. Charlottesville: University Press of Virginia, 1995. pp. 38–61.

Daniel, Janice B. "A New Kind of Hero: Harriet Jacobs's *Incidents.*" *The Southern Quarterly* 35.3 (spring 1997): 7–12.

Davie, Sharon. "'Reader, My Story Ends with Freedom': Harriet Jacobs's *Incidents in the Life of a Slave Girl.*" *Famous Last Words: Changes in Gender and Narrative Closure.* Ed. Alison Booth. Charlottesville: University Press of Virginia, 1993. pp. 86–109.

Desrochers, Robert S., Jr. "Not Fade Away: The Narrative of Venture Smith, an African American in the Early Republic." *The Journal of American History* 84 (June 1997): 40–66.

Dorsey, Peter A. "Becoming the Other: The Mimesis of Metaphor in Douglass's *My Bondage and My Freedom.*" *PMLA* 111.3 (May 1996): 435–50.

Ernest, John. "The Reconstruction of Whiteness: William Wells Brown's *The Escape; or, A Leap for Freedom.*" *PMLA* 113 (Oct. 1998): 1108–21.

Ferguson, Sally Ann H. "Christian Violence and the Slave Narrative." *American Literature* 68:2 (June 1996): 297–320.

Fichtelberg, Joseph. "Word between Worlds: the Economy of Equiano's Narrative." *American Literary History* 5:3 (1993): 459–80.

Finseth, Ian. "In Essaka Once: Time and History in Olaudah Equiano's Autobiography." *Arizona Quarterly* 58.1 (spring 2002): 1–35.

Foreman, P. Gabrielle. "The Spoken and the Silenced in *Incidents in the Life of a Slave Girl* and *Our Nig.*" *Callaloo* 13.2 (spring 1990): 313–24.

Fowler, Shelli B. "Marking the Body, Demarcating the Body Politic: Issues of Agency and Identity in Louisa Picquet and Dessa Rose." *CLA Journal* 40:4 (June 1997): 467–78.

Fulton, DoVeanna. "Speak, Sister, Speak: Oral Empowerment in Louisa Picquet the Octoroon." *Legacy* 15.1 (1998): 98–103.

Garfield, Deborah M. "Speech, Listening, and Female Sexuality in *Incidents in the Life of a Slave Girl.*" *Arizona Quarterly* 50.2 (summer 1994):19–49.

Gibson, Donald B. "Christianity and Individualism: (Re)-Creation and Reality in Frederick Douglass's Representation of Self." *African American Review* 26.4 (winter 1992): 591–603.

Golemba, Henry. "Frank Webb's *The Garies and Their Friends* Contextualized within African American Slave Narratives." *Lives Out of Letters: Essays on American Literary Biography and Documentation.* Ed. Robert D. Habich. Madison, NJ: Fairleigh Dickinson University Press, 2004: 114–42.

Hamilton, Cynthia. "Revisions, Rememories and Exorcisms: Toni Morrison and the Slave Narrative." *Journal of American Studies* 30:3 (Dec. 1996): 429–45.

Hardack, Richard. "Water Rites: Navigating Passage and Social Transformation in American Slave and Travel Narratives." *Multiculturalism: Roots and Realities.* Ed. C. James Trotman. Bloomington: Indiana University Press, 2002. pp. 49–73.

Harris, Jennifer. "Seeing the Light: Re-Reading James Albert Ukawsaw Gronniosaw." *English Language Notes* 42:4 (June 2005): 44–57.

Harrison, Suzan. "Mastering Narratives/Subverting Masters: Rhetorics of Race in The Confessions of Nat Turner, Dessa Rose, and Celia, a Slave." *Southern Quarterly* 35:3 (spring 1997): 13–28.

Hinds, Elizabeth. "The Spirit of Trade: Olaudah Equiano's Conversion, Legalism, and the Merchant's Life." *African American Review* 32.4 (winter 1998): 635–47.

Humphreys, Debra. "Power and Resistance in Harriet Jacobs' *Incidents in the Life of a Slave Girl.*" *Anxious Power: Reading, Writing, and Ambivalence in Narrative by Women.* Eds. Carol J. Singley and Susan Elizabeth Sweeney. Albany: State University of New York Press, 1993. pp. 143–55.

Ito, Akiyo. "Olaudah Equiano and the New York Artisans: The First American Edition of *The Interesting Narrative of the Life of Olaudah Equiano, or Gustavus Vassa, the African.*" *Early American Literature* 32:1 (1997): 82–101.

Jay, Gregory S. "American Literature and the New Historicism: The Example of Frederick Douglass." *Boundary 2* 17.1 (spring 1990): 211–42.

Kaplan, Carla. "Narrative Contracts and Emancipatory Readers: *Incidents in the Life of a Slave Girl.*" *Yale Journal of Criticism* 6.1 (spring 1993): 93–120.

"Recuperating Agents: Narrative Contracts, Emancipatory Readers, and *Incidents in the Life of a Slave Girl.*" *Provoking Agents: Gender and Agency in Theory and Practice.* Ed. Judith Kegan Gardiner. Urbana: University of Illinois Press, 1995. pp. 280–301.

Keetley, Dawn. "Racial Conviction, Racial Confusion: Indeterminate Identities in Women's Slave Narratives and Southern Courts." *A-B: Auto-Biography Studies* 10 (fall 1995): 1–20.

Lee, Lisa Yun. "The Politics of Language in Frederick Douglass's *Narrative of the Life of an American Slave.*" *MELUS* 17.2 (summer 1991–2): 51–59.

Levine, Robert S. "Uncle Tom's Cabin in Frederick Douglass' Paper: An Analysis of Reception." *American Literature* 64.1 (Mar. 1992): 71–93.

Ligon, Glenn. "Narratives." *Yale Journal of Criticism* 7.1 (1994): 31–40.

Lovell, Thomas B. "By Dint of Labor and Economy: Harriet Jacobs, Harriet Wilson, and the Salutary View of Wage Labor." *Arizona Quarterly* 52.3 (autumn 1996): 1–32.

Marren, Susan M. "Between Slavery and Freedom: The Transgressive Self in Olaudah Equiano's Autobiography." *PMLA* 108.1 (Jan. 1993): 94–105.

Marshall, Elaine. "Irruptions of the Grotesque in Harriet Jacobs' *Incidents in the Life of a Slave Girl.*" *JAISA: The Journal of the Association for the Interdisciplinary Study of the Arts* 2.2 (spring 1997): 17–34.

Matterson, Stephen. "Shaped by Readers: The Slave Narratives of Frederick Douglas and Harriet Jacobs." *Soft Canons: American Women Writers and Masculine Tradition.* Ed. Karen L. Kilcup. Iowa City: University of Iowa Press, 1999. pp. 82–96.

McCaskill, Barbara. "'Yours Very Truly': Ellen Craft – The Fugitive as Text and Artifact." *African American Review* 28 (winter 1994): 509–29.

McCoy, Beth A. "Race and the (Para)Textual Condition." *PMLA* 121.1 (Jan. 2006): 156–69.

Meer, Sarah. "Sentimentality and the Slave Narrative: Frederick Douglass' *My Bondage and My Freedom.*" *The Uses of Autobiography.* Ed. Julia Swindells. London: Taylor & Francis, 1995. pp. 89–97.

Mendiola, Kelly Willis. "Reading Ex-Slave Narratives: The Federal Writers' Project in Travis County, Texas." *JASAT (Journal of the American Studies Association of Texas)* 28 (Oct. 1997): 38–54.

Mills, Bruce. "Lydia Maria Child and the Endings to Harriet Jacobs's *Incidents in the Life of a Slave Girl*." *American Literature* 64.2 (June 1992): 255–72.

Moody, Joycelyn K. "Twice Other, Once Shy: Nineteenth-Century Black Women Autobiographers and the American Literary Tradition of Self-Effacement." *A/B: Auto/Biography Studies* 7.1 (spring 1992): 46–61.

Morgan, Winifred. "Gender-Related Difference in the Slave Narratives of Harriet Jacobs and Frederick Douglass." *American Studies* 35.2 (fall 1994): 73–94.

Mottolese, William. "Almost an Englishman: Olaudah Equiano and the Colonial Gift of Language." *Bucknell Review* 41.2 (1998): 160–71.

Murphy, G. "Olaudah Equiano, Accidental Tourist." *Eighteenth-Century Studies* 27 (1994): 677–92.

Musher, Sharon Ann. "Contesting 'The Way the Almighty Wants It': Crafting Memories of Ex-Slaves in the Slave Narratives." *American Quarterly* 53:1: 2001.

Nudelman, Franny. "Harriet Jacobs and the Sentimental Politics of Female Suffering." *ELH* 59.4 (winter 1992): 939–64.

Okafor, Clement A. "*The Interesting Narrative of the Life of Olaudah Equiano*: A Triple-Tiered Trans-Atlantic Testimony." *Literary Griot: International Journal of Black Expressive Cultural Studies* 14:1–2 (spring–fall 2002): 160–83.

Orban, Katalin. "Dominant and Submerged Discourses in *The Life of Olaudah Equiano Gustavus Vassa*." *African-American Review* 27.4 (1993): 655–64.

Otten, Terry. "Transfiguring the Narrative: *Beloved* – From Melodrama to Tragedy." *Critical Essays on Toni Morrison's Beloved*. Ed. Barbara H. Solomon. New York: G. K. Hall, 1998. pp. 284–99.

Phillips, Jerry. "Slave Narratives." *A Companion to the Literature and Culture of the American South*. Eds. Richard Gray and Owen Robinson. Malden, MA: Blackwell, 2004. pp. 43–57.

Potkay, Adam. "Olaudah Equiano and the Art of Spiritual Autobiography." *Eighteenth-Century Studies* 27 (1994): 677–92.

Pouchet Paquet, Sandra. "The Heartbeat of a West Indian Slave: *The History of Mary Prince*." *African American Review* 26.1 (1992): 131–45.

Rauwerda, A. M. "Naming, Agency, and 'A Tissue of Falsehoods' in *The History of Mary Prince*." *Victorian Literature and Culture* 29.2 (2001): 397–411.

Ripley, Peter. "The Autobiographical Writings of Frederick Douglass." *Southern Studies* 24.1 (spring 1985): 5–29.

Rosenberg, Warren. "'Professor, Why Are You Wasting Our Time?': Teaching Jacobs's *Incidents in the Life of a Slave Girl*." *Conversations: Contemporary Critical Theory and the Teaching of Literature*. Eds. Charles Moran and Elizabeth Penfield. Urbana: National Council of Teachers of English, 1990. pp. 132–48.

Royer, Daniel J. "The Process of Literacy as Communal Involvement in the Narratives of Frederick Douglass." *African American Review* 28.3 (fall 1994): 363–74.

Rushdy, Ashraf H. A. "The Neo-Slave Narrative." *The Cambridge Companion to the African American Novel*. Ed. Maryemma Graham. Cambridge: Cambridge University Press, 2004. pp. 87–105.

Sale, Maggie. "Critiques from Within: Antebellum Projects of Resistance." *American Literature* 64.4 (Dec. 1992): 695–718.

"To Make the Past Useful: Frederick Douglass' Politics of Solidarity." *Arizona Quarterly* 51.3 (autumn 1995): 25–60.

Sekora, John. "Briton Hammon, the Indian Captivity Narrative, and the African American Slave Narrative." *When Brer Rabbit Meets Coyote: African-Native American Literature.* Ed. Jonathan Brennan. Urbana: University of Illinois Press, 2003. pp. 141–57.

"Red, White, and Black: Indian Captivities, Colonial Printers, and the Early African-American Narrative." *A Mixed Race: Ethnicity in Early America.* Ed. Frank Shuffelton. New York: Oxford University Press, 1993. pp. 92–104.

Sharpe, Jenny. "'Something Akin to Freedom': The Case of Mary Prince." *Differences* 8.1 (1996): 31–56.

Sisco, Lisa. "'Writing in the Spaces Left': Literacy as a Process of Becoming in the Narratives of Frederick Douglass." *American Transcendental Quarterly* 9.3 (Sept. 1995): 195–227.

Skinfill, Mauri. "Nation and Miscegenation: *Incidents in the Life of a Slave Girl.*" *Arizona Quarterly* 51.2 (summer 1995): 63–79.

Slote, Ben. "Revising Freely: Frederick Douglass and the Politics of Disembodiment." *A/B: Auto/Biography Studies* 11.1 (spring 1996): 19–37.

Smith, Sidonie. "Performativity, Autobiographical Practice, Resistance." *A/B: Auto/Biography Studies* 10.1 (spring 1995): 17–33.

"Resisting the Gaze of Embodiment: Women's Autobiography in the Nineteenth Century." *American Women's Autobiography: Fea(s)ts of Memory.* Ed. Margo Culley. Madison: University of Wisconsin Press, 1992. pp. 75–110.

Sorisio, Carolyn. "'There Is Might in Each': Conceptions of Self in Harriet Jacobs's *Incidents in the Life of a Slave Girl, Written by Herself.*" *Legacy* 13.1 (1996): 1–18.

Steinberg, Marc: "Inverting History in Octavia Butler's Postmodern Slave Narrative." *African American Review* 38:3 (fall 2004): 467–76.

Wallace, Maurice. "Constructing the Black Masculine: Frederick Douglass, Booker T. Washington, and the Sublimits of African American Autobiography." *Subjects and Citizens: Nation, Race, and Gender from Oroonoko to Anita Hill.* Eds. Michael Moon and Cathy N. Davidson. Durham, NC: Duke University Press, 1995. pp. 237–62.

Walter, Krista. "Surviving in the Garret: Harriet Jacobs and the Critique of Sentiment." *American Transcendental Quarterly* 8.3 (Sept. 1994): 189–210.

Wardrop, Daneen. "'While I Am Writing': Webster's 1825 Spelling Book, the Ell, and Frederick Douglass's Positioning of Language." *African American Review* 32.4 (1998): 649–60.

Warhol, Robyn R. "'Reader, Can You Imagine? No, You Cannot': The Narratee as Other in Harriet Jacobs's Text." *Narrative* 3.1 (Jan. 1995): 57–72.

Weinauer, Ellen M. "'A Most Respectable Looking Gentleman': Passing, Possession, and Transgression in *Running a Thousand Miles for Freedom.*" *Passing and the Fictions of Identity.* Ed. Elaine K. Ginsberg. Durham, NC: Duke University Press, 1996. pp. 37–56.

Wilentz, Gay. "Authenticating Experience: North Carolina Slave Narratives and the Politics of Race." *North Carolina Literary Review* 1 (summer 1992): 115–37.

Williams, Adebayo. "Of Human Bondage and Literary Triumphs: Hannah Crafts and the Morphology of the Slave Narrative." *Research in African Literatures* 34:1 (spring 2003): 137–50.

Wohlpart, A. "James' Privatized Sentiment and the Institution of Christianity: Douglass's Ethical Stance in the Narrative." *American Transcendental Quarterly* 9.3 (Sept. 1995): 181–94.

Wolff, Cynthia Griffin. "Passing beyond the Middle Passage: Henry 'Box' Brown's Translations of Slavery." *Massachusetts Review* 37 (spring 1996): 23–44.

Worley, Sam. "Solomon Northup and the Sly Philosophy of the Slave Pen." *Callaloo* 20:1 (winter 1997): 243–59.

Yellin, Jean Fagan. "Harriet Jacobs's Family History." *American Literature* 66.4 (Dec. 1994): 765–67.

Zafar, Rafia. "Capturing the Captivity: African Americans among the Puritans." *MELUS* 17 (summer 1992): 19–35.

INDEX

abolition 2
  British 64
  discourse of 3, 35
  Garrisonian abolitionists 19
  lecture circuit of 19
  literature of 3, 70–73, 151
  poetry 71
  rise of movement 28
  slave women in relation to 232–33
  white abolitionists 3
An Account of the Life of Mr. David George 15
aesthetic (literary) value 6, 23, 196–97, 223
Africa 87–92
  African Diaspora 170
African American writers (literature) 4, 5, 112, 137–41, 147, 148–49, 150–51, 183
  African American women writers 198
Allen, Richard 95
amanuensis 241
  Gronniosaw's use of 63
  Hammon's and Marrant's use of 86
  Picquet's use of 239–41
  Prince's use of 233
  Stowe as 76
  Truth's use of 101, 235, 236
  William Craft as 238
American Abolition Society 67
American and Foreign Antislavery Reporter 18
American and Foreign Antislavery Society 18
American Anti-Slavery Society 18, 23, 28, 203, 204, 208–09, 211
American Civil War 2, 24, 34, 140, 146, 150, 175, 190, 196, 219–20
Anderson, Benedict 146
Andrews, William L. 7, 87, 89, 101
Annis, John 65

antebellum literature 116
Anti-Slavery Bugle 18
antislavery movement 11, 12, 16
  print culture of 16–17, 18
Antislavery Record 18
Anti-slavery Reporter 66
"as told to" accounts 233, 235
The Atlantic Monthly 158
Augustan ideals 66
authenticity 73–76
  see also slave narrative
autobiography 4, 13, 14, 16, 26, 46, 99–102, 207

Bakhtin, M. M. 141, 147, 148–49
Ball, Charles 25, 39, 70
  Fifty Years in Chains 24
  Slavery in the United States 23–24
Banneker, Benjamin
  letter to Thomas Jefferson 14
Barthelemy, Anthony G. 222
Baxter, Richard
  Call to the Unconverted 92
Baym, Nina 128
  Woman's Fiction 117
Belinda 13–14
Bell, Bernard W. 5
  The Afro-American Novel and Its Tradition 168–69
Benezet, Anthony 17, 64, 65
Bercovitch, Sacvan 94
Berlin, Ira 46
Bibb, Henry 18, 21, 40, 123, 146, 228
  Narrative of Henry Bibb 26, 108, 226
  on family 31–32
Black Arts Movement 169
Black Power Movement 169
Black Studies Movement 220

0 4 MAY 2018